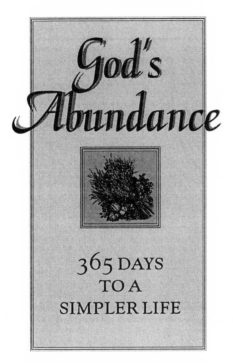

God's Abundance

365 DAYS
TO A
SIMPLER LIFE

EDITED BY

KATHY COLLARD MILLER

God's Abundance

365 DAYS
TO A
SIMPLER LIFE

Edited by
Kathy Collard Miller

STARBURST PUBLISHERS

P.O. Box 4123, Lancaster, Pennsylvania 17604

Acknowledgments

Thanks, Mother, for helping on this project.
A big thank you to the great staff at Starburst Publishers. Dave Robie is the source of great ideas. Sharon Robie is a delight to work with. I appreciate you!

Kathy Collard Miller is the author of twenty-five books, including the best-selling, *God's Vitamin "C" for the Spirit* and *God's Chewable Vitamin "C" for the Spirit*. She has written for *The Christian Communicator, Moody Monthly, L A Times,* and *Today's Christian Woman.* Kathy speaks regularly and has appeared on many talk shows including the 700 club. She lives in Placentia, California with her husband Larry. She can be reached for scheduling speaking engagements at P. O. Box 1058, Placentia, California 92871 (714) 993-2654.

To schedule Author appearances write:
Author Appearances, Starburst Promotions, P. O. Box 4123
Lancaster, Pennsylvania 17604 or call (717) 293-0939

Credits:

Cover by David Marty Design

Unless otherwise noted, or paraphrased by the author, all Scripture quotations are from the *New International Version* —Copyright 1984 by The International Bible Society and published by Zondervan Bible Publishers.

To the best of its ability, Starburst Publishers has strived to find the source of all material. If there has been an oversight, please contact us and we will make any correction deemed necessary in future printings. We also declare that to the best of our knowledge all material (quoted or not) contained herein is accurate, and we shall not be held liable for the same.

First Printing, November 1997

ISBN: 0-914984-97-7

Library of Congress Catalog Number 97-068720

Printed in the United States of America

Introduction

*A*re you looking for abundant life . . . the abundant life Jesus promised His children? Like me, do you hunger for that simple concept to be carried out in our lives? An abundant life is one that is "plentiful" and "more than sufficient" in experiencing God's love and grace. God never intended that to be complicated, only that we seek it through simple living: daily depending upon the Lord for everything we need.

When we enjoy that abundant life, we'll experience the fruit of the Spirit: love, joy, peace, patience, kindness, goodness, faithfulness, gentleness, and self-control.

The book you hold in your hands is all about living the abundant life that Jesus promised through a simple trust and obedience to Him. In the following pages you will be inspired by those who also seek God's abundant living. Your heart will be touched by the stories of those who live simple yet rich lives in God's love. And you will be challenged through practical ideas to put this abundant life into practice.

As I've been seeking and seeing progress in my own life toward this abundant life, I've grown in my ability to trust God in a simple, childlike faith that believes He loves me and wants only the best for me. Isn't that what we all desire? That is what you'll discover in *God's Abundance*.

As you journey through this book day-by-day, you'll find a year's worth of examples, encouragement, and enthusiasm for your journey toward abundant living. That is the major theme or melody of *God's Abundance*. But within each month, you'll also discover the underlying, subtle harmony of the fruits that abundance germinates. Along with the fruit of the Spirit, we'll hum the tunes of hope, gratitude and other characteristics of the simple Christian life lived in dependence upon God.

Join me, won't you, for this pilgrimage which will draw us ever closer to our Lord Jesus Christ? Life has its challenges, but focusing on the richness of God's abundant life within us will help to make the trip more enjoyable.

—Kathy Collard Miller

January

> "For I know the plans I have for you," declares the Lord, "plans to prosper you and not harm you, plans to give you hope and a future."
>
> Jeremiah 29:11

Ahhh . . . a fresh new year to allow God's Holy Spirit to flow through our lives and draw us closer to Him. We all need "new leases" on life and our Creator gives us one as, in simple ways, we make new commitments to value our relationship with Him. He wants us to live abundant lives, and fresh starts are a part of His mercy to give us all the second chances we need. As a result, we'll experience the fruit of hope in our lives.

Happy New Year!

PATTY R. STUMP

> We are not called upon to renew our minds in order
> that we may be transfigured; we are only to yield our-
> selves unto God, and He does all the rest.
> —WILLIAM L. PETTINGILL

*B*eginning a new year or a new project is always thrilling. You have chosen to begin a journey toward greater abundance in your walk with God. Congratulations! Certainly, a part of that can be beginning the new year with a resolution, which so many do, whether or not they're seeking abundance. Among those frequently considered are resolutions to lose weight, exercise, eliminate a bad habit, pursue a dream, grow up, lighten up, or look up. At the heart of a resolution is the desire to have this year be even better than the last.

Webster's Dictionary includes in its definition of *resolution* the following "a.b.c.'s": (a) the act of analyzing a complex notion into a simpler ones, (b) the act of answering, and (c) the act of determining. For the Christian, these same a.b.c.'s lay the framework for experiencing an abundant and fruitful year in one's relationship with God.

In Hebrews 12:1-2 we are exhorted to *run with endurance the race that is set before us, fixing our eyes on Jesus, the author and prefecture of faith.* Point (a) of resolution involves taking a complex notion such as *running the race that is before us* and making it manageable through simpler steps. To run the race God sets before us requires establishing Jesus Christ as our focal point. Once we invite Him into our heart to be our *Savior* we begin the journey. Yet in order to stay on course, we must embrace Him as the *Lord* of our lives; prioritizing His Word and will above our thoughts, plans, and priorities. By remaining focused on Him we are able to run with confidence, stamina, and purpose.

A second component of the word *resolution* is (b) *the act of answering*. We cannot respond to someone accurately until we first know what they have said. Psalm 46:10 instructs us to *be still, and know that I am God*. With each new day, resolve to spend time with Christ, removed from the *busyness* of life. Time spent reading the Bible, devotional books, listening to praise music, and in prayer will sharpen your ability to hear and understand God.

Finally (c) *the act of determining.* As we journey into greater abundance and simplicity, we will encounter a variety of opportunities and obstacles. Christ will give us wisdom and strength to face each situation if we are determined to seek His counsel and follow His lead. Colossians 3:2 instructs us to *set your mind on the things above.* In order to grow spiritually Christ must be at the heart of our lives, not simply a part of our lives. Commit yourself to developing a relationship with Jesus Christ.

This year resolve to know Christ more fully; running the race He unfolds with endurance! Then, an abundant life will simply and naturally flow from your relationship with Him.

Happy New Year!

The plans of the diligent lead to profit as surely as haste leads to poverty.
PROVERBS 21:5

While watching football, copy the dates of birthdays and anniversaries from your old calendar onto your new.

January 2

New Year's Resolution

MICHELE HOWE

The secret lies in how we handle today, not yesterday or tomorrow. Today . . . that special block of time holding the keys that locks out yesterday's nightmares and unlocks tomorrow's dreams.

—CHUCK SWINDOLL

*A*s I contemplate the beginning of a new year, I must admit to feeling some trepidation, for last year brought me face-to-face with great difficulties. We all face challenges every year, yet some years seem more daunting than others. At those times, the future seems forbidding. The abundant life seems difficult to reach.

Yet, I recognize now more than ever before, the need to press forward and live. Live fully. Live courageously. And most importantly, live without fear of continued suffering touching my life or the lives of those I love.

I recognize this life is peppered with pain and injustices of every sort—this is the human condition and none are immune from it. For me to hide myself away and allow part of life's ills to immobilize me would be the saddest of tragedies. In truth, it would be the greatest irony of all—for the losses would be ever more compounded if I succumb.

So this year, I choose to put behind me the fears I feel about the unknown. I consciously decide to embrace the future, facing each circumstance with joyful expectancy and hopeful anticipation rather than with fearful pausing and hesitancy. I will live my life with the integrity which can only be earned by relinquishing my selfish securities and unattainable control over the mystery of life itself. I am determined to make this the best year yet!

What fears are you facing? Let God speak hope to your heart. He knows His plans for you and they are meant only for helping you grow in abundant living.

> *You have made known to me the path of life;*
> *you will fill me with joy in your presence,*
> *with eternal pleasures at your right hand.*
>
> PSALM 16:11

> Write your greatest fear about this coming year on a piece of paper, and then burn it as a sacrifice to the Lord.

January 3

Increasing Your Effectiveness

H. NORMAN WRIGHT

Life with Christ is an endless hope; without Him it is a hopeless end.

—BEVERLY J. PLAUGHER

Would you like to get more out of your life, enjoy it more, feel relaxed, and be productive? If you said yes, consider these suggestions.

Begin each day by asking God to help you prioritize those items that need to be done. Do only those items for which you (really) have time. If you feel you can accomplish five during the day, do only four. Try to accomplish only one thing at a time.

Each day think about the cause for any potential time urgency. Write down one of the consequences of being in a hurry. If you begin to feel pressured about completing your tasks, ask yourself—*Will completing this matter three to five years from now? Must it be done now? If so, why? Could someone else do it? If not, why?*

Make a conscious effort to become a "ready listener." Ask questions to encourage others to continue talking. When someone is talking, put down your newspaper, magazine, or work and give that person your full attention.

Reevaluate your need for recognition. Instead of looking for the approval of others, tell yourself in a realistic way, *I did a good job and I can feel all right about it.*

Be self-controlled and alert . . .

I PETER 5:8

Remember your "winged" friends. Hang a cake of suet from a branch and watch the birds delight in this sweet treat!

January 4

The Pages Of Our Lives

A. JEANNE MOTT

We would come back to Thee, confessing that we are
not proud of the mistakes we have made, not too
proud of our record as we look back over the last year.
We seek now Thy forgiveness for our stupidity and
our obstinacy, for the blindness of our hearts, for the
wrong choices that grieved Thee and subtracted from
our own happiness.

—PETER MARSHALL

With every sunrise we are presented a fresh, blank page in our life's journal. The Lord is a God of new beginnings, and He gives us the freedom to fill each page with whatever we choose.

Because of the demands of modern life, with the breakneck hustle and bustle of daily existence, we often don't even skim over our journal entries at the end of the day—or week, or year. If we could review the pages of our lives up until today, would we be pleased? Is God pleased? Would we find abundant living?

If we only scribble and scurry away the years that are given us, how remorseful a thing it will be after the last page is written. When we and God look back over the scrawled pages that led up to the last one, suppose they are filled with ink that is nonsense. Suppose all the pages are blurred and have no meaning. It could easily happen—and has—and does. Page-after-page of a life filled with hum-drum existence of meaningless life. What worse thing could happen for a Christian than to live out all his pages—come to the last one, and leave behind journals only worth burning.

Instead, let's allow the Lord to lead us, inspire us, push and prod us to leave behind pages that are branded with words, deeds and prayers that influence lives for His kingdom. What else is relevant? What else will have any lasting purpose or meaning? Only God's Word and eternal souls will remain. Recognizing those priorities will help us see the importance of simplicity.

God can forgive the wasted pages of our lives and help us to savor the unblemished days ahead. We'll need to slow down and remain single-minded on Him. Let's make a commitment now to fill the unwritten pages, day-by-day, with lasting moments—ones that will influence the eternal destiny of our fellow man. And then we'll whisper, "Thank you, Lord, for abundant new beginnings. Let us walk with joy in Your Son—light through the rest of our lives' pages."

> . . . *Be very careful, then, how you live—not as unwise, but as wise,*
> *making the most of every opportunity, because the days are evil.*
> EPHESIANS 5:15,16

Take a fresh page in your journal and draw a picture that portrays an aspect of a new beginning, such as a sunrise, a baby bird in a nest, or an opening rose bud.

The Simple New Life

TONY EVANS

What oxygen is to the lungs, such is hope for the
meaning of life.

—EMIL BRUNNER

We must apply the mind of Christ by taking off the old life, saying
no to it, and putting on the new life, saying yes to it by realizing
who we are in Christ: brand-new creatures. When you're faced with
walking as the Gentiles walk, remember who you are and act on who
you are. These ideas will help:

1. If you are going to cultivate and think with the mind of Christ,
you are going to have to say no to a lot of activities, even harmless
ones, in order that you might say yes to your new life. To keep in
practice, say no to at least one thing that may be OK in itself, but is
not helping you toward spiritual maturity.

2. Since your mind absorbs whatever is put into it, you must also deal
with any negative influences that may be affecting your mind. Some are
pretty easy to deal with: Turn off the TV, close the magazine, stop going
to that place. Avoiding people who pull you down may be a little harder,
but if you know God wants you out from under their bad spiritual
influence, ask Him to show you His way of escape.

3. A lot of people are afraid to be alone and quiet because they
have never learned how to think and meditate on the important things.
Part of developing your new mind is spending time alone with the Lord
so that He can communicate His mind and heart to you. As soon as
possible, find some time to get alone and get quiet before the Lord.
Listen for the *still, small voice* of the Spirit.

*And God is faithful; he will not let you be tempted beyond what
you can bear. But when you are tempted, he will also provide a way out
so that you can stand up under it . . .*
I CORINTHIANS 10:13

> As a visible reminder that you have taken off the old life and put on the new life, find the oldest, most tattered, most worn piece of clothing you own and put it out where you'll see it every day for a while. Every time you look at it thank God for the new you!

January 6

Harvesting The Family Tree

ESTHER M. BAILEY

(Children) are . . . capable of independent and rational thought that's not attributable to any source.

—DR. JAMES DOBSON

*I*f you have a fruit tree in your yard, you probably don't eat all the fruit you pick. Some may be sour; some may be spoiled; some may be wormy or full of defects. So you separate the good from the bad, keeping the good and discarding the bad.

Did you know that your family tree could be harvested in much the same way? No doubt you have inherited some undesirable qualities from your ancestors along with the good qualities. After evaluating those influences, you may want to focus on a particular trait you wish to eliminate or one you'd like to enhance. Say, for instance, you have a tendency to pass on juicy tidbits when it's inappropriate.

First, see what the Bible says about gossip. Look up 2 Thessalonians 3:11, 1 Timothy 5:13, 1 Peter 4:15, James 1:26 and 3:5-6.

From the Scripture references select one that speaks to you most directly. Your text can be the basis of a three-step process to improvement.

1. Remind yourself. Write out your text on several slips of paper. Tape them to your bathroom mirror, your desk, and any place where you will frequently look. Remind yourself of your Scripture several times a day.

2. Pray. Pray frequently for strength to overcome your weakness. Pray when you're tempted to wait for tomorrow. Pray for grace to keep going once you get started.

3. Practice. Fortified by your Bible verse and prayer, do what you need to do. When you bridle your tongue the first time, it will be easier to do so the next time. Discipline will help you break bad habits or establish good ones.

If you work on a quality each month, you will have increased hope—one of the fruits of abundant living—as you see improvement. By the end of the year, you'll see great progress in that trait, and it will bring you closer to the abundant life Jesus promised you. Of course you may need more time to work on certain characteristics, but the main thing is that you begin now to harvest the fruits of your family tree.

Do not be like your forefathers.
ZECHARIAH 1:4

> Think of all the qualities you have observed in your family of origin. Make lists of the good ones and the bad ones. Single out one to enhance and another to eliminate.

January 7

Starting A New Year

SARAH HEALTON

God offers possibilities for a new beginning.
—REV. ROBERT SCHULLER

With the new year comes the opportunity to evaluate the year just passed and implement effective ways for a more abundant life. In making our resolutions, we think of things we plan to change. Instead of making a long list of specific resolutions, this year I made the following ones:

1. I will try not to worry. I will not allow fear or past failures to enslave me. God offers possibilities for a new beginning. This is the meaning of forgiveness.

2. I will keep my heart free from hate. Hate doesn't hurt the other person as much as it poisons me.

3. I will live simply, expect little, and not envy material things others have. I will keep myself busy doing for others.

4. I will fill my life with love. Scatter sunshine.

5. I will think of others first.

6. I will practice doing for others as I would like them to do for me.

7. I will continue to read and to seek inspiration, always being alert for something inspiring to share with others.

8. I will try to live in such a way, that when others think of honesty, compassion and integrity, they will think of me.

Resolutions like those will serve us for a lifetime of simplicity, not just for a year. Do they seem to be sound principles to live your life by? As you do, you'll experience hope in knowing that God is making changes in you.

I press on toward the goal
to win the prize for which
God has called me heavenward
in Christ Jesus.

PHILIPPIANS 3:14

Choose one of those eight resolutions, write it on a 3 X 5 card, and tape it on your bathroom mirror.

January 8

What's "Added"?

TRISHA THROOP

Remind me each day that the race is not always to the swift and that there is more to life than increasing its speed.

—O.L. CRAIN

What things are adding up in your life today? When you step on the scale do you see surprising numbers in your weight? Or when you look at your "to-do" list for the week does your mind buckle at each seemingly endless task to complete? Or are hours, days, and years piling up one on top of the other around you, imprisoning you to age—even paralyzing your dreams? At that point, a simple life is too far away.

Since this is a popular time when goals are tacked onto most everyone's jam-packed agenda, why not consider this thought: Jesus said *all these things shall be* added *to you* when God is sought first (Matthew 6:33). Christians sometimes lose themselves to the pressures of the world while forgetting too soon that their every need has been satisfied in Jehovah through Jesus Christ. The minor details of life should diminish in the light of God's salvation and the eternal destination that awaits those who believe—which is the most significant matter overall. In Matthew 6:33 "added" implies that *these things* are truly superfluous since Christians are complete in Christ both now and forever.

Make it a point today and throughout this new year to evaluate and prioritize not only your physical life, but your spiritual life as well. Try this formula for simple living: subtract extra technicalities from your routine that add nothing to your sole purpose here on Earth. Ask yourself: "How can I best glorify God; how can I serve Him with the life He has given me?" Simply seek Him above all else, and you will find abundant life through His fulfilled promises.

> But seek first His kingdom and His righteousness,
> and all these things will be given to you as well.
> MATTHEW 6:33

Plan a trip to the nearest planetarium to witness God's glory in the sky.

January 9

Choose Life

LYNN D. MORRISSEY

> One's philosophy is not best expressed in words; it is
> expressed in the choices one makes . . . . In the long
> run, we shape our lives and we shape ourselves.
> —ELEANOR ROOSEVELT

This year, instead of devising a complex list of things to do that you're bound to forget, cut to the chase and distill their essence into one potent reminder: choose life!

Before the Israelites entered the promised land, the Lord commanded Moses to tell them to choose between life and prosperity or death and adversity—between worshipping God or idols.

The advice and consequences were simple and are still true today: choose life, receive blessing; choose death, receive cursing. Why would we knowingly choose death and cursing? Because our hearts are deceitful and easily turned away by worshipping other gods or idols.

An idol is anything that replaces God in your life, thereby bringing a kind of death to your relationship with Him and destroying your sense of abundance. Idols also complicate life, by consuming your time and emotions. Some contemporary idols include the blind pursuit of prestige, power, possessions, higher education, career-climbing, indiscriminate movie-going and television-viewing, excessive shopping, eating and drinking. Of course, moderation in any would not be considered idolatrous, unless God has told you to completely get rid of it.

Apply the "choose life" principle to any questionable situation which confronts you. You're tempted to have one more drink; choose life and have apple juice or water. You're tempted to indulge in a piece of chocolate cake; choose life and eat fruit. You're tempted to spend another hour watching TV; choose life and read the Bible. You're tempted to attend another late-night meeting; choose life and spend time with your family.

Each year, life becomes progressively complicated. This year, keep things simple. Choose life in order that you may live a *truly abundant* life.

> *Now choose life, so that you and your children may live.*
> DEUTERONOMY 30:19B

Each time you "choose life," gently poke a flower seed into an indoor pot of prepared soil. Soon you'll have a blooming garden of life.

January 10

Will You Go Out Without Knowing?

OSWALD CHAMBERS

> The word *hope* I take for faith; and indeed hope is
> nothing else but the constancy of faith.
> —JOHN CALVIN

*H*ave you been "out" in this way? If so, there is no logical statement possible when anyone asks you what you are doing. One of the difficulties in Christian work is this question—"What do you expect to do?" You do not know what you are going to do; the only thing you know is that God knows what He is doing. Continually revise your attitude towards God and trust God entirely. It is this attitude that keeps you in perpetual wonder—you do not know what God is going to do next. Each morning that you wake it is to be a "going out," building confidence in God. *Take no thought for your life . . . nor yet for your body*—take no thought for the things for which you did take thought before you "went out."

Have you been asking God what He is going to do? He will never tell you. God does not tell you what He is going to do; He reveals to you who He is. Do you believe in a miracle-working God, and will you go out in surrender to Him until you are not surprised an atom at anything He does?

Suppose God is the God you know Him to be when you are nearest to Him—what an impertinence worry is! Let the attitude of the life be a continual "going out" in dependence upon God, and your life will have an ineffable charm about it which is a satisfaction to Jesus. You have to learn to go out of convictions, out of creeds, out of experiences, until so far as your faith is concerned, there is nothing between you and God.

By faith Abraham, when called to go to a place he would later receive as his inheritance, obeyed and went, even though he did not know where he was going.
HEBREWS 11:8

Memorize a Bible verse today that has the word *hope* in it.

January II

The Problem Of Being Driven

JEAN FLEMING

Enthusiasm is easier than obedience.
—MICHAEL GRIFFITH

My problem is that I'm driven, confessed a friend.

We live in a fast-paced, high-pressure society. We demand more and more of ourselves. Whether we compete to shave seconds off seconds in a race, push ourselves to check more off our "do list" than yesterday, or strive to increase our company's production, we live with a stress produced by more, faster, bigger, and better.

But is more necessarily better?

Is faster necessarily better?

Is bigger necessarily better?

Is better necessarily better?

"After all," as Thoreau reminds us, "the man whose horse trots a mile in a minute does not carry the most important message; he is not an evangelist, nor does he come around eating locusts and wild honey. I doubt if Flying Childers ever carried a peck of corn to mill."

The question is not, How can I do more? but, Am I doing the right thing?

. . .To obey is better than sacrifice . . .

I SAMUEL 15:22

> The next time you find yourself busy with worry—stop, raise your hands to the Lord and give it all to Him.

January 12

God's Protection

NELDA JONES

One on God's side is a majority.

—WENDELL PHILLIPS

*A*s I sat one day at my kitchen table, I noticed a fly crawling across the window pane with a black spider in pursuit. Each time the spider would look as though it was just about to catch it, the fly would suddenly buzz, and flit quickly out of the spider's reach, leaving the spider seemingly puzzled as to why it could not catch the fly.

I was puzzled as well, and watched the pair intently, as this episode happened several times. The fly almost seemed to be laughing at the spider, as it would buzz quickly out of the spider's reach.

Suddenly I laughed too, as I realized the window was raised and the spider was on one window and the fly was on the other, underneath the one the spider was on. The fly had nothing to fear from the spider because he was protected by the invisible pane of glass between them.

I laughed again as I realized that we as Christians can be just as secure under God's protective shield. We can laugh at Satan's puzzlement when his attempts to destroy us are thwarted by God's invisible shield of protection. A part of living the abundant life is having the hope—the assurance—that what God has called us to do, will indeed happen, even when Satan thinks otherwise.

> For surely, O Lord, you bless the righteous;
> you surround them with your favor as with a shield.

PSALM 5:12

> Set the timer for fifteen minutes and do the work you've been putting off. Having a short time to work will make it not seem so intimidating.

January 13

Living On God's Fuel

KATHRYN HARTZELL

I have a dream . . .

—MARTIN LUTHER KING, JR.

These four simple words can inspire change in ourselves, others, a nation and the world. But until each of us can stand and proclaim, "I have a dream . . ." our life remains devoid of the abundant life we're seeking.

God equips each of us with unique gifts, talents and passions. And He wants those abilities to be fulfilled in the plans that He has already intended for us. We'll experience the abundant life as we confidently live out the dreams He's birthed within us.

But we must recognize our dream, then plan for it, and finally take action to ignite God's fire within us. The hope of our dream becoming a reality is intensified when we're convinced God approves of our dream. Such approval carries with it all of God's grace and power for it to be fulfilled. When we contemplate God's hands-on involvement in our dream, the fire within our soul is unquenchable.

What is your dream? What is it inside your soul that longs to be fueled by the God who deposited that passion there?

Today, allow God to kindle the flame of your God-given dream. Take it off the shelf and examine it. Determine what must be done and when you will work on it. You'll be ready to stand and boldly proclaim, "I have a dream!"

As you take action, you'll step into God's abundant plan for you. Your hope will have become reality. And tomorrow, one person will be influenced by it. Then another and another. Only God knows the rest.

O Lord, you are my God, I will exalt you and praise your name,
for in perfect faithfulness you have done marvelous things,
things planned long ago.

ISAIAH 25:1

January 14

Trouble In Paradise

Tina Krause

To believe in heaven is not to run away from life; it is to run toward it.

—Joseph D. Blinco

"Aloha, welcome to paradise," the stewardess announced as our plane touched down on the exotic island of Maui, Hawaii.

All of my life I heard people sing the praises of beautiful, enchanting Hawaii. Some went so far as to say it reflected the beauty of heaven itself. Now it was my turn to experience it as my family and I embarked upon our first tropical adventure.

Driving to our condominium, we absorbed every morsel of scenery. It was just as I imagined—the bluest sky I had ever seen with barely a cloud to interrupt the flow of deep, rich color. Tall, looming palm trees swayed in the brisk trade winds and sun-kissed beaches lined the highway to our left while rugged mountain terrain painted a panoramic view to our right. Flowering bushes dotted the wayside as we passed by. Paradise!

Soon, however, our celestial visions shattered as Hawaii's earthly elements emerged. Shortly after our arrival, we sighted a roach in our posh, ocean-front condo.

All right, but everything else was so beautiful. Surely I could ignore one insect and enjoy . . . "What did you say was inside our living room?" I yelled to my husband from another room when I heard him mutter something. "A *lizard?*"

"No," he said loosely, "I said one of those little *geckos* seems to have made its way into our living room."

Watching the critter scamper across the ceiling, I shouted, "I don't care what you call it, it's a lizard!"

After eliminating all visible critters, I doused the floor boards and entryways with one full can of extra-strength Raid. Attempting to maintain a positive attitude, I resolved to avert any future problems by refrigerating everything. That included boxed cereals, clean glasses, the silverware and any other item that would go from hand to mouth, just in case the unwanted critters had family in the area (and they always do). But I remained positive. After all, this was "paradise."

Days later I discovered another island attraction. Gazing upward, I noticed aluminum sheeting wrapped around the palm trees. Turning to my brother, a longtime resident of Maui, I asked, "What's that for?"

"Oh," he said casually, "That's to prevent rats from climbing the trees."

"Rats?"

"Yeah, they're a problem in tropical climates."

By now, only three words expressed my feelings. Trouble in paradise!

Often we equate earthly things in heavenly terms. We clamor for a piece of heaven on earth when in reality, even the most beautiful surroundings are flawed by the results of sin. Thus, our search for perfection in a sinful, imperfect world leaves us discouraged.

Yet Christ promises us a place of beauty unequaled by anything we have ever experienced. A place where sin, sickness, sorrow, (rats, roaches, and lizards) do not exist—a true paradise—heaven.

That is the theme of this month's search for abundance: the hope—the knowledge—that one day there will be an eternity of no trouble in paradise. When this earthly life troubles you, hold onto that assurance.

Meanwhile, carry an ample supply of Raid.

In my Father's house are many rooms; if it were not so,
I would have told you. I am going there to prepare a place for you.
JOHN 14:1-2

Consider once-a-month cooking to relieve stress. *Once-A-Month Cooking* (Focus on the Family) by Mimi Wilson and Mary Beth Lagerborg will tell you how.

Keep Your Eyes On Jesus

HELEN LUECKE

The hand is quicker than the eye.

—ANONYMOUS

*A*s a child I remember watching a magic show. I raced home to tell my parents about all the wonderful things this man could do. Daddy assured me that these were all illusions. "Cozy," he said, "The hand is quicker than the eye."

Satan appears in our lives. He has had thousands of years to practice his crafty tricks. He's charming and witty as, with stunning disguises, he throws out stumbling blocks to the abundant life. They all look so real and inviting—with no hint of the consequences.

If we keep our eyes on Jesus, with the power of the Holy Spirit we can separate sin and illusion from the truths of God. There will be times when we stumble and fall. But if we look to Jesus, He will lift us up and put us back on course.

If you've slipped away from the truth that God wants you to experience the abundant life, reclaim His promise. You can have perfect peace in knowing He will work it out in you.

"Let us fix our eyes on Jesus, the author and perfecter of our faith . . ."
—JOHN 14:2

> If you're stumped by a decorating dilemma, photograph the room and carry the photo with you. It'll help you find what you need. (Roberta L. Messner)

Running The Race

PENNY SHOUP

Even the woodpecker owes his success to the fact that
he uses his head and keeps pecking away until he finishes
the job he starts.

—COLEMAN COX

"*R*un faster Penny! They're gaining on you!" The stern voice of
my coach rang above the rest of the noise.

Resisting the urge to look back I focused my attention on the goal.
*Stride, stride, stride, kick . . . I focused on my rhythm and the goal, clearing
each hurdle smoothly as it passed.*

I crossed the finish line and turned to find there was no one close
to me on the track. My coach and teammates came running out and
mobbed me, cheering and laughing.

"You just set a new school record for hurdles!" Coach Urick
announced.

I stared at her in disbelief. "You told me they were gaining! I didn't
even know I was in the lead!" I said in amazement.

"It made you run faster!" she said and we laughed.

In order for us to live abundantly, we must use the wisdom that
Coach Urick gave me: not looking back on failures of the past. God
didn't die for the righteous but sinners. We often worry that if we
weren't able to keep from sinning previously, we might fail again.
Repeat failure is always a possibility, but God will be there to pick us
up and start us on the race again.

You and I face many hurdles in life. We'll make our lives more
richly simple, if we recognize each hurdle as an obstacle to clear *one by
one* rather than as many road blocks we must face all at once. Keep
your eyes focused forward on Jesus and don't look back at failure!

*I press on toward the goal to win the prize for which
God has called me heavenward in Christ Jesus.*

PHILIPPIANS 3:14

Consider a big project like a pie: to be divided into
smaller slices!

Simple Beauty

JEREMI HARNACK

We ascribe beauty to that which is simple; which has
no superfluous parts; which exactly answers its end . . .
—RALPH WALDO EMERSON

*R*ecently I had to re-upholster my two couches. One is old-fashioned with piping and a little pleated "skirt" around the bottom. The other is plain with more open lines. I'm not a professional re-upholsterer, so I thought about leaving off the piping and skirting. Then, I decided to do it the "fancy" way just for the experience. It was hard—everything kept going wrong—but, when finished it looked fine, and I felt I had accomplished something.

Later, I blocked out time to do the second couch in the same "fancy" style. Then I began to tear the couch apart. All the time I had blocked out, disappeared into one mini-crisis after another. Suddenly, it was Thursday, and I was looking at an unfinished couch with six guests expected for dinner Saturday night. Thoughts of piping, skirting, and fancy touches left my mind. I passed off household duties to my husband and daughter, and focused all my attention on quickly doing the job. I managed to finish the job—minus the piping—a little over an hour before our dinner guests arrived. I was disappointed I hadn't been able to tie the design of the two couches together.

Later, a friend dropped by, took a look at the couch and said, "Ah, yes, clean, *simple* lines." Suddenly, I realized that the "fancy" touches on the other couch actually took away from the look of the couch. The second couch, for all its utilitarian lack of detail, was much more pleasing to the eye. I had been distracted by what I had considered my failure to make it "fancy," instead of asking God what kind of couch I needed. I had failed to appreciate the beauty of my "plain" couch.

We tend to forget the value of the simple, unadorned things of life. "Stripped down or plain" often mean "bare and unfinished," but to God it signifies "simple lines" such as truth, love, mercy, and obedience. "Fancy" is often complex, unnecessary and overdone. After all, richness and depth don't mean unnecessary complications.

It looks as though I still have some re-upholstering to do, to simplify my "fancy" couch. Maybe we should all be praying that God will "re-upholster" us to simplify our lives with clean and pure natures.

Who may ascend the hill of the Lord? Who may stand in his holy place? He who has clean hands and a pure heart, who does not lift up his soul to an idol or swear by what is false.

PSALM 24:3-4

To simplify your daily tasks: Group similar activities (like phone calls) together.

January 18

On-Purpose People

KEITH D. WRIGHT

Your mission statement becomes your constitution, the solid expression of your vision and values. It becomes the criterion by which you measure everything else in your life.

—STEPHEN R. COVEY

As we begin this new year, developing a personal mission statement can provide a "life map" that charts direction and gives purpose to your time and energy, so you can live an abundant life. After all, if you haven't defined what abundance is for *you*, you won't know what you're seeking. A "Personal Mission Statement" helps you do that.

This specialized statement is a one-page document that encompasses spiritual, social, financial, physical, and relational goals. Set aside adequate time in a quiet setting for prayer and reflection. This way you can keep Jesus Christ at the head of your life.

Here are some questions to ask yourself as you prepare your statement:

• Who has God shaped me to be at this stage of my Christian journey?

• What Christian character traits does God desire to develop in me?

• What is God calling me to do on His behalf?

• What principles will guide me to the future God has planned for me?

• What attitudes should be present in my significant relationships?

• How will I practice faithful stewardship of the gifts God has given me?

• What levels of physical fitness and financial stability will I need in order to pursue my dreams?

• What do I want to do in life just for the fun of it?

One man wrote his mission statement as: "I will be a Kingdom Builder for Christ in all areas of my life—in my marriage, family, ministry, and relationships. I will seek to consistently grow and stay open to new ideas so as to stay on the cutting edge of life and faith. I will model for others healthy relationships and approaches to ministry."

He then listed specific goals or intents (e.g., staying physically fit, spending daily time in the Word and prayer, living below his means, etc.) under each category (marriage, ministry, family, relationships) for accomplishing his stated mission.

Tomorrow we'll concentrate on your Purpose Statement. But for now, work on your Mission Statement. Once completed, refer to it often. Use it to prioritize your activities. By doing so, you will invest your time and energy toward the people and activities that are most important to you. And isn't that abundant living in its simplest form?

I am saying this for your own good, not to restrict you, but that
you may live in a right way in undivided devotion to the Lord.
1 CORINTHIANS 7:35

> Several times a year, keep track of how you spend your time. Then evaluate it for how well you're keeping to your Mission Statement.

January 19

Writing Your Purpose Statement

LYNN D. MORRISSEY

Why was I born? Why am I living?
—JEROME KERN

Sentiments like Jerome Kern's have haunted mankind throughout the centuries. Those who never come to know God by salvation through Jesus Christ miss the answer for all eternity and a truly abundant life. And sometimes even Christians puzzle over the answer.

But writing your Purpose Statement will help you to be abundantly clear about God's purposes for you.

First concentrate on why you were born. There are three main reasons: to glorify God (Isaiah 43:7), to love God (Mark 12:30), and to fulfill God's will and pleasure (Revelation 4:11). Your Purpose Statement becomes your "reason for being," based upon the type of character qualities you need to develop which will bring glory and pleasure to God. Putting it in writing simplifies life by giving you a tangible yardstick against which to measure your attitudes. Personalizing and internalizing such a statement, based upon Scripture, makes you more likely to follow it. Just like the Personal Mission Statement you prepared yesterday, referring to it often seals it in your heart and mind.

It might be helpful to consider another person's Purpose Statement. Author Anne Ortlund gives hers as, "To see self decrease and God increase, as my unpleasant characteristics are crucified and a meek and quiet spirit becomes an altar of worship to give God pleasure."

Write a brief Purpose Statement, asking the Holy Spirit to guide your thoughts. It should clearly describe personal characteristics that will help you glorify and love God, according to His will and for His pleasure. The fruit of concentrating on it will be hope and a simple—yet profound—knowledge of why God created you.

> . . . everyone who is called by My name, whom I
> have created for my glory, whom I formed and made.
>
> ISAIAH 43:7

Keep a "Victory log" in which you daily record
spiritual successes compatible with your purpose.

January 20

Is That Music I Hear?

TINA KRAUSE

Many people go to their graves with their music still
in them.

—ANONYMOUS

"Hi, Mr. Gomar!" I shouted as I passed by his house, "Beautiful day isn't it?"

"Yeah sure," he mumbled, raising his hand in disgust.

At 67 years old, Mr. Gomar is an extremely talented man. Without the luxury of taking one lesson, he plays the violin with grace and ease. His oil paintings exude warmth, character and charm. And his ability to study and retain information far surpasses his limited high school education. Yet regardless of his God-given abilities, Mr. Gomar is a miserable, empty man.

One day he took me on a guided tour of his home. As he pointed to memorabilia from his past, I noticed how many times he made reference to what he would do if he could "do it all over again." His life consists of old memories and unfulfilled dreams. His talents are left undeveloped, unused and unappreciated by the world around him, because he has never surrendered his life to the Lord.

Never fully realizing his dreams, Mr. Gomar is one who may go to his grave with music still in him.

Do you, too, believe that it is too late for God to use the gifts with which He has entrusted you? Is there a song deep within your soul, yearning to be heard? Whether we are eight or eighty it is never too late to surrender our dreams and talents to Jesus. For it is in the act of surrender that we find His resurrection power and the ability to see our dreams become a reality.

God wants you to experience the abundance of His fulfilled plans for your life. With God, all things are possible. Did you hear that Mr. Gomar? There's even hope for you.

Then let the music begin.

With man this is impossible, but with God all things are possible.
MATTHEW 19:26

> When is the last time you tried something new? Try an interesting class at your local community college.

January 21

How Content Are You?

KATHY COLLARD MILLER

A perfectionist is a person who takes great pains—then passes them on to others.
—ANONYMOUS

Our culture tells us "more" will make us happy—and if we believe its lies, God's special gift of contentment can slip from our grasp.

In order for us to live the abundant life God promises, we must fight the "more" that perfectionism requires of us. We'll attain an attitude of simplicity when we're satisfied with the best we can do.

Before you conclude that perfectionism doesn't apply to you, take this quiz developed by Sandra Simpson LeSourd in her book, *The Compulsive Woman* (Chosen Books). Check the statements that apply to you:

- If I can't do something exactly right, I won't do it at all.
- I often start things I don't finish.
- It's hard for me to relax even after my work is done.
- I am often amazed at the incompetence of others.
- I can't stand it when things are out of place.
- I find unpredictability vexing, if not intolerable.
- I have a burning need to set things right.
- I worry a lot about why I haven't done better.
- Any kind of personal failure is the worst thing I can think of.
- It seems to me that standards are slipping everywhere.

If three or more of those statements apply to you, you have perfectionistic tendencies and the abundant attitude of contentment may be difficult for you to attain.

While it is true that God wants us to be continually growing into the image of Jesus Christ, the good news for discontented perfectionists is that God already views us as perfect in our position in Christ. Someone has said, "There's nothing you can do to make God love you more and there's nothing you can do to make Him love you less." We perfectionists need to absorb that truth into our hearts. We can't make God love us by performing perfectly. God already loves and accepts us—even as He prunes the ungodly portions from our lives.

When speaking at women's retreats, I urge perfectionists to think in terms of the One Percent Principle™: seeking excellence through one percent growth. Perfectionists often lack contentment because they only value one hundred percent growth. Yet we never reach such a high standard. Instead, as we begin to ask God to help us and we are grateful for even one percent progress in an area, it'll be easier for us to live the abundant life!

> . . . *Because by one sacrifice he has made perfect*
> *forever those who are being made holy.*
>
> HEBREWS 10:14

What area would you like to grow in? Make a "one percent" improvement goal for this next week.

Begin Again!

BARBARA JOHNSON

The great thing in the world is not so much where we
stand, as in what direction we are moving.
—OLIVER WENDELL HOLMES, SR.

January is a fresh new month, the "land of beginning again." God's
fresh elastic can pull you together once more. You can make a
brand-new start in your life. No matter what has happened in the past.
No matter how much you wish the past had been different, you cannot
change what has already happened. Don't mourn over what is done;
rejoice that there is still a future! Yesterday is a canceled check,
tomorrow is a promissory note, but today is cash! Use it wisely. Today
you can have a new refreshing love, a return to Christian fellowship,
a new friendship, a new dream. Yes, you can have a fresh, new start
in January. Tear off that old calendar month, and enjoy that fresh new
page with no blot or scars on it.

God is present and ready to help you right where you are. Reach
out in a simple prayer to Jesus and feel Him now take your hand. With
His hand and power at work in your life, you, too, can have your tears
turned into joy, your night into day, your pain into gain, your failures
into successes, your scars into stars, and your tragedy into triumph.
Put the canceled checks behind you and the future in God's hands.
Enjoy the cash at hand, and your new start today!

Therefore, since the promise of entering his rest still stands, let us be careful that
none of you be found to have fallen short of it.
HEBREWS 4:1

> If you have never used or need a new prayer
> journal, treat yourself to a beautiful one that
> will inspire you to focus on God.

The Gift Of Time

DELORES ELAINE BIUS

Time is the greatest gift of all.

—ANONYMOUS

It was my privilege to care for my mother the last three months of her life on earth. When Mom became so weak that nearly all her time was spent in bed, I would pull a rattan chair in her bedroom close to her bed and sit with her. We would talk a while and then I would write letters or read while she napped. I knew my presence was reassuring to her. I also wanted to share all the time with her I could.

If only I could capture some of these hours in a magic jar or box, I thought. Then I could later bring them out and re-live them. There are so many things I want to talk about. Have we said all our good-byes and shared our love before it's too late?

One day when she queried, "Dear, are you really comfortable in that chair?" I responded truthfully, "Why yes, Mom. It's one of the most comfortable chairs you have!"

"Your grandmother bought me that chair years ago," she explained. Then Mom turned her head and looked off, as if into a distant land, seeing something I could not see. She often did this, as if Heaven were beckoning and she was more interested in it than this earth.

Abruptly, she turned back and said, "Now when I am gone, I want you to have that chair. Every time you sit in it, remember the times of sharing the Lord gave us before He took me home."

Mom died soon after that and is now in Heaven. The rattan chair is in my bedroom. I call it my meditation chair. It's where I sit and read my Bible and talk to the Lord. I recall and thank God for the very precious times Mom and I shared those last few months of her life.

One day I will join Mom in Heaven. In the meantime, my Heavenly Father and I have grown closer as He comforts me. When earthly ties are broken, the ties that bind us to God become stronger.

The gift of time—just talking and praying with Mom and even just sitting in the room with her—was probably the greatest gift I could give her.

We're living the abundant life when we recognize that time—in all it's simplicity—with those we love truly is the greatest gift of all. Will you give more of that gift this year?

Volunteer your time for at least one hour a month. That's a great gift of your time.

January 24

A Solitary Tea

EMILIE BARNES

There are few hours in my life more agreeable than the hour dedicated to the ceremony known as afternoon tea.

—HENRY JAMES

*H*uman beings crave ritual and ceremony (and loveliness) in our lives.

Tea is like that too. You may need to change your mental gears to enjoy it fully. You may need to practice waiting and learning to enjoy the repetitive freedom of the ritual. But once you do, the change of pace will renew your mind and refresh your spirit.

You don't need a lot of people to enjoy a lovely tea party. Taking the time to prepare a lovely tea just for you will calm you down and give you a wonderfully pampered feeling. Why not take a break in a long afternoon to enjoy a quiet cup in a lovely spot? Or if you have the luxury of an evening to yourself, why not prepare tea with fruit and sandwiches around five o'clock and then not worry about dinner? You'll have more time to enjoy the evening, and you'll sleep better because you ate early and light.

Here's a simple menu for a solitary tea that is easy to prepare, healthful, and satisfying.

A Perfect Pot of Tea

Orange or Apple Slices or a Beautiful Bunch of Grapes
Homemade or Store-Bought Cookies
Cream Cheese, Celery & Walnut Sandwiches
This easy-to-do sandwich filling can be made in minutes.
  1/4 pound cream cheese, room temperature
  1/4 celery heart, very finely chopped
  1/4 cup diced walnuts
White or whole-wheat bread
Parsley sprigs (for garnish)

In a small bowl, beat cream cheese until smooth. Mix in celery and walnuts. Make sandwiches with cheese mixture. Trim off crusts of bread and cut sandwiches into rectangles or triangles. Garnish plate with sprigs of parsley.

While waiting for the water to boil and the tea to steep, prepare one or more sandwiches and arrange them on a plate with the fruit and cookies. Lay a pretty cloth on a tray or on the table and add a flower or a candle for elegance. Then sit down at the table or carry your tray to a cozy spot. Enjoy!

Every good and perfect gift is from above, coming down from the Father of the heavenly lights, who does not change like shifting shadows . . .
JAMES 1:17

Send a gift of a tea bag of your favorite flavor to a special person in your life with a note of thanks.

January 25

No Second Chance

MICHELE T. HUEY

You can't turn back the clock. But you can wind it up again.
—WINNING ATTITUDES

Years ago when I was miles from home and my mother was ailing, my neighbor Mrs. Bruce became a second mother to me. She often watched my babies when I needed to make a quick trip to the grocery store and listened to me when I needed someone besides toddlers to talk to.

Then we built a house in the country and moved out of town. She relocated to a senior citizens high-rise. The children's birthdays and Christmas brought cards, often with a few dollars tucked inside, from "Grandma Bruce." I'd stop in to visit with her as often as I could, but as the family grew and the schedule became more demanding, hastily written notes and yearly Christmas cards replaced the visits.

Time passed. Her body frail with osteoporosis, she moved to a nursing home. She called me before Thanksgiving one year and I promised to free some time to go see her. I never made it. She died four days after Christmas.

I will not have another chance to take time for my friend. Has all my busy work become more important than another human being? Like Martha of old, I'm anxious and troubled about many things. I need daily to remind myself that the laundry, dishes, and cleaning will wait. Jesus Himself allowed His agenda to be disrupted while He looked to the needs of others.

It may be too late to make amends to my friend, but I can make a resolution to take time for others. Starting now.

Martha, Martha, the Lord answered, you are worried and upset about many things, but only one thing is needed.

LUKE 10:41

What visit, call, or card have you been putting off? Do it today.

January 26

An Important STEP

BILL AND PAM FARREL

God not only orders our steps. He orders our stops.
—GEORGE MULLER

In order to maintain a balanced life, it is helpful to write goals in four major life areas. Write goals that will help you take another STEP forward. You'll want to develop:

Your Spiritual Life
Your Team
Your Energy
Your Productivity

Spiritual life: This area includes goals that build a closer walk with

God—for example, a daily personal devotional time with God, Bible studies, church attendance, verses you'd like to memorize, and growth activities such as retreats, conferences, Christian radio and books you'd like to read. When you are connected to God, your perspective is renewed and your decision-making skills sharpen because you will be thinking more like God.

Team: Included in this section are goals that will build into your significant relationships, like marriage, family and close personal friends. One author recommends that we prioritize our lives by who will cry at our funeral. When you maintain healthy relationships, then you will have more emotional stability to tackle life. Your motivation for life will increase as your relationships are strengthened.

Energy: To maintain a high level of energy, you must carefully manage the areas of life that are of importance to you as an individual. These will include your personal finances, emotional well-being, physical health, and social life. It will also include those activities that are less urgent but still vital to you as an individual—your hobbies, study, sports, reading, and leisure activities.

Productivity: This area includes goals in your career, education, and ministry (both public and personal). What type of work do you want to pursue? What position do you want to attain in that field? What type of education do you need to fulfill these pursuits? Who are the people you would like to personally influence for Christ? How would you like to use your gifts in your local church ministry?

In his heart a man plans his course,
but the Lord determines his steps.

PROVERBS 16:9

Go through the STEP formula and make plans for this year.

The Lesson Of The Snow

LOIS ERISEY POOLE

And we must pass through solitude and difficulty,
isolation and silence, in order to reach forth to the
enchanted place . . .

—PABLO NERUDA

Silently, during the night the snow fell, sealing the ancient desert floor with a reflective carpet.

The emotion stirred by a full-blown snowfall is one of nature's gifts, a gift that boosts the strength in us all. The power of survival is aroused as we dig in the closet for our boots and mufflers. We take a high-stepping walk to the garage to find the dusty, bent shovel, then plod to the sidewalk and begin scooping up this timeless gift that transforms us into children again. Occasionally we pause to fashion a soft, wet ball and toss it at nothing. We laugh. We remark how this is more snow than we had last year. We play. And when our flaccid lungs and softened muscles grow weary we stamp the clotted snow off our boots and return to the kitchen for a cup of hot cocoa.

Tree branches bend, then collapse. The power goes off. We light candles and pop corn in the fireplace. Water lines bulge, then snap, and we gather snow to be melted for drinking water.

We are renewed with a spirit of worth. The world around us is cleansed of all impurities. Today we are secure as we huddle together over bowls of cold cereal and watch the dark clouds gather as more snow falls.

A neighbor stumbles through the drifts for assurance that we are safe. We dig out batteries and stuff them into the radio and wait for the weather report, secretly hoping this isolation will continue.

Worries are gone. We are one—a solid front facing the elements. Angers dissipate. Aches and pains are forgotten. Errands must wait. Decisions are shelved. We are forced to spend this time alone, looking inward.

We are useful once again. We find our value as darkness falls. We sit before a hearth warm with quiet embers and bid farewell to a primitive day of discovery. Humility is our guest as we savor fulfillment. We have learned that we are strong and capable of facing all adversities. And when we have doubts about our future; when we are sleepless with worry; when we know we can't go on, we will remember. We'll remember the day nature tested us, and we will be sustained by the knowledge that we have the inner strength to shovel away any problems in our path, while we wait for the sun to shine again.

Abundance means flowing with our circumstances and taking advantage of forced solitude. The next time you're snowed in, will you fight it or flow with it? Simplicity says, "Let God use it."

For nothing is impossible with God.
LUKE 1:37

> Whether or not you're snowed in, light a fire
> and enjoy the coziness of the hearth with family
> or friends, or with your best friend, yourself.

January 28

Breath Prayers

JAN JOHNSON

Prayer does not equip us for greater works—prayer is
the greater work.
—OSWALD CHAMBERS

Our back-and-forth communication with God might take the time-proven "breath prayer" format, repeating a familiar prayer of nine or ten syllables or less that has great meaning. To those of us who have spent our energies reciting long lists of prayer requests, breath prayers may seem hackneyed and infantile, but they aren't. Breath prayers are so simple that they're revolutionary.

What a relief to grow into a relationship with God where we don't have to go on and on explaining everything. We can rest in the confidence that God already knows and understands.

We need this simplicity in a culture that wows people with words—adorning them with graphics, manipulating and convincing people with words. Breath prayers resemble the unembellished approach Jesus recommended when He spoke of offering a simple yes or no instead of elaborate oaths (Matthew 5:33-37).

Breath prayers are very different from "vain repetitions," which Jesus described as lofty, impressive recitations made for others to notice (Matthew 6:7). They are quiet groanings of the heart that become more meaningful as we use them. As we turn these prayers over and over, they become woven through these thoughts and may even transform our attitudes.

You probably have breath prayers that you already use, but you don't call them that. Here are some that may spark your thinking.

Turn this person's heart toward You. This breath prayer paraphrases biblical statements about God's power to change motives and attitudes (I Kings 8:58, Psalm 119:36, Luke 1:17). Whether we're miffed at a government official or crusty old Aunt Franny, this breath prayer keeps us focused on God's will in the person's life. Sometimes I add, *Turn my heart toward this person*, as a prayer to empty myself of my well-researched opinion of his or her behavior. These prayers can wring the self-importance from our attitude and allow God to put within us the most loving attitude we can muster.

Do I need to change? Disturbing people or situations may signal us to look within for character flaws (I Corinthians II: 28, 2 Corinthians 13:5). Asking if we need to change lets the issue simmer on the back burner until God makes it plain whether we need to change or to turn over the thing that disturbs us.

Teach me through this negative behavior. Rather than dwelling on the inadequacies of people we find offensive, this breath prayer helps us refocus on God's desire to transform us. We ponder, *What does this person's negative example teach me about myself? What warning does his or her behavior present?* Using this breath prayer on a regular basis also rescues us from our self-righteousness—the plague of those who seek God—and calls us back to the reality that we are all flawed learners.

Thank You for this person. People who have contributed to our lives fly across our thoughts many times, and a smile of thanks can be a pleasant breath prayer.

And when you pray, do not keep on babbling like pagans, for they think they will be heard because of their many words. Do not be like them, for your Father knows what you need before you ask Him.

MATTHEW 6:7-8

For one morning or afternoon, notice your "breath prayers" and concentrate on speaking to God constantly.

The "I Can Do It All" Route To Self-Worth

LIZ CURTIS HIGGS

If you want to be respected by others, the great thing
is to respect yourself.

—FYODOR DOSTOEVSKY

Workaholism and its twin, perfectionism, are an increasing problem as we rush toward the new millennium. Paula Rinehart wrote, "Our culture seems increasingly geared to let such excesses masquerade as virtues." Working mothers are especially good at playing the "my stress is bigger than your stress" game as we compare calendars like grandmothers compare photo brag books: "Mine has more in it than yours!"

A dear friend in my profession described her urge to put too much on her calendar: "I discovered that it had little to do with financial need. It was an inner drive that pushed me to *do*, to perform to *have*, *to show that I could do it!* All wrapped up with self-esteem issues. It was a very lonely realization." Now she has posted next to her phone a copy of one crazy month's schedule from a few years back with a banner headline at the top: "*Never again! Say no!*"

Sometimes I look at my speaking calendar and cry. The tears well up from two sources: gratitude for the opportunities, and concern for my ability to pull it all off. Believe me, I love making audiences laugh and making clients happy. But sometimes, it comes at the cost of my own laughter and my own happiness. Not to mention my family's joy and contentment. Ugh.

Very slowly, I am learning that not only is it okay not to "do it all," it's dangerous to try.

Some of us even wrap our self-worth around service to the church, thinking, "If it's for God, it must be worthwhile; therefore, I am worthwhile too!" Peg Rankin, in *How to Care for the Whole World and Still Take Care of Yourself*, listed some of the seductive messages we hear concerning our spiritual areas of service:

• Take on more than you can handle. You can never do enough for God.

• Set goals and push yourself to achieve them. You want to hear "well done" on Judgment Day.

• Gauge the effectiveness of your service by concrete evidence. If you don't see results, there probably aren't any.

Ouch! These hit too close to home for this woman, especially that last one about looking for tangible, measurable results. It's hard for me to remember that, in matters of faith, invisible growth is the best kind.

If anyone thinks he is something when he is nothing, he deceives himself.
GALATIANS 6:3

Visit a used book store and see what treasures you can find.

January 30

Unexpected Miracle

MARCIA KRUGH LEASER

. . . what higher, more exalted, and more compelling goal can there be than to know God?
—JAMES I. PACKER

The air was alive with excitement and even though my friend and I had been sitting four hours waiting for the healing service to begin, it seemed like only minutes. We were a little disappointed that after arriving that early, we were still at the opposite end of the room from the stage and about twelve rows up. Nonetheless, the spirit of the Lord would not be dampened by distance, and I knew we would receive a blessing that special night.

I was awestruck as I watched the entire arena fill to capacity and beyond. "How hungry we are for You, Lord," I whispered.

My heart pounded as the wheel chairs were wheeled into the room. My soul cried out in pain as I saw the little children, with braces on their legs, hobble in and take their places. The lump in my throat grew larger as I watched the elderly being carried in on stretchers. Each of them expecting a miracle. Each one believing they would be healed before the evening was over.

I listened as the leader spoke of God's love for us and His desire to make us whole. How at the last crusade many crooked limbs were straightened, silent ears opened and deadly cancers gone. I hated to admit it even to myself, but I was skeptical.

I openly wept as I thought of all the people waiting to receive God's glory. All these were waiting for His healing touch that would awaken lifeless limbs, allowing them to leave their wheelchairs that had held them captive for so long. I covered my face with my hands and prayed. "God, these are your children. They came here expecting a miracle. They believe they will be healed. How can you allow them to leave the same way they came in? It isn't fair!" I implored.

Suddenly amid the mighty din of twenty-thousand people singing, clapping and praising God, I heard His still small voice say, "Must I still prove myself to you?"

Talk about a reality check. Of course He didn't need to prove Himself to me. He had done so . . . many years ago on an old rugged cross.

In a split second, my whole demeanor changed. Who in the world did I think I was telling God how to conduct His business? I stood amid thousands, yet felt as if I was all alone with God. But, He is so gracious. Instead of feeling small and ashamed for stepping out of bounds, I felt His warming touch of love. Just a little love tap reminding me that He is in charge and He alone knows best.

"Yes, Lord," I whispered. "Whatever is Your will."

I had known I would be blessed when I walked through the doors that evening, but I had no idea I would be one of the many that would be healed that glorious night. I was healed of something I would never have even considered laying at the feet of Jesus, my skepticism.

Does skepticism hinder your simple faith? Turn from it today and be renewed with an abundance of trust.

But grow in the grace and knowledge of our Lord and Savior Jesus Christ.
To Him be glory both now and forever! Amen.
2 PETER 3:18

As you complete this first month of focusing on an abundant life, review your progress. Have you gained an attitude of hope? Make a note in your continued growth as your journey continues.

The Rock

NELDA JONES

> Whatever is to be done at God's command may be
> accomplished in his strength.
>
> —ANONYMOUS

"If that old rock could talk, it could tell some awfully interesting stories," said my dad as we visited on the front porch of his farmhouse.

The rock to which he referred was a big, almost square rock which stands by the center of the front porch of the old farmhouse where he and Mama reared 12 children. "It has had many (foot) steps on it, and if it had eyes, it would have seen many sights," he continued.

"Yes, and I've cracked many nuts on it, too," I said, remembering my childhood.

The rock, about two feet high and three feet square, is worn smooth on top, by the feet of the many children, grandchildren, great-grandchildren, and others who have used the rock as a door-step.

When my father dug the rock out of the ground years ago, and placed it there for a doorstep, I'm sure he did not realize the significance it would later have in his life and the lives of his family.

Through the years, our family life seemed to revolve around that rock. It became something of a family center. It was a perfect place for cracking nuts, both for eating and baking. My brothers used the rock for replacing links in their bicycle chains and making wooden stilts.

The rock also made a good seat for summer visiting, or for holidays when our large family overflowed onto the porch and yard.

However, the most unexpected and significant use came in 1995, just prior to my father's death at the age of 99. Shortly before his death, due to his confusion and failing eyesight, some of us children had started taking turns staying with him.

Now, almost blind and becoming increasingly confused and disoriented, he sometimes thought his house was not the same one in which he had lived for over 60 years. When he would get confused about this, he would say, "If this is my house there is supposed to be a big rock right by the front porch."

Even though we assured him it was there, sometimes the only way to convince him was to take him to the rock and let him touch it; then he would be satisfied.

Though my dad probably had never heard of the contemporary song by Dottie Rambo entitled "I Go to the Rock," he would go to the rock in front of his house when he needed reassurance. It became a friend and an anchor to him when he was confused, just as the True Rock, Christ Jesus, had been a Friend and an Anchor to him throughout his life.

Just as Dad's life had become centered around this earthly rock, our lives must be centered around Jesus Christ, the Solid Rock. As our "rock," Jesus offers us hope that He can be depended upon. What a secure foundation for abundant living! Are you depending on that security?

The LORD is my rock, and my fortress, and my deliverer;
my God is my rock, in whom I take refuge . . .
PSALM 18:2

When returning from vacation, stop at the laundry mat to do all your laundry at once. (Sonia Lopez Brown)

February

"*I have loved you with everlasting love; Therefore I have drawn you with kindness.*"

Jeremiah 31:3

*T*ruly, February is the month of love, a significant fruit of the Holy Spirit. As we experience God's love as a part of His plan for abundance, we'll be able to love others more fully. Simple love is an unconditional acceptance that wants the best for the beloved, not just on Valentine's Day, but every day of the year. It all begins with love! Let's find in this month's readings a greater ability to love abundantly.

Appreciating The Commonplace

VEDA BOYD JONES

And God, who studies each commonplace soul, out of
commonplace things makes His beautiful whole.
—SARAH CHAUNCEY WOOLSEY

There is nothing commonplace about a crimson cardinal. And yet I
saw one in February that faded in comparison to its appearance two
weeks earlier.

The snowstorm came with big fat flakes that quickly covered the ground
and bare limbs of trees and bushes, turning the world outside my window
to pristine white. The clouds moved on, leaving us with eight inches of
brilliant snow. Imagine my surprise when a red cardinal settled on the white
branch of a bush, a flame against all that white.

I called my sons in to look at this spectacular sight. The view out the
window could have been on a Christmas card. The red bird stayed in that
bush for long minutes, and I was hypnotized by its beauty.

Two weeks later the thaw came, and the world turned back to winter
grays and browns. I glanced out my window and saw movement in the
bush. The cardinal was back. But this time it sat on a brown branch, and
although the red bird hadn't changed, the scene was quite different. There
was no brilliance, no breathtaking wonder. I didn't call my sons in to see
the red spot against the gray/brown bush in winter's silhouette.

How many other times have I seen magnificent nature against life's
fabric of changing backgrounds and not seen the beauty? From now on I
will look at life with an attitude of abundance; appreciating the
commonplace along with the unique. I won't wait for startling contrasts or
a spotlight to show me what has always been there.

If you want to have a simple appreciation for the world around you,
make a fresh commitment to stop and notice the beauty. Whether it's there
every day or only occasionally, it's God's gift of love.

From Zion, perfect in beauty, God shines forth.

PSALMS 50:2

Look around you. Is there something pretty or unique that
you haven't noticed for a while? Thank God for it right now.

Slow Down And Have Fun

BILL HYBELS

> Success in marriage consists not only in finding the
> right mate, but also in being the right mate.
>
> —ANONYMOUS

Young people are prone to distraction. Causes are great and energy is high. There is often a temptation early in marriage to let your focus wander: job, ministry, friends. There are so many paths to feeling important, respected, and valued, and the temptation is to take them all. My advice is to keep a check on your motivations, why are you working so hard, or moving so fast? Is it because you are trying to find your value outside of your relationship with Jesus Christ?

Busyness is a fun killer. And once fun disappears from a marriage, anything (or anyone) is likely to follow. It is therefore vital to balance the competing demands in your life, so you can make marriage-building a priority. Do some of the crazy things you did together when you were dating. Remember how good it feels to hold your spouse's hand on a walk around the block. Go out on picnics in the middle of the woods. Life is too short to be driven continually by Day-Timers,® calendars, and watches. Laugh a lot, enjoy each other. True love must rest on trust, honesty, and plain old fun. It is only when those foundations are built and maintained that oneness, the self-giving union of two souls, is possible.

> *Enjoy life with your wife, whom you love . . .*
> ECCLESIASTES 9:9

Regardless whether it's your mate, friend, or relative, the next time he or she tells a joke, laugh, even if the joke isn't funny.

God's Candy Box

PATRICIA A.J. ALLEN

He rolls it under his tongue as a sweet morsel.

—MATTHEW HENRY

*V*alentine's Day is fast approaching. The store aisles are filled with red hearts, hearts on teddy bears, hearts on boxes of cards, and even hearts on exercise equipment. Boxes of chocolates are themselves hearts. Regardless of the shape of the box they're in, I love chocolates. Even though I'm still trying to lose weight, I'd adore getting one of those boxes. Listening to soft music and curling up in my favorite chair, I would savor the experience. Easing up the lid of the box would prolong my anticipation of that first whiff of chocolate. I'd ponder each selection before letting the flavor and texture fill my whole being with luxury.

When I was a child, well, younger anyway, I searched the heart-shaped box and picked out all the candies that I liked best. All the nougats, the long skinny ones, went first. Then the mounded ones with the little swirl on top disappeared. After a nimble-fingered meal, I was on a sugar high, sated on chocolate, and disgusted with myself. I didn't know how to savor my pleasure.

The Word of God often got treated the same way. I picked out favorite verses and gobbled them, one right after another, until my mind was saturated. Perhaps I had done a time-consuming Bible study, but I'd filled up on "nougats." I never got into the "second layer" of deeper riches in God's Candy Box.

Learning to nibble the Bible is a luxurious experience, well-deserving of a comfortable easy chair. Studying word by word gives delight experienced in no other way. No longer am I compelled to grab whole chapters. Now, each verse or sentence fascinates me.

After choosing a verse and asking God to reveal something special for me today, I read aloud. A dictionary waits beside my chair. I look up each word that, in all honesty, I can't define. By seeing the various meanings of the words and thinking about how they might fit into God's sentence, I dive into new understandings. My mind nibbles the day's delicacies reveling in the fact that the Bible is God's love letter to me. It's abundantly better than chocolate!

Such study is simple, but not superficial. Do you value the rich taste of God's Word as much as your favorite dessert?

How sweet are your words to my taste, sweeter than honey to my mouth!
PSALM 119:103

> Listen to a Scripture song tape, as you walk or exercise, outside in God's garden.

February 4

Learn To Be Resolvers

CAROLE MAYHALL

I will not permit any man to narrow and degrade my soul by making me hate him.
—BOOKER T. WASHINGTON

This may be the month of sweethearts, but if we aren't fighting fairly, we won't be experiencing that abundant life of love. Here are "The Five R's" for resolving conflicts. They can be applied to any relationship, whether in marriage, friendship or at the workplace.

1. *Repeat* to each other what the quarrel is really about. Write it out if necessary, redefining it until both of you agree. This in itself will resolve a good many arguments.

2. *Release* it to God in prayer—separately and together. It is difficult to stay angry when you are taking it to the Lord.

3. *Reason* it through together. Identifying the problem as well as possible solutions.

4. *Resolve and leave* it. When it's over, move beyond it. Admit your mistakes, learn from criticism, and start fresh.

5. *Rebuild* the relationship afterwards.

If your partner is unwilling to work toward a solution, some of these steps will still help—defining the difficulty, praying about it, forgiving, even when the other hasn't asked forgiveness. Ask God for His wisdom on timing—when or if to bring it up again, what the next step is, what you alone can do to improve the situation and continue building the relationship in other areas. Above all, ask for wisdom in knowing when to speak and when to be still, for discernment to know if the issue should be forced into the open or put behind you unresolved.

If both of you are willing to work at conflict resolution, then you are ready to learn how to turn every argument into a *discussion*. And is that hard!

To fight—that's okay.

To fight fairly—that's growth.

But to fight with kindness and love—that's grace!

> *He who covers over an offense promotes love,*
> *but whoever repeats the matter separates close friends.*
> PROVERBS 17:9

When you're tempted to lash back at someone in anger, walk away and jog in place in private until the initial burst of energy is gone. Then return to reason through "The Five R's."

February 5

Be My Valentine

BILL AND PAM FARREL

A wise lover values not so much the gift of the lover as the love of the giver.

—THOMAS A' KEMPIS

Our favorite Valentine date was when we were struggling students and had less than ten dollars for the entire evening. Ten dollars had to cover gifts, dinner and activities. We divided up the letters in the word *valentine* and each of us took half the letters and half the money. Bill asked to arrange the food so I donated a few bucks from my share to him. Here is how the date went:

"V" was for a vase with hand-picked flowers for Pam.

"A" was for "act": they acted out Romeo and Juliet's love scene on a park stage with nobody watching.

"L" was for laugh as Bill read jokes out of a library book.

"E" was for eat—sausage on a stick from the mall while they window-shopped.

"N" was for nostalgia as they dropped off Pam's wedding ring at the jewelry store to have it cleaned.

"T" was for tapes: they went to a music store and listened to demo tapes of their favorite musicians.

"I" was for ice cream.

"N" was for a nighttime drive.

"E" was for entertainment, when Bill read Pam a love poem while they parked overlooking the lights of the city.

Each letter was a new surprise to the other person, so the evening was definitely an adventure!

> Better a little with the fear of the Lord
> than great wealth with turmoil.
>
> PROVERBS 15:16

Plan to give your spouse or a friend a Valentine gift that is from the heart, yet cost you nothing.

February 6

Language Of Love

CAROLE MAYHALL

You can give without loving, but you cannot love without giving.

—AMY CARMICHAEL

As Jack and I discussed the languages of love, we realized that one primary way Jack hears my love is by my being one hundred percent *with him*. Whenever he feels that I am not quite agreeing with what he's doing or the decision that he thought we'd agreed on, he doesn't feel truly loved. Of course we discuss everything, and of course there are times when we don't agree! But when all the discussions are over, he needs to feel that I am with him in my heart. And when he asks, a bit plaintively, "Honey, are you really with me on this?" I know I haven't communicated my loyalty and my love to him.

On the other hand, one primary way I hear Jack's love is by his *acceptance* of me. I'm kind of a nut, and I know it. I have an active imagination and sometimes ideas pop into my mind that are, well, let's say *far out*. But to my remembrance, never once in all our married life has Jack said, "Honey, that's got to be the nuttiest idea you ever came up with!" (He may have *thought* it, but he's never *said* it!) I feel his acceptance, which says to me, "I love you" (nutty ideas and all).

When we have learned our partner's language of love, then we can begin to build the secondary languages into our relationship—and have lots of creative, wonderful times doing it. But if we are missing the primary language, our partner may not feel loved in any other way and our efforts will go unnoticed.

We've heard remarks such as:

"My husband is always bringing me flowers or candy. It's like he was trying to buy me off for not spending time with our family."

"I work hard all day and then my wife criticizes me for not being romantic!"

"Why doesn't he *hold me* more when he doesn't want sex? Doesn't he realize I need more nonsexual physical touching?"

"She's always after me to tell her I love her. It's hard for me to be as verbal as she is, but I do try to keep up with all the things in the house that need attention."

Obviously, there may be much more going on in these situations than understanding the other's language. But that might be the first—and simplest—thing to check out. It may solve the problem.

It has been said, "Neglect the whole world rather than each other." Neglecting the concerted study of our love languages can be harmful to a relationship.

I wonder how many of us know our own language of love? I don't think Jack and I were even aware of how many different languages there were until we analyzed them, and even then some time passed before we realized what ours were.

> *The wise in heart are called discerning,*
> *and pleasant words promote instruction.*
> PROVERBS 16:21

Ask your spouse or best friend what makes them feel loved or appreciated and then fulfill it later on Valentine's Day.

February 7

Build Him Up

PAMALA KENNEDY

Love seeks one thing only: the good of the one loved. It leaves all the other secondary effects to take care of themselves.

—THOMAS MERTON

*A*lthough they have a hard time admitting it, men love to be bragged on in one way or another.

Praise is needed in all the little and big things they try. Somewhere I read that for women, sex begins in the kitchen. Perhaps sex begins in the garage or the yard for men.

My husband Richard is usually working on a project of some sort. His latest is restoring a '66 Ford Mustang. I can't tell you the times he has called to me, "Pam, come look at this great-looking carburetor," or he wants to show off the "illustrious interior" he has just completed. I oooh and aaah for a good amount of time, and then return to whatever I was doing before he called me from the sidelines to be cheered on.

I enjoy letting Richard know I'm enthusiastic about his efforts. He's a terrific person and I sincerely think he's deserving of all the cheering I can give him.

And he revels in my praise of whatever he is up to! The yard work, the way he plays handyman and saves us tons of money (usually), the super job he does delivering his sermon on Sunday, and especially his success on a diet. He waits eagerly to be told, "Losing those extra five pounds, Honey, sure makes you irresistible."

What kind of praise is your lover in need of today?

Your husband may be far from having the looks of Tom Selleck or the build of Arnold Schwarzennegger, but he can still be your passionate prince, your brave beloved, your exquisite enchanter, your most precious prize.

Major on any and all of the good qualities he has, physically and personally. Concentrate on his positive and not his negative attributes. Dwell on his wonderful ways and be gracious about his flaws and failures.

Practice the power of praising! It will build him up in ways nothing else can.

She brings him good, not harm,
all the days of her life.

PROVERBS 31:12

Scan the Song of Solomon and pick out several phrases that describe your husband and read them to him.

Pulse Beat

DORIS HAYS TOPPEN

At times a fragrant breeze comes floating by and
brings, you know not why, a feeling as when eager
crowds await before a garden gate.

—UNKNOWN

On a rainy afternoon in February, with Spring on my mind, I
contemplated purchasing bulbs growing in containers along the
front of the local hardware store. How many could I afford? Who all
to buy for? Which would be best?

Someone touched my arm and I turned as a sandy-haired older
lady pointed to the light-petaled daffodils mixed in with the King
Alfred's and miniatures. I eyed the woman intently, trying to understand her motions. Every now and then, a guttural sound pulsed
through her throat, excitement shining in her soft blue eyes. Her lips
pursed with a message, struggling to be heard.

I touched the pots of white-petaled bulbs with golden centers
blooming at various stages with a question in my eyes. "These are the
best?" I asked.

She relaxed her shoulders for a short moment, then began again
in childlike zeal. "Oh yes," her eyes said. Then a few more guttural
noises, her eyes spanning the sky, arms waving in a swooping motion.

I spoke again. "You have a garden full of them?" She relaxed even
more and proudly and deliberately shook her head yes.

I squeezed her arm. "I'll bet your yard is beautiful." I put several
pots in my basket and thanked her for the help.

We smiled and waved good-bye. I'll probably never see her again and
I don't even know her name. But she gave me a great gift—her trust. In
her willingness to share something too good to keep, this woman opened
herself to a stranger, risking frustration, perhaps rejection.

I will think of her each spring when the earth pulses with life,
opening to bulbs struggling to the surface, heralding spring. I will
remember the joy on her face, the beauty of her touch, the childlike
wonder in her eyes, when morning winds weave gently across the
garden path and my daffodils bloom once again.

That day, she demonstrated for me the beauty of an abundant life in her ability to risk rejection to share something important to her.

A cheerful look brings joy to the heart,
and good news gives health to the bones.

The next time you see a handicapped person, share God's love by looking them straight in the eye and smiling.

February 9

Communicate, Communicate, Communicate

BILL HYBELS

It can be said that the success and happiness of any married pair is measurable in terms of the deepening dialogue which characterizes their union.

—DWIGHT SMALL

*U*nless good patterns of communication are set up early in a marriage, a couple is probably headed for disaster. Often, in the emotion and passion of the first few years of marriage, good communication is neglected. Love—this grand adventure we have set upon together—shouldn't concern itself with the mundane. Love is supposed to conquer all. In such an exalted environment, it seems quite petty to be upset that your husband didn't take the trash out. Or that it takes your wife nearly the time it took Columbus to sail the ocean blue to put on her makeup. After all, why waste your time on such minor complaints when the bed is right upstairs?

Please, listen to me: communicate, communicate, communicate. Deal with your differences immediately. Don't store up grievances. Talk with one another about hurts, problems, and patterns of sin. If you have to schedule a time each week for a "gripe" session, free from the heat of emotions, do it. If you voice your concerns once, and the other spouse doesn't seem to get it, voice them again. Don't ever adopt the attitude "I'll just suppress the things that are bothering me until they go away." They won't. When a person hides a grievance, it will boil and stir, gather other concerns to itself, and come out much the way lava explodes from a volcano.

Not to voice concerns is to be dishonest with your spouse and to erect a marriage-threatening barrier between the two of you. This barrier, fed by other unresolved issues and grievances, will grow over time and make it impossible for you to develop oneness with your spouse. The acid of disappointment and hurt will simply be too great.

He who answers before listening–that is his folly and his shame.
PROVERBS 18:13

The next time you communicate dissatisfaction, instead of giving a "you message," phrase it as an "I feel . . . " message instead.

February 10

Gifts Of Love

PATRICIA PHIPPS

Never underestimate a gesture of affection.
— ANONYMOUS

J recently celebrated my fiftieth birthday. One of my dearest sisters in the Lord surprised me with some truly unique birthday presents. She had, over the previous year, collected fifty different items, in lots of fifty (for almost everything).

She is a tremendously talented lady and many of the items were hand made, such as crocheted book marks, coasters, napkin rings, and dish clothes. Other items which she gave were dish towels, hot pads, magnets, blank stationery notes, pencils, pens, band aids, socks, underwear, flowers. Each group of items was accompanied with a greeting card. Some of the cards were both funny and serious; some were friendship, all of which were unsigned. As she presented the last item and card, she gave me the most precious directions, "Freely you have received, freely give."

Since that time, it has been my privilege to bless others on their birthday, anniversary, wedding and Christmas. Dish towels, dish clothes, napkin rings, and coasters are an excellent wedding gift. A magnet tucked away in a card that says "I'm thinking of you" is wonderful and a bookmark laid gently inside a "Get Well" card brings such cheer. Her gifts of love have truly been far reaching.

How could you abundantly bless someone at their next birthday?

Give, and it will be given to you. A good measure, pressed down, shaken together and running over, will be poured into your lap. For with the measure you use, it will be measured to you.

LUKE 6:38

For a special relative or friend's birthday, give something that you made—maybe their favorite meal, cake or even a card.

February 11

The Symbol Of Friendship

GEORGIA CURTIS LING

Friendship is one of the sweetest joys of life.
— CHARLES SPURGEON

The fresh-baked aroma of bread always draws me to the bakery in the supermarket. It's as if it has long thin fingers beckoning me to the counter as it fills my nostrils. If I have a weakness when it comes to food, without a doubt, the answer is bread. I love it any way you slice it.

Throughout the world bread is a staple of most diets. It also carries symbols and legend with it. In ancient times many cultures believed bread was a gift from God. The Spanish saying is, "all sorrows are less with bread." Italians say, "bread is all food, the rest is merely accompaniment." To the Germans bread is a symbol of home and family. And Russian folk lore declares, "bread is the symbol of friendship."

That must be where my favorite bread gets its name, *"Friendship Bread."*

Whenever I visit my family in Kentucky, I indulge on my favorite *Friendship Bread.* A friend of the family sends it for us to enjoy. And that's just what I do. Enjoy it for breakfast, lunch, dinner and in-between snacks.

This particular bread was labeled *Friendship Bread* because you give it away to friends.

It's a yeast bread that takes a starter (usually given to you by a friend). You feed it on a regular basis and it grows and grows. It is baked several times a week and since your own family can't devour that much bread, you give it away to friends. I might add, it gets the friend addicted, anticipating week-to-week visits from a friend bearing bread gifts, joyfully unwrapping the loaf and sharing it over a cup of coffee.

Our own friendships are much like *Friendship Bread.* Friendships are formed by a starter. It may be a brief introduction with a smiling face, or a common ground or interest group like a small group study, neighbors, car pool . . . the list goes on and on. But the starter is there and someone takes the initiative to develop friendships. You never know, God may have let your paths cross for a very special reason.

Like bread, we have to feed our friendships in order for them to grow and not wither away. We need to show our love in abundant ways, and be there when asked for help, even if it's sacrificial.

And last but not least, our friendships are not gifts until we unwrap them and give them away, time and time again for all to enjoy. *Friendship Bread*—a simple starter for making abundant friendships.

Friendship. I guess I love it, even more than bread.

A friend loves at all times . . .
PROVERBS 17:17

> Reach out in friendship to someone younger or older than yourself. You'll be amazed at their wisdom.

February 12

Just Beyond The Curtain

MARCIA KRUGH LEASER

God does not make the other person as I would have made him. He did not give him to me as a brother for me to dominate and control, but in order that I might find above him the Creator.
—DIETRICH BONHOEFFER

When the phone rang loudly at 4:55 a.m. I knew it was Tammy. I was going to be a gramma!

As Bob and I hurried to the hospital, I couldn't help thinking how differently things were today than when Tammy had arrived twenty-four years earlier. I had been put into a small room and left alone with no one but a nurse allowed in to periodically check on my progress. Then when the time arrived, I was wheeled forty miles an hour down a long corridor to the room where babies were delivered—without husband or relatives near.

I was excited at the thought of being allowed to be in the birthing room with Tammy and Rod. How special this time would be for us.

As we drove through the silent night, I thought of all the things I would do to make the time more comfortable for my daughter.

I rushed into the room and found her well cared for by capable nurses.

Rod's masculine hand held Tammy's as he lovingly put a damp washcloth on her sweaty brow. "You're doing fine," his deep voice assured her.

His dark brown eyes met mine and I knew that Tammy didn't need me any more. Giving her an encouraging smile and a hearty thumbs up, I slowly backed out of the door and stood in the hallway outside of the room.

This was their time: hers and Rod's. It was time for me to realize that Tammy is no longer my little girl. She is a mother herself, a grown woman with someone else to take care of her from now on. The lump in my throat was hard to swallow, but I thanked God that Rod is the responsible, reliable person he is.

Bob and I stood outside the curtain with Linda and Sam, Rod's parents, awaiting the first little cry. It came at 10:02 a.m. and I thanked God for another life coming into this world.

It's hard to let go and suddenly become aware that our children no longer need us. I thought back to the day of Tammy's birth. How I held her tiny hand and prayed for the strength I knew I would need to raise her. Please, Lord, I prayed now, guide this new mother and father as they start out on the long road of parenthood. Make them aware of *your* presence and *your* love. And help me to always be there, Father, just beyond the curtain, to offer advice when asked, love when needed, and understanding when times seem impossible to face alone.

At times it's hard to comprehend that abundant love releases the one loved. But that simple—but not easy—act of letting go shows greater love than holding on. Is there someone you need to release? It's a paradox, but that may actually demonstrate your love more.

> So they are no longer two, but one. Therefore,
> what God has joined together, let man not separate.
> MARK 10:8-9

After receiving a prayer request on your e-mail, keep it in your active file as a reminder to pray.

Practical Steps

BILL HYBELS

> Praising a woman before marriage is a matter of in-
> clination. But praising one after you marry her is a
> matter of necessity.
>
> —DOROTHY DIX

You may have already given up, or at least determined long ago to settle for less. Your sex life, when there is any, is a matter of going through the same motions. You believe there is simply no way back to passion. I am here to tell you there is.

I am not promising it will be easy; in fact, the process will involve single-minded obedience to the will of God. But there are steps you can take to put the oneness back into marriage, and the sizzle back into the bedroom.

First, learn to communicate. Many times spouses drift away from one another simply because they don't know one another anymore. They don't know each other's thoughts, dreams, faith, and day-to-day lives. I believe it is critical for couples, regardless of how long they have been married, to have at least one date night each week, with time set aside just for talking—about goals, disappointments, hopes, grievances—yesterday, today, and tomorrow. Romance starts with the knowledge of one another, and knowledge comes through communication.

Couples should also rediscover how to court one another creatively and how to have fun together. With the pressures of raising children, holding down a job, and staying one step ahead of life, the fun often disappears. Marriage, instead of a refuge, often becomes part of the routine, another cause of exhaustion. Couples must fight the beasts of routine and stress. So go a little crazy. Rent a limousine to go to McDonald's. Jump in a lake at three in the morning on a moonlit night. Reserve a honeymoon suite, the one with fancy mirrors and a Jacuzzi, for a weekend. Take up racquetball together. Send a love letter to your spouse through the mail. The sharing of fun experiences can be a bridge to rekindling a marriage.

Serving one another is a guaranteed way of reducing the tension and building the passion in a marriage. Look for ways to be a servant. Cook your spouse's favorite meal. Wash your spouse's car. Sweep the carpet.

A man of knowledge uses words with restraint,
and a man of understanding is even-tempered.

PROVERBS 17:27

> Tell your spouse or friend that you are going to "outserve"
> them, and then look for ways to do it.

February 14

The Valentine Gift

LOUISA GODISSART MCQUILLEN

Service to a just cause rewards the worker with more
real happiness and satisfaction than any other venture
in life.

—CARRIE CHAPMAN CATT

J began my day like any other—by talking to the Lord in pre-dawn
hours. It was Valentine's Day and I felt extra-close to Him as I
dressed for work.

I hummed a worship chorus, and even lifted my hands in the air
to praise Him for several moments. Suddenly, I was dancing as well!
Around the bathroom I spun, free in heart and spirit. Inside, I felt as
though a powerful spring had activated itself.

I was embarrassed! *I must look silly*, I thought, *even to God!* Besides,
it was six o'clock in the morning—time to get ready for work.

I remembered it was Valentine's Day in time to don a red blouse
for the occasion. Then I brushed my teeth, called good-bye to my cat,
"Critter," and left the house.

While carpooling to Penn State University, I thought more about
February 14th—traditionally the biggest day of the year for sweethearts to
express their affection for one another.

Christ is the greatest love in my life. I wondered—can I give *Him* a gift
today? Just then, one of my fellow car-poolers drew me into conversation. I
forgot about giving a Valentine gift to the greatest Lover the world has ever
known.

At my office, it looked as if it might be a long day. My co-worker Carol's
new puppy, Buttons, had been killed by a huge, vicious dog. She was so
distraught that she couldn't come to work. Remembering when my dog
Jasper died, I wrote her a few words of comfort and decided to bake her a
cake when I went home.

Around noon time I heard a ragged cough coming from the next office. Sharon was battling the flu and all she managed to pack for her lunch was a bagel. In the lunchroom I could hear the gentle hum of the microwave heating my own nourishing lunch—an extra-large bowl of homemade vegetable soup. Sharon smiled weakly, grateful that I thought to share with her.

In the hall that afternoon I passed Amy, a terrific pianist for one of our department's music programs. Her fingers had fairly flown over the piano keys yesterday as I walked by the practice studio. I commented: "You play a mean piano, Amy. I'm impressed!" When we parted she was still smiling, pleased by the compliment.

At home that night I busied myself getting dinner, feeding Critter, cleaning up. For a while I worked on a new article, then went to bed. Lying there in the dark, I realized that Valentine's Day was over and I hadn't done more than think about giving Christ a gift! Now it was too late. Or was it?

My mind honed in on my awkward dance in the bathroom that morning. I had done it unto God, at a moment when my heart felt exceptionally warm toward Him. I thought of other events of the day: sharing soup with Sharon, the sympathy note written to Carol, my compliment to Amy and her happy smile as she walked away.

I smiled. I had unwittingly given Him a gift after all. As I drifted off to sleep, I envisioned Jesus smiling, too.

Though you may think you haven't invested in the lives of others, consider that Jesus values even an insignificant, simple act on our part. We won't know until heaven how God abundantly uses them to impact others.

. . . Whatever you did for one of the least of these brothers of mine,
you did for me.

MATTHEW 25:40

Call someone who is single or lonely and give them a Valentine's Day greeting.

Reminders Of God's Care

JILL BRISCOE

There is no need to plead that the love of God shall
fill our heart as though He were unwilling to fill us.
He is willing as light is willing to flood a room that is
opened to its brightness.

—AMY CARMICHAEL

*M*any a time when I have been flat on my face, God has sent
some practical expression of love to remind me that he cares.

Once when this happened I had been traveling for two weeks
straight, speaking at meetings. Somehow the tight schedule allowed
only time for talking and not much for eating! Whenever it was
mealtime, I found myself on one more airplane. On this particular day
it was hot. It was summer, and I was tired and hungry. My flight had
been delayed, and by the time I arrived at the next conference center,
I discovered that my hosts had gone to bed. (In the morning I learned
that because of the delayed flight, they presumed I would not be
coming until the following day—hence, no welcoming committee.) I
wandered around the large dining room, hoping to find something to
eat, but all the doors into the kitchen had been locked. "Lord," I
prayed, "I really don't care what I eat, but I need something—and while
I'm talking to you about this, I've got a yearning for peaches! Oh, for
a lovely, refreshing, juicy peach!" Then I smiled. That was just the sort
of prayer I counseled others against offering! I sighed, picked up my
bags, and went to my assigned cabin.

When I arrived at my room, there were my hot cakes baked on the
coals! A basket of peaches sat on the doorstep smiling up at me! I lifted
them up and felt my loving Lord's smile. (It could have been oranges
and apples, you know!) Never before or since have I received a whole
basket of delicious, fresh peaches. But he who was waiting round the
corner of my desert met and provided a sweet touch that reminded me
of his great love.

When you find yourself exhausted, burned out—look around for God's
care by some practical expression of concern through one of his children.

Since you are precious and honored in my sight, and because I love you,
I will give men in exchange for you, and people in exchange for your life.

ISAIAH 43:4

Volunteer to open your home for guest travelers at
your church.

February 16

Fit For God's Company

ESTHER M. BAILEY

Christ in His atonement has removed the bar to the
divine fellowship. Now in Christ all believing souls
are objects of God's delight.

—A. W. TOZER

Sometimes the parallel between a slice-of-life story and a spiritual
truth strikes me with such force that I consider it to be a flash
from heaven. I once had such an experience while watching the
evening news.

Perhaps the thrill of receiving fresh insight was enhanced even
more because it was surprising that I saw the program. Not only would
I normally be cooking dinner at that time, my husband usually watched
news on a different channel.

At first the theme of the story did not grab my attention. I'm not
into sheep farming and I don't know much about the culture of Peru.
The two topics are related because it is the practice of some sheep
farmers in the United States to hire shepherds from Peru to care for
their flocks. On contract for a certain number of years, the Peruvian
shepherd brings along the expertise learned in his native land.

The skill of the shepherd shows up best in the way he handles
orphaned lambs. On a large farm there usually are a few ewes that lose
their lambs. Such ewes will ignore any other lambs, even those without
mothers. Other lambs don't have the proper "scent."

But the Peruvian shepherd knows how to overcome this lack of
abundant love in the ewe. He takes the skin from the dead lamb and
places it on an orphaned lamb. The mother of the lamb that died will
then accept the orphaned lamb as her own. It is a good arrangement
for both of them. Otherwise, the lamb would die, and the ewe would
continue to grieve.

As I watched a lifesaving miracle take place, the story suddenly had profound personal meaning for me. I was an orphaned lamb, alienated from God through the fall of Adam. Left to my own devices, I would never become fit for God's company. The best I could do would be to clothe myself with filthy rags. I was headed for death—eternal separation from God, who created me to fellowship with Him.

My condition might never have changed had it not been for a pastor representative of the Shepherd. Through the pastor I learned that the Son of God became the sacrificial Lamb for me. Jesus Christ died in my place so that I might be clothed with His righteousness. As soon as I received His Son as my Savior, God accepted me as one of His children. In effect, I became covered with the Lamb's skin, making me fit to spend eternity with Him.

Do you sense a holy hush penetrating your soul as you allow the story of the Peruvian shepherd to remind you of God's abundant love and wonderful plan of redemption? He provided this simple way to have you reconciled to Him.

Just as through the disobedience of the one man the many were made sinners, so also through the obedience of the one man the many will be made righteous.

ROMANS 5:19

> Buy a dozen flowers—"today's special"—and give one to twelve different people.

February 17

Laundry Bandits and Relationships

TINA KRAUSE

Love is not only something you feel. It's something
you do.

—DAVID WILKERSON

"You can't mix three men in one dryer," Hubby mumbled as he searched through his drawer for a lost sock. It was week five and the countdown continued—four more weeks living with my parents before our new house would be ready.

"Mom must have put it in Dad's drawer when she washed our laundry again," I reasoned.

"I know," he said with a grimace. "Suddenly I have no T-shirts or socks."

We asked Mom to *please* not wash our dirty clothes; but whenever the hamper tipped half-full, the laundry bandit crept into our bedroom to nab out nighties, snitch our socks, and shrink our shirts and slacks. Since the men outnumbered the women, Jim and son, Jeff, usually came out on the short end of the scrubbing board.

"Mom," Jim called. "Do you know where my black sock is? It has a green line across the toe."

Dad overheard and responded, "I've got some of those; I could use some more."

Two families coexisting under one roof is like squeezing a size 8 foot into a size 5 shoe. After a few minutes you want to scream, flip the shoe off, and ease into a roomy pair of slippers.

It's no one's fault. We all love each other. We simply tend to guard our individuality and insist on doing things our own way. It's difficult for dissimilar individuals to inhabit the same dwelling without eventual conflict.

Church families are no different. Various people with different personalities and backgrounds gather under one roof to worship and serve God. Sooner or later, someone will unintentionally tamper with another's spiritual style or shrink someone's devout designs. After all, everyone has his or her own opinion on how to accomplish God's work.

Family unity takes work, whether in the home or in the church, but it's worth the effort. Lost socks and shrunken shirts are replaceable, but relationships aren't.

And though three men in a dryer don't mix, family and church unity is possible, even when the laundry bandit insists on doing things her way. We can live abundantly when we pour the detergent of love and grace into the washing machine of relationships.

How good and pleasant it is when brothers live together in unity!
PSALM 133:1

> To cut down on laundry time, put in a load before leaving the house and fold it later while talking on the phone.

Disney Has Nothin' On God!

LUCINDA SECREST MCDOWELL

God soon turns from his wrath, but he never turns
from his love.

—CHARLES H. SPURGEON

*A*fter 13 years of entering contests (someone had to win, why not us,
I thought?) we finally broke down and took our two girls (age 17 & 7)
to Disney World (the boys, 22 & 20, have yet to go). So now everyone asks
me the same thing, "What was your favorite site at Disney World?"

My answer comes quickly, "My daughter's face!" I spent the whole
time delighting in Maggie's enjoyment of all the fantasy, excitement, and
glitz Disney had to offer. Amidst all those distractions, the one I sought
out was her. Isn't God a lot like that?

The world seeks to entertain, tempt, dazzle and impress, but God's eyes
are always on the lookout for the most incredible sight of all—ME, His
daughter! I'm so glad He loves me (and you!) so abundantly, aren't you?

Keep me as the apple of your eye; hide me in the shadow of your wings.
PSALM 17:8

> Recall a cherished memory moment of a long-ago
> friend. Send them a memory note and a "thank-you."

Simple Love Gauge

BILLY GRAHAM

Yes, love is the magic key of life—not to get what we
want but to become what we ought to be.

—EILEEN GUDER

*I*n many of the older cars the fuel gauge used to contain a red liquid,
and its level in the gauge corresponded to the level of fuel in the
tank. As the liquid was in the gauge, so it was in the tank.

If you would know the measure of your love for God, just observe your love for your fellow men. Our compassion for others is an accurate gauge of our devotion to God.

The Bible puts it this way: "Let us love one another: for love is of God; and every one that loveth is born of God, and knoweth God . . . And this commandment have we from Him, That he who loveth God love his brother also."

This is the love for God: to obey his commands.

I JOHN 5:3

Are you planning an abundant dinner? Try using a pretty, new sheet as a tablecloth over an old door (on sawhorses) for a large dining table.

February 20

Diamond in the Sand

PETER N. ROBBINS

All individuals, like uncut diamonds, have shining qualities beneath a tough and darkened exterior.
—PETER N. ROBBINS

J recently heard of a father who took his preschool son and a playmate to the park to play. He observed the boys playing in the sandbox area with something tiny and shiny. They were banging, pounding and tossing it around, and alternately burying it.

Finally, he went over to check it out.

"Daddy, look, a ring!" the little boy held out a ring for his daddy to see. It was much more than just a ring. It was a *diamond* ring.

"Let daddy see it," he replied. The young father guessed that it was at least a full carat and put it into his pocket for safe keeping. After several weeks of futile effort to locate the owner of the ring, he took it to a jeweler for an appraisal.

"Can you tell me how much this is worth?" asked the young father. He had already explained the whole story about finding the ring.

"Well, based on your story and how badly this 1.2 carat ring has been treated, I'd say it's only worth about $50."

"$50! That's ridiculous! How can it be only worth $50?" he replied aghast.

Actually, that's not how the story went. The jeweler told the young father that it was worth about $3,500. But things of true value are not appraised based on how they are treated. Their value comes from their true essence, from intrinsic worth.

This truth is especially relevant for you in living the abundant life. Many of us struggle with low self-esteem because of how we were treated in childhood and adolescence. We may have been banged around physically, or pounded on verbally. You may not have been treated with love. As a result, you may consider yourself unworthy of living abundantly.

No matter your past, your value is not determined by how you were treated, but it is undeniable established by your Creator. His evaluation is based on two criteria: your intrinsic worth (being made in His image) and the price someone is willing to pay for your life.

What would you guess your life is worth? The fact is, your life cost the Father the life of His own Son. He gladly paid it. In short, you're priceless! Claim this truth and reclaim your true value! You can experience abundant love by simply believing you are worth it.

This is how we know what love is: Jesus Christ laid down his life for us . . .
1 JOHN 3:16

To help with a simplified life in your home, have one place designated as a desk for incoming bills, receipts and important papers.

February 21

Prayer

DEBBIE PIPER

Any good relationship depends on communication
between the people involved.

—ANONYMOUS

If we're going to live the abundant life God promised, we must have communication with Him. Since God is a living God, we can interact with Him just like we communicate with other people. But God isn't limited to needing to be physically present for us to talk to Him. Nor does He depend on the mail being delivered or getting a phone line hooked up. As believers, we have direct access to God twenty-four hours a day, seven days a week, through the presence of the Holy Spirit living within us. So we can talk with God whenever we want to, without needing a go-between of any sort. Your relationship with God will only be as strong as your communication with Him.

We've entered into a relationship with a living God who desires to get to know us intimately, and who longs for us to get to know Him intimately. And any relationship depends on communication to keep it alive and growing. The more we are with someone and spend time sharing together, the closer we are going to grow.

Prayer is the simplest basic of the Christian life. It operates just like human communication. What's the first thing two people do when they haven't seen one another in a long time? They immediately begin catching up on what has been going on in each other's lives since the last time they talked. There are always new areas to explore, new circumstances to share, and advice to be given. Communication with God is just like that.

The first and most obvious reason to pray is because we need help with daily problems, with crises, with relationships, with things we don't understand, and in making choices. But the reasons to pray go much deeper than our own personal needs.

Another foundational reason to pray is because God invites us to! He even commands it! Over and over, the Bible records God's invitation to come into His presence and get to know Him. Jesus taught His disciples to pray, to ask for what we need, and tells us to come to the Father with our needs.

And lastly, God has provided the means and the way for us to come into His presence to pray. Jesus opened the way into the Father's presence for us and is in heaven right now talking with God on our behalf. And the Holy Spirit is present within us, searching out even the deepest needs of our lives and communicating them to God when we can't find the right words to say! If God has made a point of providing the means for us to come into His presence, it must be because He thinks it is important for His children to stay in touch, and He wants to hear from us!

Have you had His attention lately? If not, He invites you to experience the abundance of sensing His presence right now.

Let us then approach the throne of grace with confidence,
so that we may receive mercy and find grace to help us in our time of need.
HEBREWS 4:16

FEBRUARY

> To simplify this daily chore, when loading silverware into the dishwasher, group similar utensils together to save time unloading.

February 22

The Taxi Driver

SANDY CATHCART

Security is having the Word of God in your own language.
Peace is having the Word of God in your own heart.
—CORRIE TEN BOOM

"Miami Airport, please," I commanded as I jumped into the front seat of the taxi. "Hope you don't mind. I get sick riding in the back."

"That's okay," the driver answered.

I detected a familiar accent. "Where are you from?"

"Miami," he mumbled.

"Born and raised?"

He straightened his cap with one hand, "You are a nosy young woman."

"Nosy perhaps," I laughed, "but not so young. Your speech sounds Russian to me."

"My name is Boris," he said. Then he told the story of how he had left a good job in Russia to immigrate to America.

"It must have been difficult to leave all your engineering training behind you," I said.

"I wanted my children to have choices." He guided the taxi through a crowded intersection. "I came to America so they could have the best of what life has to offer. My son is a doctor and my daughter recently finished college."

As I watched his fine hands working the steering wheel, I was struck with the realization of his willing sacrifice for the needs of his children. His selfless view of life was so much like that of Christ that I couldn't help but ask if he was a Christian.

"Oh no," he answered. "I was raised an atheist. I can't even understand such things."

"But I think you can," I answered. "Because Jesus calls us His children and left His heavenly home for us. Surely you can understand that kind of love after all you've done for your family. Do you have a Bible?"

He confessed that someone had recently given him a Bible but it remained unopened because he didn't think he would be able to understand it. When he pulled the taxi to the curb of the Miami Airport I turned to him. "I'll make a deal with you," I said. "There is a God in Heaven who has big dreams for His children, even bigger than you had for yours. You promise me that you will read your Bible and I'll promise to pray for your understanding."

His solemn eyes held mine. "It's a deal."

"One more thing," I said. "Promise that you will think about God."

It didn't seem like much at the time, a simple conversation with a busy man in a harried town, but looking back on it, I think I gave him the best possible gift—an opportunity to consider an abundant life in Jesus. The finest preaching in all the world can't match the simple truth of the love found in the Gospel. Whether we give the Word, live the Word, or inspire others to read the Word—even in seemingly simple, insignificant ways—the Bible is always able to reveal clear understanding to the human heart.

All Scripture is God-breathed and is useful for teaching,
rebuking, correcting and training in righteousness . . .
2 TIMOTHY 3:16

When in contact with "servers" who wear name tags (waiters, valets, clerks, etc.) make an effort to call them by name. You represent Jesus' love.

February 23

Poor In Spirit

DEBORAH SILLAS NELL

Christ says, "Give me All. I don't want so much of your time and so much of your money and so much of your work: I want You. I have not come to torment your natural self, but to kill it . . . I will give you a new self instead. In fact, I will give you Myself: my own will shall become yours."

—C.S. LEWIS

*S*ix months ago, my husband, three year-old daughter and I moved into a low income neighborhood because we felt God calling us to live among the poor and minister His love to them. God gave us the grace to move to this neighborhood and then He let me feel my poverty.

I remember sitting in our one bedroom apartment and overhearing two single moms talking to one another in the courtyard below. They spoke with one another with such ease and honesty.

How do they do that? I wondered. *They are so real, so unpretentious.*

A deep pain pierced my soul and I could not run from that pain any longer. I was confronted with a truth that my previous busyness and former environment had helped me to avoid. No longer could I avoid that truth. I felt inadequate in relating openly and honestly with other women.

You must have made a mistake, God. I have nothing to give to these women here. I feel so empty, so inept in relating to them. In my spirit I could sense God's presence and His love for me. Although I didn't hear any audible words, I did sense He said to me, "Deborah, did you think I didn't know that you would feel this emptiness within you? I've known all along about your brokenness, your difficulty in relating with other women. Will you give me your poverty and let Me fill you with my abundance? I haven't made a mistake. I have called you to minister to the people in this neighborhood. But not with your love, but Mine. Let me give you My love for them."

As tears flowed down my face, His peace and security began to fill me. I had to respond, *Yes, Lord, please take my broken, empty spirit and give me your abundance, your love for these neighbors.*

That day marked a turning point in my life. Over a period of weeks God began to fill me with His love and compassion for the people in my neighborhood. It was His compassion that compelled me to risk rejection as I began talking to my neighbors and began doing small acts of kindness for them. My fear of rejection was replaced with His compassion for the lost.

Now neighbors come to my door wanting help with learning English or with baby-sitting their children. Sometimes they just need to talk. The more I give away what God has given me—His love and compassion—the more He gives me to give away.

What a gift to see our poverty. For when we give Jesus our poverty of spirit, He gives us His Kingdom. In God's kind of economy, spiritual poverty brings abundance.

Examine your life. Is busyness and pride diminishing God's ability to produce an abundance of love and compassion for others? Let Him fill you. It just takes a simple surrender of your soul.

Blessed are the poor in spirit, for theirs is the Kingdom of heaven.

MATTHEW 5:3

> When put on hold on the telephone, find something useful to do like cleaning out a drawer or getting the bills ready to pay.

February 24

What's In A Name?

WINONA SMITH

We are not just numbers to God. He knows us better than we know ourselves.

—ANONYMOUS

Do you know someone named Kerrie? Is their name spelled with an "i.e." or is it spelled another way, such as Kerry, or Kerri? What about Susie—or maybe Suzie, or even Suzy?

There are many names that sound the same, but have different spellings. On the other hand, there are names that are spelled the same, but sound different. The way that we spell and say our name is one way that we are set apart from other people. When we are given a name by our parents, even though it might sound the same as someone else's, the people who are familiar with us know exactly who we are. Our name is unique to us and is one way that God has of letting us know that we are special, individual beings, created in His likeness. He loves each one of us individually in His own special way.

In the Bible Jesus has many different names. Some of them are: Emmanuel, Savior, Prince of Peace, Everlasting Father, and Wonderful Counselor. No matter what name we choose to call Him, He is still Jesus Christ, our Lord and King.

So, if we ever begin to feel like we've become lost in the crowd, we can remember that God knows us better than anyone elses, and since He continues to give us unconditional love, we must be unique and special to Him.

Have you allowed your uniqueness as His creation to fill you with a deep sense of His abundant love? You don't need to make His love complicated. It's just the simple truth that He created you distinctly because He loves you.

He determines the number of the stars
and calls them each by name.
Great is our Lord, and mighty in power.
His understanding has not limit.

PSALM 147:4-5

> Spend five minutes picking up clutter before going to bed, and another five minutes cleaning out the clutter in your head. You'll wake up to a cleaner house and a fresher mind that will start your day right.

February 25

The Blessing of Cancer

SANDRA HINMAN GRIESMEYER

Stop and smell the roses.

—ANONYMOUS

One of the blessings of my life has been cancer. It taught me to live an abundant life filled with love. According to my doctor, my cancer was the best kind to have—if you have to have cancer. Surgery removed it. I was back on my feet in a short time so that I could sing my solo on Christmas Day.

The "C" word caught my attention and made me pause to examine my life. I had an further opportunity to tell my two grown daughters how very proud I am of the lives they chose and the standards by which they live. I wrote to the oldest two because they were not close by. Within two months of receiving her letter, my second daughter and her only child were taken in a car accident. But I had said, "I love you" every chance I had; so there weren't any regrets.

It's simple—and an important part of an abundant Christian life—to express God's love to others. You may see a woman who has lost her usual bounce. Or a man whose usual constant smile isn't reaching his eyes today. Reach out. You have no guarantees you'll be able to do it tomorrow. I intend that when my extension on life is over, that I gave an abundance of love to those around me.

Time and three daughters have taught me that the dust bunnies will wait and gather friends. Just like laundry, pain is always there. Tomorrow, bleach can work on the stain on my shirt, but a stain on a heart needs to be taken care of today. Take time to listen to a need or share a burden. Take time to whisper a prayer for someone who's hurting. A tremendous desire to share love is the abundant blessing cancer gave me.

What will it take to motivate you to share His love?

And we know that in all things God works for the good of those who love him, who have been called according to his purpose.
ROMANS 8:28

> Do you have a friend suffering through a life trial? Make a dozen "hearts" to pass out to friends, as a reminder to pray and keep the faith of hope alive.

February 26

Triple Value

ESTHER M. BAILEY

I should kill two birds with one stone as that excellent thrifty proverb says.

—THOMAS SHADWELL

It's good to accomplish two purposes with one activity, but Maggie Johnson actually derives triple value from a single project. She turns her hobby into ministry as well as play time with her grandson.

"At this stage in life I need to get as much mileage as I can out of every moment," Johnson says with a laugh.

Actually, the stylish grandmother's hobby evolved from a simple childhood pleasure. "I liked to color so well I needed to find an excuse to continue the fun as a grown-up," she says.

Each month Maggie makes and sends thirty to forty greeting cards to people who need to know that someone cares. With approximately three hundred rubber stamps, she creates custom-designed cards for every occasion.

From the time Grandson A. J. was three years old, Maggie's hobby has provided a way of entertaining him and also something that strengthens their bond. A. J. likes to stamp the pictures and watch Grandma create a soft, delicate portrait with colored pencils. While having fun, A. J. also shares with Grandma that good feeling that comes from a benevolent act.

Johnson didn't consider her work to be a ministry until her church formed an outreach program called Open Arms to minister to shut-ins. As soon as an appeal was made, Johnson quickly volunteered to head up the card ministry.

Always on the lookout for special needs, Johnson checks the church bulletin each week and receives calls through several prayer chains in the twelve-hundred-member congregation. Her goal is to shower individuals with cards during times of bereavement, illness, or any traumatic event.

If you'd like to share God's abundant love with others in a simple way, combine ministry with other hobbies by:

• Focusing on someone's need while making a craft. Give the finished product to that person with a note: "You have been in my prayers while I worked on this."

• Shopping. Volunteer to work with the Benevolent Committee in your church. Some people are willing to provide money for needs within the congregation or Angel Tree gifts, but don't want to do the shopping.

• Reading. Write a brief synopsis of a book for the librarian, provide illustrations for your pastor's sermons, encourage others to read, donate books you've read to the library.

As you look for simple, yet effective, ways to combine your hobby with ministry, ideas will begin to flow. If you can involve your child or grandchild in the project, you may even kill three birds with one stone. That's abundance!

. . . Make the most of every opportunity.
COLOSSIANS 4:5

Concentrate on prayer requests while tending to house or garden plants. Tag each plant with the name of someone who needs your prayers. As you water and prune the plant, take the need to God. Replace with other names when situations are resolved.

Father, Forgive Them

DURLYNN ANEMA-GARTEN

To know we are forgiven means that we in turn are
able to forgive others with a similar generosity.
— DUNCAN BUCHANAN

When was the last time you chose the simple act of forgiving someone? Forgiveness is the most powerful way to show God's kind of abundant love. It requires His very power within us.

Quite often we resist forgiving because we don't want to forget how they've hurt us. We want others to forgive us. But, because of our deep wound, it's hard for us to forgive them.

But Jesus gave us the key to abundance when he told us to forgive "seventy-times-seven." Research shows that forgiveness—meaning giving up the anger and pain entirely—is good both for our spiritual and our physical well-being.

A recent study proclaimed that "holding a grudge can hinder your heart." Researchers found a direct connection between anger and an immediate change in the physical heart rate. Just think about how bitterness, the result of unforgiveness, can bring illness and depression.

Forgiveness has been defined as the fragrance flowers breathe when they are trampled upon. As you forgive, you may feel like a delicate flower which has given time and again, only to be disdained, humiliated or rejected. You have the option of cultivating the hurt or letting it go.

If you cultivate it, it will grow as a poisonous plant within. And it will grow inside *you* not your enemy. It hurts only you.

But if you choose to let it go, the burden will be lifted from your life and you will feel God's glory. You'll have freedom to be whole. That's abundant living!

Jesus is the greatest friend we will ever have. As our friend, He was suspected, deserted, tried, mocked, scourged and crucified on our behalf. He went through all that to show you His abundant love. From the depth of His agony He uttered; "Father, forgive them, for they know not what they do" (Luke 23:32-34).

Can we do less?

Bear with each other and forgive whatever grievances you
may have against one another. Forgive as the Lord forgave you.

COLOSSIANS 3:13

> Put all healthy snacks in one place and give your children permission to choose from them at any time. It'll lessen the demands upon your time and attention.

February 28

In My Corner

MICHELE T. HUEY

Friendship is to people what sunshine is to flowers.

—WINNING ATTITUDES

I am in the center of a boxing ring. My opponent is LIFE, and he deals some pretty hard blows. His strategy is not to knock me out, but to wear me down.

The bell rings to end the round. I head for my corner, but there is no one there. No one to wipe the blood from my face, soothe my bruises, massage tight muscles. No one to cheer me on, after all, everyone loves a winner. I am not winning. Not by a long shot. There is no one to spur me on, encouraging me to persist and overcome. No one to tell me, "Go get 'em!"

The bell rings once more, signaling the beginning of the next round. I drag myself out, but I am weary and broken. Is there no one who believes in me? How much longer can I last?

I step up to my opponent who is grinning. Perhaps this will be my last round. But wait. I hear my name called, faintly at first, then louder. It's coming from my corner!

Renewed energy springs up from somewhere deep within me. It's not over yet! I block punches, dodge thrusts, sidestep advances. I am still bleeding, but it doesn't matter now. Someone is behind me, shouting "You can do it!"

The bell rings once more. Amazingly I've finished another round. My bruises throb and my muscles scream with fatigue. I turn to my corner to see who has come to my side. It is LOVE.

Do you hear LOVE calling your name?

And now these three remain: faith, hope, and love. But the greatest of these is love.
1 CORINTHIANS 13:13

Send a note or card of encouragement to someone going through a difficult time.

February 29

Locked In Love

SANDRA PALMER CARR

Look to the Lord, for amid all the separations that
may come to us He will remain.
—HERBERT LOCKYER

It was bedtime for my son, Craig. Since his one-year-old brother was already sleeping soundly in the nursery, my four-year-old first-born looked forward to this time alone.

After I had read a story or two, we prayed, and then we had our nightly hugs and kisses. He always wanted one more of each and would cling to my neck as I gently loosened his grasp. This time Craig held on tighter than usual and I sensed he really needed more touching. He spoke quietly into my ear: "These are the gates of love, mom; we can't let the love go." We held onto our hug until he fell asleep.

My sons are men now. But "the gates of love" are still locked tightly. And they remind me that if there is someone in my life who needs to be touched a little more, hugged a little longer, or told "we can't let the love go," I must do it today. It's actually a simple choice of love that reaps abundant rewards.

Have you sensed that your heavenly Father never pulls away when you reach out for Him? In His eternal embrace you rest secure, knowing He is strong enough to hold you and all those to whom you reach out with His love.

Never will I leave you; never will I forsake you.
HEBREWS 13:5B

Do you have a cherished, valuable possession that is stored away for fear of it being harmed? Display it regardless, otherwise its beauty can't be appreciated.

March

"*Rejoice always.*"

I Thessalonians 5:16

Since the date for Easter changes each year, feel free to read April's offerings of peace this month if Easter falls in March. Nevertheless, this month's readings of March joy is bound to increase your simple, childlike faith in God. We all seek happiness, yet happiness is not God's primary goal for our abundant living. It's joy that will bless us more. Happiness is something that happens to us, but joy is something we can choose regardless of our circumstances. When we make that decision in God's power, we'll experience God's abundance.

The Lesson Of The Cardinal

JOAN WEAVER

Because these wings are no longer wings to fly
But merely vans to beat the air
The air which is now thoroughly small and dry
Smaller and dryer than the will
Teach us to care and not to care
Teach us to sit still.

—T.S. ELIOT

It is the beginning of March and spring has a toe-hold in the door of winter. All year long I have found simple pleasure in watching the birds flit and flutter around my bird feeders. They are a constant source of amusement and wonder. I try to keep feeders filled with different seeds so as to attract a wide variety of birds with all their colors and songs. Watching them is relaxing and often educational.

The last few days the male cardinal has been constantly flying at the bay windows. From sun-up to sun-down, he dive bombs the panes and pecks at the glass. He and the Mrs. have decided to nest in the cedar trees, and I believe they don't want me "nesting" in their territory. His ethnic cleansing of the neighborhood has already resulted in the expulsion of the blue jays. All of his persistent fussing leaves him with no time to soar or sing.

It seems my cardinal is obsessed. The fact that I have kept him well-fed all winter at a bird feeder filled with sunflower seeds does not make me any more desirable to have around. Even when he takes time away from his scoldings to drink or splash in the bird bath, he does not seem to know that the clean water is one more way I show my love for him. He does not realize that if I were to leave, as he so persistently asks me to do, his abundant life would leave with me.

But perhaps I should not be so disturbed and puzzled by this red bird's behavior, for sometimes I am very much like him. I constantly pray and hope for what I want, instead of trusting in the One who knows my needs and consistently, abundantly provides for them. How often I choose to spend my days complicating life so that I am unable to experience the beauty around me and the exhilaration of life as God's child. God offers me His abundance, yet I'm spending my short lifetime obsessed with details. Starting today, I want to take brilliant flight in my world and lift my song of praise.

As you begin this new month of abundant living, will you join me in trusting that God will provide your needs?

I will sing to the Lord, for he has been good to me.

PSALM 13:6

> Take your praise to the Lord to a new level. Choreograph a dance of worship to the chorus of your favorite praise song.

March 2

Leave Room For God

OSWALD CHAMBERS

The man or woman who is wholly or joyously surrendered to Christ can't make a wrong choice—any choice will be the right one.

—A.W. TOZER

As workers for God we have to learn to make room for God—to give God "elbow room." We calculate and estimate, and say that this and that will happen. Then we forget to make room for God to come in as He chooses. Would we be surprised if God came into our meeting or into our preaching in a way we had never looked for Him to come? Do not look for God to come in any particular way, but *look for Him.* This is the way to make room for Him. Expect Him to come, but do not expect Him in a certain way. However we may know God, the great lesson to learn is that at any minute He may break in. We are apt to overlook this element of surprise, yet God rarely works in other ways. All of a sudden God meets the life— "When it was the good pleasure of God . . ."

Keep your life so in contact with God that His surprising power may break out on the right hand and on the left. Always be in a state of expectancy, and see that you leave room for God to come in as He likes.

But when God . . . was pleased . . .

GALATIANS 1:15

> Surprise yourself with your organizational skills by having a "take along" spot in your home or office for collecting items that need to be transferred elsewhere.

March 3

Eliminate And Concentrate

PATTY R. STUMP

It is difficult to steer a parked car, so get moving.
—HENRIETTA MEARS

I enjoy spring cleaning. There is a sense of refreshment that comes from eliminating clutter as I simultaneously discover what needs to be tossed, passed on, packed up, or put to use. As I prioritize and organize, I often rediscover precious keepsakes that have been stuffed into a drawer or box, unnoticed for quite some time. Some have become weathered and worn while others continue to be carefully kept treasures. Amidst the clutter are items that are outdated and of little use, as well as necessities that I rely on day after day. Though the process is tedious, the end profits are tremendous; simplifying my household as well as my life.

The goal to clean out the clutter in order to rediscover what are genuine necessities applies to our spiritual households as well. We need to regularly take time to explore our hearts, Christ's home. In the busyness of life we can tend to stuff emotions, treasure unhealthy thoughts, hang onto habits that clutter our lives, and continue to use worn-out excuses. God's treasures for us, spiritual keepsakes, can become pushed aside and minimized as we haphazardly scurry through the days.

Spiritual cleaning requires that we take time to do a careful inventory of our hearts, discerning what needs to be tossed, replaced, passed on, and kept. Items to be tossed include harbored hurts, carefully hidden thoughts or actions, old baggage of guilt or shame, and all remnants of bitterness or unforgiveness. In need of replacement are old ways of life and possessions that crowd out heavenly gifts. Keepsakes to hang onto include truths from God's Word, daily habits that develop spiritual character and maturity, and involvement's that strengthen our relationship with Christ. Items to pass on come from the abundance of what He readily gives; keepsakes that fill our lives to overflowing. Each time we *eliminate* the unnecessary and *concentrate* on our spiritual households, we create room in our hearts for Christ to dwell in simplicity and abundance.

Create in me a pure heart, O God, and renew a steadfast spirit within me.
PSALM 51:10

> Find a photo of one of your favorite memories and send a copy with a note to each person in the photo.

March 4

Reminding Us Who We Are

JAN JOHNSON

My understanding of Christianity is God in search of lost men, not men in search of a lost God.
—RONALD R. HATCH

*F*rom God's perspective, enjoying His presence is perfectly natural—not lofty or difficult. God created us out of love and stamped us with His image. He chose for Himself the role of parent, relishing human companionship as pictured by His walking in the cool of the day with Adam and Eve in a young creation. God delights in us and wants us to connect with who He is:

"But let him who boasts boast about this:
that he *understands and knows me,*
that I am the LORD, who exercises kindness,
justice and righteousness on earth,
for in these I *delight,*" declares the LORD.
(Jeremiah 9:24, emphasis added)

Prayer isn't a performance, but "climbing up to the heart of God," as Martin Luther said. Enjoying God's presence places us squarely in God's lap, where He enjoys us:

The LORD your God is with you . . . .
He will take great delight in you,
he will quiet you with his love,
he will rejoice over you with singing.
(Zephaniah 3:17)

This awareness of God's presence is part of how we delight in God, which we are commanded to do: Psalm 37:4. Frequently, this verse is hijacked as a formula for getting what we want from God: If you delight in God, He rewards you with your heart's desires. We misunderstand the possibility that delighting in the Lord is the thing that fulfills the desires of the heart. Brother Lawrence put it this way: "Our only business is to love and delight ourselves in God."

This delight moves us toward the eternal goal, according to Revelation, of living eternally in the full presence of God by worshipping Him. In the here-and-now, it speeds us toward the goal of coming to "know Christ and the power of his resurrection" (Philippians 3:10), of coming to "know and rely on the love God has for us" (I John 4:16). In the flurry of daily events, the back-and-forth pulse of our conversation with God can bring us home to these truths about who we are and what we were created for.

Delight yourself in the LORD and he will give you the desires of your heart.
PSALM 37:4

> In your next prayer time, try to imagine yourself climbing up into God's lap in order to enjoy His presence.

March 5

Bloom Where You're Planted

PATTY R. STUMP

True contentment is the power of getting out of any situation all that there is in it.
—G.K. CHESTERTON

The diversity of the seasons is captivating. I marvel at how subtly the bleak winter days are transformed into bursting colors of spring foliage, with summer maintaining the greenery, and fall exhibiting a brilliant display of hues before creation settles once again into a slumber. The changing of the seasons is purposeful in God's master plan for creation and parallels the seasons we experience in our spiritual growth.

Like Spring, there are times when our relationship with Christ is fresh and full of newness. Spiritual summers occur; stretches when growth spurts give way to periodic dry spells. New color bursts forth during the fall seasons of our spiritual growth when the brilliance of God's handiwork captures our attention. And then winter settles in; times when we feel brittle, gloomy, or lifeless.

While certain seasons are more desirable or bearable than others, each contributes to God's master plan for our growth. There will be seasons when God is tending to our soil, planting seeds, nurturing new growth, pruning our branches, yielding a harvest, or inviting us to simply be still. In cultivating our lives towards maturity He is purposeful in attending to four vital areas:

The soil of our hearts: Matthew 13 describes four conditions of "heartsoils:" the wayside or hardened heartsoil that is casual to God's Word, the shallow heartsoil that allows little rootedness of God's Word, the thorny heartsoil that is preoccupied with the ways of the world, and the fertile heartsoil that has been regularly tended to and is prepared for growth.

The seeds of His heart: The truths of scripture are the seeds God desires to plant in our hearts. These seeds take root through time invested in His Word and personal application of His truths. Psalm 119:11 admonishes us to hide His Word in our heart that we might not sin against Him.

The light of the Son: In order for the seeds of His Word to grow in our hearts, we must be exposed to the Son. I Peter 3:15 reminds us that our hearts must establish Christ as Lord of our lives before we can experience growth. Once our thoughts, emotions, priorities, and values are grounded in Him, the seeds in our heartsoil respond to the Son.

The refreshment of living water: John 4:11 states that Jesus is the living water. He refreshes and nourishes us through spiritual soakings; times in prayer, fellowship with other Christians, worship, and Bible study. With each soaking our rootedness in Christ becomes deeper and stronger, enabling us to bear lasting fruit for His glory.

Seasons will occur in our lives; each contributing to God's master plan. Throughout each season, tend to the soils of your heart, plant the seeds of His Word, bask in the Son, and take in His refreshment. In doing so you will be able to abundantly bloom wherever He plants you, while simply representing His workmanship!

But grow in the grace and knowledge of our Lord and Savior Jesus Christ . . . .
2 PETER 3:18

Invite your child or a friend's to plant some seeds with you. As you do, share the Parable of the Soils.

Squabbles

LOIS A. WITMER

Remember, every time you open your mouth to talk, your
mind walks out and parades up and down the words.
—EDWIN H. STUART

I opened my front door and stepped into the fresh crispness of a
March morning. The forsythia bush near the mailbox showed
signs of budding. The friendly chirp of a bird caused me to turn around
to see my first robin of springtime. I breathed deeply.

Soon I became aware of a new sound. Looking skyward I not only
heard, but saw four distinct V-shaped flocks of wild geese on their trip
north, two just a bit ahead of the others. I stood looking as they flew
nearer. All of a sudden, the closest two of the V-shapes became all
mixed up with each other. Their feathers were really "ruffled." The
honking was not beautiful now. It sounded like a genuine squabble. Were
they arguing over who should be leader, or was one goose taking too
much space in the sky? Maybe a goose skipped in line. I don't know.

Gratefully, I watched as they finally settled their disagreement and
formed two V-shapes again. Now the four V's moved on together in
perfect honking harmony.

We all can learn from their example. As we choose to bring our
disagreements before the feet of the Master, our joy will be restored.
He wants our ability to forgive to represent His work in our lives. Is
there an area in your life that needs to be brought back to an abundant
"V" of concord?

How good and pleasant it is when brothers live together in unity.
PSALM 133:1

If you've had unpleasant words with someone, call, visit
or write them to make amends today.

Why Not Celebrate Passover?

MARGARET PRIMROSE

Eternal truths will be neither true nor eternal unless
they have fresh meaning for every new social situation.
—FRANKLIN D. ROOSEVELT

Few Gentile children celebrate Passover, yet an adaptation of a Jewish Seder dinner could be meaningful.

A good way to begin the evening is to have guests search for ten bread crumbs. In Jewish homes, clearing the house of leaven is always part of the preparation.

When guests are seated at the table, the hostess or mother lights holiday candles. The host, leaning or sitting on a cushion to symbolize freedom from slavery, asks the blessing. Everyone drinks grape juice (Jewish homes would have wine), and usually all wash their hands at the table.

The youngest child is coached to ask, "Why is this night different from all other nights?" Then a plate of symbolic foods is used as visual aids for the Bible story of the ten plagues, the Passover meal, and the escape through the Red Sea. It is appropriate for either the host or guests to tell or read the Bible story. Anyone may interrupt to ask questions.

These are the special foods that would be presented:

Unleavened bread, a reminder that the Israelites had no time to let their bread rise before their escape from Egypt. Matzos may be purchased in supermarkets in March or April or communion wafers could be used.

A *paste of apples, nuts, cinnamon and juice* stands for the mortar the Israelites used to build the pyramids for Pharaoh.

A *roasted lamb shank* symbolizes the Passover lamb.

A *roasted egg* is indicative of the increased endurance of the slaves.

Parsley, celery or romaine lettuce, green to represent hope, is dipped in salt water to symbolize tears.

Bitter herbs usually include horseradish.

Asking questions, sampling the symbolic foods and storytelling are unhurried, but at last an abundant meal is served. There is no traditional menu, but the food often includes chicken soup, turkey, cold fish balls, and sweet potatoes.

Though it may be kept simple, a Seder dinner is meant to be joyous. So have fun!

Remember the days of old . . .
DEUTERONOMY 32:7

Plan a Seder dinner for your family within the next week.

March 8

Communication

JACK MAYHALL

Nothing great was ever achieved without enthusiasm.
—RALPH WALDO EMERSON

Communication about what your spouse or friend wants is the first step to continued joy in your relationship. Not in generalities, but in specifics. For my wife, Carole, that takes a lot of thought, because she has a *feeling* of what she wants without much thought about what will give her that feeling. Being factual, I need her to tell me specifics.

Take some time to explore with each other questions such as: How important to you is the celebration of special occasions such as birthdays, anniversaries, Valentine's Day? What is your idea of "celebration?" What to you is "romantic?" What would you like for me to do specifically to show affection and care? (Really get down to particulars here, such as: I want you to greet me with a kiss when I come home; I'd like you to hold my hand in public; I'd like you to sit on the couch with me when we watch television.) In these specified items, which is most important to you? Least important?

As you talk to each other about these issues, talk also with God about them. Remember, God is a *creative* God and will give you new, creative thoughts if you ask Him. He is *full* of ideas! And He is waiting to reveal them to you.

Then, too, talk to older people who evidence love in their marriages. Ask them how they show their partner special love, and write down their answers. Learn from others so that you can express abundant delight in your relationship.

A fool finds no pleasure in understanding
but delights in airing his own opinions.

PROVERBS 18:2

Buy a book about marriage or friendship, and read it with the goal of loving your spouse or friend more.

March 9

Dust My Soul

JAN HOFFBAUER

Cleanliness Is Next To Godliness.

—UNKNOWN

Every Ash Wednesday I determine my Lenten resolutions and add all my broken New Year's resolutions. For a few days I manage to keep up with my monumental list but by the second week of Lent my head is splitting from sinus problems. Lent is now the farthest thing from my mind.

All I want to do is feel better. My sinuses feel as if they will blow like a volcano. The medicine I took only brings side effects and stomach problems.

Since I do not have energy for my normal tasks, I gather some of the literature and magazines that I have saved, waiting to be skimmed. As I read a newsletter, I notice the dust piled on another stack of papers. Maybe I should pick up a dust rag?

Now I have a quick spurt of energy. I bet if I cleaned out the furnace vents it would reduce some of the dust that irritates my sinus. Once the vacuum attachments are in my hot little hands I become a woman possessed. Get rid of all dust and dirt.

As the hose suction dislodges food swept under the refrigerator, I discover myself saying a prayer for the *hungry*.

In the bathroom the lint from the towels and hair spray is sucked up swiftly. My head is feeling better already. I suddenly feel grateful for the shelter I enjoy. I say a prayer for the *homeless*.

I have too many clothes to fold and iron. I clean out my closet and give some away so that others may be warm. I say a prayer for the *naked*.

I have an extra set of dishes since I received new ones for my last birthday. I clean out the cupboard. My sister might like these dishes I had stored since they had been our mother's dishes. I say a prayer for *my family.*

The clear water rinses the bathroom sink and counter. Everything is sparkling and fresh. As easily as I cleaned the sink, Jesus washed away my sins. I say a prayer for *healing.*

As I wash the windows the whole world looks brighter. My spirit is revived. My future Lenten resolution will be to spring clean. When my house is clean and healthy so is my soul. And an added benefit is that my prayers make a difference for the world.

As you spring clean your house, recognize areas of your life that need cleansing. Take advantage of Jesus' simple offer of forgiveness. It only takes a simple—yet powerful—decision to receive it. Abundant life follows.

So we make it our goal to please him,
whether we are at home in the body or away from it.
2 CORINTHIANS 5:9

> The next time you clean house, put on your favorite "Praise" album and use this time as an opportunity for prayer and praise.

March 10

Leaping Lizards!

BONNIE COMPTON HANSON

Nature is the art of God.
—SIR THOMAS BROWNE

Did you ever pet a mouse?
Did you ever pet a lizard?
Did you ever accidentally pet them *both at the same time?*

That happened to me one warm day this spring. I had propped the back door open to enjoy the sweet-smelling breezes, then sat down at my computer. Soon I was so busy writing, I didn't even bother to look down at my computer mouse each time I reached for it. (Yes, that's the kind of "mouse" I mean.)

One time, when I grabbed my mouse, I thought it felt a little different. Then I glanced down at it. It not only felt different, it *looked* different, too. For it suddenly had *two tails!*

When I opened my fingers, two bright little eyes stared through them right up at me. I don't know which of us was more surprised—me or that *lizard!* But he was enjoying the bright warm sunshine coming in my window too much to move. For all I know, he liked that "petting" a lot more than I did.

After I took the screen off the window and coaxed him outside, I marveled at how oblivious I had been to something that was literally right at my fingertips.

But it's easy to be "too busy" to see and wonder at the miracles God has placed all around us. When was the last time you lived the abundantly simple life by stopping your car to take in the full beauty of a rainbow? Or instead of spraying ant poison, paused to be reminded of the industriousness of a trail of ants? When did you last laugh with a giggling child instead of frowning over such silliness?

All of these are ours to see, cherish and hold tight to our hearts. Even friendly lizards.

> Come and see what God has done,
> how awesome his works in man's behalf!
>
> PSALM 66:5

When you are out driving today, stop for just five minutes by the side of the road to enjoy some view that you usually take for granted.

March 11

Joy Through Greater Intimacy

BILL FARREL

> Joy is the standard that flies on the battlements of the heart when the King is in residence.
>
> —R. LEONARD SMALL

There are some common tactics that are thought to be useful but which actually disrupt the process of intimacy:

1. Avoid saying, "I know just how you feel" and "I understand what you are feeling." This is an impossibility. For instance, I will never understand what it is like to be a woman because I am not a woman. I will never know the tension of putting my career on hold for eleven years while waiting for my kids to start school. The only way I can relate to these influences in my wife's life is to listen to Pam and let her explain to me what it is like to be Pam.

2. Avoid asking, "Why do you feel this way?" The answer is, "I don't know." Our emotions have never had the ability to think. We feel what we feel because of past influences and developmental factors. Emotions are not rational in their makeup, and so they don't think before they express themselves. The goal in intimate conversation with your spouse is not to analyze emotions and come up with some kind of solution that will make your spouse never feel this way again. The goal is simply to grow a little closer and reaffirm your love. This love you share with your spouse can be worn down over time. If you are not careful to reaffirm it often, it loses its vitality and can be swallowed up in life. When, on the other hand, you maintain the habit of often reestablishing the bond of love that drew you together, you can experience a growing joy with each other. And that is better than "finding a solution."

3. Don't try to fix your spouse. Your husband may say, "I am often intimidated by my boss." Do not respond with, "There is no reason to be intimidated. You are bright, intelligent and talented. Your boss is just threatened by how good you are. Be brave, honey. It will be all right!" In doing so, you shut him down. Your husband is probably trying to get a conversation started with you that is bigger than work. It probably has to do with his lack of confidence or lack of understanding of how competition works in an adult world. Or he may be contemplating a job change and be checking to see how accepting you may be of having that conversation. Or he may be intimidated by you, and he is trying to lead into the conversation by talking about his boss first! Whatever the case may be, you will never know if you attempt to fix him rather than let him work through the process of healing with your listening help.

The tongue has the power of life and death,
and those who love it will eat its fruit.
PROVERBS 18:21

Plan a get-away for you and your spouse. If finances are low, ask some good friends whether you can stay at their home while they take care of your children at yours. And then return the favor for their get-away.

Memorable Laughter

PATSY CLAIRMONT

Man is distinguished from all other creatures by the
faculty of laughter.

—JOSEPH ADDISON

*L*aughter can make moments more memorable. Whether laughing
alone or with others, it helps us feel good about our memories.

I remember walking through the mall once when I noticed a quarter
on the floor. Had it been a penny, I might have passed it by. But a quarter?
No way. I stooped down and swooped my hand across the floor to scoop
up the coin, but it didn't budge. I tried again. I could hear laughter coming
from a nearby ice cream shop, but I didn't look because I was focused on
the shiny coin. I tried to pick it up again, but it held fast. I tried prying it
with my nails. I even took out my emery board and used it like a crowbar,
trying to dislodge this gleaming coin.

As I stared at George Washington's immobile silhouette, I thought
I saw him smirk. Then I realized George was not alone. The laughter
nearby had grown to unbridled guffawing. I looked up and realized
five teenagers were watching me and laughing at my financial struggle.
It was the kind of laugh that told me they knew something I didn't.

I could have flown off in a fury or resented their intrusion. Then
again, I could find out what was so hilarious and join the fun.

I asked, "Okay, what's the deal?"

One girl confessed they had glued the quarter to the floor and
had been watching people try to pick it up. The kids dubbed me the
"most dedicated to the task." I giggled with them as I thought about
my 25-cent antics.

Laughter is an incredible gift. It helps us to not take ourselves too
seriously and makes it possible for us to survive life's awkward moments.

. . . a time to weep and a time to laugh . . .
ECCLESIASTES 3:4

Is there someone you know that could use a good laugh?
Send them a humorous card or note today.

Time Tithing

RENEE MCCLELLAN

Abundant life is doing God's will, God's way, in
God's time with God's power.

—RENEE MCCLELLAN

"It's working, and it scares me to death!" I confided to my spiritual
advisor last week.

"What's working?" she inquired.

"Everything," I replied. "Maybe what I'm experiencing is joy!"

"What *is* working?" I mused later that afternoon. I've been on a
spiritual adventure the last eleven years. It started with a silent prayer
for more energy.

By trial and error I've developed a routine that works for me. I
start my day by reading a daily devotional. Then I say a prayer where
I turn my day and my way over to God. I give Him my marriage, my
children, my other relationships, my things, my attitude, and my
schedule for the day. I ask Him to empower me to do His will, His way
in His time.

My prayer while I shower is: "My Creator, I trust You completely. I
am entirely ready to have You remove any false beliefs, adjust any attitudes
and remove any ineffective behavior that stands in the way of my
usefulness to You and others. Empower me to know, love and serve You
with my whole heart, mind, soul and strength. Empower me to cherish,
protect and share my creativity and sensitivity. Empower me to be Your
voice to the world directly, honestly and appropriately. Amen."

My half-hour prayer walk is my favorite part of my morning ritual.
As I walk down an asphalt road to a nearby creek, I repeat, "Speak,
Lord, your servant is listening." I listen with my eyes, skin and nose
as well as my ears. On the way back, half the time I repeat an
affirmation, "Jesus empowers me, His Holy Spirit inspires me." The
other half I spend praising God and praying for others.

As I get to my front door, I pray, "Do life through me, Lord—do
woman, wife, mother, bookkeeper, and writer. I can't, You can, help
me let You." With that, I make breakfast and get my two daughters off
to school.

Since I work out of my home, I schedule rest time after lunch. I lay down for twenty to thirty minutes, focus on the cross on my bedroom wall and be with God.

When I go to bed at night, I read a short devotional and write a letter to Jesus. "Thank You," "Please advise," "I'm sorry," and "HELP!" are my most frequent statements.

I realized recently that I spend approximately ten percent of my waking hours in prayer and meditation—I tithe my time. As a result, I seem to have the energy, desire and time to share my creativity and heart knowledge of God with others. I'm so very grateful for this tremendous joy God is giving me. The abundant life is possible. The plaque by Serenity Inc. I received as a gift years ago seems to say it all: "God saves the very best . . . For those of us . . . Who leave the choice to Him."

Are you leaving the choice up to Him? If you do, you will experience His great joy . . . in abundance!

> *. . . Seek Me and live.*
>
> AMOS 5:4

Write out a "Joy List" of those things that you appreciate about God's work in your life. Refer to it several times a day.

March 14

Giving God Offerings

PENNY SHOUP

> Make all you can, save all you can, give all you can.
> —JOHN WESLEY

Yesterday we concentrated on tithing our time to bring joy into our lives. Today, we'll consider tithing our finances. Tithing is the minimum amount God expects. Above that falls another category that is a little more vague. I have seen many examples of this type of giving in the lives of Christians and it thrills my heart. I feel strongly that if you approach God with an open mind He will speak to you about when, where, how and how much to give. This type of giving needs to be done in secret as much as possible.

I have an incident I want to tell you about but I am hesitant to because we are instructed to do our giving in secret. However, I need an example. Several years ago I owned a horse that I loved. But she would do very dangerous things when she got scared. With the help of trainers, we tried everything we could think of; but the problem didn't get better. Ultimately I faced the fact that I had to sell her or someone was going to get seriously hurt. Then God showed me a beautiful way in which I could use the money from my horse and give something to someone else.

There was a group of five ladies in the church who were good friends of mine. We all had small children and, as most mothers, they put their children first and rarely did anything just for themselves. I arranged a day and took them to dinner. At dinner I told them we were going to go shopping and get each one a new dress. Not just a dress but shoes and purses to match. But they had to keep it a secret. They objected but I explained that it wasn't me but God that was doing it for them. We had so much fun.

Several months later my friend Ellen pulled me to the side after church and whispered to me, "Look how nice Sally looks. I've noticed that since that day we went shopping she seems to be taking better care of herself and her appearance. I'm sure it's because she has a better self-concept of herself."

I looked at Ellen in awe. She was right. Sally did look pretty and she seemed happier. I was filled with joy thinking that God had used me to give abundance to someone else.

God loves a cheerful giver. How would you characterize your giving lately? I challenge you to be open to His leading. You'll experience greater joy and will see others blessed.

But when you give to the needy, do not let your left hand know what your right hand is doing, so that your giving may be in secret. Then your Father, who sees what is done in secret, will reward you.
MATTHEW 6:3-4

Give an unexpected gift (whether small or large) to someone today, and make it anonymous.

Then I Saw Him Smile

DORIS HAYS TOPPEN

When saving for old age, be sure to put away a few
pleasant thoughts.

—ANONYMOUS

"Grandma, I'm serving lunch in cooking class next week. Mom
and Dad both have to work and can't come. Would you be the
guest at our table?"

Would I? Of course. Brad was a senior in high school and explained
that groups of four were serving their guests and would be graded on
their efforts.

I dressed carefully, in my best suit, wanting Brad to be comfortable
and proud of his grandmother in front of his friends.

Following explicit directions, I arrived at the school and found my
way to senior hall and room 208, "Creative Cooking."

Then I saw him smile. There was a dance inside my chest as he walked
toward me. Six foot four, dark curly hair, translucent blue eyes that looked
at me with all the love in the world. "Hi, Grandma." Brad took my arm
and guided me through the door. "Hope you like what we made."

Young men bustled about the room, seating guests, creating last
minute centerpieces with scarlet, gold leaves and candles, taped music
with a mellow beat played in the background.

Other parents in Brad's group were unable to attend. So I was the
only guest of honor. One boy lit the candles and brought tea to me,
another crackers and cheese. Brad and his partner carried in the main
dish. A tray of the most beautiful hero sandwiches I have ever seen.

Sitting in the midst of those boys, their eyes radiant with achievement and delight, I bit into the most delicious concoction I had ever
eaten. Meats piled high with onion, tomatoes, olives, pickles and
cheese, slathered with mustard, and mingled between buns of sesame.

We talked of the boys' plans after graduation, the football team,
how "Creative Cooking" had rounded out their credits and was more
fun and interesting than they had expected. Banana pudding piled
high with whipped cream complemented the homemade almond roca
I had brought.

I listened to the hum in the room, the sounds of life, the laughter, and let the cranberry scent and glow of candles wash over me. My grandson's invitation was such a great gift that I could be included in his busy world among his peers.

Too soon it was time to leave. As I walked through the school grounds I clutched a maple leaf, feeling as if I were holding the world in my hand. In that moment, I realized that the abundant life can—and must—include wonderful memories of the joys God gives us. And mine today was seeing the love in my grandson's eyes. Now I can choose joy any time I desire, just by living this moment again in my memory.

If you're low on joy today, why not recall some precious memory of earlier days? You'll sense God's smile.

I have not stopped giving thanks for you, remembering you in my prayers.
EPHESIANS 1:16

Secretly tape your next family celebration. Then make copies for all to enjoy for years to come.

March 16

Joyful Tomatoes

MARCIA VAN'T LAND

The surest mark of a Christian is not facts, or even love, but joy.

—SAMUEL M. SHOEMAKER

J make room for one tomato plant in my small flower bed by our front door. I, and my children, tend and nurture that tomato plant. The other day our eleven-year-old came in the house saying that there were twenty-four tomatoes and blossoms on that one plant. We are learning much patience as we wait for the delicious red tomatoes. The results don't come overnight but we have the faith that they will come eventually. We and the plant work together on this project.

So it is with Christian joy. It doesn't happen overnight. We cannot sprout joy in our lives. We must prepare our lives—like the rich flower bed—so that we, with God's help, can experience joy. Joy is very important to God because he mentions the word "joy" and "rejoice" about three hundred times in the Bible.

Joy doesn't mean we must be laughing, giggling, and kidding around. Joy is not the same as happiness. Things may not be happy but there can still be joy. True joy gets us through tough situations. It occurs right in the middle of serious trials.

Joy is based on who we are and not what we have. It is the underlying foundation upon which faith is built. To choose joy is a commandment from God—it is not optional. Joy can happen in the kitchen, barn, backyard, office, or wherever we are. It is the master gift of the Christian lifestyle and brings us into the realm of the abundant life.

As we see God bear the fruit of joy in our lives, we must not be selfish with that gift. The purpose of joy is to serve others. We must give of ourselves, talents, time and money.

We must also expect that Satan will work hard at snatching our joy. Nothing aggravates Satan more than when he sees a joyful Christian. True, abundant Christian joy comes when we let God fill us with his life.

Whenever I eat a tomato, even when it isn't off our own plant, I am reminded that God and I are working together on this "joy" business.

You have filled my heart with greater joy . . . .
I will lie down and sleep in peace, for you alone,
o Lord, make me dwell in safety.

PSALM 4:7-8

It's hard to have joy when you're exhausted. Pay attention to your body's internal time clock and find greater joy.

March 17

This Transient Life

LYNN D. MORRISSEY

It goes so fast. We don't have time to look at one
another . . . Do human beings ever realize life
while they live it—every, every minute?
—THORNTON WILDER (*Our Town*)

Time waits for no one. How keenly aware I was of this truth as I watched my "baby" daughter, Sheridan, blow out the fourth candle on her birthday cake. Each candle was a year of her life blazing brilliantly, only to be extinguished too rapidly.

When I left a twenty-year career to nurture Sheridan before she entered kindergarten, five years equaled eternity. Yet how grateful I am now to those mothers who encouraged my transition, realizing the fleetness of time.

Actually, it's not so much that time fleets, but that we, ourselves, are fleeting beings. Because our earthly existence is relatively short-lived, we attempt to slow time by efficiently managing it, overloading pregnant schedules with additional activity—cramming more into less time.

From a Christian perspective, I've found the key to joy lies not in time management, but in life management—not in handling time efficiently, but in living proficiently.

From the world's perspective, motherhood's repetitive ministrations tally in life's debit column. Compared to acquiring an education, pursuing a glitzy career, and outdistancing the "Joneses," wiping sticky hands, bandaging scraped knees, and saying "no" for the umpteenth time, result in decided loss. Yet God keeps a topsy-turvy scorecard, where loss is gain, last is first, and dying to self is living for God.

So how do we manage life and confront transience?

1. Put God first. Follow His *general* will for your life: live in personal relationship with His Son, Jesus Christ, glorify Him, read His word, pray, fellowship with other believers, and evangelize the lost.

2. Discover God's *specific* purpose for your life, employing your spiritual gifts in serving the church in His assigned ministry.

3. Write a personal mission statement (check back in January for how to do that) and evaluate your activities against it. Avoid following rabbit tracks. Relinquish the better for the best.

4. Eliminate "life-wasters" such as watching soap operas and other "mindless" television, reading dime store romance novels, excessive shopping, etc.

5. Keep short accounts with God by confessing sin and restoring fellowship. Do the same with others.

6. Enjoy where you are on the way to where you're going. Don't confuse "waiting time" with wasting time. And don't waste waiting time. Rest in the Lord, wait patiently, and enjoy His company and lessons along the way. If you are in His will, He'll use all your experiences to contribute ultimately to your life's mission.

7. Rather than be depressed about life's brevity, delight in its beauty. Don't take *anything* or *anyone* for granted. Be alert to life. Appreciate its wonder. Tell people you love them and praise their efforts. Tomorrow might be too late.

If you follow these seven guidelines, you will experience God's abundant joy and you'll have a full life, with no regrets in the end.

Show me, O Lord, my life's end and the number of my days; let me know how fleeting is my life. You have made my days a mere handbreadth; the span of my years is as nothing before you. Each man's life is but a breath. Selah.

Prepare for each day the night before. Lay out clothes, prepare a to-do list, center your trust in the Lord for the next day.

March 18

Taught By Surprise

JIM SCHWEITZER

When a man is wrapped up in himself, he makes a pretty small package.

—JOHN RUSKIN

My family planned to spend some time at the Saturday Market in Portland, about 90 miles north of our home in Albany, Oregon. I was driving my daughter's van and dropped everyone off, except a sleeping grandson. I finally found a parking space which needed feeding. I found my pockets empty and no trace of coin in the van.

I stepped out to the meter to ponder my dilemma. Soon I heard a crying grandson. I wrapped him up and together we waited for my prayers to be answered. I noticed what I knew was not "the answer" and turned my back to the approaching "bum." He stopped to ask for change for a cup of coffee, and I explained my situation. He got a big grin on his face, reached into his pocket and pulled out a handfull of loot. He deposited the coin I needed and graciously accepted my heartfelt blessing.

Later in the morning, as we were leaving the area, we passed the same man pushing the same grocery cart. I was tempted to stop and return his gift; a stronger urge within me said, "Let the man enjoy the feeling of having made a difference in someone's life."

The Lord taught me that day through a surprise encounter that some people have more abundance than they let on.

A man's pride brings him low, but a man of lowly spirit gains honor.

PROVERBS 29:23

Do a "Random Act of Kindness" for a stranger today.

React Or Respond?

LAURA SABIN RILEY

> Since we cannot change reality, let us change the eyes
> which see reality.
>
> —NIKOS KAZANTZAKIS

*S*ome days I have a difficult time reacting *spiritually* to my responsibilities as a stay-at-home mom. I struggle to find the redeeming qualities in picking up dirty laundry, scrubbing floors and cleaning hand prints from windows. "Why am I doing this?" I wonder aloud as I work on a sticky window, "I'll only have to do it again tomorrow." In the midst of wiping up yet another glass of spilled milk, I find myself grumbling instead of praising God for my work.

I'm sure I'm not the only mother of young children who's been tempted to turn in her dish rag for a business suit a time or two. That temptation comes with the territory. It's tough to see the joy in the job when you can't even see out the windows. My natural instinct is to react to the circumstances around me, rather than to respond to the knowledge of God's Word. I know I'd experience more of the abundant life Jesus promised if I did. The Bible tells women to be workers at home in Titus 2:5. So, if that is the reality of Scripture, I wonder, "Why then, is it so difficult for me to find joy in my situation when I know that I'm doing what God wants me to do?"

I found the answer during a break in my daily duties one quiet afternoon. Looking at the sticky kitchen floor and feeling overwhelmed with the never-ending task of taking care of a home and family, I decided I needed a Bible break. I Corinthians 15:46 spoke to my heart: "However the spiritual is not first, but the natural; then the spiritual." I understand that I am run more by my natural desires than my supernatural, because I often give in to my fleshly emotions and reactions, which are usually negative—like grumbling and complaining. I have to make a conscious effort to overcome my natural because it always shows up first.

The only way I can overcome my negative attitude about certain responsibilities of my job, such as housework, is to seek God and ask Him to replace my natural reactions with spiritual responses. I can meditate on His Word and ask the Holy Spirit to bring those truths in Scripture to my mind when I am building up a bad attitude, which diminishes my awareness of my abundant life. I have to ask God to help me see my circumstances through His eyes rather than mine. I can choose to respond to what God's Word says about what I am doing, "being a worker at home," rather than react to some of the negative circumstances surrounding it. When I *respond*, I am acting or behaving as if in answer to someone or something, as opposed to *reacting*, which is acting often in opposition to someone or something. Given that definition, I know I don't want to be in opposition to God's Word. Over time, I have learned that if I respond to the Scriptures, rather than the dirty laundry surrounding me, I can find joy in even the most mundane of tasks.

Will you take a Bible break today in the midst of your activities? If you do, you'll find it easier to center yourself on the abundant spiritual life, rejoicing in the tasks God has given you.

Do everything without complaining or arguing.
PHILIPPIANS 2:14

Decide right now the time you'll break later for five minute Bible reading to check on your "abundance attitude."

March 20

Less Cost, More Satisfaction

PATRICIA A.J. ALLEN

I believe the right question to ask, respecting all ornament,
is simply this: Was it done with enjoyment . . . ?
—JOHN RUSKIN

We all assume that eating out is more expensive than eating in, but is it? Learning why you eat out and doing personalized market research may prove that a restaurant meal is often your best economy.

My husband and I eat out as a form of recreation. We compared restaurant costs with normal expenses of other forms of entertainment and relaxation. We chose only enjoyable items for which we are equipped. Some local sports cost more than a restaurant meal. Some entertainments cost the same while others are much less expensive.

To balance our investigation, we also explored creative celebrations of individual holidays. For example, on my birthday, my husband wanted to take me to a gala Oriental restaurant because I love Chinese food. When he learned that my favorite Chinese dish is one I can enjoy cooking myself, I bought supplies. He dressed up for dinner and presented me with a small corsage. Uncommon tenderness and romance transformed the familiar dining room.

David and I wanted to eat out as much as possible. We looked for ways to cut our restaurant expense. Evaluating the type of restaurant we frequented has saved us the most money. We asked ourselves these questions. Is this a higher class restaurant than our situation requires? Is fastest food always the cheapest? What types of food give us the most pleasure? We learned that a burger and "the works" costs us more than a Chinese buffet, and much more than a soup and salad lunch-time special at a fancy Italian restaurant. We discovered the least expensive shop to grab a sub sandwich and found we enjoy picnics. Our actual needs and the offerings of the local eateries now guide our choices. We invest our hard-earned money in areas that truly satisfy and bring us joy.

Have you learned that abundant dining can include variety and choices?

Why spend money on what is not bread, and your labor on what does not satisfy…?
ISAIAH 55:2

> Instead of waiting for an open slot in your schedule to clean the whole refrigerator, clean one shelf at a time when waiting for food to cook.

March 21

The Button Box

MICHELE HOWE

Depth not length, is important. Not how long you
take to talk but how much you say. Not how flowery
and eloquent you sound but how sincerely and succinctly
you speak . . . that's what is important . . . that's what
is remembered. Two memorable minutes can be more
effective than two marathon hours.
—CHUCK SWINDOLL

There were three constants in Grandma's house when I was a child. I could always count on Grandpa sitting at the kitchen table with a portable radio, earplug in place, as he listened to the Detroit Tigers baseball games. There were the puffy, sweet homemade sugar cookies filled with a moist raisin center. And then there was the button box . . . an old cardboard box filled to the brim with every kind of button imaginable.

I remember seeing my Grandma cutting all the buttons off an old work shirt one afternoon. I asked her why she bothered since she already had so many in her box. Her eyes opened wide in disbelief, and she said, "You never know if you might need just this size button" as she held up her most recent orphaned button. After that, I never questioned Grandma about her practical ways. She was just too nice.

Besides, my brother and I had our own uses for that old box of buttons. Time and again, we'd visit and make our way to Grandma's small store of toys. This meager selection consisted of a partially rusted blue truck similar to the Tonka's of today; a box of Lincoln Logs (which I still can't master well enough to build a suitable log cabin); and several thick books filled with cherished stories about King Midas, The Water Babies, and a lonely little girl visiting a farm.

After we'd played out our imaginations, we'd begin to slowly meander around the house with something more dreadful than trouble on our minds . . . boredom! I guess it was just instinctive but Grandma always could tell the right moment to pull out the button box. She would call us out to the kitchen where Grandpa still sat, earplug in place, and we would start stringing buttons.

What fun we had making all kinds of different designs and sometimes fighting over a particularly unusual button. I can't remember hardly ever going to my Grandparents' house without spending time stringing and re-stringing buttons. It seemed a shame to spill them all out once our string was full, but then again Grandma would remind us that the buttons weren't going anywhere and would be waiting for us the next time around.

Over fifteen years have passed since Grandma died, but every day I have a reminder of the simple joys of childhood inspired by a loving, creative lady. On my kitchen counter, in a glass jar, lovingly sits the same buttons waiting for some child to get bored and start stringing.

What joyful memories are you making with the important people in your life? You'll find greater abundance when you make them a priority, and they'll bless you for it.

The memory of the righteous will be a blessing.

PROVERBS 10:7A

> Try an excursion to an antique shop, and see if you can find a memento from the past, that opens the door to one of your childhood memories.

March 22

Pursuing Contentment
And
Growth—At The Same Time

DOUG SCHMIDT

Inventions have long since reached their limit;
I see no hope for further development.
> —JULIUS FRONTINUS,
> ROMAN ENGINEER, FIRST CENTURY A.D.

Julius Frontinus was content. He had established himself as one of the Roman Empire's leading engineers and was satisfied that there wasn't much more he could do to make his world a better place. Tweak an aqueduct here and there, fill in a crack or two on a Roman road . . . not much more. Anything significant had already been accomplished.

Howard Hughes was never content. He was a man driven to grow, to constantly make himself bigger in the eyes of himself and others. He never had enough money, enough possessions, enough friends, or enough love. He died alone and despairing, never achieving the sense of satisfaction he longed for all his life.

If we ever reach a state of contentment, do we have to stop growing? Must we perpetuate a gnawing, sense of inadequacy to motivate our growth? Where is the balance as we seek the abundant life?

Contentment and growth are great friends. In fact, apart from one another they can hardly function. Contentment without growth leads to complacency; growth without contentment leads to insatiable dissatisfaction.

Personal godliness is the key to pursuing contentment and growth simultaneously. A simple, loving relationship with God not only provides a refuge of contentment in a hectic world, but also perpetuates a healthy desire to build and advance his Kingdom.

Where are you in seeking a balance between contentment and growth? You'll know you're nearing it when you experience abundant joy.

But godliness with contentment is great gain. For we brought nothing into the world, and we can take nothing out of it.
I TIMOTHY 6:6-7

Buy yourself a "Special" coffee mug or tea cup and learn to enjoy life's simple pleasures.

March 23

The Far View

MURIEL LARSON

Heaven will be the endless portion of every man who has heaven in his soul.
—HENRY WARD BEECHER

*M*y husband was considering a pastorate of a country church. The couple with whom we were staying overnight took us to see the parsonage. I couldn't believe my eyes! It was an old, partly-whitewashed, pieced-together stucco shack with a tin roof.

"It doesn't look like much on the outside," said the lady apologetically, "But it's not too bad on the inside."

"And it does have hot and cold running water and an indoor bathroom," added the man. At the time I didn't realize that was more than some parishioners had.

Then the lady tapped me on the shoulder. "Turn around," she said, "and look!" She waved her arm in a sweeping motion. "Isn't that the most gorgeous view you have ever seen?"

We looked out from that high ridge upon miles and miles of fields, trees, and valleys. "You can even see the next state from here," declared the lady. "And look off in that other direction." That view almost took our breath away, it was so majestic.

My husband was called by the church and accepted the pastorate. His salary was low, but farm products such as meat and vegetables would be given by the people. A wood-burning stove in the living room heated the house. And we had resident black spiders about as big as a quarter. Also, that area was well-known as rattlesnake country.

But oh, the far view! How it thrilled and rested my soul to look out at it for any and all reasons. During the winter, the dark outline of trees stood out starkly from the sparkling white snow, with an intensely blue sky overhead. During the spring, wherever he or she looked, one could see the white and pink blossoms of apple and cherry trees, the lime-green of freshly-budded foliage, and new shoots of corn coming up in the fields. In the summer the corn grew tall, the blackberries down in the valley ripened, and cows grazed contentedly. In the fall, the maples were a riot of color as were the sunsets. Yes, the far view was beautiful.

For the person who lives for Jesus Christ, so also is the far view beautiful. If we live for this life only, we may enjoy temporal conveniences and pleasures. But if through reading God's Word we get a glimpse of the glory awaiting those who suffer with and for Christ, then the beautiful far view will keep our eyes on the goal our Lord has set for us. And wouldn't we have more abundance and joy in our lives if we would get our eyes off present distressing circumstances and rest them on the far view?

How do you want to improve your far view vision today? Can you see eternity peaking at you, wondering whether you'll respond with joy regarding your distressing circumstances?

For our light and momentary troubles are achieving for us an eternal glory that far outweighs them all. So we fix our eyes not on what is seen, but on what is unseen. For what is seen is temporary, but what is unseen is eternal.
2 CORINTHIANS 4:17-18

As an object lesson in the "far view," wear someone else's glasses for a few moments and remember that's how we view life's difficulties when we don't take into account our future in heaven.

March 24

It's A Matter Of Attitude

JOAN CLAYTON

There is more joy in Jesus in twenty-four hours than
there is in the world in 365 days. I have tried them both.
—R.A. TORREY

Did you ever have someone remark to you: "You look tired. Are you feeling well?" Immediately you think, "I must look awful" or "I really do not feel well." The funny thing about it is, that before you heard that remark, you felt great! The power of suggestion has a stronghold.

Have you ever had a trusted friend make a catty remark behind your back? It hurts, but how you react is determined by your attitude. You can avoid that person or you can overlook the offense, realizing that you must look for the beam in your own eye.

I can learn a lesson and guard my mouth and speech by not doing the same thing they've done; thus I can avoid hurting someone else with my tongue.

How this has simplified my life! I do not have to worry about something I may have said to someone else.

Do you look for the good in bad situations? A friend had a bad case of the flu. She said, "I'm surely glad I had the flu shot. Look how sick I would have been without it!" Now, that is looking for the good!

Two prisoners looked out the window through bars. One saw mud . . . the other saw stars! One had the right attitude.

Attitude determines success in life. An attitude of unforgiveness makes you the slave to the person you have not forgiven. Bitterness creates an attitude of cynicism, eating away joy. Besides, unforgiveness is very unhealthy. A recent television show had a clip on forgiveness and how it improves one's state of health. Guess what? "Forgiveness" has always been in the Bible. God was the first one to say it!

Whatever the situation, you have the power to choose your attitude. Misery accompanies the person with a bad attitude because from their perspective nothing is ever right. Talk about an abundance-stealer.

But you and I can *choose* to be joyful in distressing circumstances. The mature Christian living the abundant life sees the hand of God in all events—and He knows the good He'll bring from each. So, rejoice! It will simplify your life. It's all a matter of attitude.

But thanks be to God, who always leads us in triumphal procession in Christ and through us spreads everywhere the fragrance of the knowledge of him.

2 CORINTHIANS 2:14

Start a "Love Box" for yourself. Each time you receive a card, note or other encouragement—add it to your box. It's a great spirit-lifter for those "Blue Days."

Does Wealth Bring Happiness?

GLORIA H. DVORAK

That money talks
I'll not deny,
I heard it once:
It said, "Goodbye."

—RICHARD ARMOUR

Ecclesiastes 5:16 tells us that *chasing after money is futile, like chasing after the wind.* If you took a survey of what most men and women want out of life, wealth would definitely be at the top of the list. Those who hoard their money and those who lose it soon learn what Solomon learned that when we leave this life, it will be worth nothing, not even the shirt on our back.

Ecclesiastes 5 tells us the truth about vanities and riches which fade away and are meaningless. Instead of riches, Solomon elaborates on three of God's gifts which should make life abundant.

Verse 18 talks of the gift of *satisfaction.* Our world offers us many temptations of what the "good life" is supposed to be. It entices us to make lots of money. The belief that wealth will solve all our problems, however, is the great lie. A true test of satisfaction is when we can say, "If what I have now is all I'm ever going to have, then it's enough."

Verse 19 tells us that *God lets us enjoy whatever wealth we have.* But wealth doesn't always have to be money. If we are healthy, have work we enjoy, and a happy family, that's lasting wealth. Abundant thinking acknowledges our joys with or without financial riches.

Verse 20 encourages us to *find joy in working and accepting our lot in life.* Happy is the man who is content with his work. Contentment is a rare commodity in life today. Most of us are driven to reach and grab onto things we do not need. Barbara Johnson, the Christian humorist who survived many personal devastating experiences, says, "Pain is inevitable but misery is optional." Her example encourages us to pick the flowers instead of the weeds.

Wealth, when used wisely can do much good. But when it is used to excess, it can cause much harm. It is better to put our hope in God who will supply our every need. Being assured of that will increase our ability to live the abundant life in joy.

Command those who are rich in this present world not to be arrogant nor to put their hope in wealth, which is so uncertain, but to put their hope in God, who richly provides us with everything for our enjoyment.

I TIMOTHY 6:17

> Keep track of everything you spend for a week and then evaluate where changes need to be made.

March 26

An Attitude Of Joy

RUTH E. MCDANIEL

That thou art happy, owe to God;
That thou continuest such, owe to thyself,
That is, to thy obedience.

—MILTON

It takes all kinds of people to make up our world. If there's one thing we have plenty of, it's diversity. Often, the greatest differences lie in their attitudes.

We've all known people who were old by the time they reached their fiftieth birthdays. Others seemed young at eighty. Invariably, the youthful ones have certain things in common—exuberance, a zest for life, and a positive attitude. I believe these are manifestations of the joy of the Lord.

As I was driving home today, I saw something that perfectly illustrated my point. Two elderly men were in their front yards. They looked to be about the same age, height, and weight, but that's where the similarities ended. The first man was seated in a chair, hunched over, with his chin propped on a cane, staring off into space. The second man was walking across his lawn, pushing an electric mower with one hand and steadying himself with a cane in the other!

Now, if you were told to interview one of those men, which one would you choose? Chances are, you'd pick the plucky one. First impressions can be wrong, but I'm almost certain the active fellow would have a more interesting tale to tell than the motionless man. Plus, you have to admire the groundkeeper's spunk. Anyone with that kind of zest must have a positive attitude, and most people with positive attitudes know the joy of the Lord.

The Bible teaches that *the joy of the Lord is your strength* (Nehemiah 8:10). When you're filled with the joy of the Lord, you can't help but show it. A joyful Christian is an active Christian, serving God in every way possible—even to mowing the lawn with one hand as a witness to passersby of an indomitable spirit. That's abundant living—even when using your cane!

> *But may the righteous be glad and rejoice before God;*
> *may they be happy and joyful.*
>
> PSALM 68:3

If you don't truly need something from a mail order catalogue, recycle it. Don't let it lie around tempting you. (Jeanne Zornes)

March 27

In All Things

ROBERT YOCUM

Life is like riding a bicycle. You don't fall off until you stop pedaling.

—CLAUDE PEPPER

Since God promises us in Romans 8:28 that He works out everything for our good in all of life's experiences, we must accept the good and bad times as part of the abundant life. At the beginning of WW II, I was ordered to have a physical examination for service in the military. At the conclusion the doctor said: "Disgustingly healthy!" That has characterized most of my life. I had very little time or patience for anyone who had an illness until a major illness came my way.

In 1981, I was diagnosed with lupus and that was a devastating experience. My plans and goals were interrupted and I knew that I would never see them completed. As a result I chose early retirement without achieving my "nest egg" and targeted income. My most agonizing thought was, "How can I live on that income?"

I moved to a new community and developed a philosophy for retirement: I will be content within my income, find constructive ways to help others, and serve my community through my church and other organizations. To my pleasant surprise, I am able to live within my income, generously help others in need and also save for future needs. Yes! God abundantly supplies our every need.

During my ten-year struggle with lupus on three different occasions I spent three months in bed. Though they were difficult times, God taught me precious lessons I would never have learned otherwise I needed those times in bed and I discovered that they are part of the abundant life.

I have used some of the lessons God taught me to help others. A friend's family walked out on him. I shared with him what God had taught me in my despondent times and God spoke to him through it. Months later, our paths crossed and he thanked me for the day I encouraged him. He told me that was the turning point in reconciliation with his family.

Although lupus is supposed to be an incurable disease and many have a tough time dealing with it, I can only say that I needed my illness. As a result, I have learned a new perspective of the abundant life Jesus promised.

If you are ill and the abundant life escapes you, look for the ways God is bringing good out of it. If you are healthy and fear becoming ill, trust that if God allows it, He knows the way He plans to use it.

For our light and momentary troubles are achieving for us an eternal glory that far outweighs them all.
2 CORINTHIANS 4:17

> Have a separate address book for businesses and services you frequently call or use in order to save time looking it up in the Yellow Pages.

March 28

Positive Mental Outlook

ANNIE CHAPMAN

Love, in the divine alchemy of life, transmutes all duties into privileges, all responsibilities into joys.
—WILLIAM GEORGE JORDAN

*A*ll of us know people who seem to have a positive mental attitude no matter what the circumstances of their life. Though hard times and tough situations confront them, they face life with optimism.

These people, whether they are Christians or not, truly believe and follow the basic premise of Minirth and Meier's book: *Happiness is a Choice.* Rather than buckle under the pressure of life, they choose to face their circumstances squarely and deal with problems positively.

As Christians, we are mandated to make this same choice. That doesn't mean our life will be problem-free. And it doesn't mean we should wear a perpetual smile and deny the reality of our daily challenges. For instance, if I discover a lump in my breast I need to say, "This could be cancer, and I need to have it checked, instead of thinking, 'God wouldn't let anything bad happen to me, so I don't need to worry about this.'"

The fact is bad things do happen to us. But as Christians, we have an inner peace and joy that says, "God is in control. Even though I don't like what is happening, I know I can trust Him." When we live like this, those who know us will see that, although we hurt at times, we have a place to bring our pain.

Optimists are often called idealists, as if their joy were based on some false sense of hope and they were not grounded in reality. Granted, there are those who deny reality and pretend that nothing bad ever happens to them. Joy like this is about as sturdy as whipped cream. Once the sun comes out and heats it up, it melts away.

A true healthy mental outlook, on the other hand, recognizes life's challenges, deals with them appropriately, and continues moving through life with a sense of peace that God is working to bring good out of difficult situations.

Consider it pure joy, my brothers, whenever you face trials of many kinds.
JAMES 1:2

Make yourself feel "Special" tonight, by using cloth napkins and the good china!

March 29

A Ten Minute Vacation

SUSAN TITUS OSBORN

A bird doesn't sing because he has an answer—he sings because he has a song.

—JOAN ANGLUND

With today's busy schedule, I always seem to be in a rush. To keep an abundance of joy, I've found that it helps to take a ten minute vacation now and then.

My vacation retreat is a beautiful gazebo that my husband built at the edge of our property overlooking a wildlife preserve and a golf course. When I go out there and sit in my hammock swing, there are no interruptions. I can't hear the doorbell, and the phone doesn't reach. Although I live in the middle of a large metropolitan area, I don't hear the rush of traffic. In my gazebo I escape from the busyness of life for my ten minute vacation.

In my private hideaway, I marvel at God's creation. I watch the birds eat from my hanging feeder—sparrows, wrens, doves, and swallows. I listen to the water in the creek a hundred feet below as it plunges over the spillway on its way to the ocean. If I am very still, I can hear frogs croak and crickets chirp.

When I rush around all day, I often lose touch with abundant living and listening to God. It has been my experience that He doesn't speak very loudly. In my gazebo hideaway I always feel close to the Lord. The soft breeze brushes my face, refreshing me. I am still and in tune with God. My muscles relax, and tension drains from my body.

A few minutes later, I return to the house and my business responsibilities, feeling relaxed and refreshed after my ten-minute vacation with God.

When you're feeling stressed, find a hideaway and rediscover abundant joy through a ten minute getaway.

Be still and know that I am God. I will be exalted among the nations, I will be exalted in the earth.

PSALM 46:10

Postcards are still the best mail bargain. Keep some in your purse or glove compartment for taking advantage of small bits of time. (Jeanne Zornes)

March 30

God, Please Make It My Friend

DIANE LEHMAN

When life gives you lemons, make lemonade!

—ANONYMOUS

*L*ike watching a movie in slow motion, I felt detached as the doctor gave me his diagnosis: "Mrs. Lehman, you have Muscular Dystrophy!" It was as if someone suddenly knocked the air out of me. Would I be an invalid in my thirties? Would I even live to see my children grow up?

As a child on a swim team something had puzzled me. It was impossible for me to crawl out of the pool without a ladder. No one else seemed to have that problem . . . but then again, no one else had trouble chinning themselves, doing pushups or climbing the rope for gym.

Our doctor said that I had undiagnosed polio, and it was too late to do anything about it. So, I just focused on the things that I still could do.

However, after the birth of my second child, I knew something was wrong. At first I thought it was the trauma of a difficult pregnancy and delivery. But the nagging thought that it was something more led me to the specialists—and the doctor's alarming announcement.

Still numb, I tried to regain some control by asking the doctor how I could help myself. His insensitivity stunned me, "There is nothing to do but monitor the deterioration and have you come back when you need a wheelchair!"

Dazed and alone, I turned to God. "Jesus, dear Jesus, help me keep my eyes on you . . . and make this disease my friend." I knew it was a choice: to learn and grow from this new challenge or be overcome with fear, anger, and grief. It would strengthen my relationship with God, or destroy it.

Like a robot on remote control I drove home, repeating that prayer over and over again. An amazing thing happened during that long drive. The love of Jesus surrounded and comforted me. He filled me with a sense of incredible peace and joy. I knew He cared and was answering my prayer.

God did not cure me of my disease but He has helped to make it my friend. That is abundant living. I've learned to marvel at the human body and how miraculously it adapts. My disease has taught me to appreciate and focus on what I *can* do. I have learned how precious and fragile life is, and I try to enjoy what I have while I still have it. It has tempered my workaholism to help me prioritize the important things in my life: my faith, my family, and helping others. It has helped me to be able to empathize and relate to others who have chronic, untreatable conditions. It has forced me to rely more on God, which has helped me grow spiritually. And it makes me look forward to heaven with great anticipation of finally having a "body" that is strong.

Abundant living doesn't have to include being able to do everything everyone else can. It's a perspective of life that rejoices in what you indeed can do.

But he said to me, "My grace if sufficient for you,
for my power is made perfect in weakness."

2 CORINTHIANS 12:9

For items that get easily scattered, find wire baskets or
other holders at garage sales, flea markets or discount
stores to group them together.

March 31

One Isn't Always The Loneliest Number

LUCI SHAW

He who neglects to drink of the spring of experience is
apt to die of thirst in the desert of ignorance.

—LING PO

*M*ost of us think of being alone as a negative. After Harold died, I realized that being alone didn't necessarily mean I was lonely. I came to enjoy the advantages of only having to care for myself at the end of a long day. If I was hungry, I could eat what I wanted, when I wanted. I could sleep when my body decided it needed rest. There was definitely a relief in not having to justify myself and my actions to anyone else!

It was during this time of freedom that I learned the difference between loneliness and solitude. Solitude is finding a wholeness, a completeness, a richness within myself. I value solitude because I'm a busy person, and I'm involved in many people's lives. I'm energized by people, but I'm also energized and recharged by being alone. For me, solitude means enjoying my own company because I feel self-contained and contented. Loneliness, on the other hand, comes when I recognize a lack of resources within myself. When I'm lonely, I want to reach out and make contact with other people because within myself I feel inadequate.

I didn't realize my own spiritual and emotional inadequacies until after Harold died. He was always such a strong, giving person, and whenever I would have difficulties or questions, I would confide in him and find understanding and comfort. When he died, I lost my human intermediary, and I was forced to go to God directly. In many ways, loneliness served a critical purpose in my spiritual development. It wasn't until I began to bring all of my needs to God that I began to see how He truly does fill every void.

Claiming God's presence and actually feeling it are two separate issues. I spent many months asking God to fill my heart's desires before I began to see He really was there for me. Now, when I look back in my journal, I realize that in a larger sense, God was there caring for me and planning my life all along—I just didn't realize it at the time. There is no sure-fire formula for achieving intimacy with God. But as long as our hearts are crying out for a close relationship with Him, we can be confident He will satisfy us in His own time.

Loneliness and a sense of lack isn't always a bad thing. It reminds us that life is a series of losses and gains—light and darkness. Just as a tree needs the stresses of the elements, such as wind and rain and drought, so, too, we need the stresses of life to mature. We need loneliness to appreciate the blessings we do have. And if we allow ourselves to absorb the feeling of loneliness and reflect on the experience, God can use it to teach us many new things about ourselves and about Him.

Blessed are those who mourn, for they will be comforted.
MATTHEW 5:4

The art of "Bonsai" is a great example of endurance and beauty—spring garden shows are a wonderful place to witness this joy.

April

"Therefore, having been justified by faith, we have peace with God through our Lord Jesus Christ."

Romans 5:1

*A*bundant peace is what April is all about. The sacrificial death of Christ brings a simple peace so that we can know without a doubt that we are reconciled to God through the forgiveness of our sins. Then the victory of Jesus' resurrection assures us death has no power over us. We have peace about our eternal future in His presence. Let this month's readings fill your heart with abundant peace.

Spring Renewal

LIBBY C. CARPENTER

> One life to live, will soon be past. Only what's done
> for Christ will last.
>
> —UNKNOWN

*M*any Christians across the world observe the forty days before Easter as the Lenten season. Named for the time of year when the days begin to lengthen, Lent has been observed since 200 A.D. The season begins with "Ash Wednesday" and concludes with "Holy Week." It is a time of preparation for Christ's suffering and death. In some churches, on Ash Wednesday the sign of the cross is placed on the forehead using ashes from the previous year's Easter celebration. This is to represent humility and repentance.

As I began my Lenten journey this year, attending Ash Wednesday service started out as merely the annual ritual. Soon after the service began, the time came for the mark of the cross to be placed on our foreheads. I rose from my seat with the others. But as we began filing to the front of the church, I felt something was totally different. Walking forward I realized that in this same fashion, we as believers will some day line up and approach the Father on Judgment Day. That will be the time to answer for our actions during our earthly pilgrimage. Only the acts we performed of eternal value will count. All else will be burned away.

As the minister smudged the sign of the cross on my forehead, I made a vow. A vow to use my life in commitment to His service, and His alone. I left with a new attitude and burning desire to invest my life in the important things—the things that will build His kingdom.

Have you made such a simple—yet incredibly peaceful—decision? It's the only way to experience the abundant life Jesus promised.

For we must all appear before the judgment seat of Christ, that each one may receive
what is due him for the things done while in the body, whether good or bad.
2 CORINTHIANS 5:10

> If your church doesn't practice the sign of the cross on the forehead, consider doing it yourself as a sign of commitment and love for the Lord Jesus who died for you.

Lenten Sacrifice

KITTY BUCHOLTZ

It is only through the mystery of self-sacrifice that a
man may find himself anew.

—CARL GUSTAV JUNG

During the Ash Wednesday message last year, the priest challenged
each of us to give up praying for ourselves for the entire Lenten
season. We were to pray only for others, or in thanksgiving. At first, I
resisted the idea. My husband and I were having some severe financial
hardships and had just begun new jobs. It was flu season. I could not
imagine giving up praying for myself.

As a child I memorized the Bible verse about praying without
ceasing, and over the years it had become a way of life. I prayed for the
people I passed on the road, the homeless people I saw on the street,
my neighbor yelling at his wife. I also prayed constantly for myself: for
finding my car keys, losing weight, getting to work on time.

But I could feel the urge to accept the challenge tickling the inside
of my head. *Okay, God, I relented. I get the feeling You want me to try
this.* And with that I left church feeling lighthearted and ready to pray.

I never would have imagined how hard it is not to pray for yourself.
I came down with the flu two days later and started to pray, *Dear Lord,
please help . . . John to not get sick.* I was driving to work, and realizing
I would be late, began, *God please . . . thank you for helping me to be on
time most of the time.* I spent a lunch hour working on a new book idea,
trying to find that illusive thought I'd been waiting for for days. *Lord
. . . Thank you for all the ideas in my head. I know I'll find the right one.*
It was getting easier. While paying our bills, I thought about how much
we were short and thought to pray for help, but instead prayed, *Dear
Lord, thank you so much for always helping us and never letting us down.*

I prayed for others more than I ever had before. I prayed for my
co-worker and her teenage daughter. I prayed for my manager and his
wife and newborn baby. I prayed for my friend who was in a car
accident, and for my friend who had two horses fall on top of her.

And I began to feel the abundance of praying for others and
thanking God for what I have without asking for more: God answered
my long-standing prayer to feel more peace and contentment in life. I

am more understanding of people because I spend more time praying for their problems. I worry about things less because I "can't" pray for them, so I thank God instead for the blessings I already have. I am truly turning a new page in my life's chapter of abundant living.

I never would have imagined that such a simple step could have created such abundance in my attitudes. I challenge you to make a similar experiment. You may be surprised at how God uses it.

> . . . Pray continually, give thanks in all circumstances,
> for this is God's will for you in Christ Jesus.
>
> I THESSALONIANS 5:17,18

If you feel a similar challenge, try refraining from praying for yourself for a designated period of time. Instead, only give thanks. Record your responses in your journal.

April 3

Born For Adversity

RUTH M. RINK

I am still learning.

— MICHELANGELO

*L*ate as usual, I grabbed my coat, balanced a hot casserole along with my purse, and hurried off to deliver dinner to a shut-in. Seconds later, I slipped on my icy back steps, bumping one by one to the bottom. Although free from pain, I noticed my right foot felt disconnected. Could my leg be broken?

Inch by inch, I dragged myself down my driveway to the street. After waiting what seemed interminably long, a neighbor appeared, followed by others. As they helped me, I couldn't help but think, "They're all here to help at this moment, but where will they be a month from now? Who has time for a retired, 70-year-old school teacher, living alone with a broken leg?"

Following X-rays at the hospital, the surgeon said, "Your leg is broken in two places. You face five to six months in a cast, on crutches." My church friends prayed with me one more time before leaving. "Lord Jesus, provide for Ruth's every need during this difficult time."

A week later, another ambulance delivered me to a nursing home where I joyfully watched as an attendant displayed my stack of get-well cards, flowers, plants, and gifts. Different friends poked smiling faces through my doorway, each of the thirty days I was there.

Eagerly, I anticipated going home. My best friend from third grade was scheduled to fly East to care for me. Her phone call devastated me. "Ruth, I can't come right now. Family problems, dear. Can you possibly make other arrangements for the next ten days?"

"Of course!" I chirped over the phone, wiping away a stray tear. I hung up the phone, feeling suddenly empty of my faith in a God who cares. But that very day, a former high school student of mine, and also a good friend, arrived and asked, "How would you like to come home with me, Ruth?"

I accepted, humbled by God's loving concern.

Ten days later, my elementary school friend arrived and remained nine weeks. When she left, I flew to Florida for loving care by still another friend. Returning home minus my crutches, I was hopefully, forever convinced that friends are God's gift of abundant love.

If you wonder whether God will provide for you in some difficulty, let your heart be at peace. He is faithful and good.

A righteous man is a guide to his neighbor . . .
PROVERBS 12:26

> In preparation for Easter, read your children the book by Liz Curtis Higgs, *The Parable of the Lily*, (Thomas Nelson, 1997).

April 4

Look Again And Consecrate

OSWALD CHAMBERS

Worry is the interest paid by those who borrow trouble.
—GEORGE LYONS

A simple statement of Jesus is always a puzzle to us if we are not simple. How are we going to be simple with the simplicity of Jesus? By receiving His Spirit, recognizing and relying on Him, obeying Him as He brings the word of God, and life will become amazingly simple. "Consider," says Jesus, "How much more your Father who clothes the grass of the field will clothe you, if you keep your relationship right with Him." Every time we have gone back in spiritual communion it has been because we have impertinently known better than Jesus Christ. We have allowed the cares of the world to come in, and have forgotten the "much more" of our Heavenly Father.

Behold the fowls of the air—their main function is to obey the principle of life that is in them and God looks after them. Jesus says that if you are rightly related to Him and obey His Spirit that is in you, God will look after your "feathers."

Consider the lilies of the field—they grow where they are put. Many of us refuse to grow where we are put, consequently we take root nowhere. Jesus says that if we obey the life God has given us, He will look after all the other things. Has Jesus Christ told us a lie? If we are not experiencing the "much more," it is because we are not obeying the life God has given us, we are taken up with confusing considerations. How much time have we taken up worrying God with questions when we should have been absolutely free to concentrate on His work? Consecration means the continual separating of oneself to a particular thing. We cannot consecrate once and for all. Am I continually separating myself to consider God every day of my life?

If that is how God clothes the grass of the field,
which is here today and tomorrow is thrown into the fire,
will he not much more clothe you, O you of little faith?
MATTHEW 6:30

Take a 3 X 5 card and write STOP in big letters on one side. On the other side write out Matthew 6:30. Whenever you notice worry stealing your peace, pull out your card and say out loud, "Stop!" Then turn the card over and meditate on the Scripture.

April 5

The Lesson Of The Easter Eggs

LOIS ERISEY POOLE

Very little is needed to make a happy life.
—MARCUS AURELIUS ANTONINUS

"Grandma? Can we color Easter eggs this afternoon?"
Why, hadn't I remembered to buy egg dye when I was at the market?

I asked myself. Living in a rural area makes one alert to grocery lists and necessities. We don't run to the market for any little item that suddenly pops into our minds.

I wracked my brain for an idea. Then, I recalled my childhood Easters. We always had eggs dyed with onion skins, and I had a bin filled with dry husks of yellow onions from our garden.

I prepared a large enamel pan with water. Then we wrapped each egg in a small square of cheese cloth which had been thickly layered with the dried onion skins. Tying each package with string, I dropped them into the water and boiled them for 20 minutes.

"But Grandma, this isn't any fun. I wanted to dip them into the cups of colors," she whined, impatiently.

"Wait until they're cool, honey, then you can unwrap them and you will be very surprised."

My comment fell on deaf ears and disappointed glances.

As we waited, I recalled how impatient I, too, could be; impatient with cold weather, adjusting the furnace, gathering up heavy coats, and scraping ice off car windows.

And then one day lady Spring tiptoes down the road through our back gate where she sprinkles the lawn with green "hellos." She wraps the edges of the days with warmth. The sun becomes a little brighter and the birds begin to sing.

But best of all, Spring brings Easter, a delightful season each year that reminds us that we are capable of bearing any cross of despair, because we now have an opportunity to begin life anew.

When the eggs had cooled we began to cut the string and unwrap them.

"They're so pretty!" my grandaughter laughed. "These are the prettiest eggs I've every seen."

We giggled together as we continued to open each soggy little bundle. The contents were startling and surprising. Some eggs were a deep brown like ovals of mahogany; others were veined with yellows and greens. We polished them to a high gloss with vegetable oil and arranged them on a bed of parsley in a crystal bowl. Later, our guests delighted in them.

My granddaughter learned, and I was reminded, that we all are capable of accomplishing wonderful feats with whatever God gives us. That's one of the rules for simple living: being at peace, knowing God can use "nothing" to become something of value.

This is the day the Lord has made; let us rejoice and be glad in it.
PSALM 118:24

> This year, color your eggs with onion skins.

Needing Acceptance

KITTY BUCHOLTZ

A man who was completely innocent, offered himself
as a sacrifice for the good of others, including his
enemies, and became the ransom of the world. It was
a perfect act.

—MOHANDAS K. GANDHI

One year, on Ash Wednesday, I was leaving church with my friend
Linda and said to her, "I'm never sure whether to say anything or
try to hide the fact that I've given up sweets for Lent. It says in Matthew
6 that when you pray or fast, you should do it in secret and God will
reward you. But it also says to let your life reflect your beliefs so that
others will come to know God. With food in the office all the time,
people are bound to wonder, and I don't want to lie. Plus, it seems like
this is the perfect time of year to try to share my beliefs."

Linda nodded her head. "I've thought about that, too."

If you offer a sacrifice to God in secret, I mused, *He rewards you. If
you also obey God by openly sharing His word and His love with others—
even if it means sharing your secret offering, are you then nullifying the effect
of your sacrifice?*

Ever since I started giving up something for Lent, I have struggled
with whether to keep it a secret at all costs, or to witness in whatever
way I could, even if it seemed to dampen the beauty of my offering.
Two years ago, I heard God answer my question.

I had never been willing to "sacrifice" what people thought of me;
I could never just start talking to people about God for fear I would
be ostracized. But one of my friends, also a Christian, asked me why
I had given up chocolate for Lent. After a quick prayer for courage I
began to tell him.

"Since Jesus calls us to follow Him in leading a different life and
leaving behind our worldly desires, I give up something I enjoy—eating
chocolate, reading fiction—to remind myself that I am willing to change
my life for Him."

I spoke briefly, waiting for him to turn the conversation elsewhere,
but soon there were four or five people standing around talking about

Lent and Easter and Jesus! My heart began to sing as I realized God was at work!

I had prayed and when I heard God's voice, I obeyed, even when it seemed contrary to what I thought I ought to do. It was then that I found God helping me to make a simple, yet greater, sacrifice, one that *really* showed I loved Him more than myself: I gave up needing the acceptance of my peers. Choosing to value God's approval brought an abundant peace that was far more valuable.

If you are weighed down with a need to please others, make the same choice I did. God's peace will be your reward.

. . . Does the Lord delight in burnt offerings and sacrifices as much as in obeying the voice of the Lord? To obey is better than sacrifice . . .

I SAMUEL 15:22

> If you desire to sacrifice for Lent, consider something that isn't a "thing," but the correction of an attitude or behavior.

April 7

The Challenge Of The Cross

RUTH M. RINK

I have been driven many times to my knees by the overwhelming conviction that I had nowhere else to turn . . .

—ABRAHAM LINCOLN

When I was a teenager, a group from our church presented an Easter pageant entitled "The Challenge of the Cross." I was given the role of the penitent sinner who came down the aisle singing, "I am Coming to the Cross." It was a thrilling experience for us even though, I am sure, it fell short of a perfect performance.

Today, the Cross's outstretched arms still challenge those of us who have never known the peace of a daily walk with God, to kneel at its foot, inviting Jesus to come into our lives to be present with us always.

I believe the Cross challenges those of us who have become complacent and are following "afar off" to come rededicate our lives and recapture the joy and peace that we once knew.

We should all be challenged to covenant with God to pray more earnestly for our church, our community, our country and our world. God calls us to repentant prayer in 2 Chronicles 7:14: *If my people, who are called by my name, will humble themselves and pray and seek my face and turn from their wicked ways, then will I hear from heaven and will forgive their sin and will heal their land.*

When that event occurs, let us strive to be ready, individually and as a church, to enter into a time of revival and renewal. Only then can God's abundant peace surround us.

Come to me, all you who are weary and burdened, and I will give you rest.
MATTHEW 11:28

> Pray today specifically for some member of our government and for revival in our land.

April 8

The Secret Of Sharing

HELEN KESINGER

Little is much if God is in it.
—AMERICAN PROVERB

"Psst, Karen . . . " I whispered as I leaned over the pew to get the attention of a young single mother. I knew she was strapped for money. "What are you doing for lunch today?"

"I don't have anything planned. Why?"

"I've got a platter of ham left over from last night's church dinner. I surely could use some help eating it." I didn't tell her, but that's *all* I had in the refrigerator or likely would have until payday.

"Sounds great! I have a tray of deviled eggs I was going to take last night, but I ended up staying home because my daughter was sick."

Another single-again person sitting down the pew from me leaned forward, "I'm stuck with a potato casserole."

"Come on over," I replied jubilantly.

"Hey, don't leave me out. I've got a head of lettuce," added a college student.

"And I've got some tomatoes and carrots," came a voice from the pew behind me.

A shy, awkward man cleared his throat nervously. "Uh . . . I can stop at the store and pick up . . . Uh . . . a chocolate cake . . . if that's all right. I mean, would you mind if I came over, too?"

The church service had not yet begun, but I was getting excited to see the Lord already at work. I guess He knew something about the domino theory. The momentum grew until I was wondering if I had enough room for everyone. But somehow I knew it would turn out just right.

The simple gesture of sharing a little turned into an abundant feast as single adults filled my home to celebrate Easter Sunday and the risen Christ, the master of all giving. Who can you reach out to so that the peace that Jesus offers can be shared with others?

> . . . Practice hospitality.
>
> ROMANS 12:13

If you're a single, then start a regular holiday gathering for other singles. If you're not single, invite a single person to your Easter celebration.

April 9

Rehearsal Or Reality?

CORA LEE PLESS

Jesus was crucified not in a cathedral between two candles,
but on a cross between two thieves.
—GEORGE F. MACLEOD

"You're supposed to cry out as though you're really in pain," our pastor instructed the teenagers.

Our youth group was rehearsing a drama about the Crucifixion and Resurrection, and we had come to the part where the legs of the criminals were broken.

Following the instructions of our pastor-director, one of the "soldiers" had approached one of the "thieves," drawn his makeshift sword and struck the wood of the cross behind the boy's legs. The impact resulted in a loud whack. The thief was then supposed to emit a scream of pain, but instead he only let out a feeble cry.

That's when the pastor stopped the rehearsal and instructed the thief to make his cry more realistic.

"Let's try it again," our pastor said.

Once again the soldier approached the cross and struck with his sword. This time, the thief screamed out as though he were in actual agony.

"Much better!" the director said, pleased.

"It should be!" the thief exclaimed. "This time he missed the cross. He really hit my leg!"

Remembering that event causes me to smile but also to think. How often do I go through the motions of observing this special time of year without contemplating the reality of what my Lord endured?

As I take time to ponder the depth of Jesus' suffering, I begin to appreciate the abundant gift of peace He offers me. Because He took my place of suffering, I have peace with God. My sins are forgiven and I no longer need to condemn myself.

Have you received the free gift of peace God makes available through Jesus?

But he was pierced for our transgressions, he was crushed for our iniquities;
the punishment that brought us peace was upon him,
and by his wounds we are healed.

ISAIAH 53:5

As you view a cross this Easter season, try to imagine for one full minute the agony that Jesus suffered in your behalf.

April 10

The Easter Egg Legend

JOAN K. WEAVER

Look at the sequence: risen from the dead, therefore alive forever; therefore our contemporary; therefore able to confront us face to face.

—JAMES S. STEWART

This week children everywhere will be dyeing colorful eggs for the Easter celebration. They will put food coloring or those little tablets in a cup of water and vinegar believing this is the way it has always been done. However, synthetic dyes have only been around for 125 years. Early settlers to this country brought natural dyeing techniques with them from their home countries. This year, it might be fun to experiment with some traditional dyes. And as long as you are in a mood for "eggs-perimentation," pick up a dozen, old-fashioned brown eggs and dye them along with the white ones. Here are some recipes to try:

Yellow
1 tsp. powdered turmeric
2 cups water
1 tbsp. vinegar
2 pinches of alum

Green
4 cups chopped spinach, birch or elderberry leaves
water to cover
1 tbsp. vinegar

Blue
1 cup red cabbage leaves, chopped
2 cups water
1 tbsp. vinegar

Red-Brown
2 cups yellow onion skins
3 cups water

Gently simmer the ingredients in a stainless steel, enamel, or glass pan to extract color. When water is richly colored, strain out any plant material, add raw eggs and simmer 10 minutes.

Or use precooked, hard-boiled eggs with the liquids that follow. Just dip or soak the eggs for the desired shade.

PURPLE: grape juice concentrate
RED: juice from fresh beets, smashed raspberries or strawberries
TAN: tea, coffee or liquid saved from boiling walnut or pecan hulls in water
BLUE: juice from smashed blueberries

At Easter time we remember that Christ came so that we can be reborn and made new also. Just like the simple egg, we are made beautiful in Christ.

Therefore, if any one is in Christ, he is a new creation;
the old has gone, the new has come!
2 CORINTHIANS 5:17

> While you and your children are concocting these natural dyes, it would be a good time to talk about how the springtime is a time for eggs to hatch, for baby bunnies to be born, and for flowers to bloom.

Easter With The Family

MARGARET PRIMROSE

Christ is risen! Christ is risen!
Celebrate and sing.
Jesus died and rose to save us.
Proclaim Him as our King.

—ANONYMOUS

The resurrection of Jesus was the greatest event in history. Without it we would have no hope of life after death. Then why shouldn't families do more to celebrate it than any other holiday of the year? That need not mean elaborate decorations, expensive new clothes or big dinners. There are a lot of simple things we can do to make it memorable.

Plan a treasure hunt. Instead of the usual hard-boiled or candy eggs, fill plastic eggs with an Easter balloon or sticker and a piece of paper on which you have written an Easter scripture.

Dramatize parts of the Resurrection. It doesn't require elaborate props or scripts. Let children imagine an empty tomb and run to tell their friends about it. One of them could play Mary when she discovers that Jesus is alive and that she just talked to Him. "Doubting Thomas" could also react to seeing Jesus and His scars.

Use objects that suggest scenes from the Easter story. A list of suitable objects include a bag of silver (Luke 22:3-6), a sponge and a jar of vinegar (John 19:38-30), a basin of water and a towel (John 13:1-5), grape juice and bread (Matthew 26:28), a stone (Mark 16:2-4), and spices (Luke 23:55-56).

The list is adaptable. Use these objects for a scavenger hunt. Or have the family search for Scriptures listing the items and read the verses that show how the items figure in the Easter story. Another idea is to read the Easter story and let children score points for being the first to link a passage with something in your collection. Whatever the approach, talk about the significance of what was listed or collected.

After Easter, continue to capitalize on the post-Resurrection appearances of Jesus. A family fish fry by the lake would be a good time to talk about Jesus' command to "feed my sheep." Or take an "Emmaus walk" in the country.

With enthusiasm and a simple imagination, we can make Easter the most special celebration of the year. Victories are for celebrating.

. . . Death has been swallowed up in victory.
I CORINTHIANS 15:54

> Consider having a family sunrise service. Revel in the first rays of the rising sun while you read the Easter story. Sing a few appropriate choruses and have prayer. This will set the tone for the remainder of the day.

April 12

Peep Checkers

JOANIE PRICE BROWN

My business is not to remake myself but to make the absolute best of what God made.

—ROBERT BROWNING

*M*y brother-in-law, Bruce, devours purple chickens; but he'll eat pink ones too. Bruce gobbles those tiny marshmallow chicks with black beady eyes in one quick gulp. I bought him a package of the purple peepers, wrapped it in purple paper and gave it to him Easter morning.

Bruce and Judy, along with my husband and I, sat around the small patio table we use for a kitchen table. Bruce surveyed the little package of staring peeps and found one with uneven eyes; he held the sticky purple treat between his fingers as he talked.

"Before these tiny chicks ever reach the shelves, inspectors—peep checkers—examine their tiny black eyes to see if they are evenly aligned. If one eye is slightly askew, the chicks are thrown back into a boiling pot, melted down and re-formed into perfect peepers. Guess they missed this one," he surmised.

We eyed Bruce with suspicion, not realizing he was quite serious.

He continued, "Oh yes, they carefully inspect each eye, plucking and shucking the imperfections while only the best of the litter pass on."

"Aren't you glad God didn't throw us back into the pot?" I laughed.

That evening, I remembered our conversation. I thought of my own flaws, like ugly words spewed out in moments of uncontrolled anger. *I'm glad God doesn't throw us back into the kiln,* I mused. *He accepts us as we are with our imperfections and human limitations. That gives me such peace.*

I spoke with Judy a week later. "Remember Bruce's purple chick with the uneven eyes?" I asked. "I've been thinking about that chick and how my learning disabilities are like those uneven eyes. God takes my disability and views me through the eyes of Jesus. How wonderful that He sees my 'purple chick' eyes in perfect alignment!"

A few weeks later, Judy sent me a refrigerator magnet with a paraphrase of 2 Corinthians 12:9 "My grace is all you need for my power is strongest when you are weak." It reminds me when "I can't, God can."

When imperfections hinder and frustrate us, we can have peace knowing God gives us the power to work within our boundaries and beyond with His power.

If some limitation diminishes your trust in God's power to use you for His glory, be confident knowing He uniquely created you for an abundant plan. Nothing can prevent that from happening, except you!

> *But he said to me, "My grace is sufficient for you,*
> *for my power is made perfect in weakness. . ."*
>
> 2 CORINTHIANS 12:9

Write down the things you don't like about yourself. Then beside each one note how God has used it for good.

April 13

Visiting With Luke

ROBERTA L. MESSNER

Too often we underestimate the power of a touch, a
smile, a kind word, a listening ear, an honest compliment,
or the smallest act of caring, all of which have the potential to turn a life around.

—LEO BUSCAGLIA

One chaotic spring day, when I was trying to juggle the responsibilities of work, home, and graduate school, I was assigned to care for a patient diagnosed with incurable cancer. Luke was so despondent, he refused to talk to anyone. When I made my initial home visit, I felt woefully inadequate for the task ahead.

I learned that for the first time in Luke's hardworking 55 years, he'd finally been able to buy a brand new truck. But now, because of the gravity of his condition and the medications he was taking, he couldn't even drive it.

I wanted so to communicate with Luke, but nothing in my professional career had prepared me for such a challenge. When I asked the Lord to help me, an inner voice urged: "Ask Luke to show you that new shiny red truck of his."

What difference could that possibly make? I inwardly debated. I decided to give it a try, though, and before I knew it, the two of us were climbing inside. Luke had settled for junk heaps his whole life and was so thrilled with all of its exciting features.

From that day on, whenever I called on Luke, he'd be waiting in the driver's seat with a thermos of coffee and two empty mugs. In the cab of that truck, we watched the crocuses, hyacinths, and tulips break through the barren ground. Luke was a different person there, somehow more in control and anxious to chat. Our "truck talks" eventually progressed to more serious matters . . . Luke's fear of dying, leaving his wife behind, and our shared assurance of eternal life.

I've never forgotten the lesson I learned that Easter season about helping people who are coping with any devastating circumstance. Like Jesus, when He was facing death in the garden of Gethsemane, He simply asked His disciples to stand watch with Him and pray.

Today, those who are ill are asking that we simply be there. By meeting Luke just where he was, a harried nurse and a terminally ill patient experienced the miracle that is Easter.

The next time a friend of yours is in need and you feel inadequate to comfort or guide, give the gift of your presence. It's a simple response with an abundant result.

Then he said to them, My soul is overwhelmed with sorrow to the point of death. Stay here and keep watch with me.
MATTHEW 26:38

> The next time you have the privilege of ministering to someone in difficult circumstances, listen more than you talk.

April 14

Prevent Ambition From Stealing Your Peace

BILL AND PAM FARREL

We have all of a few moments in life of hard, glorious
running; but we have days and years of walking—the
uneventful discharge of small duties.
— ALEXANDER MACLAREN

*A*mbition can be a good thing. It gets us out of bed each morning.
It gives us the desire to do our best at whatever task is ahead.
But blind ambition can be a cruel taskmaster, driving you past your
personal limit and beyond your ability to cope with life. Chasing the
almighty dollar or the next promotion can drive a person to the point
of collapse and ruin an otherwise healthy marriage.

Ask yourself these questions: Does this desire match Scripture?
Does it match my ability to achieve it? Does it allow me a stress level
that I can handle? Does it transcend my decision-making ability? Does
it fall well within my skill level?

Yes, God can stretch you and help you grow. But God usually
stretches people in small increments. God doesn't send you out to fail.
Often we are in a hurry and don't want to earn our way to the top.
We want it handed to us on a silver platter.

It is the process of day-in and day-out service and decision-making
that brings spiritual advancement. The forging of our character
day-after-day prepares us for more responsibility.

The plans of the diligent lead to profit
as surely as haste leads to poverty.
PROVERBS 21:5

If you have a desire that seems monumental because it is
stealing your peace, write it down on a piece of paper and
surrender it to God by burning it.

Being At Peace With God's Assignments

JEAN FLEMING

The morality of an action depends on the motive
from which we act.

—SAMUEL JOHNSON

Jesus did not heal everyone. He did not meet the needs of all the poor, or cast out all demons. I cannot meet every need I'm aware of. I cannot exploit every opportunity. At times, I must prune away good, worthwhile branches to insure that the trunk and limbs are more prominent than the ever-expanding branches.

The goal of much that is written about life management is to enable us to do more in less time. But is this necessarily a desirable goal? Perhaps we need not to get *less done*, but the right things.

When Mother Teresa received the Nobel Prize, a reporter asked a stinging question: "How can you receive this award when you've helped so few of the world's poor?" Mother Teresa replied that she couldn't accept responsibility for all the world's poor; she could only help those God asked her to be responsible for. We, too, can content ourselves with doing what God asks *us* to do.

> . . . and Joshua did it; he left nothing undone of all that the
> Lord commanded Moses.
>
> JOSHUA 11:15

> ". . . and on the seventh day, He rested." —Learn to
> "contemplate boredom" and take a half hour leisure break.

A Simple Secret

GLENDA SMITHERS

Worry is interest paid on trouble before it becomes due.
—WILLIAM R. INGE

"*A*re you going to grow with this experience," demanded my husband "Or just grow gray over it?"

A recent hospital stay was most revealing to me; for, as discomforting as the tests and diagnosis, I learned an important secret of health. How to keep calm. For 50 years I've hated needles and being calm inside a hospital wasn't on my patient chart—or so I thought.

With my health rebounding, I can take a clinical look at three things that kept me from anxiety during a week's stay in the hospital. I experienced the abundant life while there because of three simple things: the snow at night, the corridor's light, and my dear 70-year-old mother.

The snowflakes softly drifting against the window by an all-wise Creator, simply fulfilled God's purpose for them and fell with beauty. They reminded me to relax in God's care, knowing He is aware of every one of them and also me.

The corridor's light warmed me with confidence that God provides professional care. I could count on nurses and doctors to meet my needs. With the push of a button, an angel of mercy would be at my bedside.

There, too, is my mom. She'd serenely sit or stand by me, reminding me that if one's roots of faith are anchored in the promises of prayer and scripture, all will be well.

God provides whatever we need to remain calm in the midst of life's storms in order that we can continually experience His abundant life. It may be something as simple as a vision of beauty (rain, snow, flowers, cards, etc.). It may be faith in other people who come to your aid. It may be the love of family.

If I must return to the hospital, I'll go with infinite peace, knowing the Lord will supply a simple example of His sovereign control.

When I am afraid, I will trust in You.
PSALM 56:3

Habit-Forming Tips: Look ahead, Identify conflicts, Work out compromise solutions, Promptly contact all parties, and Avoid suprises. (*Finding Time*, Paula Peisner)

April 17

Teach Me To Pray

DEBBIE PIPER

Hurry is the death of prayer.

—SAMUEL CHADWICK

*A*lthough prayer is a simple form of communication with God, as a part of the abundant life, we can often make it complicated. As a result, it can diminish the peace we experience because it becomes intimidating.

We may have concerns about the *how* of praying because as children we learned to pray in ways that seem inadequate now. We may have learned "poem-prayers:" "Now I lay me down to sleep, I pray the Lord my soul to keep," or "God is great, God is good, Let us thank Him for our food." Or perhaps we've heard prayers using formal, elegant language far removed from our everyday vocabulary. "Thee" and "thou" were used in common daily speech in the 1600s, and while people may use these words in an honest desire to honor God, there is nothing inherently holy about them.

The secret to prayer is *honesty* and *humility*. God simply desires an honest expression of what you are thinking and feeling as you come to Him in prayer, He wants you to be aware of your need of Him in your life.

Prayer, talking with God, is as simple as talking with another person. In this case, it's God, and not someone sitting across from you. But God is your Father and your friend. He cares about you, and He's eager to hear from you. So you don't need to have any anxiety about talking with Him. There are no special formulas, no fancy words, no religious rituals necessary.

You can start with what you are feeling this very moment and go from there. Sometimes you'll come to God eagerly, looking forward to your time together; other times you'll come with anxiety because you failed to reach His standard. It doesn't matter to God. He still wants to talk with you.

You don't need to be in any special position to pray. You don't have to kneel, stand or sit cross-legged. You don't have to be in a special place—you can be at home, in the car, outside, at school, or in your office. You can pray with your eyes open, or shut. You don't have to use fancy religious words. You can call Him Father, Lord, God, Jesus, or Holy Spirit! You can pray silently, aloud, or by writing down your words. You can express your emotions freely—your joy, anger, fears, confusion. You can tell Him all your thoughts, including your doubts and uncertainties. Sometimes you will come to Him for a regularly-scheduled time of prayer. Other times you will call out to Him in a crisis. You can follow a set pattern in your prayers or you can just tell Him what's on your mind at the moment. God isn't as concerned with how you pray as He is with simply *hearing* from you. He wants to give you His peace.

As you reach out to Him in any or all of these ways, you will experience the abundant life.

> . . . *Pray continually.*
>
> I THESSALONIANS 5:17

Buy or check out a book on prayer from your church library.

April 18

Turn Up The Volume!

LAURA SABIN RILEY

> Praise is more spontaneous when things go right; but
> it is more precious when things go wrong.
>
> —ANONYMOUS

Ever have days of total chaos in your household from the time the sun rises to the time it sets? When it seems as if everyone wakes up on the wrong side of the bed and stays there all day? Or your kids are just plain mischievous and determined to stir the pot? That kind of day just drags along as we wish it would end. We think, "This definitely isn't the abundant life Jesus promised!"

It was during one of "those days" that I discovered a very simple way to change the atmosphere in our home for the better. The secret is praise. Praising God even in the worst of circumstances seems to change things. It doesn't change the circumstances but it does change our attitude about the circumstances.

I have found that when the atmosphere is looking bleak around our house or the kids are out of control, I need to change the atmosphere. One great way is to play praise music. Some days I play praise music on our stereo all day long, whether it's softly in the background of another activity or loudly while the kids and I sing and dance to the music. I have discovered that when my children are rambunctious and full of mischief, the praise music quiets them right down. The tone in our house will suddenly change, and we begin to experience abundant, peaceful living again.

The next time you need to turn down the volume on the attitudes and actions of the members of your household, turn up the praise music and watch God work!

> *From the rising of the sun to the place where it sets,*
> *the name of the Lord is to be praised.*
>
> PSALM 113:3

> Always carry a book in the car, you never know when you'll have a few minutes to read.

April 19

Give Us Our Daily Bread . . .

DURLYNN ANEMA-GARTEN

> Instead of comparing our lot with that of those who
> are more fortunate than we are, we should compare it
> with the lot of the great majority of our fellow men. It
> then appears that we are among the privileged.
>
> —HELEN KELLER

*H*ow often have you stood in a grocery line with two or three people ahead of you and become impatient? "After all," you tell yourself (or anyone else within hearing distance), "I am too busy to wait in line."

I frequently did that until I traveled in Eastern Europe and Russia several years ago. Imagine standing in line for an hour or longer *each* day to buy that evening's meal. As you stand there, you hope enough meat or vegetables will be available when you finally arrive at the counter. Women who must wait in those lines accept it as a way of life—perhaps complaining only to themselves or their husbands later in the day.

Yet, as I watched those faces staring straight ahead with little emotion, I recognized a spirit of peace hidden behind their facades. Many were the same women I saw in churches—even when those churches were forbidden. They knew the bread of life was far more than the physical entity they would purchase that day.

In churches throughout these countries I observed women kneeling in prayer. Their quiet spirit patiently waited for those prayers to be answered, even as their physical bodies waited for another day's meal. They believed Jesus' promise of *I am the bread of life...* (John 6:35) and that He would meet all their needs.

Unfortunately, we often confuse needs and wants. We don't starve and we don't stand in long, endless lines to purchase our food. Yet, we fret. We think having enough money to buy all the vegetables and meat we want is the criteria for abundant living. We complain about buying small items and why we can't have what others have.

Will we need shortages and lines before we realize that an abundant life can be ours even if we must stand in long lines? The people of the countries I visited have already learned that lesson. I saw a strength of character in them that we lack.

Let's stop thinking that an abundance of food or material possessions gives abundant Christian living. It's actually our simple belief in Jesus' words that gives fulfillment.

> *Then Jesus declared, "I am the bread of life.*
> *He who comes to me will never go hungry,*
> *and he who believes in me will never be thirsty."*
>
> JOHN 6:35

Have you tried bartering for some of your needs? Find those who offer what you want and want what you can do for them.

April 20

Let God Do The Worrying

JILL BRISCOE

There are two days in the week about which I never
worry. Two carefree days kept sacredly free from fear
and apprehension. One of these days is yesterday—and
the other day I do not worry about is tomorrow.
—ROBERT BURDETTE

*J*esus said in the scriptures that we mustn't worry about things that must be done. That worry is, in the end, a lack of trust in our heavenly Father, who knows all our needs and has promised to meet them. (In another Scripture he told us to look at the birds and realize that our feathered friends don't worry at all and yet are wonderfully cared for.) When we are trying to prioritize our priorities, we should remember Jesus' point: There are many things we should do, but there is *one* thing we *must* do, and that is to put Him first, at the very top of the list of "things I should do today." We must make sure we meet with Him, and that meeting is called "worship." If we don't do this, we will soon be running on empty.

Jesus used Mary as a model for Martha. *Mary has chosen what is better,* he explained. She met with Him, spent time with Him.

We have a choice. (We always do.) We can worry or we can worship. Strangely enough, busy people find it a whole lot easier to worry than to worship. When we worry, we feel we are still in control, even if we are worrying about things out of our control. At least we feel we are doing something about the situation. We are worrying.

When we worship, however, we ask God to take control and we let him do the worrying for us. He is concerned for us with a deep anxiety, a deep concern. The problem is—Marthas like to be in control. Notice in Luke 10:38, Martha didn't say to Mary, "You take over and tell *me* what to do." No, she wanted Mary to help her. She wanted to stay firmly in control. It's hard to give control up to someone else. Worship says, "Dear Lord, you are quite capable of controlling this situation. I should have asked you what you would like to eat, not provided seven courses that you might not even want. You are the Lord; I am the servant—direct me."

What the wicked dreads will overtake him;
what the righteous desire will be granted.

PROVERBS 10:24

> When worry seeks to overwhelm you, think of the worst possible thing that could happen if your worry occurred and then think of ways God could use it for good.

Tackle The Problem

MURIEL LARSON

Take plenty of time to count your blessings, but never spend a minute in worry.

—Anonymous

One night while I was reading in bed I heard a loud insect noise. "Creek, creek," it went. I got up to investigate. The noise stopped. Back I went to my reading. "Creek, creek!"

If I was going to be able to sleep, I had to do something. Crouching by the closet, I waited quietly. "Just one more 'creek,'" I said softly, "and I'll have you!"

"Creek, creek!" Out of the corner of my eye I saw the cricket, perched on the molding by the closet door. I'm ashamed to admit that I let the poor thing have it. But at least I slept good that night.

Do you have a problem that keeps you fretting? Perhaps it keeps you awake at night, tossing and turning. Maybe day after day it troubles you—sort of like a chirping cricket that starts up just when you begin to relax. Maybe it's a person who drives you crazy, a distressful situation, or a feeling of guilt, real or imagined. Whatever it is, it robs you of peace and the abundant life.

I've found that the best way to handle such things is to deal with them. On my study wall I have the "Prayer of Serenity" plaque: "God grant me the serenity to accept the things I cannot change, courage to change the things I can, and the wisdom to know the difference." It works!

For some things, such as car trouble or a toothache, I know just what I must do: take it to be worked on. If there's a task that needs attending to, I do it.

If something comes between the Lord and me, I seek to make it right and ask His forgiveness, for "He is faithful and just to forgive us our sins and cleanse us from all unrighteousness" (1 John 1:9). There's no sense in allowing guilt to keep weighing us down. Why should we sacrifice God's peace and joy by continuing to grieve Him?

If something comes between me and someone else, I obey the Scripture: "Go to your brother and get it settled." Jesus also told us to forgive one another and to love and pray for those who use us.

In fact, Jesus laid out in His Sermon on the Mount just about everything we need to know as far as our relationships with God and man are concerned—and it's usually in these two areas that we experience the most anxiety. He told us to seek first the kingdom of God and God would provide for all our needs (Matthew 6:33). What could be plainer than that? Being right with God takes care of guilt (because He forgives), depression (because He fills our hearts with faith, peace, and joy), and our earthly needs (because God provides for His own). By simply seeking to follow Christ's precepts in His Sermon on the Mount, I have saved myself much unrest. Then God's abundant living takes over again.

Which of Jesus' principles from His sermon are needed in your life today to experience greater abundance? If you ask, He'll provide the strength.

Come to me, all you who are weary and burdened, and I will give you rest.
MATTHEW 11:28

Answering phone solicitors with a "Please put me on your no-call list" legally obligates them to omit your name. (Jeanne Zornes)

April 22

The Decision Tree

CARL WESTLING

To know the will of God is the greatest knowledge! To do the will of God is the greatest achievement.
—GEORGE W. TRUETT

*D*ecisions can be complicated enough, even when a crisis is not at hand. Regardless of the pressures, it helps us to think like a chess player. This is another brick in the foundation for our abundant life.

Tournament class chess players pride themselves on their ability to think five, six, seven or more moves in advance. This preplanning allows them to avoid potential pitfalls that would not show up in just a few moves. The winner of a tournament is generally the one whose moves are planned farther ahead than their opponent.

This same logic can be used in daily activities that involve making multiple decisions. One simple way of doing this is by building a decision tree. You may choose to experiment with this concept before applying it to real life.

Here is how it works: Let's assume you have been offered a job in another city. First, draw a vertical line to represent a tree trunk. Next, put a fork on the trunk and label each of the two branches. Label one "move," the other "stay." On the move branch add additional branches sprouting from it for each added decision you will be required to make as a result of the move. Do the same with the stay branch.

Each added branch will have a name like: new living quarters, change banks, new friends, church, and so forth. Likewise, the stay branch will be labeled with your existing circumstances; same job, church, friends, living quarters, and on and on. The number of branches for each of the forks will only be limited by your imagination and present circumstances.

Just starting to label these new branches will bring new thoughts to mind, as well as make you consciously think of the less obvious factors of your present circumstances. And remember, most of these branches will have sub-branches. Just taking the time to begin sketching a decision tree will bring a degree of rationality to your ultimate decision, whether you are in the midst of a crisis or facing a decision in a non-crisis situation.

If you have asked the advice of others as you build your decision tree, remember one important fact: you are the one that will have to live with your decision. Though your friends and relatives will help you consider options, you are the one that will have to determine the merits of each option.

As you follow through on developing this simple, yet effective decision-making tool, pray that God will enlighten your mind and give you peace about the way He wants you to take. By surrendering your own desires, He will guide you. That's a promise in God's abundant living program.

Make level paths for your feet and take only ways that are firm.
PROVERBS 4:26

Don't make major decisions in times of crisis unless it is absolutely necessary.

The Simplicity Of Service

CAROLYN C. WILSON

True service comes from a relationship with the divine urgings. Energy is expended but it is not the frantic energy of the flesh.

—RICHARD J. FOSTER

On the cold New Year's Eve morning of 1990, I rushed outside onto a thin coat of invisible ice on our front steps. When my right foot touched the ice it spun wildly, and I crumpled to the cold concrete. I could not get up. I looked desperately around but there was no one to help me. My heart pounded loudly in my ears. *Help me,* I cried.

In my fear, a still small Voice calmed me: *My help comes from the Lord who made heaven and earth.* I found that I could move if I kept my leg straightened in front of me. Inch-by-inch, I scooted myself back inside the door, pulled a phone from a shelf, and dialed 911.

Today I look at that event as my life's watershed moment. It changed me forever as God taught me to listen to his Voice and be *still and know that I am God* (Psalm 46:10).

Before my accident I had been intent on advancing my career as a university instructor. I spent my days surrounded by college students and most evenings writing, grading papers, and planning classes. I preferred to be busy even though I had little time to spend with my husband or our two grown children. But that didn't bother me since they also were busy.

After my accident and surgery, I was confined to bed for a number of weeks. At night I slept fitfully because of the pain and prayer seemed to be the only thing that brought me peace. I finally learned to listen to God's voice.

The Voice asked, "Why are you so busy? What are you doing in your busyness? What are you living for?"

I felt indignant and replied, "I am helping your children, these college students, Lord. You put me in this position. I am busy for You!"

Gently, God showed me that my busyness was motivated by me, not God. I had kept myself busy serving for many years but I had no time for praising, adoring, and listening. Like Martha of the Bible, I had scurried around doing much for God. Now I know He didn't want my work; He wanted my devotion, affection, and love.

After my recovery, I resigned my university position to begin a small private practice in speech-language pathology. Now, my husband and I spend our evenings together and have time to devote to our two beautiful grandchildren. My daughter and I have become close, enjoying good times together chatting, antique shopping, and traveling.

I'm learning that listening leads to obeying. For example, early this morning the Voice urged, "Get up. Write down your thoughts. I gave them to you." After a few minutes of rationalizing why I should go back to sleep, I sat up instead. It was such a simple thing, I'm embarrassed to tell it, but as my feet touched the floor, I heard a glorious Hallelujah within me.

The still small Voice is the source of abundant life. Listen! Make sure you're not too busy to find peace through the simple, important things of life like relationships and worship.

Take my yoke upon you and learn from me, for I am gentle and humble in heart, and you will find rest for your souls.
MATTHEW 11:29

When the Lord brings to mind someone you know, pray for them. Then send a note telling them God thought of them this day.

April 24

A Comforting Thought

DORIS CRANDALL

If you forget everything else, remember one thing; Almighty God loves you.
—BILLY GRAHAM

Some children were performing the Passion Play for our church congregation. In the play, Jesus brings His disciples to Gethsemane and tells them to wait while He goes ahead to pray (Matthew 26:36).

"Peter, you and James and John come with me," said the small boy who had earned the honor of playing the part of Jesus. "Stay here. Stay awake with me," he told them.

Then he went down stage, fell face down on the floor, and prayed just as the Bible says Jesus did. Soon he returned, found the three disciples asleep, and forgot his well-rehearsed lines. Undaunted, he ad-libbed, "Boy, they sure don't make disciples like they used to."

Many things aren't like they used to be, but one thing won't change—Jesus Christ. How comforting it is to know that our Heavenly Father won't fail us. That's a simple, yet profound, truth that guarantees a peaceful, abundant life when we truly believe it.

Jesus Christ is the same yesterday and today and forever.
HEBREWS 13:8

> Realize that the "unforgettable times" are usually "moments" not days.

April 25

The Glory Of Solitude

JANE E. MAXWELL

When it seems that every meeting with another person has been a collision, we need the still waters of solitude to restore our soul.

—PHILIP KOCH

Solitude was virtually unknown to me as I struggled through my younger years trying to keep up with my four energetic children. My stress level often sky-rocketed as my inner buzzer flashed "overload, overload, overload." This led to depression, exhaustion and a lack of peace. I couldn't comprehend that there was something called an abundant life.

Some years later I discovered how periods of solitude could simplify my life as they simplified my harried mind and calmed my anxious spirit. Those days of utter frustration have disappeared.

Thomas Merton once said, "Not all men are called to be hermits, but all men need enough silence and solitude in their lives to enable the deep inner voice of their true self to be heard at least occasionally."

Solitude is a conscious disengagement from other people and places that allows us to attune our hearts and mind to our inner spirit. In solitude we become attuned to our inner self and our relationship with our Heavenly Father. We are able to see joys and sorrows woven together into His complete pattern. During this time of abundance, we escape to a solitary place that provides a restorative respite from our busy world and a healing to our spirit.

These periods of solitude may be so sublime that we long to stay there, but we are not meant to stay. Jesus felt the need to be alone more than once but he later returned to the crowds to nourish them. In a similar manner, after our renewing, we also return to our family and friends to bless them with the abundant life we've discovered.

I once felt that I didn't have time for solitude. Now I feel those periods of solitude stretch my time because it is there that I can clear my mind, focus on the important things, and see God's pattern. It's God's plan that, by simplifying, I am actually more effective. Sometimes the periods are only a half an hour, other times much longer, but all need to be without interruptions. I have found as Mary Sarton wrote, "being with people or even one beloved person for any length of time without solitude is even worse than loneliness. I feel dispersed, scattered, in pieces." With solitude I feel that my restless mind is put at rest and my weary spirit restored.

If you'd like to simplify your life through solitude, consider going to a special retreat cottage, the mountains, or lakeside. But you don't have to go to a distant place to enter into that special time with God. You can enjoy it in your own home. A special "set apart room" or corner of a bedroom, where you consciously shut out the world outside, can serve as your sanctuary.

But Jesus often withdrew to lonely places and prayed.
LUKE 5:16

Have a file available labeled with each child's name. When they return home from school, they can file the material they need you to review.

First The Good News

JULIE MARIE CAROBINI

The nature of bad news infects the teller.

—SHAKESPEARE

If Shakespeare's comment is true, then no wonder today's newspapers often read like a horror novel.

Even so, many of us do not hesitate to pick up the newspaper the first thing each morning and scan its pages. Unlike the Bible, "daily's" are not filled with love, wisdom, and hope. They more often contain stories of ravaged hearts, pain and despair.

That is why my husband and I decided to make a change: we now avoid the world's predictions until after we have read God's Word. With young children in the house and hectic schedules, it is not always easy to carve out that niche of time to spend in Bible study. Sometimes it seems simpler to flop open the paper in the midst of pouring cereal and juice, just long enough to run our eyes over those sobering headlines.

Yet we have learned to resist that temptation and it has made a refreshing change. Instead of facing the day with fear and turmoil, we are reminded of the ever-present Spirit of God who offers abundant life. He's just waiting to carry our family through the hours ahead.

How do you start your day? Why not start it by ignoring the bad news and focusing instead on God's good news? You'll have more peace.

Great peace have they who love your law, and nothing can make them stumble.
PSALM 119:165

> Do you struggle with change? Try focusing on the next step instead—it will make the process easier.

In His Name

MARCIA KRUGH LEASER

God's promises are like the stars: the darker the night
the brighter they shine.

—DAVID NICHOLAS

*A*bout a year ago, I experienced a tremendously difficult time and it caused me to have insomnia. I would awaken after only an hour or two of fitful sleep and be haunted by the silence of the darkness around me. My mind filled with unkind thoughts and was taunted by past failures.

This went on for several weeks and began affecting my relationships at home, at work, and with my Lord. I would pray for a good night's sleep and close my eyes confident that I would awaken with the sun shining in my bedroom window. Instead, I found myself two hours later staring into the blackness of yet another sleepless night.

I believed that *Greater is He that is in me, than he who is in the world* (1 John 4:4). I belonged to Jesus and nothing could harm me. Yet, here I was being hindered by this spirit of sleeplessness. How could this be?

I poured over my Bible searching for an answer. John 15:16 came to life as I read, "You did not choose me, but I chose you and appointed you to go and bear fruit—fruit that will last. Then the Father will give you whatever you ask in my name." I sat silently mulling over those words. He had chosen me, and anything I asked for, using His name would be given to me. *His* name . . . Jesus. Unlike my name which is simply used to identify myself, Jesus' name is power and authority! I felt assured that the abundant life God desires for me stems from using that power and authority.

That night I spoke these mighty words: "Spirit of restlessness, be gone in the name of Jesus. Spirit of fear, be gone in the name of Jesus." I had an entire list of negative things that I felt could have been robbing me of my much needed sleep and was prepared to say every one of them. It was not needed, however, because after only two or three commands, I fell into a relaxing sleep and awakened to the sound of the chirping birds welcoming another day.

Since that time, whenever I have been troubled by negative thoughts that cause me restlessness, I know I can call on God's power. His power is greater than anything this world can throw at me. He chose me and I will achieve what He has chosen me to do in this lifetime.

Although not all sleeplessness has a spiritual cause, use any time of wakefulness to relax in God's watchful care over you. That'll bring peace—and a good night's sleep.

If you remain in me and my words remain in you,
ask whatever you wish, and it will be given you.

JOHN 15:7

> When was the last time you went for a ride in country? Try it this week with your family—who knows what you'll discover?

April 28

Pressure Is Normal

EDWIN LOUIS COLE

It is impossible to have the feeling of peace and serenity without being at rest with God.
—DOROTHY H. PENTECOST

Jesus was without personal stress in Himself, though He bore the sins of the world. Admitting that He was only doing what he saw the Father do, relieved Him from the pressure of having to perform on His own. He had the backing of heaven for all He did (John 5:19-20). Regardless of the turmoil in the world around Him, He was without feelings of insecurity. Neither was He insecure in His identity. His open confession of Himself came from His established heart (John 10:30-42). Spoken with perfect equanimity, His testimony was attested by His deeds. *Believe me for what I say, or believe for my work's sake,* He told people (John 14:12; 10:37-38).

He never manipulated, threatened, or gave ultimatums to those who heard Him. He spoke *as one having authority, and not as the scribes* (Matthew. 7:29). This authority came in part from His knowledge of who He was, His purpose in life, and an identity with which He was in perfect agreement.

Real men are Christlike. Identified with Jesus, secure in that identity, acting in faith on God's Word, believing God will perform what He says. They move through life's trials and circumstances with confidence and face adversity with courage.

Pressure is normal and even needed in life. The right amount of tension in a guitar or piano string is necessary for fine tuning. Too much and it will snap. Water, steam, and ice are made from the same substance, as are carbon, graphite, and diamonds. It's the pressure that makes the difference. The more pressure matter is able to withstand, the more valuable it becomes. It's the same with people.

If we are in Christ, and Christ is in us, then God cannot deny us in our time of trouble or temptation. If He did He would be denying Himself; and that He will not do.

Our personal feelings, sentiments, attitudes, or emotions do not annul the promises of God.

If you falter in times of trouble, how small is your strength!
PROVERBS. 24:10

> Open large manila envelopes or bubble-wrap parcels carefully and use them again with a 3 X 5 card covering the old address. (Jeanne Zornes)

April 29

Focus On The Needs Of Others

ANNIE CHAPMAN

Whenever you are too selfishly looking out for your own interest, you have only one person working for you—yourself. When you help a dozen other people with their problems, you have a dozen people working with you.

—WILLIAM B. GIVEN, JR.

I've found that when I focus on the needs and the problems of others, I seem to worry less about myself. Perhaps part of our tendency to worry stems from thinking too much about ourselves. On the other hand, when we're focused on giving to others, we're much more apt to praise God and recognize His hand in the world.

I once heard a story about a man who was robbed. Instead of fretting about the terrible thing that had happened to him, he had four praises: This was the first time he had been robbed; the thieves had taken his money instead of his life; he didn't have much money for them to take; and he was the one being robbed instead of the one robbing.

For every circumstance that appears as a misfortune on the surface, there is a flip side—one that induces praise and thanksgiving. When it comes to combating the habit of worry, we need to be dwelling on that new perspective.

Each of you should look not only to your own interests,
but also to the interests of others.

PHILIPPIANS 2:4

> Fly a kite today and envision your worries being "flown away."

April 30

Writing Your Dreams

LYNN D. MORRISSEY

We are such stuff as dreams are made on.

—SHAKESPEARE

When God shows you your life's mission, He also gives you special dreams that will accomplish it. God's timing isn't always your timing; so you'll need to fight anxiety as you wait for Him to work. But when the "going gets rough," dreams will give you hope and momentum to "keep on keeping on."

In order to recognize your dreams, ask if they have inspiration. Are they worthy of God and in line with His principles? Also, do they have imagination? In other words, do they cause you to think creatively and stretch beyond your present potential, completely relying upon God's strength?

As you further evaluate your dream, it should excite you and motivate you to take steps to achieve it even over a long period of time. God will most likely have already given you the abilities necessary, but if not, He'll guide you to the training you need.

In order to realize your dreams, you must delight in fellowship with God through Bible study and prayer, learn as much as possible by talking to mentors and reading books, stay focused and dare to launch your dream.

You'll most likely receive other people's affirmations that this is God's plan that you must be willing to persevere regardless of any discouragement or obstacles you encounter.

Even though you find all this confirms your desires, some-times—often, because of impatiently jumping into ideas—you may find that the dream dies. In that case, you must let it die a natural death. You may have misunderstood God's direction. Don't despair. Trust in His sovereignty and love. He'll accomplish what's best for you. Sometimes when you've surrendered your dream to God and allowed it to die, He mysteriously resurrects it through new opportunities.

The important thing is to let God fulfill His desires in His timing. He wants only the best for you. Will you cooperate with Him? If you do, you'll experience a peaceful abundance of seeing Him use you in mighty ways.

In his heart a man plans his course, but the Lord determines his steps.
PROVERBS 16:9

Keep a "dream journal" to record and date your dreams. It's exciting to see God bring them to pass.

May

"Strengthened with all power, according to His glorious might, for the attaining of all steadfastness and patience . . ."

Colossians 1:11

Mother's Day. What fun to honor those who gave us life. For those of us who are mothers, what a challenge to exhibit the fruit of the Spirit—patience—toward our children. You'll find in this month's readings, touching stories, and inspiring practical ideas for expressing love and patience toward the most important people in our lives, our families—and friends, too. And since they are the ones who try our patience the most, these readings will energize you toward more abundant living in your relationships.

Anonymous Joy

VEDA BOYD JONES

He called the flowers, so blue and golden,
Stars, that in earth's firmament do shine.
—HENRY WADSWORTH LONGFELLOW

It has been a tradition in my family to share May flowers with our neighbor. My sons make the May basket by curling a piece of construction paper into a cone and stapling it to hold its shape. They punch a hole through the open end and thread yarn through it. After tying the yarn, which forms a loop to hang over a doorknob, they are ready to pick flowers from our yard to fill the basket.

The fun comes from running to a neighbor's door with a fragrant bouquet, hanging the basket, and ringing the doorbell. What a scramble for the boys to get out of sight before the door is opened.

Never have they been caught. Never have they received a thank you, because their gift is anonymous. And the thing that keeps them doing this year after year is when they peek out from their hiding place and see the beaming smile on the neighbor's face.

The first day of May is a special day for taking a simple moment to show God's abundant fruit of love toward others. Maybe for you it'll be expressed in patience toward someone who usually irritates you. Why not commit to showing them grace and love?

Flowers appear on the earth;
the season of singing has come, the cooing of doves
is heard in our land.
SONG OF SOLOMON 2:12

Even if you don't have children in your home, take some flowers to a neighbor or friend.

Giving God The Best Dish

JILL BRISCOE

It is possible to be so active in the service of Christ as
to forget to love him.

—P.T. FORSYTH

We need to make God a promise to set aside part of each day for him. In Luke 10, Jesus told Martha that Mary had "chosen what is better;" she had chosen to serve him the "best dish." That was Mary's *choice*. If we can come to the point of making that choice, too, then it will help to make Christ a promise about it. Make him a promise in prayer. Then see that you keep it. Someone has said, "Martha ticked and kept time." When your life sounds like a clock that keeps perfect time, you will need to make a deliberate choice to set aside some of those carefully calculated minutes in your well-ordered day just for God.

Secondly, we need to get organized about that promised time. We need to *listen*. If there is anything that is hard for a Martha to do, it is to listen. Marthas usually are so busy barking orders all day long that the very practice of listening is totally foreign—an unlearned art. (To learn "Mary's way" think through some "listening" steps.)

First, make your body listen. That means getting comfortable so you can forget your physical being. If you have a bad hip or back, don't kneel to pray. You won't be able to stay with Jesus very long if you're hurting; you'll be thinking of all your aches and pains instead of him.

Next, make your mind listen. Read lots of Scripture. A few verses won't do it. Let the Word of God wash over your hurried thoughts, sitting them down and talking to them. Be systematic. Read "around" the verses for the day. If you are in an epistle, and it's only four or five chapters long, read the whole thing. Listening with your mind means concentrating on his Word untill you succeed in shutting out other people's words. This takes time and effort.

Finally, make your heart listen. What has God said to you? What is His personal word in your ear? What application must be drawn from what He has said? Ask yourself, "What does he want me to do about this?" or "What does he want me to believe?" or "What does he want me to think?" Don't dare get up before you've figured this out as best you can. It helps to capture the thought in one sentence and write it down. So buy a little notebook and jot down these things.

It's so simple. You make a promise to meet Him; you keep it—and you get organized. If you are a Martha, you should be able to organize your time with Him as efficiently as you organize everybody else's time.

Taking the time you need to really grasp what the Lord is saying to you means the difference between knowing the Bible and knowing the Lord of the Bible.

Not everyone who says to me, "Lord, Lord," will enter the kingdom of heaven, but only he who does the will of my Father who is in heaven.
MATTHEW 7:21

> Start a baby-sitting "co-op." It's a great way to get free baby-sitting and socialize all in one.

May 3

God's Timing

ROSALIE J.G. MILLS

God's will, done God's way, by God's appointed person(s), in God's timing, will get God's results.
—RON SMEDLEY

"Is it time yet?" the buds anxiously asked the Master as He walked through His garden, greeting each one in turn. They'd been told of the gentle breeze which, after they bloomed, would delicately brush by, carrying their fragrance to expectant noses earnestly anticipating the first signs of Spring. "Not quite," cautioned the Master, their Creator.

"I want to bloom." complained one impatient bud. "It's time."

"Not quite yet," cautioned the Master, "Just a little longer."

"But I want to bloom *now*." retorted the bud, pushing out of her pod.

"I had great plans for you," sighed the Master. Suddenly a blast of frigid air caught the new flower by surprise. She tried to return to her pod, but was left at the mercy of the merciless wind.

"Master, help me." cried the little flower, shivering in the cold.

"I can't," He replied sadly. "You bloomed too early, and now must endure the cold unprotected."

The little flower shivered as her petals fell, victims of the last frost. "If only you had waited," wept the Master. "If only you had listened."

Soon the Master's voice called, "Come to me my flowers. It's time to blossom." A fearful bud peeped out cautiously. He heard the Master, but his eyes fell on the fallen petals of the impatient flower and he pulled back into his pod. *I'll wait here until I'm sure the frost is over,* he thought.

Now deeply surrounded by his fear, he couldn't hear the Master's final call, "The winter is over, come to me and blossom, my flowers."

As He said this, one patiently waiting flower heard a melody so sweet the birds hushed their singing. Stretching out of her pod, her radiant blossoms flooded the air with fragrance and the afternoon breeze caressed her petals with life-giving warmth as she basked in the Master's presence.

"I'm here, little flower, to add you to the bouquet at the Father's table." The new flower quaked with delight as the Master gently cut her loose from the bush. "We're missing two flowers," He said. "One bloomed too quickly and froze in winter's final blast, and the other wilted, afraid to come out of his bud. But you have blossomed exactly on time, and to perfection. The Father will be very pleased."

He looked sadly at the frozen petals and the wilted bud; both had fallen to the ground. As He stooped to retrieve them, He said, "Still, I can use these to fertilize the ground for next year's blossoms." And He walked into the Father's house, carrying the beautifully blooming flower.

How often do we impatiently push ahead, not waiting for the Lord's perfect timing, or we procrastinate, afraid of failing? Instead, let us bloom right on time. If there's an area of your life in which God seems to be working too slow, can you believe He knows the best way? Then you'll experience the abundant life, eliminating distrust and hurry.

> *But I trust in You, O Lord; I say, "You are my God."*
> *My times are in Your hands . . .*
>
> PSALM 31:14-15

Plant your favorite flower and meditate on some area of your life where you're not waiting peacefully for the Father's "go-ahead."

Hands Of Love

RUTH M. RINK

In all things we learn only from those we love.

—GOETHE

*M*y childhood training was like a yellow line down the middle of the highway: straight, narrow and even.

I can still see Mother sitting at our large, round dining-room table, table cloth pushed back, creating special occasion poems, humorous true-to-life memories to read to the Ladies Literary Club, and newsy letters to relatives separated from us by many miles.

The screeching squeal of her dip ink pen announced that Mother was busy tabulating sums as treasurer of the Foreign Missionary Society, wrestling for hours in search of a stray penny. As year's end approached, I traveled throughout the village with her, her sturdy hand knocking on doors to dauntlessly collect delinquent dues. Then an accountant would arrive and help Mother close the yearly report. For 20 years, all our household sighed with relief every time the accounts were finally balanced.

Her rough and work-hardened hands diapered, scrubbed, cooked and mended for our family of five. But her stubby fingers grew more gentle each time she caressed my hair or wiped away my tears.

The long, slender, tapered fingers of my dentist father contrasted Mother's. Somehow he was able to make the pain more bearable as he deftly drilled, picked, and probed in my small mouth.

The memory of his hands, folded in prayer before our evening meals, also remains with me. I wonder how many prayers father raised on my behalf before that winter night when I was ten. That evening, after thirteen straight nights of revival services at our white-steepled Methodist Church, father noticed tears flowing down my cheeks. He gently clasped my hand in his, and with mother following, we stepped down the long aisle to an over-crowded altar. Turning around, we knelt at the front pew. Father rested his hands on my forehead and prayed the most meaningful prayer of my young life, asking Jesus to come into my life as Savior.

Two parents, laughing joyfully, pulled me home on my sled after the service. I hugged myself with glee and smiled up as soft, friendly snowflakes drifted down on my face.

At 86, I still remember the bright beauty of that frosty night, especially the warmth of father's hands upon my forehead as he interceded for me.

How blessed to be raised in the hands of parents who will hand your life over to the Lord. Because they were patient with me, I believed my Heavenly Father was patient with my stumbling efforts to please Him.

Even if you weren't reared by loving parents who prayed for you, Jesus intercedes before your Heavenly Father's throne right now. He will steadfastly guide you.

They will still bear fruit in old age, they will stay fresh and green.
PSALM 92:14

> Write out a prayer for each of your children or an important person in your life and mail it to them—even if they live in your home.

May 5

From Purpose . . . To Time Management

PATRICK M. MORLEY

Not failure, but low aim, is crime.
—JAMES RUSSELL LOWELL

Bill Bright closes his letters, "Yours for fulfilling the Great Commission in this generation." I imagine that comes as close to a Written Life Purpose Statement as we'll ever find (see Matthew 28:19-20). Dr. Bright knows his life's purpose. That makes setting priorities and time management a lot easier.

A couple traveling through the countryside was lost. They spotted an old man on the side of the road and asked, "Where are we at?"

"Where are you going?" came his reply.

"We don't know," they said.

"Then it doesn't matter."

When we don't have a sense of where we are going, where we are now isn't that important. Only when we know our purpose—where we are going—can we make heads or tails out of how to use our time.

Follow this progression: Our purpose helps us prioritize. Our priorities form solid ground for us to stand on when we make plans and set goals. Time management is no more nor less than strategically "engineering" this progression: from purpose to priorities to plans and goals.

God always provides enough time to accomplish God's plans. We've got the time—we just need to use it more productively. We need to stop always going for the "long bomb" and run more dependable short yardage plays. We need to block and tackle better. If we do, we will have all the time we need. If we don't, we'll have to punt. "Little things done in a single direction"—that's the way.

Whatever your hand finds to do, do it with all your might . . .
ECCLESIASTES 9:10

Give yourself credit for what you have accomplished. *How Do You Want Your Room . . . Plain Or Padded?* (Jo Ann Larsen & Artemus Cole)

May 6

Just A Mom

RUTH E. MCDANIEL

God bless my mother; all that I am or ever hope to be
I owe to her.

—ABRAHAM LINCOLN

"I'm just a mom," the young woman shyly replied in response to my question. It was the first time I'd met the members of an ongoing Bible study group, and I wanted to know something about them. Were they married? Did they have children? Did they work outside of the home? Her answer stunned me.

"Just a mom?" I replied. "Don't you realize that you have one of the most (if not *the* most) important jobs any human being can have?" At that moment the group leader started the Bible study, so our private conversation ended. But her comment haunted me for days.

How many other mothers feel that way? How many women have bought into the idea that stay-at-home-moms have little value? If even one woman believed that lie, it would be too many.

What a privilege it is to become a mother. And, what an awesome responsibility. For the first nine months of their lives, a child knows only one person—his mother. He snuggles beneath her heart, he listens to her voice, and he responds. If Mom is upset, he's afraid. If she's happy, he's content. His mother's moods directly affect him—now and through birth, infancy, and beyond.

A mother is responsible for her child's early development—physically, emotionally, and psychologically. If she does her job well, the child will grow up well-adjusted and happy.

Studies have shown that children begin learning while still in the womb. If every mother would lovingly read the Bible to her unborn child, then continue after birth and on through puberty, can you imagine what the next generation would be like?

The Lord has provided each mother with instincts to love, nurture, and protect her child. God entrusts each mother with the care of His greatest blessing—a child. A mother's job is indispensable. Would anyone consider that mother to be of little value?

I can't wait to talk to that young woman in Bible study again. Just a mom? Name me one other occupation in which children arise up and call you blessed.

If you sometimes feel like describing yourself as "just a mom," especially because you sometimes become impatient with your children, know that God will help you grow stronger in reacting in a calm way. He's not finished with you yet.

Her children arise and call her blessed . . .
PROVERBS 31:28

Write a letter to your mother and mention the ways she has blessed your life—even if she wasn't perfect. If she is deceased, write it anyway as a part of your healing.

May 7

Maintaining A Proper Perspective

LUIS PALAU

The man who comes to a right belief about God is relieved of ten thousand temporal problems, for he sees at once that these have to do with matters which at the most cannot concern him for very long.
—A.W. TOZER

Did you know a single cup of coffee contains enough moisture to blanket your entire neighborhood with fog 50 feet thick?

It's amazing how such a small amount of water spread out so thinly can hinder our vision almost completely.

We tend to get upset when fog hinders our pilgrimage, but we forget the sun is still shining overhead, burning it away. Why do we get upset? Because we fail to maintain a proper perspective.

British statesman William Wilberforce once commented, "The objects of the present life fill the human eye with a false magnification because of their immediacy." Problems and concerns often act like fog to obscure our present situation. They keep us from seeing things in proper perspective.

Psychologists tell us that 45 percent of what we worry about is past, and 45 percent is future. (30 percent concerns our health alone.) Only one in every 10 things we worry about will ever come to pass and we usually cannot do anything about it anyway.

Sometimes we treat problems and trials as if we were on a television commercial. We rush around thinking we have to solve everything in 30 seconds. When we can't, we panic.

We try every option we can think of to overcome our problems and difficulties. When none of them work, we reluctantly turn to God as a last resort.

But there are no emergencies in heaven. God is aware of our problems (1 Peter 5:7). He did not create us to be self-sufficient to meet our needs. He created us to depend on Him.

Do you face a difficult situation, my friend? Has your way been covered by a heavy fog? God has not allowed this situation to come into your life to discourage or defeat you. Every trial you and I face is an opportunity for God to demonstrate who He is to us—the One we can always depend upon, no matter what. Be patient. He will reveal Himself and the way out. Your abundant life will be strengthened as you wait patiently upon Him.

Do not be anxious about anything, but . . . present your requests to God.
PHILIPPIANS 4:6

For a pick-me-up, rent your favorite movie and watch it with a friend.

The Rose:
In Memory Of Elizabeth Crudup

BRENDALYN CRUDUP MARTIN

And in the end it's not the years in your life that
count. It's the life in your years.

—ABRAHAM LINCOLN

I awoke with mixed feelings on Mother's Day, the memories of my
mother's death still heavy on my mind. It would be two years in
July, yet in some ways it seemed like yesterday. Shortly before her death,
I shared with her a special Mother's Day poem I wrote for her.

I still remembered the look on her face as I read the words to her.
I told her how much I loved her and what a beautiful inspiration she
was to me. Tears filled her eyes, but I knew they were tears of love.

Thinking again of my loss, I dreaded facing this day. As I prepared
for church, I feel sick and almost convinced myself not to go—how could
I enjoy the service in this condition? In the back of my mind was the
vision of a white rose.

It is tradition in my church to pin a rose on all the mothers in the
church. You receive a red rose if your mother is alive, a white one if
she is deceased. I didn't want to look at all those red roses while they
pinned a white one on me.

I couldn't feel sorry for myself all day, as if only I felt her loss.
Today, my whole family would share her loss with me. Despite this
reminder to myself, my feelings were mixed as I finished dressing. The
drive to church was quiet and solemn.

Listening to the music and prayers, I tried to ignore the white rose
pinned on my shoulder. The pastor spoke of the loss of her mother
and how she felt both sorrow and joy. Her words touched my heart as
I realized, "someone else understands my feelings. She knows what
I'm going through. I'm not alone."

God was speaking to me through her and suddenly my loneliness
was pushed aside by many happy memories. Both my parents had
always been there for my brother and me. They filled our childhood
with memories of a loving family. I thought, "My real loss would have
been not to have known her love at all."

My heart grew lighter. No longer painful, the loving memories that filled my heart were reminders of the gift of love God gave me in my mother.

If you've lost your mother, focus on the blessings of your memories of her and try to let go of the pain. God knows your heart. He understands and wants to comfort you. Little by little, your joy will return, as will your abundance.

> *You turned my wailing into dancing: you removed my sackcloth,*
> *and clothed me with joy.*

PSALM 30:11

Express some kindness to a mother whose child has died.

May 9

Mother's Special Flower

NAOMI WIEDERKEHR

Just as the carnation never sheds a petal, so mother love never dies.

—UNKNOWN

Did you know that the carnation is the flower most often used at Mother's Day? Do you know why?

Many years ago, in 1908, a lady named Anne Jarvis, was asked to arrange a church service in honor of her mother. Her home church in Philadelphia was so happy with the thought of honoring mothers that they wanted to make it a yearly event.

In 1914, Congress passed a law declaring the second Sunday in May as the national day to observe Mother's Day. The second Sunday in May was chosen because that was the birthday of Miss Jarvis' mother, and the carnation was chosen as the floral symbol because that was her favorite flower.

Here's how to tint carnations.

1. Leave carnations out of water for a while.

2. Cut the stems diagonally with a knife leaving a six inch stem.

3. Take a drinking glass, fill half full of warm water, and pour in food coloring. The flowers draw the color up, the stronger the dye the more it colors.

4. The tips of petals will start to tint in one hour and the flower

will be fully tinted in two to three hours. Or if you want more color, leave the dye in longer.

> Honor your father and your mother, so that you may
> live long in the land the Lord your God is giving you.
>
> EXODUS 20: 12

Color some carnations for your Mother's Day celebration bouquet.

May 10

Mother's Day And Love

DURLYNN ANEMA-GARTEN

> Someday, when my children are old enough to
> understand the logic that motivates a mother, I'll tell
> them: I loved you enough to bug you, about where you
> were going, with whom and what time you would get
> home.
>
> —ERMA BOMBECK

Whenever I think of Mother's Day, I think of the greatest mother of all—Mary who had to undergo so many trials. Through all of them she retained her strong faith in God. Think about those trials . . .

. . . trying to tell your husband-to-be you are going to be a mother

. . . watching your child go off into the desert

. . . hearing the taunts about your child

. . . and finally, bearing the sadness of His death upon the cross.

But Mary knew the mysteries and "pondered it in her heart." She knew how special it was to be a mother—an exceptional mother.

Aren't we all special? Even in our times of trial and sadness?

I never dreamed of being a mother when I was young. I had too many other plans. But I praise God each day that He gave me motherhood and all it represents. I always told myself I only "borrowed" my children for 18 years, but what a great 18 years. I will never forget the picnics, bike rides, parties, and those quiet times reading together or simply talking. We had a good time together, even as I made many mistakes.

That's one thing about children; they know our mistakes, but they also know the love. Even when we are impatient, our love still seeps through. Children go on loving you, forgiving, and coming "home" because they love you as you loved them.

Jesus taught us to "love one another." To be a mother is to learn the true meaning of love—just as we learn it when we view how much Christ loved us.

And Mary said: 'My soul glorifies the Lord and my spirit rejoices in God my Savior, for he has been mindful of the humble state of his servant. From now on all generations will call me blessed.'

LUKE 1:46-48

If you find yourself focusing more on your mistakes as a mother (or friend), make a list of the things you've done right and focus on them instead.

May 11

Student Training In Motherhood

GEORGIA E. BURKETT

One of the greatest gifts God ever gave a woman is motherhood.

—UNKNOWN

The Bible tells us that according to Egyptian law, Moses should have been killed as soon as he was born, like all other male Jewish babies. But Moses' mother, Jochebed, hid Moses in the bulrushes along the Nile River.

However, the task of watching over him was given to his big sister, Miriam. What a scary job that must have been. To be found protecting her baby brother in that reed patch would have been cause for severe punishment.

I can sympathize with that young baby-sitter. When I was a youngster, I was the baby-sitter for my two little brothers. We lived in an apartment house in mid-city Philadelphia, but we had no yard to play in. Mother was often quite ill, so I would put the boys in our big baby carriage, and push them around the city streets. We didn't have to worry about street crime then as folks do now, but there was plenty of danger in the bustling city traffic.

Realizing the danger we faced, Mother asked God every day to protect us—and He did, just as He protected baby Moses and his sister. Nobody ever bothered us, and we crossed the countless busy streets as easily as when Moses led the Israelites across the Red Sea. I still marvel at God's blessed protection and that I could be so patient with them.

My baby-sitting days seem like ancient history now, but God knew what he was doing when he gave me my job as baby-sitter. What better opportunity could I have had to learn diapering, feeding, and caring for the six babies he gave my husband, Dewey, and me? I'll admit I often felt my life was an endless round of laundry, cooking, dirty dishes, and nights spent in soothing sore throats and earaches. And at times, I felt impatient. But I learned to be a good mother.

My children are all adults now, with families of their own. I thank God every day for those wonderful days of my own childhood, when he gave me my "student-training" in motherhood.

Now I know that patience is a "learned" skill. If you're in "student-training" to be more patient, don't give up. You only learn by being tested.

As a mother comforts her child, so will I comfort you.
ISAIAH 66:13A

Who has had the greatest impact in teaching you mothering (or friendship) skills? Call or write them to let them know you appreciate their influence.

May 12

Mother's Hands

LOUISA GODISSART MCQUILLEN

God pardons like a mother, who kisses the offense
into everlasting forgiveness.
—HENRY WARD BEECHER

Night after night she would come to tuck me in, even long after my childhood years. Following her long-standing custom, she'd lean down and push my long hair out of the way, then kiss my forehead.

I don't remember when it first started annoying me—her hands pushing my hair that way. But it did annoy me, for they felt work-worn and rough against my young skin. Finally one night I lashed out at her impatiently: "Don't do that anymore, your hands are too rough."

She didn't say anything in reply. But never again did my mother close out my day with that familiar expression of her love. Lying awake long afterwards, my words haunted me. But pride stifled my conscience, and I didn't tell her that I was sorry.

Time after time with the passing years, my thoughts returned to that night. By then I missed my mother's hands and goodnight kiss upon my forehead. Sometimes the incident seemed very close, sometimes far away. But always it lurked, hauntingly, in the back of my mind.

The years have passed and I'm not a little girl anymore. Mom is in her mid-70's, and those hands I once thought to be so rough are still caring for the people around her.

Now my own children are grown and gone. Mom no longer has Dad either, and on special occasions I still find myself drawn next door to spend the night with her. So it was late one Thanksgiving Eve, as I drifted into sleep in the bedroom of my youth, a familiar hand hesitantly stole across my face to brush the hair from my forehead. Then a kiss, ever so gently, touched my brow.

I reacted involuntarily. Catching Mom's hand in mine, I blurted out how sorry I was for that night I said, "Your hands are too rough." I thought she'd remember, as I did. But Mom didn't know what I was talking about. She had forgotten—and forgiven—long ago. She had been patient with my immaturity, and I hadn't appreciated it.

That night I fell asleep with a new gratitude for my patient mother and her caring hands. And the guilt I had carried around for so long was nowhere to be found.

If you've recently expressed impatience with someone, they most likely have forgiven and forgotten. But to be sure, ask their forgiveness. Feeling guilty takes away our sense of *abundance*. But being forgiven expands it.

She watches over the affairs of her household . . .
PROVERBS 31:27

Reminisce about your childhood by looking back through photo albums.

May 13

The Tradition Of Tea

EMILIE BARNES

Somehow, taking tea together encourages an atmosphere of intimacy when you slip off the timepiece in
your mind and cast your fate to a delight of tasty tea,
tiny foods, and thoughtful conversation.

—GAIL GRECO

When we do things a certain way, the way we have done them in
the past, the way others before us have done them, something
deep in our spirits is comforted.

Children instinctively know this; that's why they delight in family
traditions. Teenagers may rebel against established customs, but they
create their own. (Watch a teenager get ready to go out in the evening
and you'll know how important ritual is to him or her.) Most of us, as
we grow older, also grow to cherish the rituals of our lives.

Another satisfying aspect of a ritual lies in its repetition. We
quickly learn what to do; we can almost do it without thinking. So
after a time, the ritual performs the valuable function of occupying
the body and the senses while freeing the mind and spirit.

Have you ever noticed that your mind seems to work better when
your body is occupied with something it's done before—like taking a
walk, washing dishes, or mowing the lawn? The same thing happens
to me when I'm rinsing out a teapot, cutting the crust off little
sandwiches, or arranging tea things on a tray. The little repetitive
actions of preparation and serving tea become as a reassuring soil out
of which thoughts can grow, and conversations can spring.

There's no hurry about any of this, since you can't go ahead with
the tea until the water is boiling. And there's more waiting to do even
then, because the tea leaves or teabags must steep in the pot. But while
you are waiting for the liquid to turn its fragrant amber, you can carry
the tray to a comfortable nook and wait in peace. If you are with
friends, this is a wonderful time to reconnect with one another. If you
are alone, you can read, think, pray, or just "be."

The brewed tea is too hot to gulp, but it will cool. You can simply sit
and wait until the boiling liquid settles into comfortable warmth. Maybe

you can read yet another page of your book. Or you can politely pass the cream and sugar and cookies or fruit to your friends—more ritual.

Then your cup is ready to enjoy. And somehow, as you sip, your mind continues to settle out of its habitual rush. Your words and your musings slow down and sift deeper. Your relationships—even your relationship with yourself—are granted space for a leisurely stretch.

And the beautiful thing is: All this slowness takes so little time.

Enjoying a cup of tea is not like taking a summer off or going away on a retreat. It's an island of calm you can reasonably visit in the course of your busiest day.

If you have to, you can have a tea break in twenty minutes. Thirty is better, an hour ideal. But no matter how much time you take, you won't catch the calming spirit of the tea party unless you let yourself slow down and enjoy it.

> *Blessed are those who hunger and thirst for righteousness,*
> *for they will be filled.*
>
> MATTHEW 5:6

Whether you enjoy tea or coffee, take a few minutes out of your busy schedule to enjoy a cup and meditate on how to be more patient today.

May 14

The Simple Difference

DR. JAMES DOBSON

> One reason sin flourishes is that it is treated like a
> cream puff instead of a rattlesnake.
>
> —BILLY SUNDAY

I heard about a missionary in Africa who returned to his hut late one afternoon. As he entered the front door he was confronted by a huge python on the floor. He ran back to his truck and retrieved a .45-caliber pistol. Unfortunately, he had only one bullet in the chamber and no extra ammunition. Taking careful aim, the missionary sent that single shot into the head of the reptile. The snake was mortally wounded, but it did not die quickly. It began frantically thrashing and writhing on the floor. Retreating to the front yard, the missionary could hear furniture breaking and lamps crashing. Finally, all was quiet, and the man cautiously reentered his house. He found the snake dead, but the entire interior of the hut was shattered. In its dying moments, the python had unleashed all its mighty power and wrath on everything in sight.

Later, the missionary drew an analogy between the python and the great serpent named Satan. Our adversary has already been mortally wounded by the death and resurrection of Jesus Christ. Thus, the serpent's days are numbered and he knows it. In a final desperate effort to thwart the will of God and deceive His people, Satan has unleashed all his fury. He is fostering hate and deceit and aggression wherever human interests collide. He especially despises the institution of the family, which is symbolic of the relationship between Jesus Christ and His church.

How can we survive in such a dangerous environment? How can we cope with the fury of Satan in his final days? Admittedly, we would stand no chance in our own strength. But listen to what Jesus said about His followers: "My sheep listen to my voice; I know them, and they follow me. I give them eternal life, and they shall never perish; no one can snatch them out of my hand. My Father, who has given them to me, is greater than all" (John 10:27-29).

Because of the Redeemer, we need not fear the great deceiver—the father of lies. We are promised throughout Scripture that we are never left to fight our battles alone.

That is great news for all who are weary and burdened by the stresses of living. It all comes down to this simple concept: God is not against us for our sins. He is for us against our sins. That makes all the difference.

Therefore, since we have been justified through faith, we have peace with God through our Lord Jesus Christ.

ROMANS 5:1

> For two to three days, keep track by the hour of how you spend your time. Then evaluate how you need to make better choices.

Be Still

MARCIA KRUGH LEASER

Be it ours, when we cannot see the face of God, to
trust under the shadow of his wings.
—CHARLES H. SPURGEON

Enjoying working in my garden, I turned my face upward to allow
the fresh breeze to blow through my hair. My eyes caught sight of
a small blackbird flying majestically through the blue sky overhead. It
was carrying a piece of straw in its beak to build a nest, and I smiled.

Suddenly a huge gust of wind came from nowhere and blew the
tops of the trees wildly. My eyes were still on the bird and I was
surprised at his reaction. He relaxed completely, not fluttering a
feather, and allowed the wind to carry him along. When the gust
subsided, he resumed his journey rested and relaxed.

That fragile bird displayed a greater faith than I often do. How many
times do I relax when the winds of life threaten my plans? How often do
I patiently ride out the storm, knowing that it will soon pass? Not often.
I fret and worry . . . then, when the storm subsides I find myself worn
out and weak from the strain of fighting something I can't control.

Knowing the difference between battles I can win and ones I
should not be fighting at all is a part of experiencing the abundant life.
It's the difference between "God" being in control and "me" being in
control, it's such a simple thing, and yet don't each of us find it hard
at times to apply? Let's allow God to be God and patiently relax in His
power to ride the winds of earth's difficulties.

You will not have to fight this battle. Take up your positions;
stand firm and see the deliverance the Lord will give you . . .
2 CHRONICLES 20:17

Write down the difficulties you're facing in two columns: those
you can do something about and those you can't. Ask God to
help you release to Him the ones you have no power over.

May 16

Turn Irritation Into Insight

BILL & PAM FARREL

The test of a man or woman's breeding is how they
behave in a quarrel.

—GEORGE BERNARD SHAW

Whatever you appreciate most about your spouse (or anyone) could be the point of highest irritation.

If you listen to these irritations and are willing to look beyond your anger to the qualities in your spouse that are so vital to your own life, you will find you can build your marriage even as you struggle. Your irritations can be the springboard to new conversations of intimacy.

To turn your irritations into insights, try the following:

1. Make a list of the characteristics you appreciate most about your spouse. Keep this list in a place where you can review it often. Reminding yourself that you love your spouse is one of the best ways we know of to lasso the whirlwind of modern life.

2. When you begin to get angry, ask yourself, "What did my spouse say or do that has got me so upset?" Something was done that triggered strong emotions in your soul. These strong emotions can either be seeds of anger or bridges of intimacy. If you can identify the trigger event, you will be close to turning it to your advantage.

3. Ask yourself, "What positive quality in my spouse's life is this irritation related to?"

4. Repeat to yourself at least seven times, "I love _____ for . . . " (inserting their name and the quality that attracted you in the first place).

*In your anger do not sin: Do not let the sun go down while
you are still angry, and do not give the devil a foothold.*
EPHESIANS 4:26-27

Right now, write down five things you like best about your spouse or significant person in your life. When you feel impatient with them, check to see whether it's related to one of those characteristics. Then turn your focus back to seeing the positive.

Have You Ever Been Alone With God?

OSWALD CHAMBERS

I have more trouble with D.L. Moody than with any other man I ever met.

—DWIGHT L. MOODY

*J*esus does not take us alone and expound things to us all the time; He expounds things to us as we can understand them. Other lives are parables. God is making us spell out our own souls. It is slow work, so slow that it takes God all time and eternity to make a man and woman after His own purpose. The only way we can be of use to God is to let Him take us through the crooks and crannies of our own characters. It is astounding how ignorant we are about ourselves. We do not know envy when we see it, or laziness, or pride. Jesus reveals to us all that this body has been harboring before His grace began to work. How many of us have learned to look in with courage?

We have to get rid of the idea that we understand ourselves, it is the last conceit to go. The only one who understands us is God. The greatest curse in spiritual life is conceit. If we have ever had a glimpse of what we are like in the sight of God, we shall never say, "Oh, I am so unworthy," because we shall know we are, beyond the possibility of stating it. As long as we are not quite sure that we are unworthy, God will keep narrowing us in until He gets us alone. Wherever there is any element of pride or of conceit, Jesus cannot expound a thing. He will take us through the disappointment of a wounded pride of intellect, through disappointment of heart. He will reveal inordinate affections—things over which we never thought He would have to get us alone. We listen to many things in classes, but they are not an exposition to us yet. They will be when God gets us alone.

But when he was alone with his own disciples, he explained everything.

MARK 4:34

Ask your spouse or a close friend for a suggestion about one characteristic of yours that you need to work on changing with God's help.

Thoughtful Living

JEAN FLEMING

I find that doing the will of God leaves me no time for disputing about His plans.

—GEORGE MACDONALD

The Scriptures prod us to thoughtful living: *Be very careful, then, how you live—not as unwise but as wise, making the most of every opportunity, because the days are evil. Therefore do not be foolish, but understand what the Lord's will is* (Ephesians 5:15-17).

These verses usually spur us to redouble our efforts, increase our speed, and expand our territory. However, three phrases from this portion should slow us down for reflection:

1. Be very careful, then, how you live,
2. Not as unwise but as wise,
3. Do not be foolish, but understand what the Lord's will is.

First, the Apostle Paul cautions us to give serious attention to how we live. Careful living requires thought. Earlier in his letter to the Ephesians, Paul tells us to become imitators of God, and live as children of light. It takes time to look for and at God so that we can be like Him.

Second, Paul tells us to live wisely. But how do we gain wisdom? James 1:5 comes to mind as nearly everyone's favorite verse on wisdom: *If any of you lacks wisdom, he should ask God,. . . and it will be given to him.* Unfortunately, some people hold James 1:5 in reserve with the intention of setting it loose like a genie for their next crisis. God is gracious, and does sometimes intervene in catastrophes when his poor, ignorant people wail for help. We have all experienced this kind of help.

But this is not the pattern God has ordained for acquiring wisdom. In fact, Proverbs 1:23-33 teaches that if you have not made the pursuit of wisdom the direction of your life, God does not obligate Himself to run to your rescue. Proverbs is a wonderful book to study to gain insights on living wisely.

Third, we must understand what the Lord's will is so that we can make the most of every opportunity. The emphasis is not on learning to pack more into each day, so much as learning to order our day according to God's will. We must recover our time from wasteful activities, and liberate it for God's purposes. Again, reading the Bible and considering His truths are essential.

If you've identified yourself as too busy, step off that jet-propelled treadmill. Take some time to catch your breath and confront the condition of your soul, your relationships, and your work for God. Be very careful, then, how you live.

. . . being strengthened with all power according to his glorious might so that you may have great endurance and patience . . .

COLOSSIANS 1:11

Cut down on the time it takes to run errands by finding resources closer to home.

May 19

Puzzled?

LUCINDA SECREST MCDOWELL

The faith of Christ offers no buttons to push for quick service. The new order must wait the Lord's own time, and that is too much for the man in a hurry. He just gives up and becomes interested in something else.

—A.W. TOZER

When was the last time you put together a jigsaw puzzle? That's right—the ones that come in boxes covered with a gorgeous scene usually including lots of trees, clouds, or water broken into a *bajillion* pieces of cardboard. They say that all those pieces are guaranteed to come together to produce that beautiful picture on the cover. But they usually forget to mention that it takes at least 119 hours of hard work and multiplied patience to accomplish that feat.

Every summer, during family holiday, I beamingly produce yet another challenging jigsaw puzzle, much to the moans and groans of our teenagers. Yet, somehow during the week everyone is lured into the act, perhaps by the sheer improbability that we will ever be able to put it together. For one thing, many pieces have been cut in the same shape and therefore appear at first to be a perfect fit. It takes patience to find the right piece.

Last summer we did a 1000 piece round puzzle of North American birds. (Think of all those feathers.) What a sense of accomplishment to see it completed. In the process, God taught me some important lessons. Too often my own life seems to be in a million pieces which make no sense at all. It seems like it'll just take too long to put them together. But then, over time, I patiently gather a godly perspective from my friends, family and other Christians to understand God's will for my abundant life.

Are you feeling impatient about putting the puzzle pieces of your life together? If it seems it's taking too long before the picture is revealed, just hang on. You're learning patience and growing closer to your Sovereign Lord. He has a master pattern for you and He promises to fit everything together.

And the glory of the Lord will be revealed, and all mankind together will see it . . .
ISAIAH 40:5

As summer approaches, be on the lookout for a unique puzzle that will occupy and teach patience to your family members. To save money, check at thrift stores.

May 20

The Fastest Way To Get Nowhere

OLGA FLORES

Feather by feather the goose is plucked.
—JOHN RAY

"If you're in a hurry, slow down," was my mother's free advice to people who were always rushing through life. In her words, taking your time would prevent mistakes or could get you where you were going slowly, but surely. Somehow her advice didn't make sense to me then.

These days everyone seems to be in a hurry to get somewhere. Nowhere is this more evident than in traffic. Take for instance, the young woman who was determined to get ahead of everybody in heavy morning traffic. She moved from behind me and squeezed her way between two cars, only to move to the next lane after narrowly missing the car in front and causing the car behind her to screech to a halt. Then she was gone, or so I thought.

A long line of cars had formed in the exit lane, and a second line of impatient drivers trying to merge into the line slowed down all traffic lanes. As I drove past a huge trailer in the line, I saw the young woman's car, caught between the trailer and a truck. She didn't want to exit. She wanted to merge into traffic, but her blinking light could not be seen until it was too late to stop and let her in.

As I passed her car, I recognized her. She was the young executive who had joined the company where I used to work, about a year before I retired. I recalled how much she wanted to get to the top. But in her eagerness, she took off too fast and did not stop to ask for directions or to see who else was on the road. At first she rose like a skyrocket, but quickly reached a dead end, where she has been for the past five years.

I wondered, *Do we drive like we live, or do we live like we drive?*

Now my mother's advice makes sense. The young executive is still rushing. She will someday find out, like I did, that the abundant life is not achieved through going fast but slowing down—and being patient with those around us.

How's your driving lately? Is it representative of how you live? If you're weaving in and out of traffic—and life—slow down. In doing so, you'll reach your destination of simple abundance sooner.

> *So the last will be first, and the first will be last.*
> MATTHEW 20:16

Though it may seem impossible, commit to not going over the speed limit for a week and see whether you enjoy life more.

May 21

Vertical And Horizontal Sighs

MARCIA VAN'T LAND

> The real voyage of discovery consists not in seeking
> new lands, but in seeing with new eyes.
> —MARCEL ROUST

It was one of those crazy school mornings when everyone was rushing around, not accomplishing much. As our fifteen-year-old daughter went out the door, she tossed me a bundle of dirty clothes from her school bag and asked, "Mom, will you wash a load for me?"

I had just finished a load of laundry for her. I said nothing but I sighed deeply at her disorganization. Our ten-year-old picked up on my impatience and matter-of-factly said as she went out the door, "It must be hard to be a mom."

Was that the message I was giving? I wanted to run after that school bus and tell our children that I loved being their mom and wouldn't change that fact for anything.

I sighed deeply again as I poured myself a cup of coffee. Then a quote on our refrigerator hit me like a ton of bricks. It read: "We cough to clear our throats; we sigh to clear our hearts." I was certainly sighing.

Suddenly, I made the connection. There are horizontal, earthly sighs directed toward men. There are also vertical sighs directed toward God when we're in pain and troubled. I wonder how often I make God sigh?

When you find yourself sighing because of frustration with another person, meditate on God's goodness and patience with you. Not only will you grow in patience, you'll have greater abundance by not concentrating on their inadequacies.

> . . . He is patient with you, not wanting anyone to perish,
> but everyone to come to repentance.
>
> 2 PETER 3:9

Send a Mother's Day card to someone who may not be a mother, but has mothered or nurtured others.

May 22

Grandma Took Time

D.J. NOTE

Our deeds determine us, as much as we determine our deeds.

—GEORGE ELIOT

"I can't," I complained.

"Can't never accomplished anything," Grandma lovingly scolded me. "Where there's a will, there's a way."

I loved to watch Grandma crochet, but learning how myself seemed impossible. Grandma held her hook in the wrong hand. She was right-handed and I was left-handed.

Grandma patiently placed her crochet hook in my hand, hoping I might catch on. I tried, but I continued to "throw the thread over" the wrong way, or "go into the loop" backwards. My frustration mounted. I convinced myself I was just plain stupid.

Still Grandma didn't give up. Grandma lowered her hands and studied me through her bifocals. "Sit on the floor facing me."

I sat cross-legged on the linoleum.

"Now watch my hands." She picked up the crochet hook with her right hand and paused. I copied her with my left. "Pick up your thread with the other hand," she said. The colorful Red Heart yarn threaded through the fingers of her left hand. I held my frayed "practice" orange thread in my right. "Put your hook into the next stitch like this."

I slipped my hook into the stitch as she instructed. "Throw your thread over and draw it through." She spoke patiently. My inexperienced hand held a death grip on the hook as I brought the thread through the loop. I could hear the rhythmic ticking of the antique clock.

"All right," Grandma said, "throw your thread over again. Now draw it through. See how I did that?" She smiled. "Now throw your thread over and draw the hook through both loops." The threads of her yarn formed a perfect stitch.

"I can see it." I hollered. By sitting on the floor in front of Grandma, the crochet hook appeared to be in her left hand. My stitches were uneven and the tension sloppy, but I was really crocheting.

Grandma leaned back on the couch with a contented smile, "Remember Honey, 'can't' never accomplished anything."

I did remember. Thirty five years later, I can still see her tender smile and hear those sweet words of encouragement echoing down the tunnel of time. At ninety-seven-years-young, this grand lady is still sharing old-fashioned values with a patient spirit. She recently surprised me with a gift of her crochet hooks. I'm grateful to have these special keepsakes. They remind me that Grandma took time. And those old hooks don't seem to mind at all going in the opposite direction.

As you instruct others, are you demonstrating an abundant life through patient and persistent encouragement? Don't say you "can't" be patient. Where there's God's power, there is a way.

The wise in heart are called discerning,
and pleasant words promote instruction.
PROVERBS 16:21

Some of the most beautiful quilts and sweaters have been made from leftovers. Give it a try.

To Build A Christian House

DURLYNN ANEMA-GARTEN

A man builds a fine house; and now he has a master,
and a task for life . . .

—EMERSON

Deciding to build a house is both a positive and negative experience. It is positive because it is yours from the beginning; negative
because of the headaches in timing and incorrect construction moves.

We were fortunate because our contractor, who is a Chrstian,
demonstrated how to build a Christian house. And God became the
master of our house rather than the house becoming master of us.

"You'll have a Christian house," our contractor said as we finalized
building plans.

We nodded. "Of course, we try to maintain a Christian home."

"Not home," said our contractor, "but house. Let's pray and
dedicate this house to our Lord."

Thus began the story of our Christian house, a house not only blessed
from the beginning but exuding that blessedness on all who enter.

When we decided to build we asked three contractors to bid, two
of whom were Christians. It hurt to tell one young man we couldn't
use him, but the older man, who also was a member of our congregation,
not only presented the lower bid but had over thirty years experience.
When he bowed in prayer before we began, we knew we made the
right choice.

From the beginning, he demonstrated his serious dedication to
Christianity. And he also chose Christians for most of the subcontracting.
If a worker was not a believer, we shared God's love and he eagerly listened.

What started as merely another house quickly became an experience in developing abundant patience and love for all concerned. It
was an experience to begin talking to a subcontractor about his work
and end up discussing the work of our Lord.

How do you accomplish this same experience?

The first step involves prayer. We turned over both our house
search and land search to our Lord. When the time was propitious,
He led us to the piece of property we knew was for us. Planning the

house involved some frustration, but we learned greater patience as we eventually designed a house to fit our needs.

The second step is selecting a contractor. The contractors presenting bids were a varied group. We had no idea where our Lord would lead, but knew what we could spend. The one we chose came through with a unique bid that saved us almost $20,000. That meant additional stipend for our Lord's church.

Through patient building, our new home was finished. Our minister dedicated it to our Lord and we rededicated ourselves. As we stood in the middle of the living room holding hands, we felt the strong presence of the Holy Spirit who will never leave the house. When people enter the door, they don't just "ooh" and "aah" at the appearance of our house, they say quite honestly, "There seems to be something different."

We smile, "That's the Holy Spirit, our daily companion in this house built by our Lord and a witness for all who enter through its doors."

Anything worth building—whether a structure, a business, a ministry, or a relationship—is worth the patient endeavor put into it. If you're feeling frustrated because of circumstances delaying the fulfillment of your plans, persevere. You *will* receive the blessing of the Holy Spirit "inhabiting" your completed goal.

Unless the Lord builds the house, its builders labor in vain . . .
PSALM 127:1

Play a board game instead of watching television tonight.

May 24

Snatches Of Time

MURIEL LARSON

You can't kill time without injuring eternity.
—HENRY DAVID THOREAU

*A*ll of us have experienced the frustration of waiting to be called into the doctor or dentist's office. It feels like we're wasting time. There are always moments when time is passing in front of our eyes and it can't be used for anything good. But if we'll just think creatively and make some simple choices, we can "redeem" those moments by using them to memorize Scripture.

One of my friends uses the time waiting for an appointment to go over the verses she uses for witnessing. At one time I worked at a place that was only a mile from my home, so I walked to work every day. Each day I assigned myself one or two more Bible verses to memorize and went over those I had already learned. I added more than two hundred Bible verses to my memory bank that way.

Not only that, I soon discovered that the world of nature that the Lord created was never so beautiful as when I was thinking about His Word. Roses looked lovelier. The birds sang sweeter. The air smelled fresher. And I always seemed to get to work before I knew it.

These were just some side benefits from using available minutes to memorize God's Word. I know the Lord used those verses to draw me closer to Himself and grow in Him then. Through the years He has spoken to my heart through them.

Another important benefit came in my witnessing to non-Christians and encouraging fellow Christians. Ever since that time I have had verses for every opportunity. The Lord uses His Word to convict me, too, to make me a better Christian. For instance, when I get angry with someone, I sense the withdrawal of God's peace from my heart. Then the Spirit reminds me of what Jesus said: *But if you do not forgive men their sins, your Father will not forgive your sins* (Matthew 6:15). Believe me, I get right fast.

Think back—how much time have you spent waiting in lines, in offices, and for other things during the past year? Might those waits have added up to perhaps thirty hours? You, and I, can make a wise choice to use it effectively by hiding God's Word in our hearts. Plus, it'll help us be more patient when life hands us delays.

> *. . . making the most of every opportunity, because the days are evil.*
> EPHESIANS 5:16

If you don't regularly memorize Scripture, plan to learn one verse this week.

Times Of Our Lives

SANDRA HINMAN GRIESMEYER

It is more important to gird ourselves for the grind of
life than it is to throw ourselves into high gear only
for the grandiose affairs of life.

—CHARLES CALDWELL RYRIE

*A*s little children, we wish time would pass so Christmas would be
here, or school would start. When we are a little older, we wish
summer was here, so school would be out. We are often impatiently
looking to the future for some great event, wishing away the time.

Every minute is the same as the others of its kind. Yet some are longer,
filled with pain, and some all too brief, when filled with joy. These are
the times of our lives, each governed and guided by the wisdom of the
Lord. He makes them not too long otherwise the joy might become boring
or commonplace. But not too brief so that it won't be missed.

Yet, if we neglect that simple truth, we will impatiently look to the
future and not enjoy the moment we have right now. That will steal our
"abundance" outlook on life because we'll never be satisfied with the
present. Even when the favored event arrives, our focus will instantly
change to the next anticipated event.

Does this describe you? If so, sit still in this moment. Camp at this
moment. Savor it. Enjoy it. Revel in it. Don't switch your focus to the future.
Squeeze every last bit of joy out of right now. Patiently breathe in this
moment's abundance and allow God to fulfill His plan for right now.

When times are good, be happy; but when times are bad, consider:
God has made the one as well as the other.
Therefore, a man cannot discover anything about his future.
ECCLESIASTES 7:14

Start a gardening plant exchange with your neighbors or friends.

Come Away With Me

JUNE L. VARNUM

Flee for a while from your tasks, hide yourself for a
little space from the turmoil of your thoughts. For
a little while give your time to God, and rest in
him for a little while.

—ANSELM (1033-1109), ARCHBISHOP OF CANTERBURY

I pushed myself out of bed and glanced at the to-do list propped
by the lamp. I know it by heart—finish a writing assignment, mop
floor, vacuum, dust, grocery shop, prepare dinner, do Bible study,
review Sunday school lesson, drive ninety mile round trip to take Mom
to her doctor. *How can I do everything? I already feel like giving up.*

While showering, I continued to review the day's tasks. Nothing
could be left undone. *I'll just have a mug of coffee, a few minutes to read
and then tackle that list.*

Slipping into my rocking chair, I opened my devotional book.
Halfway through the passage, my thoughts became so jumbled I
couldn't remember what I'd just read. Returning to the verse, I tried
again. All I could think about was that list. *How can I get everything
done?* pounded through my head.

*I'll sit quietly for a few minutes, then get to work. God will understand,
I'm sure.* Taking a sip of coffee, I glanced at the clock. Tick, tick, tick.
It seemed to shout, "You're wasting time, wasting time, wasting time."

I gave up and headed to the computer. It refused to obey me. After
a half hour I gave up. Household chores didn't go much better when
my impatient actions pushed over a vase and broke it. Sinking down
to the floor, tears flooded onto my cheeks. That's when I heard the
whisper, "Go outside now. Get away for a bit."

Why not? I thought, *I'm sure not accomplishing anything here.* With
swimming eyes, I found my way to the back porch and flopped into a
lawn chair. Facing east, I watched the sun climb higher. A few wispy
white clouds tinged with pink drifted along slowly across the mountain
tops. *That's neat, Lord. You care, don't you?*

Closing my eyes, silence surrounded me. Soon I could hear gurgling
water from the nearby creek. *How nice, Lord.* And I sat. Just sat.

Slowly, lazily, I opened my eyes. *How lovely everything looks.* Smiling,

I began humming a praise chorus as I headed back to the house and that trying list. The chores still waited to be done. But now I understood the important ones would be accomplished. The rest weren't worth being impatient over.

When your to-do list begins to monopolize your life, creating impatience and distance from God, remember God's abundance principle for patience: "I will give you enough time to do what I want you to do. All you need to do is obey Me."

Come with me by yourselves to a quiet place and get some rest.
MARK 6:31B

> Instead of trying to keep up with placing photos in albums, label a box for each child and place photos and papers important to them in their box. Then present the box to them when they leave home.

May 27

A Place For Everything

CHER HOLTON

It takes a great man to give sound advice tactfully, but
a greater to accept it graciously.
—J.C. MACAULAY

*M*ay represents patience and we need to gain control over the frustration of our cluttered desks or offices. I recently worked with a professional organizer and have experienced amazing results in just a few days. Once I got over the embarrassment of letting her see my cluttered office, we were able to roll up our sleeves and make some simple changes that have created unbelievable results in terms of not only my organization, but my peace of mind as well.

The biggest "a-ha" for me was to implement the maxim "a place for everything." By identifying the clutter and determining specific locations to house it, I have eliminated a major source of my frustration: paper avalanche. Now, for example, I have a shelf spot for reading material (and when it's full, it's time to throw some away); a lateral file on my desk to hold folders for "Calls Pending, To Review, Calls to Make, File in Tickler," etc. I love the fact that my professional organizer did not force me to have a clean desk. She recognized my need to have some things at my fingertips and worked with me to develop a strategy that would fit my work preferences.

The concept I resisted most was the File Directory, yet it has become my greatest friend. No longer do I wonder where to file something, or where to find it. The best part of using a professional organizer was that she made all of the labels and got my files into shape in no time. We chose files in beautiful colors, so now I actually enjoy working with them. I feel as if I have been given the gift of more time to focus on what I do best.

If you're feeling frustrated because you can't find what you need on your desk, consider getting assistance. Wise people seek help and there may be someone in your life who has a gift for organization. Call upon them and you'll find greater abundant patience. You may actually quickly find that piece of paper.

He who obeys instructions guards his life,
but he who is contemptuous of his ways will die.

PROVERBS 19:16

Evaluate your office or desk space. What one thing will you do today to get control over clutter and gain more peace?

May 28

God's Waiting Room

L. PAMELA WAIAN

We ask for miracles not because we need it for our faith,
but because through them we can share with others the
glory of God.

—ANONYMOUS

*H*ave you ever prayed for so many years for a person or situation that you thought your impatience would cause you give up? I have. And every time I felt the lowest, I would repeat God's words to myself, *Men and women ought to pray, and not faint or give up.* Across my mind would always march the Parable of the Unjust Judge. The widow petitioned the judge over and over again. I would then tell God, "I will go to my grave still asking."

A twelve-year-long prayer began when my daughter reached maturity, moved out on her own and decided not to embrace mom and dad's religion anymore. After four years and marriage to the man of her choice, she became lonely and decided to return to church. She attended for a few months and began to consider making a commitment. But her husband decided he wasn't ready to have a religious wife.

My daughter called us in tears, realizing she had to choose between her husband and attending church. We proclaimed our unconditional love but encouraged her to make the choice herself. She made the decision to stay with her husband and stop attending church.

Though weary at times of praying for my son-in-law's changed heart, I continued through the many years that followed. At times there were small bursts of light in the darkness and my daughter and I especially grew closer spiritually. We were asked by them to offer a prayer of thanksgiving and blessing on the purchase of their new house, on the birth of their first child, anointings when sick and prayers over meals.

Over the years, acceptance and love for our son-in-law has had many positive benefits. During our last visit, he told us he wanted his daughter to grow up with Christian values. Recently, they all began going to church and enjoying it.

All this has taken more than twelve years of faithful praying and not letting my occasional impatience with God's timing distract me.

If you have been praying for a situation or person for a long time, remember God's timing and wisdom is perfect and He loves you. God will answer. He promises it as a part of the abundant life He wants for us. So continue to pray . . . as you wait patiently in the "waiting room."

May our Lord Jesus Christ himself and God our Father,
who loved us and by his grace gave us eternal encouragement and good hope,
encourage your hearts and strengthen you in every good deed and word.
2 THESSALONIANS 2:16-17

Since Memorial Day will be celebrated soon, inquire at local cemeteries about helping to put out the crosses.

Search The Scriptures

LAURA SABIN RILEY

A man travels the world over in search of what he
needs and returns home to find it.

—GEORGE MOORE

What is God's will for your life? This age old question has plagued God-seeking people for centuries. Most of the time, we can find God's will quite easily. It's actually simple, but because most of us think it should be complicated, we impatiently go on a search, seeking other authorities and opinions. But the only opinion that really matters is God's. We can find all of the answers we are looking for in one place: His Word.

Every time I am feeling confused about God's will, I find the answer when I patiently take time to look in the Bible. That transformation of my mind takes place as I fill it up with the Scriptures. To "transform" implies to bring about a change either in external form or in inner nature. When God's Word changes our inner nature, then our external form is affected as well—the way we act, speak and treat others. Simply put, to borrow a popular slogan, if we want to live an abundant life, we should "just do it." Just follow the principles in God's Word.

If you've been struggling with determining God's will, go to the Scriptures and let them transform your mind. Everything can be tested against God's Word. For instance, if you're wondering whether it's God's will for you to have that new dining room set you want (and it just went on sale), but you must pay with your credit card, look at Proverbs 22:26 and Romans 13:8. Wondering what God's will is concerning the discipline of your children? The answer is in Proverbs 13:24 and 22:15. What about that relative who is in financial trouble and has come to you for a loan? See 1 Timothy 5:8.

The examples are endless. All the answers we need in life are in God's Word. Life doesn't have to be complicated nor do we impatiently have to seek everyone's opinion. We never have to go searching for His will as long as we search the Scriptures.

Do not conform any longer to the pattern of this world, but be transformed by the renewing of your mind. Then you will be able to test and approve what God's will is—his good, pleasing and perfect will.

ROMANS 12:2

> It's not a new concept but it brings simplicity: a place for everything and everything in its place.

May 30

God's Gooey Gum

ANDREA BICZO

> God can make you anything you want to be, but you
> have to put everything in his hands.
>
> —MAHALIA JACKSON

It was a warm Spring day and all the kids were in the front yard running through the sprinklers. Morgan suddenly appeared at the screen door, calling "I'm all sticky, Mommy, help." I swung open the screen door and was horrified to see my two-year-old daughter nearly mummified in a cocoon of bubble gum. She was wound up from the top of her head to the tips of her toes in hot pink bubble gum smelling of the sickening sweet aroma of strawberries.

As Morgan stood there, stuck to the welcome mat, struggling like a fly caught in a web, she yelped once again, "Sticky, Mommy, help." I felt weak as I thought, "How am I going to free this helpless child from her gooey web?"

Moments later, Morgan stood howling in the bathtub. I had poured a large bottle of vegetable oil over her and she dripped from head to toe. I started to peel away layers of bubble gum when I realized she couldn't even see. Her eyelashes were glued shut from the bubble gum. After she recovered from bubble gum blindness, she calmed down and stopped howling. She realized the damage was only temporary and began to relax and cooperate with my picking and pulling.

Later, as I thought about Morgan's dilemma, I realized that sometimes my eyes have been sealed shut with a spiritual blindness that resembles a sticky wad of bubble gum. I impatiently lose sight of God's abilities to remedy my sticky situations. Panic sets in and I howl with discomfort. Like a big bottle of oil that slowly and gently releases my impatience, God removes my sticky, uncomfortable situations. But I must simply relax and cooperate and realize He is in control. If I fight Him, I only wind myself up tighter in a web of discomfort.

Are you impatiently struggling with some circumstance today that is blinding your eyes to God's plan for abundant living? Stop trying to fight it yourself. Let His Holy Spirit pour His balm of truth over you, releasing you of self effort. The battle is His. Cooperate with His directions. Wait patiently for His plan to be fulfilled.

Commit to the Lord whatever you do, and your plans will succeed.
PROVERBS 16:3

> Pick out three recipes that are quick to fix. Always keep the ingredients on hand for last minute cooking.

May 31

Instant Fix It

LILLE DIANE

There is little you can learn from doing nothing.
—ZIG ZIGLER

We live in a drive-thru society, with countless time saving devices and overnight express promises. We don't even have to get up to change the television. Pour the machine bread mix into the bread-maker and several hours later, out pops a perfect loaf of bread. No kneading or picking the dough out from underneath your finger nails—all the great smells and flavor of homemade, but *no* work.

We have convenienced ourselves into a people that are overweight, sick and tired. The problem with this style of living, besides being unhealthy, is impatiently thinking we can correct the problem quickly. We may join a local gym only to discover there are no instant results, so we drop out. The same applies to diets. We make a great start but find that a long term commitment is needed.

Here are four affirmations for making healthiness a daily part of your life. Use 3 X 5 cards to copy the following tips and place them where you will see them often.

1. I will dedicate an entire year to eliminating unhealthy habits and replace them with positive actions.

2. Losing weight is not a quick fix. Staying fit is a life-style.

3. I will stop the Stop-Start-Stop habits created by losing weight for a special occasion.

4. I will lose weight for me and no one else.

Making those four attitudes a way of life will eliminate the impatience of wanting unrealistic results. As a result, you'll experience an abundance of control over your eating.

He gives strength to the weary, and increase the power of the weak. Even youths grow tired and weary, and young men stumble and fall; but those who hope in the Lord will renew their strength. They will soar on wings like eagles; they will run and not grow weary, they will walk and not grow faint.

ISAIAH 40:29-31

> If you don't have it in your house, it can't tempt you. Don't bring unhealthy food home from the store.

June

"And be kind to one another . . ."

Ephesians 4:32

$\mathcal{E}$ach of us hunger for kindness to be expressed toward us. Hopefully, our human father expressed the fruit of the Spirit that results from abundant living. But if not, we can experience it from our Heavenly Father. This month's readings will strengthen our ability to live in *simple abundance* and as a result, we'll see more gentle responses toward others.

A Day With The Sand Terns

KATHRYN PRESLEY

It is life near the bone where it is the sweetest.
—HENRY DAVID THOREAU

*A*s we begin this new month in our journey toward greater abundance, today let's make our lives abundantly simple by focusing on kindness within our families. That can be communicated through a simple statement we've all heard, the "best things in life are free." My family had occasion to prove that in our one-income household when our children were small. I interrupted my career to stay home until our children were in school. I loved being a home-maker, and, although it wasn't easy, I knew it was the right decision. We lived very "close to the bone" during those years: eating a lot of peanut butter, driving the wheels off a battered old Volkswagen, running out of money before we ran out of month, gathering coke bottles and milk bottles to sell. I worried that we were not able to provide our gifted children with advantages they deserved. Our vacations were usually short camping trips, the children wore a lot of homemade clothes (I'm not a gifted seamstress), and Christmas at our house was lean compared to other homes on the block.

Imagine my joy when I recently overheard our children discussing their "nearly perfect childhood." They are parents now and enjoying many of the same things with their children that we loved to do with them: camping trips, picnics on the beach, fishing, hunting, making Christmas gifts, and gardening. They often reminisce about the long camping trip to Yellowstone, watching the sun come up over the Grand Canyon, and the trip we made to Canada with just $60 (we caught and ate fish three meals a day).

But one trip to the beach really stands out. It was a raw, windy day and we had planned to picnic and fly kites. After all, poor food (Vienna sausages, peanut butter and jelly) tastes better on the beach. That particular day, our daughter stumbled over a nest in the sand. Suddenly, we saw the beach was alive with hatching birds. Sand terns had built their nests all along the beach and we crawled around for hours, careful not to disturb the nests, watching baby birds struggle into the light. It seemed a miracle of life and turned our hearts toward the Creator.

Thirty years later, our children don't remember or care that our furniture was old and shabby, that they had no designer labels in their clothes, that we never bought new cars, or that their bicycles were always "recycled" ones. However, they do remember the time we spent with them, the joys we shared, and the Creator who "gives us richly all things to enjoy."

If you're feeling discouraged or like a failure for not providing your children everything the proverbial "Jones" have, take heart. They are much more interested in time spent with *you* than the things you might provide for them. Your kindness provides abundant security for them.

> And my God will meet all your needs according
> to his glorious riches in Christ Jesus.
>
> PHILIPPIANS 4:19

Plan a trip for your family and see how little you can spend.

June 2

Abundant Spiritual Gifts

TONY EVANS

To give real service you must add something which cannot be bought or measured with money, and that is sincerity and integrity.

—DONALD A. ADAMS

Will Jesus Christ announce you as a winner at His judgment seat? Or will He strip you of your medal? If you want to be a winner on that day, make Him the object of your first love today. I hope these ideas will help you avoid loss of reward in heaven by running according to the rules here on earth:

1. If you want to have a very interesting family conversation at your next meal together, ask each member to try to identify his or her spiritual gifts and then talk about ways God can use each of you to put your gifts to work for Him. Read Jesus' parable in Matthew 25:14-30 and stress the importance of using what He entrusts to us.

2. Is there a gift or ability you know God has given you, yet you are hiding for whatever reason? Then get your shovel out. Dig up your "talent" and ask God for an opportunity to serve Him with it. Then be alert for the answer.

3. We as Christians differ in gifts, abilities, and financial resources—but we can all be faithful. Look around you and take note of the people

whose faithfulness to the Lord and His people blesses your life. Make it a point to let at least three of these people know how much you appreciate them.

We have different gifts, according to the grace given us . . .
ROMANS 12:6

> Take a piece of paper and write down three or four areas of your life (e.g. marriage, ministry, financial stewardship) where you especially want to hear Jesus' commendation, "Well done, good and faithful servant." Now opposite each item list the things you are doing *now* to reach your goal.

June 3

Beauty Escapes

PAMALA CONDIT KENNEDY

Just as you have to let a computer cool down occasionally, the same goes for the human machine. Small cool-downs help prevent meltdown.

—JUDITH WATERS

We all must spend time pampering ourselves on occasion. The quick hop in and out of the shower we ritually go through each morning cannot be compared to the relaxation of a hot, bubbly bath. A bath is not just sitting in your own dirty water, as some might mournfully moan. It can be soothing, satisfying, sensual and sumptuous.

Can I tempt you to run to the nearest drug store and load up with wonderful bathing delights such as mineral salts, softening oils, a stimulating body brush, a great magazine or two, and, of course, sparkling cider?

Water has deep relaxing qualities. Whether the crystal tepid bath in the privacy of your own home or a natural mineral-saturated hot springs, your body will respond to the free-moving waves about you. The hustle of the day is washed from your mind and body as you lie back and enjoy the warmth that penetrates deep into your senses.

To get the full treatment of a luxurious bath, you may want to apply a facial mask and deep-condition your hair as well. You must give in completely to the solitude of this moment and refrain from mentally formulating a to-do list or worrying about tomorrow's responsibilities. Make the most of this calming time, and for a nice change, light a candle and play quiet, romantic music. Instructions must be given to all family members that this is a "Do Not Disturb" time for Mom.

Many women have a difficult time giving themselves a gift of kindness and feel guilty for any personal time they take. But if you make the time to treat yourself some type of calming experience, you'll give more abundantly of yourself.

Before a girl's turn came to go in to King Xerxes, she had to complete twelve months of beauty treatments prescribed for the women, six months with oil of myrrh and six with perfumes and cosmetics.

ESTHER 2:12

Either today or tomorrow, take a soothing, lingering bath.
Don't forget to light a candle and take a good book with you.

June 4

Speaking Your Spouse's Language

H. NORMAN WRIGHT

Communication is depositing a part of yourself in another person.

—ANONYMOUS

Speaking your spouse's language includes not only vocabulary but also the person's packaging. Packaging refers to whether a person is an amplifier (sharing great volumes of details) or a condenser (sharing little more than the bottom line).

If he's an amplifier, go for it. If he's a condenser, keep it brief. Neither men nor women want to hear a monologue of the reasons they need to fulfill a request.

Amplifiers give a number of descriptive sentences as they talk, while condensers give one or two sentences. In approximately 70 percent of marriages, the man is the condenser and the woman is the amplifier. Neither is a negative trait, but the amplifier wishes his or her partner would share more, while the condenser wishes his or her partner would share less. It is only when each of you adapts to the style of your partner that real communication occurs.

And don't spend time recounting all the times your partner didn't come through for you or did it wrong. You'll just reinforce the possibility they'll repeat what you don't want to happen. Always, always talk about what you want and present it in such a way that they catch in your request the belief that they can do it.

Reckless words pierce like a sword, but the tongue of the wise brings healing.
PROVERBS 12:18

Are you an amplifier or a condenser? Evaluate your spouse or the significant person in your life, and change your communication to fit their needs.

June 5

A Little Bit Of Heaven

CHRISTINE R. DAVIS

Earth laughs in flowers.
—RALPH WALDO EMERSON

I begin thinking about my summer flower garden long before the winter snows disappear. I study the "zillions" of mail order catalogs that clutter the house. It's a monumental task just to decide what types of plants and seeds I want to grow. Flower gardening is hard work, but it's one of the most enjoyable and rewarding jobs I know. Gardens offer a restful spot to spend quiet, reflective time away from the phone and TV.

Like everyone else, there are times when I feel stressed by the demands of a busy day, or when I get angry or upset about something. To clear my head, it helps me to go outside and get busy in the garden. I may just pull a few unwanted weeds, water the plants, or pick a sweet-smelling bouquet, but the physical activity and surroundings take my mind off troubles.

When I step out in the garden, it's easy to forget problems. How can I stay troubled or angry surrounded by all the beauty and activity in a garden? My dark moods seem to lift almost immediately when I'm there. It's a delight to enjoy the cheerful purple and orange blooms of cosmos, wisteria and marigolds and watch butterflies and humming-birds visit in search of nectar among the blossoms. There's even a tiny green frog that makes his home in a shallow container pond nestled under some ferns.

In this little version of "heaven on earth," I feel very close to a kind God who provides such beauty. I marvel at the mystery of His universe and every living thing when I see His handiwork. It's His garden and He wants me to feel His presence there and find laughter, comfort and enjoyment in something simple like flowers.

When was the last time you enjoyed the simplicity of working in your garden or yard? Do it soon and enjoy God's kindness in providing something that easily soothes stress. You may find yourself passing along that kindness to others.

> *How many are your works, O Lord. In wisdom you made them all . . .*
> PSALM 104:24

If you've been putting off planting some flowers, plan an hour or two soon when you'll enjoy getting your hands into God's earth.

June 6

Floral Notecards

CHRISTINE R. DAVIS

To assert that a world as intricate as ours emerged
from chaos by chance is about as sensible as to claim
that Shakespeare's dramas were composed by rioting
monkeys in a print shop.

—MERRILL C. TENNEY

*Y*esterday we talked about enjoying God's creation through our gardens. Today let's discover how to preserve those flowers so that they can be shared in your own handcrafted notecards.

Many flower types (daisies, roses, pansies, etc.) can be pressed easily between the pages of old books if they are allowed to dry. This can take several days to several weeks, depending on the size and thickness of the flowers. Check on them periodically.

Supplies needed:

Flowers: pressed; dried flat.

Blank notecards: these can be purchased at craft and hobby stores in a variety of colors, or you can use heavy stock paper or construction paper.

Glue

Toothpicks

Paints: acrylic, watercolor, etc.

Markers

Raffia

Directions: Position and arrange your flowers on the front of the card in a pleasing design. With a toothpick, apply tiny dots of glue to the backs of the flowers and gently position on the card. Allow to dry. Paints, markers, and small raffia bows can also be used to decorate the cards.

Write a kind, loving message or verse inside the card and share your abundance of summer flowers with others.

In the beginning God created the heavens and the earth.
GENESIS I:I

> Create your own cards with flowers you grow or buy.

June 7

Walking In Beauty

JOAN K. WEAVER

There is beauty before me, there is beauty behind me
There is beauty above me, there is beauty below me
I walk in beauty . . .

—NAVAJO PRAYER

*T*hus begins the Navajo prayer which reminds us that we can choose to stand centered in the beauty of God's creation no matter where we find ourselves. One small way I have found this to be true is on wash day. Like many other people, my modern lifestyle has necessitated several moves to new cities and houses. Within weeks of moving day, I have always had my husband erect a sturdy clothes line in backyards from Michigan suburbs, to New Mexican desert, and finally Kansas prairie.

Obvious economic and environmental benefits exist for using a "solar" clothes dryer and saving on utilities. But there are other reasons as well. My love affair with the clothes line probably began with the image of my mother walking in the sunshine with a large wicker basket full of damp dungarees and cotton, sashed dresses. Like most people,

I also love to crawl into bed between fresh-smelling, line-dried sheets. I even prefer the stimulating roughness of a stiff, sun-baked bath towel to the overpowering perfume of a fabric-softened one.

I have always enjoyed the act of hanging out the clothes. My mother taught me to have a neat clothesline—one where the socks are mated and like articles are always hung together. Sheets and pillow cases go in the back, towels and washcloths next, shirts and jeans, and finally the little articles of underwear and socks hang in front. Cloth diapers always got the most direct sun for bleaching.

Through all these years, the clothes line has brought some symbolic order to my life. Problems and little imperfections seem to be washed away. When the clothes are hung, at least for a little while, a sometimes hectic and chaotic world slows down and finds order.

But what I have appreciated the most is the actual pinning of the clothes to the line. It is a fact that clothes lines have to be high or the sheets will drag on the ground. Each time I reach up to pin a garment, my eyes naturally look up into the sky where I see the clouds, butterflies flying, and the swaying branches of trees. I feel the sunshine on my face and hear the birds singing. It is my perfect time to praise God for creation's beauty and thank Him for my blessings. When I return to the house, I am refreshed like a sheet and sun-bleached by His kindness and mercy.

What routine, simple task do you do that reflects God's kindness to you? Instead of complaining about it, enjoy it. And also concentrate on how you need to be kind to someone today.

I lift up my eyes to you, to you whose throne is in heaven.
PSALM 123:1

If you don't already have one, put up a makeshift clothes line so that you can hang your laundry on it this week.

June 8

Rhythms Throughout The Day

JAN JOHNSON

When we ask Christ, "What next?" we tune in and give Him a chance to pour His ideas through our enkindled imagination.

—FRANK LAUBACH

*B*etween morning and evening, tiny Sabbaths occur all day long. Some Christian traditions have structured these Sabbaths into seven times of prayer scattered throughout the day. These are called the Daily Office, and Psalms are used as prayers. (The term *office* is derived from the idea that prayer is our work.) Based on the verse *Seven times a day I praise you for your righteous laws* (Psalm 119:164), the Daily Office occurs at such times as daybreak, 6:00 a.m., 9:00 a.m., noon, 3:00 p.m., dusk (or the end of the workday), and before bed. These moments of prayer "punctuate the day, corresponding both to natural rhythms as well as to events in the life of the historical Christ." We may want to follow that tradition or find Sabbaths within the natural rhythms of our day—before rising, parking a car at work, coffee breaks, noontime, dinnertime, moving from one task to another. Every transition is a time for a comment to God ("I don't like meetings anymore."), a request ("Please help me remember . . ."), or a question ("How can I show love to a friend?").

It's easy to see why Psalms are the prayers chosen for the Daily Office. These slim, unsophisticated scriptural prayers teach us down-to-earth patterns for Heavenly conversations:

• effervescing with thanks for deliverance from yet another difficult situation;

• honoring and applauding God for His relentless love, quiet power, and mysterious majesty; or

• pouring out the soul in anger and anguish.

These are things that friends do together, are they not? Friendship with God is not only possible, but it is God's will.

You know you have a real friend when the two of you can pass time quietly doing nothing and saying nothing clever. It's enough to be together. Having a friendship with God means that we can relax with Him and enjoy His company in the in-between moments all day long.

I no longer call you servants, because a servant does not know his master's business. Instead, I have called you friends, for everything that I learned from my Father I have made known to you.

JOHN 15:15

For several days, designate a time when you'll pause in your work or play to focus on God for five minutes—that is not your regular devotional time.

A Full Man

SANDRA PALMER CARR

For if ever an earthly father was worthy of the confidence
of his children, surely much more is our Heavenly Father
worthy of our confidence.

—HANNAH WHITALL SMITH

*A*s we draw closer to celebrating Father's Day, focus on the
following characteristics which hopefully were demonstrated by
your father. But if not, be assured they are by your Heavenly Father.

LOVE – You know love when your father introduces you to the
love of Jesus before you can talk.

JOY – You feel joy when your father sings and whistles every
day because he can't keep it inside.

PEACE – You experience peace when you're frightened and
your father comes to your rescue.

PATIENCE – You learn patience as your father holds you,
struggling in his arms.

KINDNESS – You touch kindness when your father eases a
painful or difficult time for you.

GOODNESS – You see goodness when your father does what is
right because it is.

FAITHFULNESS – You understand faithfulness if your father is
faithful to your mother.

GENTLENESS – You touch gentleness when your father hears
your side of the story before he passes judgment.

SELF-CONTROL – You comprehend self-control if your father
exercises it when he disciplines you.

Dad, thank you for teaching me to know love, feel joy, experience
peace, learn patience, touch kindness, see goodness, understand
faithfulness, touch gentleness, and comprehend self-control. You are
a "full" man—a man filled with the Spirit of God.

Even if your father wasn't perfect in these areas, show God's
kindness to him by expressing your appreciation for whatever goodness
he gave you. Verbalizing or writing those positives doesn't mean you're
approving of anything wrong he has done. Your kindness might be
used by God to break through distance or bitterness.

But the fruit of the Spirit is love, joy, peace, patience, kindness, goodness,
faithfulness, gentleness and self-control. Against such things there is no law.
GALATIANS 5:22-23

> If you are a father—or a mother—which of these characteristics
> are you strong in and which do you need to grow in?

June 10

Safely Truckin'

HEIDI JOY CRESSLEY

The supreme happiness of life is the conviction that
we are loved.

—VICTOR HUGO

When I was growing up, summer vacations meant truck rides, ice cream and waiting. Dad would come into my dark room at 3 a.m. to kiss me on the cheek. "Time to get up my truckin' girl," he would whisper.

Oh how proud I was climbing up into that 18-wheeler while the rest of the world slept. I loved watching Dad handle the big rig. His muscular arms worked around the steering wheel like a baker kneading bread dough. As we rode for hours, I often glanced at Dad and he'd smile. This was the safest place in the world.

Sometimes we would enter an industrial plant that did not allow children in the loading areas. Dad would reluctantly leave me sitting in an office or hallway. It really didn't bother me, because I knew he'd come back for me as soon as he could. I'd watch every truck come out of the plant with great anticipation. When Dad's truck pulled up, excitement rushed through my veins. He'd hurry to hug me tight. Then we looked for the closest ice cream stand.

Dad's kindness taught me a lot about my Heavenly Father. I grew up to understand the security of God's love. I know that first hug from Jesus someday will remind me of my earthly father.

If you still have your father today, consider the things he taught you. Thank your Heavenly Father for them and how he has empowered you to experience the abundant life.

> *But you are a shield around me, O Lord;*
> *you bestow glory on me and lift up my head.*
> PSALM 3:3

June II

Symphony

LYNELL GRAY

The rain is raining all around, it falls on field and tree.
It rains on the umbrellas here and on the ships at sea.
—ROBERT LOUIS STEVENSON

I am chanting the lines of that Robert Louis Stevenson poem remembered from childhood. A summer rain gently dampens the earth. My two-year-old daughter, Christy, sitting demurely on her small chair on the patio, nods solemnly. After a silence, she says in a little voice, "Birds . . . song."

She has brought her puppet out to see the rain, too, and now she motions for me to put him on my hand. He comes alive, gesturing dramatically and squealing his unconcealed delight over the rain. We are both charmed. He feels a raindrop on his head and covers it with mock alarm, then peers out and laughs to reassure us he is only playing. We want to forget that he is a puppet and so, for the moment, we do. He is our friend, and we love him for his funny, wonderful ways.

"Oh, smell the rain." he insists. Breathing deeply, we drink in the fresh, earthy scent.

My daughter wanders off, and I lean back to look up at my canopy of green. The tree which overhangs the patio has made a perfect covering and I am suddenly grateful. Grateful to its Creator for making it so, and grateful that I can sit under it, watch the rain, and have so much enjoyment from such a simple thing.

Christy is bringing me treasures now, as she loves to do. Leaves wet with rain, sticky dandelions—all these things are special wonders to her, and I look at them with new eyes.

The rain has lightened to a drizzle now, and the sun is brighter behind the gray layers of cloud. The world seems to stir from its lull of wet sleep. The birds are more eloquent than ever. A breeze is rustling the leaves, shaking drops down on me.

It has been like a symphony this morning. First, a single note, a hushed beginning, melodious, and perfect. Then a quickening and a bursting forth of life, the symphony full of movement and energy.

And now the drops, fat and heavy, are falling again. The sky darkens. The breeze has died to unpredictable wisps. The symphony is drawing to a hush.

Whenever I take the time, I will find that the music has never stopped, and is never quite the same. It is the song of God's creation, the life-giving rain as an emblem of His great kindness poured out upon us.

As we stop to enjoy such simple gifts from God, we come away renewed, restored, refreshed. That's the core of the abundant life: stopping to hear God's gentle whisper in the rainstorm, then turning to breath out His kindness to those around us.

> . . . All the earth bows down to you. they sing praise to you, they sing praise to your name. Selah.
>
> PSALM 66:4

The next time it rains, stand outside and really hear the symphony it expresses in praise of its Creator. If you're brave enough, do it without an umbrella.

June 12

Preparing For Pets

ESTHER M. BAILEY

> The sovereign God has permitted us to have a measure
> of conditional sovereignty, a mark of the divine image
> once given at the Creation and partially lost by the Fall.
> —A. W. TOZER

As summer vacation nears, this is a good time to think about integrating pets into the family when children have time to spend with the newcomers. Pets can be a powerful teaching tool for children to learn kindness. But without proper preparation, though, parents may be stuck with a job they don't want.

The child thinks only of the good times he or she can have with the dog. Sharing love and games with a puppy can be fun, but when the reality of regular feeding, bathing, and clean-up duty sets in, interest often wanes.

To prevent such conflicts, my friend Molly Wolf uses a system worth passing on. She puts her two girls through an extensive orientation process before allowing them to bring any living creatures into the home.

One of the girls wanted gerbils.

"I'm not fond of gerbils," Molly said, "but go to the library and read up on them. Tell me everything about them. If you still want them and will take complete care of them, okay."

The required research did not dissuade the ten-year-old. Two gerbils moved in without upsetting the household because the child was prepared to deal with the problems. Two parakeets became members of the family in the same way.

The orientation process could be carried a step further with practical experience. For instance, the child who wants a dog might volunteer to walk the neighbor's dog for a month. If the desire for canine companionship survives thirty days of tending to mundane tasks, the child is a good candidate to become a dog owner.

Some time before a pet is actually purchased, reading and discussing Genesis 1:24-26 will help children realize that the responsibility to care for a pet is God-given. Ask, "How did God feel about the animals He made?"

Explain that God will be disappointed if we aren't kind to the animals He made. Ask, "How would you feel if someone knocked down the tower you built?" Encourage the child to pray for wisdom in caring for the prospective pet. This will reinforce recognition of the need for total commitment.

Pets can either add to or subtract from the harmony in a home. If you decide to allow pets in your home after careful planning, the results are likely to be on the positive side, teaching kindness and self control. Animals do add to to a family's fullness: the abundant life.

Suppose one of you wants to build a tower.
Will he not first sit down and estimate the cost . . . ?

LUKE 14:28

The next time you have a picnic, pass around the ice cream maker, and let each person take a turn at turning the handle. You'll be able to enjoy this sweet treat sooner.

Melt The Icy Differences

CAROLE MAYHALL

> People can't get your goat if you don't tell them where
> it's tied up.
> — BUNNY WILSON

In every relationship, there are going to be differences. We can either practice kindness in responding to them and do ourselves a favor, or react with anger. Since we want to concentrate on kindness this month, especially in our relationships, here are a few suggestions for melting the icy differences:

Set objectives. Write down practical steps you can take to grow in relating. Plan to attend a marriage seminar; do a Bible study on the person of Christ (to see the perfect balance in a life, for instance); memorize together some verses on understanding; pray together daily concerning understanding. Have someone close to you check up on your progress.

Start now and do it. A godly friend of ours was asked by a young woman, "My mother and I fight all the time and clash every single day. What can I do?" His advice to her was, "Stop it."

Remember, we *can* if we will. Our wills are involved in the process of putting into action what God wants us to change.

Finally, *celebrate* your differences.

Toward the end of her life and a second marriage, Catherine Marshall wrote, "Husbands and wives are basically incompatible . . . . That's why the home is His classroom for molding and shaping us into mature people."

Let's celebrate God's molding.

Carl Rogers uses this analogy: "When I walk on the beach to watch the sunset I do not call out, 'A little more orange over to the right, please,' or, 'Would you mind giving us less purple in the back?' No, I enjoy the always-different sunsets as they are. We do well to do the same with people we love."

Let's celebrate God's unique designs.

> *Love . . . keeps no record of wrongs . . .*
> I CORINTHIANS 13:4-5

June 14

Simple Training

VEDA BOYD JONES

Turn, turn, my wheel. Tis nature's plan
The child should grow into the man.
—HENRY WADSWORTH LONGFELLOW

In the summers when my sons are home for the long school vacation, they help with the cooking, and in so doing, learn more kindness and cooperation. Once a week each boy is required to plan and cook a meal. Although it really doesn't give me time out of the kitchen, since I'm the technical advisor, it gives the boys confidence that they can manage a simple survivor skill of cooking for themselves and others. They also learn the importance of complimenting other cooks' hard work in the kitchen.

Okay, I'll admit we have a lot of hamburgers and macaroni and cheese in the summer. Occasionally I'll require them to cook something brand new from a cookbook. That teaches them the importance of following directions.

By summer's end the boys have more respect for how hard it is to cook for a family and how rewarding it can be.

If you have children at home, teach them greater kindness through a summer of cooking.

Train a child in the way he should go,
and when he is old he will not turn from it.
PROVERBS 22:6

Buy a feeder for hummingbirds and enjoy seeing those delightful birds visiting you this summer.

Irregularities Can Be Gifts

MARTHA B. YODER

Mankind cannot judge the way our Heavenly Father
deals with His creation.

—RAYMOND P. BRUNK

Irregularities can be gifts from a kind God. When God sends
unpleasant curves or the challenge of a handicap into our formerly
settled lives, He also sends gifts of comfort and kindness we can share
with others.

One father of a Down's Syndrome son began a workshop where those
with limited mental abilities could do simple tasks and feel productive.
He also organized and led a support group of interested adults who had
handicapped family members.

Writing of her experiences with depression gave one lady therapeutic
outreach. As a result, she had new opportunities to encourage others as
she corresponded with those who responded to these articles.

One person forced to limit her walking, uses a battery scooter. It
fascinates children and has made her their special friend as she rides
around at their eye level. Making story tapes for the children has widened
her gift of kindness and increased children's affection for her in return.

A young man with speech limitations, along with other minor
irregularities, is very perceptive to children who have handicaps. Parents
of a fretful Down's child were relieved when he asked to hold the child.
Though strangers, they were comforted by his kind gift of "comfort."

An epileptic used his gift of comfort and help by asking to clean the
paint brushes for a volunteer clean-up crew each evening, making the
brushes clean and soft again for their work as they returned to a flood site.

A family with a visible genetic disorder readily shares their gift of love
by explaining the disorder to those who rudely stare and point. In this
way barriers are broken down and self-pity is not allowed to sprout its
ugly seeds.

There is no limit to the ways one can use these gifts of comfort.
Irregularities come to us as painful inconveniences, but Jesus is there to
turn them into His special gifts of comfort to be shared. We can either
consider them cruel punishment from a mean God, or the kind gift
from a loving God who has a plan for good. The former opinion steals

our abundance but the later creates abundance-centered attitudes. Which one will you choose?

> Praise be to the God and Father of our Lord Jesus Christ, the Father of compassion and the God of all comfort, who comforts us in all our troubles, so that we can comfort those in any trouble with the comfort we ourselves have received from God.
>
> 2 CORINTHIANS 1:3-4

> While supervising children in a bathtub, bring in a drawer and clean it out.

June 16

Hospitality

DORTHA EDITH OSBORN

> He was a wealthy man, and kindly to his fellowmen;
> for dwelling by the side of the road,
> he used to entertain all comers.
>
> —HOMER

When I was a new Christian, a widow in our church invited the single women for supper once or twice a month before the midweek meeting. We enjoyed good fellowship around food and read from God's Word after the meal. How much this meant to me as a new believer needing friends and emotional support. She also provided food when someone was ill, for church suppers, and other occasions. She's 85 now, still preparing food for the sick, hosting a meal now and then, and baking her wonderful pecan caramel rolls for special occasions. Now that I've begun to show hospitality on a regular basis, her example has modeled the abundant life of giving to others.

Months ago, while visiting friends in another city, I bemoaned the fragmentation in our church. We were socially close before nearly everyone married and had children. Now the married ones are wrapped up in their own families and activities. As a result, most of us see each other only at meetings, where conversations "on the run" prevail.

My friend suggested I work on a Bible study on hospitality and begin to practice it on a regular basis. I started by working through the Bible study she gave me, praying for the Lord's direction. Now I invite eight or ten people at least once a month for a meal. Through this, new and long-time friends are enjoying each other and fellowshiping in the Lord. I hope it starts a trend among our body of believers.

Hospitality draws lost people to Christ and brings saved people close to Him and each other. It can be inconvenient, and it costs effort, time, and money to prepare and clean-up after meals, or to house people temporarily. But hospitality brings great blessings, especially when we do it in the name of Christ. And He told us to. We may even be entertaining angels unawares (Hebrews 13:2).

When we're feeling lonely or alienated ourselves, it's often a signal to be hospitable to others. Would God like you to share His kindness with others in this way? Instead of waiting for someone else to start, how about you? You may find a new page of abundant living has been turned in the book of your life.

Offer hospitality to one another without grumbling.
Each one should use whatever gift he has received to serve others,
faithfully administering God's grace in its various forms.

I PETER 4:9-10

> Stop trying to be perfect, be joyful instead.

June 17

Pen Pal

SUSAN KIMMEL WRIGHT

He prayeth best, who loveth best
All things both great and small;
For the dear God who loveth us,
He made and loveth all.

—COLERIDGE

Some time ago, an elderly widow in another state fell and broke her hip. She had no children or close family, so it wasn't until a day or so later that someone found and sent her to a nursing home to recuperate. Shortly afterward, I received a note from her nephew. She'd made sure he'd let me know her change of address.

I didn't know her in the usual sense, but I'd been writing to her for some years. She was one of a number of shut-ins I've enjoyed corresponding with, just sending cards, notes, accounts of daily events. Sometimes my penpals write back. Often they're unable to, but that's all right.

It doesn't take much time or money to send a brief note. Occasionally, I enclose a photo or one of my kids' drawings. My reward is knowing that I'm directly touching another life with God's love. It's in realizing how much pleasure there is in receiving mail, especially for folks who are confined most of the time.

Once in a while, my reward comes in the form of a return note. Sometimes, my pen pal will write. Often, the note comes from a relative or health-care aide, letting me know of a hospitalization or surgery or just telling me how appreciated those little notes are.

My elderly friend with the broken hip used to write back to me, letters laboriously hand-pecked on a manual typewriter. Eventually, some time before her fall, the letters had stopped altogether. Her nephew's note told me that she still looked forward to receiving mine.

One day I received another note from her nephew. His aunt had died in her mid-nineties. He said my letters meant so much. It was a simple act of kindness to write them, especially when I didn't write as often as I should have. Still, they were something. I was glad I wrote them.

Who could you show kindness to today through a note or through even becoming a pen pal? It may not seem like much to you, but to them it'll give a burst of abundance.

I tell you the truth, whatever you did for one of the least of these brothers of mine, you did for me.
MATTHEW 25:40B

Choose some of your early blooming flowers for drying. Tie them in bunches and hang them upside down in the garage, barn or basement.

June 18

Responding In Love

MARJORIE K. EVANS

God records every act of service done in His name—even a "cup of water."
—JOHN HASH

One day, while diligently working on a devotional article about God's love, the insistent ringing of the telephone interrupted my thoughts.

Oh, dear, who can that be? I sighed. *I really need to finish this article today so I can read it to the critique group tomorrow and then mail it out.*

The caller was a worker from a local rehabilitation center asking if I'd had a chance to sort any good used clothes or household items since her call of the week before. She again reminded me they were in dire need of clothing and that the truck would pick up items the next day. I apologized for forgetting about her previous call and told her I was too busy to sort over anything that day. Graciously she replied, "I understand. I'll call again."

So I went back to my writing, but ideas refused to come. Suddenly I was conscience-stricken as I thought of Jesus' teaching in Matthew about being kind to those who are needy and thus doing it for him.

Full of remorse, I thought, *How can I write an article about God's love when my life doesn't exhibit love towards those who need help?*

"Forgive me, dear Lord," I prayed in deep repentance. Then I called the rehabilitation center and told them I would have a box ready for the truck the next day.

Peace came as I took time out from writing to fill a large container with clothes. And with the peace came new ideas for the article.

Is there a way you can show God's abundant living today by reaching out to those less fortunate? Your kindness will bless your heart and theirs too.

. . . Lord, when did we see you hungry and feed you, or thirsty and give you something to drink? When did we see you a stranger and invite you in, or needing clothes and clothe you? When did we see you sick or in prison and go to visit you? The King will reply, "I tell you the truth, whatever you did for one of the least of these brothers of mine, you did for me."

MATTHEW 25:37-40

Read *Loving God With All Your Heart*, a compilation of Andrew Murray's writings, by Judith Couchman (Vine Books) 1997.

Asking For Help

JUNE HETZEL

Many hands make light work.
—GRANDMA PLAUGHER

I am part of the fifteen percent of the general population that prefers to work alone, and so I often forget the concept of teamwork. In my mind, I think I am responsible for every aspect of household chores, schoolwork, and business. I tend not to ask for help, but instead, attempt to carry the load alone. Nothing could be more exhausting.

My husband, Geoff, has helped me learn that sharing household duties can be liberating and fun. Geoff often does the grocery shopping, cooking, and/or clean-up for meals. When we first got married, I had some difficulty accepting that he actually wanted to be in the kitchen. I felt obligated to be in the kitchen and fought for control at all times.

Over the last seven years of marriage, I have learned to "let go" and share the joys and challenges of household tasks. I now find that I can come home from a hard day's work and enjoy a meal my husband has cooked. It's okay to take turns with household duties and to deviate from traditional roles. I have also learned to say, "I need help. We are having company tonight, and which part of this list can you do honey?"

Because we all have different gifts and preferences, your household's sharing of tasks will look quite different than mine.

If it's difficult for you to accept the kind help of others, why not say, "Thanks, yes, you may," instead of "No, I can do it." They may not do it the same way you would, but they'll appreciate being involved. Teamwork makes the load light. If we deprive others of the opportunity to share, we're stealing their opportunity for abundant living.

. . . so in Christ we who are many form one body, and each member belongs to all the others. We have different gifts, according to the grace given us . . .
ROMANS 12:5-6

> Consider the truth of this German saying:
> "When one is helping another, both are strong."
> How could you apply it to your day today?

Write That Note

ROBERTA L. MESSNER

Unlike the phone, a letter is never an interruption. A
letter doesn't require immediate attention; it can be
saved for the appropriate time and place and savored.

—ALEXANDRA STODDARD

Nothing quite equals the quiet encouragement of a handwritten
note. Yet many Christians who care deeply about others resist
putting their hearts on paper. The secret to elevating this dreaded task
to a rewarding ritual is convenience and a conviction that your words
can make a difference. Here are some suggestions to help you along:

1. Organize writing materials in a basket, box, or drawer. If you
have to search for a stamp, addresses, or pen every time you get the
notion to scribble a few words, it will likely slip to the bottom of your
never-ending "To Do" list. If you spot the announcement of your
neighbor's 50th anniversary in the newspaper, clip it out and put it
right with your correspondence supplies.

2. Write in a conversational tone. Try penning the words simply, as
if you were talking to that person, rather than resorting to tired clichés.

3. Be specific. Rather than writing, "My thoughts are with you at
this time of sorrow," ask the Lord to help you recall a special memory
that will comfort the bereaved person: "Your dad always sat in the pew
behind our family at church. Every Sunday morning, just as the organist
began her prelude, we could count on him to slip us a roll of cherry
Lifesavers. To this day, I never see a roll of candy without remembering
his giving ways."

4. Never ignore the urge to let someone know you care. It may well
be just the spirit-lifter he or she needs at that moment in their life.

I once dismissed the feeling that I should write a note to a dear
lady who always brought me a chocolate egg with my name on it at
Easter. Having a name like "Roberta" and being one of four children,
it made me feel so special and has prompted me to give similar gifts
as an adult. I thought I'd get around to it someday, but she died
unexpectedly before that nebulous day arrived.

5. Give the gift of a second "Thank You." Has the bread machine
your Aunt Sue gave you for a wedding present greatly simplified your

life? Write her *again* and tell her how your company raved about that loaf of Italian bread.

Your words may never command $77,000.00 at auction like the love letter Abraham Lincoln once penned to his future wife; but your ministry of kindness and encouragement will surely be an investment of eternal significance. Don't wait. Someone is waiting for your signature touch.

Therefore encourage one another, and build each other up . . .
I THESSALONIANS 5:11

> Sometimes the hardest thing to accept is help. It's even harder to ask for it. Think of it as a gift to allow others to be generous.

June 21

A Simple Trip

JOAN CLAYTON

Scars are evidences of great love.
—ANONYMOUS

Our last child had left home. I was really into the "empty nest" syndrome. The empty closets and the quiet house were almost more than I could bear.

"Let's get in the pickup and go for a drive," my husband said, brushing away my tears.

"But I have so many things to do," I protested.

"Do them another time," Emmitt responded.

I reluctantly grabbed my sweater and ran to the pickup.

"Where are we going?" I asked with a despondent air.

"I don't know," Emmitt replied, "but we are going to have some simple fun."

This excited me. I loved it when we didn't make plans and just let life happen.

We headed west. We talked about things on the way and reminisced as we drove through the little town we grew up in.

Before we knew it, we were 75 miles from home. As we approached a lake we'd taken our boys to many times, Emmitt exclaimed: "Let's stop and look around."

I bounded out of the pickup eagerly and said: "Remember when we used to find turtle rocks here when the boys were little?"

"Maybe we can find one now," my adoring husband said as he grabbed my hand.

Then I saw it. This huge, beautiful piece of gnarled white driftwood was scarred from nature and mankind, but its scars only made it all the more beautiful. The bleached white wood reflected in the glistening sunlight.

"I'll get the shovel," Emmitt said noticing the gleam in my eye.

He worked hard to dig that gnarled piece of wood up just for me. He tied it in the back of the pickup and we headed back home.

We stopped and had a hamburger in the little town where we grew up. We even found the tree where Emmitt carved our initials so many years earlier. We sat on the rock wall that surrounded our high school and held hands again.

It was dark when we finally arrived back home. What a wonderful time we had had that day. Now we regularly take time off for unplanned adventures. It has simplified our lives and has brought us so much joy. When Emmitt shows me kindness and says, "Let's go," I leave my work and away we go.

We put our driftwood "treasure" in our front yard. It is still there, reminding us that we can have wonderful, simplifying times just being together, doing little simple things.

When was the last time you left everything behind and went off for a simple adventure? Try it soon.

Therefore, as God's chosen people, holy and dearly loved, clothe yourselves with compassion, kindness, humility, gentleness and patience.
COLOSSIANS 3:12

> When you hear of a hospitalized friend, prelabel several get well cards so that it will be easier to send them.

June 22

Vanity, Oh, Vanity

JUDITH HAYES

Conceit is the finest armor a man or woman can wear.
—ANONYMOUS

*V*anity is a funny thing. I seem to fluctuate between two very opposite attitudes and emotions. One moment I feel a bit superior and self-confident, and the next totally insecure and intimidated by another woman's beauty. As a young woman, I tended to judge other women by their "cover," but as an older, and hopefully wiser woman, I've learned life and human beings are much more complex than mere outward appearances.

I have a friend who is very cute, petite, slender, and dresses like a Barbie doll. I am, conversely, fairly tall, round and curvy, and wear whatever I can find that adapts well to my bumps and curves.

Ever since I met my petite bubbly friend, I have felt a bit envious of her. Then one day she invited me to share a room together at a weekend women's retreat. While there, I learned some valuable and unforgettable lessons. I soon discovered that my friend and roommate maintained her slim girlish figure through bulimia. I also learned that her pretty smile was made up of a full set of dentures. My friend also shared her make-up tips with me, and I soon discovered she was not the "natural" auburn-haired Barbie doll I had presumed. Suddenly, all of my lumps, curves and imperfections didn't seem so bad after all.

Realizing that my friend was real, human, and flawed just like me taught me a good lesson. I was not less, nor was my friend more. We are both imperfect human beings living in an imperfect world. I also learned that I can never again judge a book or a person by their "cover." It is just that—something that is used to protect, conceal, or hide whatever is underneath.

Could it be that you've hesitated to be kind to others because they have intimidated you in some way through their "cover?" Share the abundance within you by reaching out to them. They may be more needy than you think.

. . . The Lord does not look at the things man looks at.
Man looks at the outward appearance, but the Lord looks at the heart.
I SAMUEL 16:7

One of the greatest gifts you can give is a compliment. Give one today.

Mama T

CORA LEE PLESS

A faithful friend is an image of God.

—FRENCH PROVERB

She swept into the house, blown by the wind of love.

My father-in-law had died that morning and Alice Templeton, a long-time friend of the family, was one of the first to be notified. Now, only hours later, she had driven the distance to be with us.

"Well, it didn't take you long to get here," someone said with a smile.

"As soon as I heard, I picked up a few things and out the door I went," Alice stated.

She plopped a shopping bag onto the kitchen table and like a modern-day Mary Poppins, began pulling things from it.

First came a pack of trash bags.

"You always need these," she said.

Then came a box of tissues, already opened. "Picked this up on my way out the door."

Finally, she reached into the depths of the bag and pulled out a six-pack—of toilet tissue. "You tend to forget about getting toilet paper at a time like this," she declared. "And I sure didn't want to run out of it."

Alice stayed for several days, doing those things she thought needed to be done. As we greeted people at the funeral home, Alice brought peppermint candy to soothe our dry throats and stood guard over my mother-in-law to keep her seated and off her feet.

She entertained and loved our kids who were soon calling her by her grandmother name, "Mama T." She took my dad to the church and looked after Aunt Sadie who was confined to a wheelchair.

Throughout those days, she reminded us that Christians have joy even at a time of death. Alice lifted many burdens, and she did it all with a smile.

My young daughter summed up our feelings as she confided to me, "I really like that 'Mama T' person."

Through simple acts of kindness and words of courage, Alice brought love, compassion, and hope into our world during those difficult days. Even after she had left, the sunshine of love that surrounded her remained, giving abundance to our lives.

How can you reach out in kindness when others are hurting? Or maybe you need to receive someone's kindness in your time of hurting. Both will allow God's abundance to be seen by many.

Carry each other's burdens, and in this way you will fulfill the law of Christ.
GALATIANS 6:2

> People in grief seldom have the energy or inclination to care for their home. Give the gift of a clean house as a labor of love to someone in need.

June 24

In The Midst Of My Reality

COLLEEN FRAIOLI

God works best in the middle of chaos.
—ANONYMOUS

There is an unsolved mystery in our home—a natural phenomena that occurs between 4 and 7 p.m. Just the other day while meditating on a casserole recipe, it hit. Like "The Bermuda Triangle," my kitchen and family room jumped into another dimension.

All of the possible variables converged: PMS, low blood sugar, diaper aversion. Why it came as a surprise, I don't know. Perhaps it's like the frog in the kettle coming to a slow boil, never noticing until it's too late.

The scenario began slowly with the usual whining and complaining, shortly followed by arguing and accusing. I felt sucked in by a force bigger than myself. The noise level grew. I checked-out.

I slid down the counter and onto the floor while my offspring ran amok. I tried to focus: A naked two-year-old. Pots and pans banging out war cries. Kids shrieking. The dog brandishing a dirty diaper.

Sensing my powerless state, the mutiny gained momentum, growing from bedlam to hostile takeover in seconds. Experiencing newfound liberation, the children shrieked "I just can't wait to be king."

Still sitting on the floor in the kitchen, two impulses came to me: *I could either have my nervous break-down now, or I could run.*

At the peak of insanity, I tried something different—I prayed.

"God, right here, right now, I need you. I'd like to see what you can do in the middle of this chaos."

Then the thought came to me: *Wait a minute, I'm the mom here. How did I become the helpless victim?*

With a surge of power I leaped up, snapped off the TV, kicked the dog out, disposed the dirty diaper, grabbed the pots and pans, and pinned the kids to the couch. I informed them that their behavior was unacceptable and they would be spending time in their rooms until Mommy regains composure.

Picking up the fragments of my family room, I mentally surveyed the damage. All inclinations toward denial fled. I admitted to myself that the kids ruled and I had let them. I confessed my expectations: a continual state of tranquillity; a stress-free life. Unreality. Especially with a two-year-old. I asked God for the power to deal with my reality and establish patterns of order rather than reacting to whatever the day brings.

That day became my turning point.

I began to strategize. By analyzing my routine, I saw modifications I could make that changed the entire outcome of the day (like preparing casseroles in the morning). I committed to being more kind but firm in following through with consequences for disobedience.

I figured if God created the world out of chaos in three days, establishing order in my home shouldn't take too much longer.

Tranquillity? Not necessarily, but my home is now characterized by order the majority of the time and more kindness as I'm not feeling so out of control. Most of all, afternoons are no longer an unsolved mystery.

If you're the mom of young kids and find your abundant life is running out the door because of the chaos inside, evaluate how it happens and what needs to change. Then you'll turn chaos into kindness and abundance will again feel welcome in your home.

She is clothed with strength and dignity; she can laugh at the days to come.
PROVERBS 31:25

For a good laugh, read the book, *How Do You Want Your Room . . . Plain or Padded?* by Jo Ann Larsen & Artemus Cole.

Sixty-Six Words

MARGARET PRIMROSE

To be a Christian without prayer is no more possible
than to be alive without breathing.
—MARTIN LUTHER

The Lord's Prayer is short and simple—only 66 words. We can repeat it in 25 seconds or less. Yet now and then it is good to ask ourselves if we are really *praying* or just *saying* the well-known phrases of the Lord's Prayer:

Our Father, who art in heaven, Hallowed be Thy name. At the offset, it is good to notice that this is a prayer for "us" and "our," not just "me" and "mine." When we think about who He is—our Father—and where He lives—in heaven—how could we not say, "Hallowed be Thy name? How could we not praise Him for who He is and what He does for us?

Thy will be done. How many of us have said this with a whine? I have. Sometimes, though, I remember a college professor who said, "Pray 'Thy will be done' with the ring of a victor in your voice." If His will be best for us, and it is, why shouldn't we make sure we are ready to accept whatever God has for us?

Give us this day our daily bread. Glasses won't help us if we are so far-sighted we can only focus on tomorrow, next week, or next year. We can only become more near-sighted by drawing closer to the Lord. That may keep us from asking for "chocolate cake with thick icing" when all we actually need is a slice of toast.

Forgive us our trespasses, our debts, our sins, our shortcomings or however else it may be translated. It has all fit us at times.

As we forgive. The Lord did not tell us to excuse sin—that is spineless—but He can give us the backbone to forgive sin whether we feel like it or not.

Deliver us from evil. Once we have experienced His forgiveness, asking for grace to overcome the things that led to our downfall should be a priority.

How grateful we can be that God is not unrealistic in His demands of our prayers. He provided a simple—yet effective—model for prayer. And we can take longer than 25 seconds if we need to—to say those 66 simple words from the heart. The abundant life comes from saying the Lord's Prayer once *from* the heart rather than a thousand times *by* heart.

You will seek me and find me when you seek me with all your heart.
JEREMIAH 29:13

Read *Prayer* by Richard J. Foster (Harper Collins)
1992.

June 26

A Poem Ministry

NANETTE THORSEN-SNIPES

> There never was any heart truly great and generous,
> that was not also tender and compassionate.
>
> —ROBERT FROST

In April of 1981, my two sisters and I were no longer members of a church. When my mother passed away, the Lord surrounded me with His grace and love in a very powerful way. It was as though His arms embraced me, His wandering child, and kept me safe.

After another tragedy a couple of years later, I made a conscious decision to serve the Lord again. With the blessing of the Lord still refreshing my soul, I began to feel His urging to write poems for those in pain. I wanted to comfort them just as the Lord had so graciously comforted me.

Once, I gave a framed poem to the mother of a young woman who was ill with kidney disease. She gave it to her daughter who placed it beside her bed. In time, I lost track of mother and daughter. During the years that passed, I gave framed poetry to many people; some of whom I knew but many I did not.

One day I was working with my friend, Barbara, when she received the news that a friend of hers had died from kidney disease. After the call, she related the story, and I discovered it was the daughter of the woman to whom I'd given a poem several years before.

Barbara attended the memorial service the following day. Later, she called me and said, "The minister read your poem at Renita's service." I was saddened by the loss of this young woman I'd met only a couple of times. At the same time I felt humbled and honored that she wanted the poem read. God, in His infinite wisdom, allowed my poem to bring comfort not only to Renita while she was alive, but to those who mourned her passing.

You may not be able to write poetry but God can guide you to some form of compassion and kindness to help others. He wants all of us to extend His hand of love and comfort because that's an important part of the abundant life.

He who oppresses the poor shows contempt for their Maker,
but whoever is kind to the needy honors God.
PROVERBS 14:31

Remember the mothers who are also "fathers" this month. Invite them to spend Father's Day with your family for dinner.

June 27

Doers Of The Word

MARJORIE K. EVANS

Do all the good you can, By all the means you can,
In all the ways you can, In all the places you can,
At all the times you can, To all the people you can,
As long as ever you can.

—JOHN WESLEY

One Saturday morning my friend, Gloria, called and said, "Marge, I'll come by in an hour, and we'll go to the store."

Alone, and the sole support of my baby and my little boy, it was difficult for me to do the weekly grocery shopping without a car. But it was also hard to accept Gloria's generosity and kindness week after week, for I was not used to receiving help from others.

Later, as we unloaded the groceries, I said, "Gloria, thank you so much. I wish there were some way I could pay you for gasoline and for times you baby-sit for me."

"Marge," she replied, "don't even think about paying me. It's a joy to be able to help you and your children. Someday your circumstances will improve. Then you can help someone else. Just pass it on."

Through the years I've remembered Gloria's remarks. And, as my circumstances improved, and I "passed it on" to others, I realized that not only had I been fortunate in accepting Gloria's kindness, but that she, too had been blessed. Both of us learned what our Lord meant when He said, *It is more blessed to give than to receive* (Acts 20:35).

As she and others helped me in my time of need, they experienced the abundant life of being not just a hearer, but a "doer." Now I'm inspired to be a "doer."

You, too, can be a "doer." Here are suggestions.

• Send cards to sick or bereaved neighbors, fellow employees, and people at church.

• Think of new and creative ways to let your husband, your children, and your parents know you love and appreciate them.

• Call friends who are discouraged. Let them know you are thinking about and praying for them. Invite them over for coffee or tea.

• Take people without a car to church, the store, the doctor, or wherever they need to go.

• Prepare a meal for someone ill or just home from the hospital.

• Baby-sit without pay for a young couple or single parents.

• Include single parents and their youngsters when you and your family go on outings.

• Invite lonely neighbors over for lunch or supper.

• Read the Bible to older people who have trouble reading.

• Take flowers, a pot of soup, or a bowl of fruit to elderly neighbors or shut-ins.

• Invite single, widowed, or lonely people to spend holidays with you and your family.

I'm sure you can think of many additional ways of kindness in which you can help friends, neighbors, and acquaintances. As you ask the Lord to make you more sensitive to others' needs, you'll become a "doer." And you'll experience "joy unspeakable and full of glory—" the abundant life.

Do not merely listen to the word, and so deceive yourselves. Do what it says.
JAMES 1: 22

> To each of us, God has given a talent—share yours today.

Kindness To The Rescue

JULIE MARIE CAROBINI

No act of kindness, no matter how small, is ever wasted.

—AESOP

*R*ecently my mother planted herself in the nineties and purchased a cellular phone—for emergencies, of course. Thankfully, flat tires in the middle of nowhere are rare in our family, but that doesn't mean Mom's cell phone never gets used. In fact, on this particular occasion, her call could not have come at a better time.

"I'm in the vegetable aisle at the grocery store," she whispered into the tiny phone. "Can I get you anything while I'm here?"

"Oh, would you?" I answered. The next morning I needed to send snacks to my son's preschool class. I had planned to stop at the supermarket that evening but Mom's offer was too good to pass up.

Later that day, my phone began ringing over and over again. As the Wednesday night Service Coordinator for my church's children's ministry, it's my responsibility to provide enough volunteer teachers. For some unforeseen reason, four out of six teachers canceled at the last minute. Suddenly, my relaxed evening turned chaotic as I searched for last minute substitutes and I would need to be one of them.

The toddlers I cared for that evening were precious, but busy, busy, busy. By the end of the evening, all I wanted to do was flop into bed.

It occurred to me then that Mom had really saved me from further stress. Her simple phone call, made on a whim, relieved me from having to stop at the store after a very full day.

Everybody's life is chaotic at times and in need of a "stress buster." Wouldn't life be more abundant for everyone if we all followed those inner urgings to be kind to a friend or family member, as my mom did on that day?

Do not withhold good from those who deserve it, when it is in your power to act.
PROVERBS 3:27

> Is there a particular act of generosity that was a blessing to you? Give to to someone else.

Smiley Face Pancakes

INA GESELL

Those who bring sunshine to the lives of others cannot keep it from themselves.

—JAMES M. BARRY

*H*ow about a special weekend breakfast that's easy, your kids will remember forever, and you probably have the ingredients in your kitchen right now? Want to make your kids smile at breakfast? How can they avoid smiling when their food is smiling back at them?

Why not start the weekend with a smile with Smiley Face Pancakes? They're so easy, they take very little extra time, and the kids love them.

Use the pancakes batter you usually do, but get the griddle hot. Take a teaspoon and drizzle two dots of pancake batter for eyes and a curvy line for a smile on the griddle.

Then pour the quarter cup of pancake batter over that to complete the pancake. The eyes and smile brown first and stand out on the face of the pancake when you flip it over, to the absolute delight of the kids.

If you want to experiment, you can also write a short name on the pancake, or a short message, like "I Love You," but you have to remember to do it mirror image. That's a fun challenge for you, but the kids will "eat it up."

How can a weekend that begins with so much simple fun not continue to be an abundantly fun weekend? The kids will tuck it away in their memory banks. Mine did. And there isn't a simpler way to tempt a smile at breakfast time.

He will yet fill your mouth with laughter . . .

JOB 8:21

Family time around the kitchen table is always time well spent.

Unexpected Gifts

ELAINE NAVARRO

> God, give us grace to accept with serenity the things that
> cannot be changed, courage to change the things which
> should be changed, and the wisdom to distinguish the one
> from the other.
>
> —DR. REINHOLD NIEBUHR

This verse from "The Serenity Prayer" arrived in some mail early one morning. Every day the mail includes unsolicited items. Angel pins, cards, requests for donations, and calendars are just a few of the items that show up each year.

As Christians, we strive to have the kind heart of Christ. Even so, what should one do in the face of such an abundance?

Here are some satisfying solutions.

• When the mailbox is overflowing with requests for money, I pick the familiar charities and send my donation to them. I pray for the remaining organizations and those they represent, to know the abundance of God.

• Since there is no obligation to pay for what is unsolicited, I enjoy those that I can use, such as name labels. It's been months since I've had to write a return address on an envelope.

• Some unsolicited items come just at the right time, as if divinely inspired. The quote by Dr. Reinhold Niebuhr, for example, came at a time when I had difficult decisions to make. I was uplifted by it and inspired to send back a donation to its point of origin.

Since kindness is one of our fruit of abundance, we don't want to be unkind as we respond to so many requests. But since we can't give to each one, we must obey God in what He wants us to and then trust that He'll provide for the remaining needs He finds worthy. Out of His abundance, He will provide.

For I testify that they gave as much as they were able, and even beyond their ability . . .
2 CORINTHIANS 8:3

A favorite childhood pastime is daydreaming. Allow yourself this pleasure today. Dreams are a gift from God.

July

"*And let us not lose heart in doing good, for in due time we shall reap if we do not grow weary.*"

Galatians 6:9

In the midst of this summer month, we celebrate our country's birth. God is good toward us in blessing us with such a wonderful country. But this month, we'll concentrate on more than that blessing; we'll focus on doing and being good. It's really about making wise choices. The more we have a simple dependence upon God, knowing He asks us to obey His loving commands, the more we'll experience an abundant life.

Porch Sitters

RUTH M. RINK

Lost: Yesterday, somewhere between sunrise and sunset, two golden hours, each set with sixty diamond minutes. No reward is offered, for they are gone forever.

—HORACE MANN

This is the beginning of a new month, July. And with it comes the heat of summer and hopefully, being good to ourselves with vacation and added leisure time. And what could be more leisurely than sitting on a porch visiting with family, friends or neighbors. Will you reminisce with me about those glorious years when houses had spacious, winding porches and families used them from early spring through long summer days and lengthening evenings? Can you hear the faintly sad chirp of the crickets? The not-so-pleasant hum of mosquitoes? Can you picture the flashing of lightening bugs with their lanterns darting here and there?

I smell the fragrance of climbing roses on the porch trellis. If I listen carefully, I can hear again the voices of children playing hide and seek and calling out "Ali-ali out in free" and demanding calls of mothers getting louder and louder as their shouts go unheeded. The pleading "Aw, just a few minutes more, Mom" drifts back to my ears.

My parents' home, shaded by maple trees and a haven from the world, sat back from the street sufficiently to offer privacy from curious passers-by. I remember times of being bone-weary and sinking into the arms of our porch glider and giving over to its comfort and restoration. Ah, the sheer ecstasy of it.

One of the joys of porch-sitting was the contact with neighbors. The family directly across the street was especially enlivening as they called back and forth, teasing and friendly. Two neighbors had a standing rivalry over their tomato raising, going to such lengths as tying ripe tomatoes on the vines earlier than the other's tomatoes could ripen.

Is porch-sitting a forgotten joy, a custom lost to future generations? Frank Trippert, an essayist for *Time*, summed it up best when he wrote that air conditioning has "seduced families into retreating into houses with closed doors and shut windows, reducing the commonality of neighborhood life and all but making obsolete the society whose open, casual folkways were an appealing hallmark of a sweatier America."

Indeed, would *Gone With the Wind* have had the same sex appeal if Scarlet were sitting inside next to a humming air conditioner rather than flirting and fanning herself out on the verandah? I think not.

However, as I drive through new developments, I am heartened to see many new homes displaying winding porches. Probably the change has come from the desire of more and more people to get back to nature, seeking the elemental life with its values of the past. Whatever the reason, I am grateful that present and future generations will not be denied the neighborliness of porch sitting.

Why not be good to yourself and enjoy a session of porch sitting?

Be devoted to one another in brotherly love.

ROMANS 12:10A

Even if you don't have a porch, surprise your neighbors by sitting in a chair in your front yard and greeting them as they drive by.

July 2

Good Giving

BILL AND PAM FARREL

I do not believe one can settle how much we ought to give. I am afraid the only safe rule is to give more than we can spare.

—C.S. LEWIS

*A*re you frustrated because you cannot give as much money as you would like to the causes you think are important? Do you wish you could give more to your local church? Have you felt empty because you couldn't help someone in need? Do you feel, at the same time, a pressure to increase your standard of living with each increase in pay?

One man committed himself to God to give a certain percentage of his income as long as he lived. From his first week's pay he gave $1 to the Lord. Soon his weekly offering had increased to $10. As time went on, he continued to prosper. Before long he was giving $100 a week, then $200, and in time $500 a week. This process started out as an intense joy, as he felt his hard work was making life better for many people. But after a while he found himself in conflict. He began to think that it was, after all, his money, and that he shouldn't be giving away so much. Finally he called a close friend.

"You remember the promise I made to God years ago? How can I get released? When I made the promise, I only had to give a dollar, but now it's $500. I can't afford to give away money like that."

His wise friend said, "I'm afraid you cannot get a release from the promise, but there is something we can do. We can kneel down and ask God to shrink your income so that you can afford to give a dollar again."

Seek to live a life that enables you to give to others and to the causes you believe in. Money is a cruel master. If it dominates your decisions in life, you may find yourself struggling with discontent, jealousy or simply the continual search for more wealth or possessions. If, on the other hand, you are able to discipline your financial life so that you can give, you will find joy and freedom.

At the present time your plenty will supply what they need, so that in turn their plenty will supply what you need. Then there will be equality.
2 CORINTHIANS 8:14

The next time you have an opportunity to give, show your gratitude for God's goodness by giving just a little more than you normally would.

July 3

A Church In The Wild Woods

PAT VERBAL

Who builds a church within his heart
And takes it with him everywhere
Is holier far than he whose church
Is but a one-day house of prayer.

—MORRIS ABEL BEER

Does your family like to camp? Well, mine sure did. I should say my father did. At least, I thought he did. Actually, I learned later in life that it wasn't that my parents liked to camp so much; it was that we didn't have enough money for motels. (I also thought my mom liked picnics.)

Every time we arrived at a new campsite, my parents let us know that "out of the goodness of their hearts," they would give us kids a very important job to do. We had to scout out the area for just the right spot to have church. Since our parents agreed to meet anywhere we selected, we took our responsibility very seriously. It had to be the most beautiful, most inspirational, most adventurous spot in the whole territory.

We rarely failed to satisfy our own expectations—or those of our parents. We had church in caves way up the sides of purple mountains. We had church on huge logs extending over rushing white rapids. We crossed pastures to meet near herds of cows and found ripe blackberry patches where we could snack during worship.

The curious thing was that while we thought we were leading our parents on a wild-goose chase to far-off places, we were always eager to have church while we were out camping. There was none of this "Oh, no, why do we have to have church on our vacation?" No, when we all got in semi-comfortable seats and Dad began to read from the Bible, the nature surrounding us became holier. And when Mom started a song in her low alto voice, the streams and birds seemed to join us in worship. The wind and the swaying trees echoed God's majesty.

Each spot was somehow anointed. It was always perfect. Our parents praised us for picking such a special place to worship. Sometimes we camped with family friends. Then we had to show other kids how to pick out the spot. They would say, "Wait a minute. My mom will never climb up there." But when it came time for church, everyone always did.

I'm glad I have worshipped in some of the most beautiful sanctuaries in the world . . . while sleeping in a tent. I never realized how God was using my parents' "goodness" to draw us closer to God. Parents—and God—sure can be clever. And actually, goodness is always meant for our *good*, anyway.

. . . Burst into song, you mountains, you forests and all your trees . . .
ISAIAH 44:23

The next time you vacation, ask your children to pick out the spot for worship—even if it's in a city.

Our Adopted Country

MARY LOU KLINGLER

Men and nations sink or soar, survive or perish, as
they choose to be dominated by sin or righteousness.
— A.P. GOUTHEY

God has given us a good gift in our country. Today is the anniversary of our country's birth. Since men and women fought for our independence and won it, thousands have come from other countries to enjoy God's goodness here. In 1819, a two-year-old girl named Jane Dupre, came with her family to America on a ship from France seeking religious freedom.

The family settled in Chillicothe, Ohio, which was the state capitol at that time. Jane's father found work and established residence for three years; then he applied for citizenship to this wonderful country. Evenings he studied the history and government of America and was ready to be questioned.

When the day came for Papa Dupre to take his oath of loyalty, Jane begged, "Papa, I want to go, too!"

Papa smiled at his five-year-old daughter and agreed she could go.

They went to the capitol grounds where the court was held. Jane watched, not missing anything. Papa said, "It's a rule we have to take off our shoes and stand barefooted on American soil to take our oath of loyalty."

Jane unbuttoned her shoes and slipped them off just like Papa. As Papa made his oath, Jane held his left hand and he raised his right hand as he pledged to be true to America, his adopted country, and to swear to give up his loyalty to the country that he came from.

Papa and his family were now citizens of the United States.

Jane lived to be 106 years old but never forgot that special day when she and Papa stood, barefoot, on American soil, to become a part of their adopted country.

The United States and Canada have welcomed immigrants from all parts of the world. These people have brought new skills, ideas, different foods, music, and religions to our country. North America is a nation of immigrants.

Some people are unwilling to accept new aliens, but we must

remember that we are all descendants of immigrants. Being a good citizen means we should help others and welcome them as we would like to be welcomed.

For the Christian, even though we enjoy our freedom here, our citizenship is in Heaven. Though we love our homeland and do all we can to make it better, we have something better to look forward to.

> *But our citizenship is in heaven. And we eagerly await a*
> *Savior from there, the Lord Jesus Christ.*
>
> PHILIPPIANS 3:20

Make a study of your ancestors and discover your roots.

July 5

Setting Goals

ROBERT SCHULLER

You are smarter today than you have ever been before.
—ROBERT SCHULLER

*B*efore you set goals, begin to potentialize by opening your mind to real creativity.

Ask yourself these questions:

· What would I try to do if I knew I might succeed?
· What goals would I set if I knew I could not fail?
· What price am I willing to pay?
· What sacrifices am I willing to make?
· Would I be willing to move?
· Where would I go?
· What if I changed vocations?
· What could I do?
· Where could I go?
· What could I become?

Write the answers DOWN. Do it NOW! You'll feel better about yourself.

> *It is not good to have zeal without knowledge,*
> *nor to be hasty and miss the way.*
>
> PROVERBS 19:2

July 6

The Cellular Phone Reminder

ED HORTON

You don't need to work harder, you need to work smarter.

—ANONYMOUS

Recently I enjoyed an evening of good music at the elementary school where my wife teaches. Moms and dads, grandparents, and invited guests packed the audience. I relaxed as the director waved her arms, leading the children in a familiar song.

Chirrrrrp . . . Chirrrrrp.

A muffled warbling sound interrupted my listening.

Glancing around, I spotted a young woman dressed in a navy business suit, extracting a cellular telephone from her purse. Although several people chuckled as she fumbled with the contraption, the device's aggravating chirp distracted many of us. The young executive answered and then whispered for several minutes.

"Did you have to call now? My daughter's class is about to sing," she said. However, instead of hanging up, she continued the annoying murmur while she rummaged through her handbag in search of pad and pencil.

A third grade class entered the platform and took their place on the risers. I wondered if one of the children belonged to the cell phone lady. It didn't take long to get an answer.

The exuberant children searched the audience for familiar faces. One little girl caught my attention. Her face reflected dejection as she eyed her mother busily scribbling and talking, oblivious to her presence on the stage. The child lost her enthusiasm for performing.

This incident reminded me to keep my priorities centered on the things that matter most—God, family, career. I work smarter when I confess my weaknesses. If I allow God's power to flow through me, He will strengthen those weak points and help me to focus on Him.

There are times when I need to realign my priorities before I clearly communicate with God and those around me. Like the young woman with the cell phone, I can get so caught up in the successes and challenges of a busy career that I ignore doing good to the people who are of greater importance. If I seek God with my whole heart, He provides the strength of character and wisdom I need to keep things in perspective.

The other morning a coworker told me she had arrived at the office before 5:00 on a Monday morning.

"Why were you here so early?" I asked.

"To catch up on a few things," she said. "I had planned to come in Saturday and work for several hours. As I was getting ready to leave, my eight-year-old son reminded me that it was his birthday. I was embarrassed that I'd forgotten. I changed my plans and spent the day with him."

I'm glad my friend showed goodness to her son by valuing him above her career. Let's all seek abundant simple living by asking God to show us if we're aligning our priorities incorrectly.

Then you will call upon me and come and pray to me, and I will listen to you.
You will seek me and find me when you seek me with all your heart.
JEREMIAH 29:12-13

Take that important person in your life out for an ice cream cone tonight.

July 7

Vacation Choices

JOY P. GAGE

Life is like money. You can spend it anyway you like,
but you can spend it only once.

—ANONYMOUS

Have you ever wished for more vacation dollars so that you could take that "dream vacation"? Our family learned that planning such a vacation is not always a matter of making more money. Sometimes it's a matter of making good choices.

We had two daughters in high school when we began planning a European trip. From the start, it was a family project. For fifteen months we poured over copies of *The National Geographic*, Eurail schedules, and Arthur Frommer's budget guide to European vacations.

Our budget for the trip divided itself into three major items: the charter air fare to Europe, Eurail passes for travel in Europe, and the per day amount suggested by Arthur Frommer for meals and lodging.

We faced a major challenge, for there was little money from our regular source of income to cover such a trip. One daughter, who was working full time during her last semester of high school, paid her own way. The other saved all her spending money. Book royalties covered all expenses for one person. Making tough choices enabled us to pay for the two remaining persons.

One of the lasting benefits of the experience was the opportunity to teach our daughters a practical lesson on making choices. "We have a choice here," we explained. "For the price of a color television, one person can go to Europe. For the price of the cheapest used car we can find, another person can go to Europe. We can buy a new television and we can look into a second car, or we can go to Europe. But we can't do both."

We have never been sorry that we made the necessary choices in order to take our European vacation. The benefits of our trip far outweighed the sacrifices. We saw tears in the eyes of our teenagers as we visited the home of Ann Frank. We experienced a sobering day long visit to Dachau. We viewed the great art treasures at the Rijks museum. And we remember two weary teenagers falling asleep in the Louvre as we waited for our tour to begin.

Most of all, we remember how our girls learned through the experience that the Gages didn't have to spend their money like everyone else. We could make our own choices. As we made those good choices, our daughters also learned a cold hard fact. You can spend your money anyway you like, but you can spend it only once. Seeking a simple abundance will result in wise spending decisions.

Be very careful, then, how you live—not as unwise but as wise,
making the most of every opportunity, because the days are evil.
EPHESIANS 5:15-16

You may not be able to go to Europe, but there may be a traveling museum of art from Europe. Visit a museum this summer.

Compensations

CAROLE MAYHALL

> People are lonely because they build walls instead of
> bridges.
>
> —JOSEPH FORT NEWTON

God leads two people together so one can compensate for the other's weaknesses. If we are not giving the good gift of listening to the person who loves us the most, has our best interests at heart, and is in the best position to see our faults, sins, and inadequacies, then we can be weakened by several deficiencies.

First, we will not be "sharpened" by that relationship as God intended.

Second, our prayers could be hindered. Peter cautions husbands in I Peter 3:7: *Husbands, in the same way be considerate as you live with your wives, and treat them with respect as the weaker partner and as heirs with you of the gracious gift of life, so that nothing will hinder your prayers.* In verse 8 he sums up by exhorting "all" to be harmonious, sympathetic, loving, kind-hearted, and humble. How can our married lives be harmonious and kind, how can we be truly good for them, if we do not *listen* to our partner? And if we are not understanding, God says our very communication with Him might be hindered.

And third, we might end up a nervous wreck. Living with someone twenty-four hours a day who disagrees with you about important issues will affect your physical, mental, or emotional health.

Finally, we may miss out on the complete will of God for our lives.

If we are listening in order to understand—or *heart-hearing*—we will be able to put ourselves in the other's shoes and take into serious consideration that person's thoughts and feelings in making decisions. Tragically, some Christian men feel that if they have simply listened to their wife's words, then they have adequately considered her viewpoint. Then they go ahead and make decisions independently.

Listening, according to *Webster*, means "to make a conscious effort to hear; attend closely;" but the second meaning is, "to give heed; take advice."

God calls us to be one in marriage. Some husbands know that, but somehow think *they* are the "one." Oneness means a lot of things, but certainly it means to be intertwined both in heart and in mind.

Therefore, agreement on major decisions is essential before action is taken. If that's done, we know we're making the simple, wise decision that will bring good for all concerned.

Do two walk together unless they have agreed to do so?

AMOS 3:3

> As you look back on your marriage or relationship with a friend, how has God used a difference in your personalities to bring about something good? Write a note about it, thanking him or her for it.

July 9

Pruning Life

SUSAN KIMMEL WRIGHT

A tree has significance if one sees it against the empty face of sky. A note in music gains significance from the silences on either side.

—ANNE MORROW LINDBERGH

"You'll be sorry," our friends said when we mentioned driving across the country to visit my brother-in-law in Colorado. "Kansas never ends."

Our friends were in a hurry. They'd seen the plains from the interstate and now preferred ignoring them from the air.

We saw Kansas from the ground, driving those roads that slice across farmland and somehow miss the shopping malls and industrial parks. To a child of the Pennsylvania mountains—forever hugging, like an effusive aunt—Kansas had an aloof, unearthly beauty.

For days on the road we rolled across the flat treeless acres, passing corn spread like an open bolt of fabric, soybeans, and sunflowers. Miles away, a pickup truck approached, stirring up dust on a narrow side road. At night, our headlights picked out a jackrabbit, racing soundlessly ahead of us, arrow-straight into saturated darkness.

Day by day my vision lengthened. Eyes straining ahead, I could almost see buffalo, a Ute encampment, cavalry on horseback, a lurching line of covered wagons. I could almost see the Rocky Mountains and the ocean beyond.

Late one evening, we drove into the endless sunset while an

electrical storm played along the southern horizon. Our radio picked up a program of classical guitar music and we drove for hours. Andres Segovia filled our ears while the lightning danced beside us and the sky ahead stormed through rose and gold before sinking into amethyst and peach.

Back home, my world is crowded again. Like Anne Morrow Lindbergh, it grieves me to realize my daily life "lacks this quality of significance and therefore of beauty, because there is so little empty space. The space has been scribbled on; the time has been filled." I need to prune my engagements, to turn off the TV and listen to the silence.

Whether or not you plan to take a cross-country trip, be good to yourself with plans for a simple life during this summer month. How could you make life less complicated, even today?

Be still and know that I am God.

PSALM 46:10A

> What fun thing this summer have you been delaying until your schedule "opens up?" Make plans now to do it.

July 10

Think On These Things

NANCY E. PETERSON

The music in my heart I bore, long after it was heard
no more.

—HENRY WORDSWORTH

Here's a Christian twist to the subliminal tapes you see advertised, and it has brought goodness into our family. If you want constant positive input in your life, keep Christian CD's or tapes playing in your home. The ones we prefer are contemporary Christian and Jewish Messianic mixed in with the old stand-by's like "Rock of Ages" and "It Is Well." The variety keeps us from getting bored with the music and, at least some of it appeals to each of us. My husband prefers the older works while I prefer the Jewish Messianic sound. We also have a teen so we try to make sure things he likes are on the CD changer. We put it on "shuffle" and "repeat" and let it go all the time from first thing in the morning until bedtime. It's really hard to be cruel, sinful, or snippy toward each other when you have God's Word being sung in the background.

My husband and I each drive a lot so we enjoy the music in the car, too. It's funny how the long drives turn from boring to peaceful when God's music is playing. It especially helps when someone cuts us off during our commutes. We're a little more inclined to be good to our enemies by not getting angry.

You might be too if you surround yourself with music that draws your thoughts closer to the Lord.

Speak to one another with psalms, hymns and spiritual songs.
Sing and make music in your heart to the Lord, always giving thanks to
God the Father for everything, in the name of our Lord Jesus Christ.
EPHESIANS 5:19-20

Be adventurous. Buy some new Christian music in a style that you don't usually listen to. Give it a fair try before passing it along to someone else.

July II

Morning And Evening Rhythms

JAN JOHNSON

Those who have the gale of the Holy Spirit go forward, even in sleep.

— BROTHER LAWRENCE

Abiding in Christ develops a rhythm of its own more easily when propelled by morning and evening patterns. Donald G. Bloesch writes, "Luther suggested that prayer should be 'the first business of the morning and the last at night.' He advised: 'Cultivate the habit of falling asleep with the Lord's Prayer on your lips every evening when you go to bed and again every morning when you get up. And if occasion, place, and time permit, pray before you do anything else.'"

A word of caution about respecting one's body rhythms is appropriate. Plenty of us who are night people wake up slowly, and we have felt undue guilt that we don't think about God when awakening. Instead, we may need to ooze into the day with a simple acknowledgment of God's presence. As the morning unfolds, we can offer to the Lord the day's schedule—the scary risks, the emotional stretches, the boring tasks: "Every morning I lay out the pieces of my life on your altar and watch for fire to descend."

The quiet moments before sleep are an ideal time to ask, "Where was God in this day?" This is also a time to resonate with gratitude on the day, recalling tasks, welcoming smiles, or delightful stories told. We can thank God for God, and His unending companionship throughout the day.

Instead of feeling guilty if we "fall asleep on God," we can count it as a credit that God can bring rest. Words from hymns and worship songs may play in our thoughts through the night and continue their rhythm when we awaken.

The Lord replied, "My Presence will go with you, and I will give you rest."
EXODUS 33:14

> As you fall asleep tonight, be meditating on your favorite Bible verse.

July 12

Satisfying Life

JEAN FLEMING

It's about time we gave up all this theological grand
opera and went back to practicing the scales.
— VAN HAVNER

Our attempts to control and regulate life, no matter how good we are at it, leave the inner man fragmented still. The simplicity man seeks is not organization and management, but of relationship.

The answer for satisfying living for the Christian lies not in organizing, managing, or controlling life, but in focusing life. The Bible teaches that our relationship to God must take absolute precedence over everything else in life.

But what does it mean to "seek first?" Certainly it doesn't mean seek God first, then scratch that off the list and pursue the rest of life. We never complete our obligation to seek Him. Seeking God first is not a matter of order, but of focus.

Christ must not become simply another item in our life—not even the most important item. He did not come in order to be the most crucial piece of our fragmented life; He came to absorb all of life—our family, job, talents, dreams, ministry—into Himself and impress on it His mark.

To add Christ to our already busy life is to complicate living; to allow Christ to absorb all the elements of our life is to simplify it. Life is simplified when there is *one* center, *one* reason, *one* motivation, *one* direction and purpose.

> But seek first his kingdom and his righteousness,
> and all these things will be given to you as well.
>
> MATTHEW 6:33

Find a children's museum (if there's one in your area) or an adult museum to give your children some culture this summer.

July 13

Doing What Our Father Says

LUIS PALAU

Spiritual maturity comes not by erudition, but by compliance with the known will of God.
—LEONARD RAVENHILL

*M*ore than 90 people conducted an all-night search for Dominic DeCarlo, an eight-year-old boy lost on a snowy mountain slope. Dominic, who had been on a skiing trip with his father, apparently had ridden on a new lift and skied off the run without realizing it.

As each hour passed, the search party and the boy's family became more and more concerned for his health and safety. By dawn they had found no trace of the boy. Two helicopter crews joined the search, and within 15 minutes they spotted ski tracks. A ground team followed the tracks, which changed to small footprints. The footprints led to a tree, where they found the boy at last.

A hospital spokeswoman said the boy was in fine condition, so he wasn't even admitted.

Silbaugh explained why the boy did so well despite spending a night in the freezing elements: His father had enough forethought to warn the boy what to do if he became lost, and his son had enough trust to do exactly what his father said.

Dominic protected himself from possible frostbite and hypothermia by snuggling up to a tree and covering himself with branches. As a young child, he never would have thought of doing this on his own. He was simply obeying his wise and loving father.

Dominic reminds me of what we should do as children of our loving and infinitely wise Heavenly Father. We are not to walk according to the course of this world, which is passing away. Instead, we are to walk in obedience to the Lord's commands. After all, He knows what is best for us.

In a world full of deceptive detours and confusing paths, let's trust our Father and do exactly what He says. When we do, we'll be exhibiting the fruit of goodness which abundance produces.

As obedient children, do not conform to the evil
desires you had when you lived in ignorance.
1 PETER 1:14

Read *Anywhere He Leads* Me, a compilation of the writings of Corrie ten Boom by Judith Couchman (Vine Books).

July 14

Spiritual Housecleaning

NELDA JONES

My conscience is captive to the Word of God.
—MARTIN LUTHER

As I swept the living room floor, I noticed a cobweb between the legs of a table in front of the window. I swept it away with the broom and continued with my cleaning. A few days later, as I was sweeping the same floor, I noticed another cobweb in the same place. This time, after sweeping away the cobweb, I knelt on the floor to get a closer look. Sure enough, I finally found a tiny spider, barely visible to the eye. Apparently I had not killed the spider the first time. I had only swept away the cobweb, the visible evidence of his presence.

This is the way we do so often in our "spiritual house-cleaning." We only sweep away the cobwebs, or the visible evidence of sin in our lives. We fail to "kill the spider," or get rid of the root of sin which caused the problems in the first place. Then the evidence of Satan's presence soon returns—bigger and stronger than ever.

Just as the spider was more easily found on my knees, so are the "spiritual spiders" more easily found by spending time on our knees in prayer.

Have you been examining your heart thoroughly in order to keep it clean and pure before the Lord? In order for us to experience abundance, we must make sure that the source of any sin is removed.

Test me, O Lord, and try me, examine my heart and my mind.

PSALM 26:2

Do you have a bad habit you'd like to change? Then be open to the Holy Spirit's "nudging" each time you slip. Forgive yourself and try again.

July 15

At Home In Heaven

ESTHER M. BAILEY

How would you fit in heaven if you were placed there right now?

—REV. PAULINE M. MAXWELL

Elmer's funeral was a victory celebration because family and friends knew he had gone to be with the Lord. His death was rather sudden but not surprising for a man who was nearly 102 years old.

The pastor mentioned Elmer's devotion to the Word of God. At age 95 he purchased a new study Bible to augment his understanding of Scripture. "Elmer will feel right at home with God because the two of them got well acquainted here," the pastor said.

The idea of feeling at home in heaven should challenge us to ask ourselves: Are we too wrapped up in the here and now to transfer our focus to the hereafter? Jesus emphasized the spiritual nature of His kingdom. Even though we live in a materialistic world, we can focus on spiritual matters. To check ourselves in this area, we can ask: How much do our possessions grab our hearts? Would we be willing to give them up for God? If we hold earthly treasures too tightly, we might miss their presence throughout eternity.

We can attain the holiness required to enter heaven only through the blood of Jesus. But while still on this earth, so that we can make right and good choices, we must ask: Would our language fit in heaven? Our thoughts? The kind of entertainment we enjoy? Could we share our attitudes with Jesus?

Much of the activity in heaven centers around worship of God. How eager are we to participate in private as well as corporate worship?

If Heavenly praises flow from our hearts here, we will be ready to join the angels in everlasting adoration of God.

Our goodness does not earn God's gift of salvation, but our deeds will affect our future reward. All our selfish effort will benefit only our existence on earth, but what we do for the kingdom of God will net us treasure in heaven. In eternal assets, are we millionaires or paupers?

With enjoyment of heaven in mind, we can frequently examine our lifestyles. When we find inconsistencies with biblical directives, we can seek to alter our deeds, thoughts, and words to fit heaven's environment. Not only will we then experience abundance in heaven, but on earth as well.

> *Now we know that if the earthly tent we live in is destroyed,*
> *we have . . . an eternal house in heaven, not built by human hands.*
> 2 CORINTHIANS 5:1

Read *Eternity* by Joseph M. Stowell, (Moody Press, 1995).

July 16

Ali-Anna, A Lesson In Listening

CHERYL WILLIAMS

Being a Christian is a way of life, not a method or a technique, but a life-style all its own.

—FEMI ILESANMI

Some time ago, my husband bought two Hereford calves for the children and I to bottle feed. In keeping with the theme of our Arabian horse farm, we named them Ali-Oop and Ali-Anna. They were like two large puppies, laying in the front yard for us to lean against when we rested under the big old shade tree. They'd even bang on the door to get in when it rained. Ali-Oop could be found grazing while wearing a cowboy hat. When Ali-Anna reached breeding age, I was anxious for her to have her own calf.

My husband made arrangements to take Ali-Anna to a local Hereford breeder and leave her with his bull. I was ecstatic—until I went to pick her up and could not find her. It seemed like there were at least a thousand Herefords in the large pasture. Ali-Anna had appeared so distinct in my herd of two with her dark mahogany color. But here amongst so many, I roamed fruitlessly through the large herd, returning with only a broken heart and tears in my eyes. I had lost my beloved Anna.

The head rancher told me to just pick out any heifer I wanted. He didn't understand my love for Anna, but my husband did. He was a horse rancher and not cattleman, therefore he had trained our cows to trailer load like horses. Quietly he fetched a bucket of grain and opened the horse trailer door. Together we began to call out "Ali-Anna, Ali-Anna." Suddenly Anna came bursting forth from the large herd, ran toward us, jumped into the trailer and began to eat her grain.

The cattlemen shook their heads in absolute disbelief while I jumped up and down with joy. My husband smiled that confident little smile of his.

As we live the abundant life, we can be assured that God knows and loves each one of us individually. While in the midst of earth's difficulties, we may not stand out, but when the time comes to be taken to heaven, God won't have any difficulty finding us.

He calls His own sheep by name and leads them out.
JOHN 10:3B

> Memorize the fruit of the Spirit in Galatians 5:22-23.

July 17

What Should I Pray About?

DEBBIE PIPER

Since the lines have been cleared between the Lord
and me, the telephone has never stopped ringing.
—BERNARD L. CLARK

One of the abundant life's main foundational stones is laid through a close relationship with God through prayer. Whatever is going on in your life, whatever concerns you, is something to talk to God about. That includes, but isn't limited to, your relationship with Him, your relationships with others, your daily needs, your job, your financial needs, your desires, hopes and dreams, and your frustrations, big and small.

Some specific things that the Bible tells us to pray for are wisdom (James 1:5), our daily needs (Matthew 6:11), forgiveness (Matthew 6:12), protection from temptation (Matthew 6:13), growth in spiritual understanding (Ephesians 1: 17-19, Philippians 1:9-11), help when we are in trouble (James 5:13), and for openings to tell others about Jesus (Colossians 4:3-4).

But communication involves more than just asking for what we need. It also involves sharing our thoughts about life, our feelings, asking for another's input, asking about their dreams and concerns, telling them what they mean to us. In the same way, a healthy prayer life will include more than just telling God what you need. It will also include time spent thinking about who God is, and telling Him what it is about Him that means so much to you. That is often referred to as praise or adoration and involves simply remembering the attributes of God and the difference He has made in your life.

Often, as you come into God's presence and consider who He is, you will be struck by the contrast between God and you, and your need of Him. Tell Him where you see your need to grow, how you've failed to live up to Christ's character. That's called confession: agreeing with God about the reality of your daily life and where you've fallen short of His ideal. He'll then forgive you.

Time with God will also bring up memories of what you have asked Him to do for you in the past, and how He has answered those prayers. As you remember what God has done for you in the past and as you think of your needs for today, you'll also want to ask Him to be at work in the lives of those around you.

Drawing closer to God in prayer will enable you to recognize His hand at work in your life and to make good choices. Begin to experience the abundant life today by talking with God in a real and personal way. Prayer is really that simple.

Cast all your anxiety on him because he cares for you.

I PETER 5:7

Read *31 Days of Praise* by Ruth Myers (Questar Publishers).

July 18

The Joys Of Journaling

ROBERTA L. MESSNER

A simpler life is one in which the knowledge of what
matters dictates all that surrounds us. It is a life lived
with the courage to let go of what our hearts know
does not belong. It is a more balanced life, not a more
expert balancing act.
—ANDREA VAN STEENHOUSE AND DORIS A. FULLER

A growing number of people are finding that journaling makes
life less complicated and helps to bring abundance. Here's how
it can become one of your simple pleasures:

1. *Use your journal to record your journey.* Record those moments
when joyful things happened, when you evaluated and changed an
unwanted habit, or when the Lord spoke to your heart.

2. *Bring order to your days with a journal.* Much of our stress is due
to disorganization. But did you know the word "ordinary" comes from
the word "order?" When you begin to really notice the ordinary events
of life, you are creating order out of the chaos of everyday experience.
There's something about writing it all down that brings understanding, especially when you revisit your journal weeks or months
later. It's like the backside of a piece of needlework. At first glance, it
appears to be a tangle of threads and colors. But turn it over and
examine it, and you discover the exquisite pattern that stitch by stitch
has emerged.

3. *Don't strive for perfection.* This begins with selecting a journaling
method that works for you. If a composition notebook or computer is
more to your liking, don't feel compelled to purchase a fancy journal.
The same goes for pens. Choose one that feels right and gives you
pleasure. You don't have to write every single day, either. Let the words
flow without concern for grammar or correct spelling. If you worry
about being "proper," you'll shut down your creativity as well as your
enthusiasm for journaling.

4. *Don't be afraid you have nothing to say.* In these hurried times,
it's easy to forget that each of us is unlike any other person who has
ever lived. If life (and the Lord) speaks to you through the seasons of
your garden or through preparing meals for your family, tell it to your

journal. There are profound lessons in the every-day-ness of our lives, if we will only listen.

As journaling becomes a habit and friend, you'll find it records your growth and maturity toward goodness as God works in your life. And that will encourage you to grow even more.

Then the Lord replied: "Write down the revelation and make it plain on tablets . . ."
HABAKKUK 2:2

> Have a washcloth available by the bathroom sink to wipe off the counter each time it's used. The counter will stay cleaner longer.

July 19

In Our Shoes

LOUISA GODISSART MCQUILLEN

Because He walked in my shoes, I will follow in His footsteps . . .

—ANONYMOUS

I had picked up some paperwork from Ann in the copy center. Then I wound my way down the stairwell, heading for my office several buildings away. Suddenly a young student narrowly missed me as he barreled up the steps. "Where's he going in such a hurry?" I wondered. At that thought, my imagination kicked in. My mind's eye saw *me*, not the student, rush past a slow-moving woman at the landing.

I felt a gentle nudge in my spirit: "*Walk farther in his shoes . . .*" The challenge seemed intriguing. My imagination even supplied a reason: "I'm late for class, but I'm also worried I won't graduate."

The boy appeared to be my son's age. I wondered, *Does his family pray for him daily as I do for Pat?* "Stay in your own shoes," I mumbled. I stepped out the door into a cloud of cigarette smoke. An employee leaned against the building, and I couldn't resist imagining her thoughts: "I'm cold out here. I wish I could give up these cigarettes."

Wow. I was getting into this thing of "walking" in other people's shoes. An older gentleman came toward me with the shuffling gait of the severely impaired. Did I have the courage to slip into his shoes? Before I could decide, a boy with headphones on his ears jogged by. The music was deafening—I sure didn't want to try *his* shoes.

Soon I was back in my office, thinking about the various shoes in which I had walked. Although mine were strictly imaginary, each person's steps could well have been my own.

Like that young student, sometimes I tend to forget about others. I had even forgotten to hold the door open for the woman behind me. Also, I don't smoke, but I have other poor habits that have a grip on me.

As I remembered the uneven steps of the impaired gentleman, I realized I'm sometimes out of step in my Christian walk. I even identified with that fellow wearing headphones—sometimes I tune *out* things I need to hear.

What had I accomplished by my imaginary steps in others' shoes? For one thing, a better understanding of people. And a greater desire to treat them with respect and goodness. Even with our differences, we're all part of a family called humankind.

An old proverb warns not to judge others until we've walked in their shoes. What would it be like to walk in Jesus' shoes? I never could, of course. My imagination would just burn out. And yet . . .

I imagined a cobblestone road winding out of the city, and a weary, disheveled man struggling along with a heavy beam on his back. He stopped to rest, looked up and saw me in my office window. Then he smiled, straightened, got a firmer grip on the beam. Before moving on, he pointed downward.

I looked at his feet and saw my shoes.

Jesus took our place so that we might have abundance. Then He desires to share that abundance with others through understanding what they're going through—walking in their shoes. Have you done any of that kind of walking lately?

He has shown you, O man, what is good. And what does the Lord require of you? To act justly and to love mercy and to walk humbly with your God.
MICAH 6:8

Place seed out for the birds and enjoy their fun.

July 20

Do You Want The Best?

CRANE DELBERT BENNETT

A little with God goes farther than a lot without God.
— ANONYMOUS

*J*f you want the best for yourself, give the best you have. Does that make sense? If you give of your best, how can you have the best left?

The Word tells us that we should bring all the tithes (ten percent according to Webster's dictionary) into His storehouse and He will pour out a blessing upon us. If I give God ten percent, I will only have ninety percent left. How can my resources stretch far enough when I only have ninety percent of the one hundred percent I had previously?

The words "tithe" and "tithes" appear over thirty times in the Bible, so tithing must be extremely important. I personally came to this conclusion at a bad time. We were married, my wife quit her job reducing our income substantially, and we were expecting our first child. I prayed about it, suggesting to God that when we were in a better financial condition we would start tithing. I read the Bible some more for support for my decision, but I could find no place in the Word that I could put off tithing until it was more convenient.

Then my wife and I talked it over and prayed about it. We determined we would begin tithing right away, taking the ten percent right off the top of our income and making do on the ninety percent left over. Since that time we have consistently paid ten percent of our income into God's storehouse before making any other expenditure. And we've made a wonderful discover—ninety percent with the Lord's blessing goes farther than the one hundred percent without His blessing.

Why should we tithe? Because we love the Lord and want to do good. When we tithe for that reason, God does bless us, physically, mentally, spiritually, and materially. I have no doubt that my wife and I have been blessed abundantly by giving priority to tithing our income.

All that we have comes from God. He gives us one hundred percent and only asks for ten percent in return. No one can beat that. And we've found that giving ten percent right off the top is the best and least complicated method of following God's direction for our lives.

If you don't yet tithe, then you aren't yet experiencing total abundance. Step out in faith, you'll find God is good and generous.

"Bring the whole tithe into the storehouse, that there may be food in my house. Test me in this," says the Lord Almighty, "and see if I will not throw open the floodgates of heaven and pour out so much blessing that you will not have room enough for it."

MALACHI 3:10

Encourage your children to give a tithe from their allowance.

Home-Made Cards

JEANNE ZORNES

When you care enough to send the very best.
—RETAIL SLOGAN

I don't hang around card shops as much as I used to. For years I've created a lot of my own greeting cards at a fraction of the cost. Plus, "homemade" carries a message that you cared enough to spend that precious commodity called "time." This is one of my ways of abundantly doing good for others.

I make many cards out of extra snapshots or pictures cut out of magazines, catalogs and newspapers. They're pasted on folded construction paper or on card stock bought in quantity from my local printer. Sometimes my cards are simply a cover picture and witty remark inside. For example, for a friend who's a dentist's wife, I saved a magazine picture of an eccentric dentist, wildly beckoning to his chair. Inside: "The tooth fairy wishes you a happy birthday." It was exactly right for her.

Another time I pasted an aerial picture of a lake on the front of nice card stock. Inside I wrote a letter of encouragement to a friend on the first anniversary of her husband's death. Her husband loved to fish; I told her the picture reminded me of his new celestial perspective, where delights surpass any "catch" down here. Within the week she called me and said she'd kept the card in view on her kitchen counter.

Sometimes I'll paste pictures into booklets made of typing paper folded in half and tied with yarn. I enjoy giving these for "significant" decade birthdays (30, 40, etc.), filled with old ads clipped from mail-order catalogs. I label the cover (usually of black construction paper) as "House of Karen" (or whatever the person's name is)—"Discreet Shopping for the Older Woman" (or Man). The booklets always get a hoot, especially the last page which advises them to place their order by calling "1-800-I-AM-OLDER" and to have their Medicare number available for the waiting operator.

I usually send serious cards to the ill or injured. One time, though, I obeyed an inner nudge to make a funny card for a friend hospitalized after an auto accident. She was so depressed she didn't even want visitors. I made a booklet of hospital jokes (a glass of water with "Eat all your cream of water soup"), and for the last page rigged up a recycled electronic song disk. The previous page warned her I was sending a little music to brighten her day. The "happy birthday" disk was incongruous—but helped her laugh. At the end, I wrote a serious note assuring her of my prayers. She later told me it was her best get well card ever.

When a neighbor turned 90, I went to the bank and got 90 new pennies which I attached with a hot-glue gun to poster board in a big "90." He displayed it for months.

The rare times I get a homemade card from somebody, I really feel honored. We care enough to send the best when we send ourselves, no matter how homely the trappings. The next time you need a greeting card, consider making one yourself. Your effort will be appreciated.

Therefore, as we have opportunity, let us do good to all people,
especially to those who belong to the family of believers.
GALATIANS 6:10

Train your children in the art of cardmaking. Their creativity will amaze you.

July 22

Drink Your Milk

MARGARET PRIMROSE

Tell me the story simply, As to a little child.
—KATHARINE HANKEY

It was fun to watch our farm's two "bottle babies" when they were being called. They did not just answer with a lusty "Baa-a-a." They scampered to their dinner as fast as their little hoofs could go. Then attacked their bottles vigorously.

One's attack was a little too vigorous for Rita, a child who lived on an adjoining farm. Her father did not have any sheep, and so feeding one of our babies seemed like an adventure to her.

If the lamb knelt as he began gulping his milk, he did not stay on his knees long. Capering right and capering left, he almost seemed to dance. The problem was that he jerked at the bottle as he danced. Though Rita clung to it, off came the nipple.

Maybe there was no use to cry over spilled milk, but the lamb did not know that. He was also ready to show Rita that he still claimed the bottle. Fortunately, mother was there to save some of the milk from becoming part of a mud puddle. But dinner was over before Lambkin was ready to accept that. He would rather have had seconds than to go back to his pen to play.

God wants all Christians, young or old, to have healthy appetites for the milk of His Word. It is as essential for spiritual health and abundance as milk is to a lamb. We would not be normal without it.

It is also important to remember that we do not outgrow our need for milk. Fruit, vegetables and meat are indeed important in the diet, but so is calcium. Adults who do not drink milk are likely to have osteoporosis when they age. Height shrinks, shoulders become rounded and bones get brittle.

Likewise, even mature Christians should still have the desire to hear the profound but simple stories they loved as children. Simple truths are the milk that satisfy basic needs when we cannot digest deep theological thoughts.

Are you getting enough milk? If you do, it'll grow the spiritual bones of doing good and right.

> Like newborn babies, crave pure spiritual milk,
> so that by it you may grow up in your salvation.
>
> I PETER 2:2

Read the story of Joseph in Genesis and get a fresh "dose of spiritual milk."

July 23

The Purple Ribbon

MARGARET PRIMROSE

> I pledge my head to clearer thinking, my heart to
> greater loyalty, my hands to larger service, and my
> health to better living, for my club, my community, my
> country, and my world.
>
> —4-H CLUB PLEDGE

One summer I worked very hard on a dress, blouse, and lingerie to enter at the county fair. I received good ratings on everything except the blouse. Why? I had neglected to tie knots at the beginnings and endings of seams. The stitching might ravel.

It didn't matter that I had learned to make bound buttonholes and edged a collar on the dress with lace. What should have been a lot easier became my downfall on a simpler garment. I had not done the "clearer thinking" to which I pledged myself at every 4-H meeting.

It is human to want to exhibit our skill in something complicated and showy. The "great" of Jesus' day had that problem, too. They wanted their faces to show they were fasting. They gave their alms publicly so that others would see them. As long as their real motives did not show, they seemed to think that all was well. They thought God was not interested in the many regulations they added to His commands. But He looked *inside*, just as the 4-H judges did.

God looks on the inside of us too to see the motives for our goodness. Are we doing nice, right things because we love God or because others will praise us for it? Let's not look for the approval of men for our good deeds. God does a more abundant job of rewarding us anyway. Let's seek His approval.

And now, O Israel, what does the Lord your God ask of you but to fear the Lord your God, to walk in all His ways, to love Him, to serve the Lord your God with all your heart and with all your soul . . .
—DEUTERONOMY 10:12

> The best way to keep organized, is to keep it simple. Baskets are not only beautiful, but adaptable to many organizational needs.

July 24

Becoming A "Fred"

SANDRA HINMAN GRIESMEYER

A rose by any other name is still a rose.
—ANONYMOUS

She was only four and we lived in Italy. It seemed like she was always getting into trouble. One time Cyndi got off the bus before her stop because she wanted to visit a friend's house. I had to leave work to get her and she knew she was in "hot water."

The next day, Cyndi's teacher told me, "Cyndi told the other children that some day, if she was really good, she might get off 'striction.'"

I replied, "Don't count on it."

Later that day, someone else came by the store where I worked and found out I was Cyndi's mother. She explained that Cyndi had told the children at preschool that there were dragons in the small lake near our villa, a story she got from her sisters. The woman's child, who was in Cyndi's class, was now afraid to cross bridges, because the water beneath them might be connected to the lake. As they drove, her son nearly had to be sedated.

When I got home that evening, I hollered Cyndi's full given name, a certain sign of major trouble. She dragged herself to the car. "I hate being Cyndi Florence Griesmeyer. Every time I'm Cyndi Florence Griesmeyer, I get in trouble."

It had been a long week. It was Thursday, she still had a day to go. God gave me abundant understanding and I replied, "So who do you want to be? Fred?"

From that day on, whenever Cyndi Florence Griesmeyer got into too much trouble, my daughter became Fred. It acknowledged the problem and gave her another chance to begin again.

Because God knew we couldn't be good all the time, He made it possible for us to assume another name. Just like Cyndi needed to be shown mercy and called "Fred," so you and I are shown grace and called "Christian" if we know Jesus as Lord and Savior. This other title gets us out of trouble with God because He mercifully sees Jesus' robe of righteousness surrounding us. (But we still must seek being like a "good" Cyndi.)

Blessed are the merciful, for they will be shown mercy.
MATTHEW 5:7

Create a "secret garden" for a child. Make it as simple or elaborate as you like.

July 25

Safe In God's Hand

DEBBIE PIPER

If those who believe in Christ receive God's righteousness through faith in Christ, then nothing can add or improve to that.
—RICHARD A. SEYMOUR

The year was 1971. The warm Hawaiian trade winds swept past me carrying the scent of tropical flowers—plumeria and ginger. I stood in the shade, out of the hot sun, waiting for the bus to arrive. And still the thoughts raced inside my mind.

No matter how hard I tried, it seemed I couldn't live the perfect life I knew God required. Even though I was a Christian, I still struggled with a sense of sin and guilt. *Why couldn't I get along with my parents? Why did I always feel guilty? Why couldn't I do everything God wanted me to do? And why was temptation so . . . well, so tempting?* It seemed like I was all alone in my struggle. No one in the youth group at church talked about struggling with sin. *I guess they don't have the same struggles I do.*

Then came the vision. In my mind I saw a hand, God's hand, reaching down from heaven. And I saw myself clinging desperately to His fingers, legs kicking, trying with all my might to scramble back up to the safety of His hand. But I was losing my grip. That's when the thought came. *Maybe I should stop trying to hold on to God, and let Him hold onto me.* The picture changed. Now I was seated in the palm of His hand, safe and secure. A sense of peace briefly filled me.

The year was 1985. I'd been studying the gospel of John, when suddenly I read Jesus saying, *I give (my sheep) eternal life, and they shall never perish; no one can snatch them out of my hand. My Father, who has given them to me, is greater than all; no one can snatch them out of my Father's hand* (John 10:28-29). Again the picture came. Again the sense of peace. Only this time the Holy Spirit impressed upon me that the security I have in Christ is no fleeting thing, but reality. I am His forever and ever.

The years continued to pass. And along the way I learned that living the Christian life isn't following a list of do's and don'ts, but living in relationship with the God who loves me unconditionally. Not because of my ability to live the perfect life He requires, but because of my trust in His Son Jesus Christ who lived that perfect life, took the punishment for my sin on the cross, and freely offers me His perfection in exchange for my sin, simply through trusting in Him.

What freedom. What peace. What hope. What abundance to exchange guilt for grace, fear for freedom, a life of being graded for a life of gratitude.

You can experience the same abundance in knowing that you are secure in His power to hold you.

Therefore, if anyone is in Christ, he is a new creation; the old has gone, the new has come.

2 CORINTHIANS 5:17

July 26

Spiritual Nutrition

TAMMI EASTERDAY

If we would accomplish anything for God, we need to
carve out spaces of time when we can be alone with
Him. There's no shortcut, no substitution to taking
time with God.

—DICK JOHNSON

*H*ave you ever found yourself rummaging through the fridge or
the kitchen cabinets searching for that scrumptious morsel that
will satisfy the relentless, uncontrollable hunger within you?
Hmm—would some chocolate chip cookies do? How about a bag of
chips? Ice cream sounds good. You snack and munch but you still seem
to have a feeling of hollowness deep inside.

Could that persistent feeling of emptiness possibly be coming from
your soul rather than your stomach? Might you be longing for something spiritually satisfying and nutritious?

In Deuteronomy 8:3, we read that God actually caused the
Israelites to hunger then gave them manna to teach them that the
importance of depending upon God. Maybe that aching hunger within
you is also the Lord. Remember He longs for us and wants to fill our
emptiness with a loving relationship with Him.

Our communication with the Father through Bible reading and
prayer enables us to more easily deal with all the difficulties that
confront us. Christ Himself depended on His time with God for
strength and guidance. He often drew away from the crowds and
sought out time with the Father. We, too, also need to carve out time
in our day to spend with Him.

You may be wondering where you will find the time. You might
find that reading and prayer first thing in the morning gets your day
off to a good start. Or use the minutes before going to sleep at night.
If these times don't work for you, why not consider communing with
the Lord while you're waiting for an appointment or during your lunch
break? What about listening to tapes of the Scriptures as you get
dressed in the morning or travel from place to place in your car? Prayer

can be done most anywhere and anytime throughout the day. In maintaining a recommended daily time with Him, we receive nourishment for our spirit and fill that yearning void inside.

Seeking Him in these ways is a good thing to do and it also becomes a source of our strength. For truly, we will not have an abundant life without spiritual nourishment.

The next time you find yourself going through the fridge looking for that quick-fix to satisfy those munchies, stop and think . . . could I actually be longing for more than something to eat? Have I been feasting upon God's word lately and being filled with that which truly satisfies?

He humbled you, causing you to hunger and then feeding you with manna which neither you nor your fathers had known, to teach you that man does not live on bread alone but on every word that comes from the mouth of the Lord.
DEUTERONOMY 8:3

If you destest weeding—keep up by pulling a few every evening, as you take a stroll.

July 27

Following The White Lines

RUTH GIAGNOCAVO

Real goodness does not attach itself merely to this
life—it points to another world.
—DANIEL WEBSTER

I finished my grocery shopping and loaded the bags into the car. As I pulled out of the parking lot of the store, I noticed that a heavy fog had descended during the time I had been shopping. I wasn't too worried though, because the road was familiar and the five miles home shouldn't be too difficult.

When I reached the stretch of newly-laid asphalt on the main highway however, I realized with a sickening feeling that no yellow or white lines had been laid yet.

The night was dark, the fog was dense, the road was black, and there were no lines to guide me. The road lay ahead with no way to determine where it ended. It was one of the most frightening experiences I can remember.

How much more dangerous it is to journey through life with no guiding lines. The night is often dark. We can't see the road ahead, either to keep us on the right way, or to avoid the dangers ahead.

I can remember how, as a teenager, I rebelled at the lines that were placed to keep me from wandering into the unknown. To me they were just so many restrictions on my freedom.

As I grew as a Christian, I learned to value those guidelines, especially in the Scriptures. God has given them to protect us and teach us to be good. Ignoring His rules will leave us falling helplessly into a wayside ditch, or may even lead to death. Goodness is not just some plan by God to keep us on our toes, but is meant for our *good*.

From the list of the Ten Commandments to the Sermon on the Mount and the letters of the Apostles, the rules for living life abundantly are clear and compelling. We ignore them at our risk. God has supplied them because he loves us, not to give us a hard time.

Trust in the Lord with all your heart, and lean not on your own understanding; in all your ways acknowledge him, and he will make your paths straight.

PROVERBS 3:5-6

Establish a prayer counsel of friends to hold you accountable and pray you through your life's work.

July 28

Dear God . . .

MICHELE T. HUEY

A servant's heart remains the rarest jewel on earth.
—WINNING ATTITUDES

I'm tired, Lord—in body, mind, and spirit;
It's not that I'm ungrateful for all the blessings.
It's just that life can be so overwhelming at times—
A new baby on the way,
Trying to get moved upstairs—after living in the basement
for four years—
Trying to keep a balanced, sensible budget on one income,
Trying to meet my family's needs,
Trying to keep in touch with You.
I feel like such a failure,
I can't keep up with it all:

Church responsibilities, club responsibilities—
My outlets to the world outside,
My keeping in touch with the person I am inside,
Besides being someone's wife and someone's mother.
And now, Lord, another one is on the way.
More needs to be met,
More giving of my precious time.
My guitar will have to idle in a forgotten corner,
My music on a dusty shelf,
My crochet and stitching
In a bag beginning to smell like mildew.
While my fingers busy themselves
With diapers and vacuum cleaners,
Dirty clothes and lunch buckets,
Checking homework and peanut butter and jelly,
While yesterday's dishes wait in the kitchen sink.
In the midst of it all, Lord, I see You on the cross;
And I hear Your voice:
"If any man will come after Me, let him deny himself,
And take up his cross, and follow me."
And again:
"The Son of Man came not to be served;
He came to serve and to give His Life for many."
Is this what it means to "die to self?"
Then, Lord, I don't know
If I want to give up *Myself* just yet.
Myself is so strong,
It doesn't want to be quenched
Beneath the humbling load of the everyday.
Myself flares up, rebels, and seeks recognition.
Myself makes myself so miserable—and others, too.
Help me to surrender, Lord,
The dreams of self-gratification.
Help me instead to give
Without seeking recognition,
Without complaining.
Help me to say,
"Not my will, Lord, but Thine be done,"
And mean it in my heart.
Love,
Michele

Take time to list the ways your family has been a blessing to you.

July 29

Showing You Care

L. PAMELA WAIAN

Giving and caring for others is a way for us to a get a glimpse of what God feels.

—ANONYMOUS

Showing how to care has always been a favorite subject of mine. Especially as a woman, we are often very concerned about our relationships, and God made us with the desire to show we care.

Showing someone you care is to highly regard their desires as important to you. You are sensitive to their cares, feelings and needs. One biblical example is when King David was thirsty and wanted a drink from a particular well. One of his soldiers risked his life to go behind enemy lines to bring King David a drink of water. David was so moved he couldn't drink it. Instead, he offered it to God.

There are many different ways to show you care. Words are not always enough and must be accompanied by acts of goodness. Gifts always come to mind, but how about the gift of spending time (your life) and effort (your energy) to show you care.

Something to remember when doing good for others is that we want the caring to meet the emotional needs of the other person. We can discover their needs by asking them how they would show care to someone else. For example, to find out how your daughter wants to be loved, ask her how she would show love toward a friend. Would she buy gifts, would she send cards, or would she want to talk with them and give them a hug? By her answer, you will determine the kind of goodness she values.

We were good to someone in our family at their birthday by preparing their favorite dinner with the freshest ingredients available. We spent both time and effort.

We also helped each of our children fulfill their individual goals and dreams. Even though they are grown, when we visit them, we give of ourselves in time and effort for their projects, repairs and creative endeavors. The key for us is Time + Effort = Caring.

We want to show them that not only do we have caring words, but we have caring action too. In essence, we're "putting our money where our mouth is." That's abundant goodness in action.

How are you doing in showing goodness to others? The abundant life expresses love in the way the other person values.

. . . conduct yourselves in a manner worthy of the gospel of Christ.
PHILIPPIANS 1:27

> Diluted milk makes a great houseplant leaf cleanser and leaves plants with a healthy glow. (Lille Diane)

July 30

Ducks And Eagles

DAVE GETZ

From the summit of power men no longer turn their eyes upward, but begin to look about them.
—JAMES RUSSELL LOWELL, 1870

The fishing at Lake Mary had slowed. I gazed across the waves shimmering in the Arizona sunshine. A flock of ducks attempted to take flight from the lake. Their little webbed feet churned the water into foam while their wings beat furiously at the air. They were the definition of effort. They finally managed to become airborne for about thirty yards. The birds then settled back onto the water, satisfied their mission was accomplished.

Meanwhile, a bald eagle soared with majesty above the ducks. Without ever flapping his wings, the eagle spiraled ever upward until he became a black dot against the distant white clouds. He was a perfect picture of serenity.

What was the difference between the two types of birds?

The ducks relied upon their own strength and hard work to lift themselves from the water. But the eagle rested in the power of a warm-air thermal which carried him to tremendous heights.

Christians are often like the ducks, and rely too much on self effort. We try to see what *we* can do for God and end up struggling to accomplish very little. Life becomes difficult and the abundant life we hunger for is beyond our spiritual fingertips. Our Heavenly Father wants to show what *He* can do *for* us through the Holy Spirit. This will happen only by presenting ourselves to God in the knowledge that we are weak. Then—like the eagle—we can soar to the great heights of God's abundant peace while resting in the Holy Spirit's power.

I came to you in weakness and fear, and with much trembling. My message and my preaching were not with wise and persuasive words, but with a demonstration of the Spirit's power, so that your faith might not rest on men's wisdom, but on God's power.

I CORINTHIANS 2:3-5

One childs definition of the word *vibration:* "A motion that hasn't figured out which way to go"—Think about it.

July 31

Man Is A Hard Audience To Please

JEAN FLEMING

Thou hast made us for Thyself, and the heart of man
is restless until it finds its rest in Thee.

—SAINT AUGUSTINE

*I*t is impossible to please all the people all the time; we can't even please *one* person all the time. Even loving parents can find it difficult to respond rightly when a child surprises them with breakfast in bed and then spills the maple syrup on the bedspread. Or when a child, after hearing dad talking about how badly the house needs painting, decides to tackle the job himself to lighten the load—but instead of paint, he uses varnish.

The heart was right, but the outcome was a sticky mess. Man looks at the results; God looks at the desire and motive. Since we have such a gracious audience in our God, aren't we foolish to make men our focus?

Francois Fenelon, the Archbishop of Cambrai until 1715, gave good advice when he said, "Do not be vexed at what people say. Endeavor to do the will of God and let them speak. You will never succeed in pleasing men, and it would not be worth the trouble if you could . . . We must love our fellow beings without depending upon their friendship . . . Fix your attention upon God alone in your connection with them."

Even the good we do (pray, fast, give to the poor) receives no reward from the Heavenly Father if the motivation is to impress people. When we determine our audience, we determine our reward. If we play our life to men, we receive the kinds of rewards men give; if we focus on pleasing our Father in Heaven, we receive the kinds of rewards God gives.

When God calls us to pray, fast, and give "in secret," He speaks not of the secrecy of the spy, but the secrecy of the lover. He calls us to withdraw from the tensions of pleasing others to His private, hidden, inner garden with luxuriant foliage, bubbling springs, and fragrant blossoms; to leave behind ambition, fear, and reputation and develop an intimate relationship with Him.

A secret shared fosters intimacy. To be the first to know a friend is engaged, is expecting a child, or has received a promotion, makes us feel especially close. In the same way, when we live with the inner purpose of pleasing God in what we say and do, the relationship deepens.

The Lord detests all the proud of heart. Be sure of this:
They will not go unpunished.

PROVERBS 16:5

Buy a bird bath or set out a large tub of water. Your feathered friends will love you.

August

"Be faithful until death, and I will give you the crown of life."

Revelation 2:10

*G*od's plan for our abundant living includes our faithfulness. That's a characteristic that is often lacking in our responses toward family and friends, and in the workplace. Being faithful means simply keeping our promises and fulfilling the plans we make. As we appreciate God's loyal friendship with us, we can grow in our ability to pass it along to others. That's abundant living.

A Mirror For Others

LYNETTE S. MCBRIDE

The greatest characteristic a Christian can exhibit is completely unveiled openness before God, which allows that person's life to become a mirror for others.
—OSWALD CHAMBERS

How are you doing in your journey toward abundance? As we begin another month, it's a fresh reminder that we always have new beginnings. As the year continues, August's fruit of faithfulness is so appropriate. For we need to be faithful in seeking simplicity, even if we don't arrive immediately at our goals.

And our overall goal as Christians should be to let God have total control of our lives so that we may be an effective witness for Him. We must faithfully live our lives as an example to others of what Jesus, Christ is all about. My personal desire is to be so excited about Jesus and to live so totally for Him, that other people will know, just by being around me, that I have something very special. My hope is that they will want to know what that something special is so that they, too, may experience it.

One of the best ways I have found to accomplish this goal is to have time alone with God every morning. Having a morning quiet time has been, for me, the most special time of the day. By praying and reading Scripture I have been able to draw close to God and know His heart, and prepare myself for another day of serving Him. This special time each day gives me strength and courage to go out into a world that can sometimes be very unfriendly.

After spending some time in prayer first and then in reading God's word, I take a few minutes to reflect upon the day ahead. I focus on the things I will be doing and the people I will meet, even though I don't always know who they will be. Then I end my quiet time with the following prayer, or something close to it:

"Lord, make this Your day in my life. Make the words that come from my mouth be Your words and not mine, that they would be edifying to others. Help me to be kind, patient, and gracious to those I come in contact with today. Help me to love them as You love them, and to see them through Your eyes. Today, let Jesus so shine through me, that they see Jesus and His love. Use me today in some way for Your glory. I just want to be Your servant."

This helps me draw close to Jesus and get myself ready for the day. I am able, then, to anticipate meeting people, knowing God will fulfill His plan in my life and theirs.

Try this for yourself. If you faithfully meet with Him, it will give a new boost to each day, and you just may be surprised at how our awesome God works.

> *Therefore, as God's chosen people, holy and dearly loved, clothe yourselves with compassion, kindness, humility, gentleness, and patience.*
>
> COLOSSIANS 3:12

> If you do not have a regular quiet time with God, make a new commitment to spend seven minutes with Him daily for the next seven days.

August 2

Lemons and Life

GEORGIA CURTIS LING

> Believe that life is worth living and your belief will
> help create the fact.
>
> —WILLIAM JAMES

It's neat to find out what your child really enjoyed during the summer when you read his report, "What I Liked Most About My Summer."

Believe it or not, it wasn't the fun-filled, action packed trips we crammed in during the summer months. It was a simple, one-afternoon entrepreneurial endeavor: a lemonade and cookie stand.

Our six-year-old son, Philip, was so excited as he planned this business adventure before summer, but with our busy schedule he had to postpone it until August. But that didn't dampen his spirit. He made arrangements weeks in advance. He had it all set up at his Dad's office, scheduled the table and location, made reminder calls, and on the morning of the big business he baked the cookies, cut fresh lemons for his lemonade, and went to the bank for change for his customers.

Now this was scheduled for Thursday afternoon. The previous

Monday night at bedtime, Philip said, "I wish I could sleep through until Thursday. I'm so excited, I can hardly wait."

Needless to say, Thursday morning he was up at the crack of dawn, ready and raring to go.

He did a great job. He even went the extra mile and made personal deliveries to some offices as he juggled lemonade in one hand and cookies in the other. It was a day he'll remember for the rest of his life.

Philip's example of faithfulness made me realize that a change from the ordinary usually rekindles excitement for me. I love it, but I have to confess, it's sometimes bad for my health. I'm up hours on end night after night with my brain working overtime, planning my next strategic step.

I sometimes have to take inventory in my daily Christian walk and wonder—no—I guess I know, that I need to rekindle that childlike excitement and commitment I made when I first became a believer. It may be a fresh devotional book to add to my daily reading, or stepping out of my comfort zone to share what I've found in Christ, or being involved in a different ministry, that will add new zeal.

What rekindles that childlike excitement in you? A new business, an engagement, a promotion, a new home, a new addition to your family, or a fresh start?

Whatever it is, take it from me, it's never too late to flame the fire. Look around you, see the need, and make an endeavor to make a difference. You'll be so excited, you won't be able to sleep because you'll be experiencing the abundant life, just like Philip.

Commit to the Lord whatever you do,
and your plans will succeed.
PROVERBS 16:3

What new venture has God been prompting you to step out into, in faith? Go for it.

Know His Purpose

MARILYN WILLETT HEAVILIN

The time a Christian gives to prayer and communion
with God is not meant for his natural life, but meant
to nourish the life of the Son of God in him.

—OSWALD CHAMBERS

J have a little dog who is a real character. Captain has learned that
if he comes near me in the morning when I'm having breakfast,
every once in a while I might drop a little crumb for him. Well, instead
of just hoping he finds one on the floor, or hoping he happens to be
there at the right time, the minute he smells the toast in the toaster,
he is next to me. He follows me to the table. He sits right in front of
me, following my every move . . . just waiting. His eyes never leave my
hand. If I move my hand up, his eyes go up. If I move my hand to the
left, his eyes follow my hand. He is watching because I have food for
him, and he does not want to miss even one crumb.

That's the way I think we should be with our Heavenly Father.
Our eyes should be on Him constantly, and we should be eagerly
awaiting every morsel. We should let Him see that we are excited about
what He might give us and that we understand our food, our joy, our
confidence, and our peace all come from Him.

Each time I pray, I create a setting or picture in my mind. Jesus
and I may be sitting in my office or some other place in my home, or
I may see myself entering His throne room and bowing before Him.
Whatever the setting, I focus on His face. I do not see an image I could
draw for you, and generally not even an image I could describe in
words, but I concentrate on the image He gives me of Himself. I often
pray, *Dear Jesus, let me see Your face. Let me sense the response of Your
eyes as I talk with You. Keep me sensitive to Your responses that we may
always be in tune with each other. In Jesus' Name, Amen.*

Look to the Lord and his strength; seek his face always.
1 CHRONICLES 16:11

> The next time you pray, begin by spending one minute imaging Jesus' face as you think of Him interacting in one of the stories from the gospel accounts.

August 4

Bagel Memories

MARY BAHR FRITTS

> Whatever we possess, becomes of double value when we share it with others.
>
> —ANONYMOUS

Several summers ago while on vacation, my family and I were lunching at a truck stop.

A trucker, eating silently at the table next to ours was an attraction to our boys with his tooled leather boots, golden belt, and western hat. Throughout the meal, they barraged him with chatter while we tried to contain them, thinking he might want to eat in peace. They stopped only when we paid our bill and left.

As we were loading the "troops" into the van, we saw the trucker leaving too, motioning us to follow him. We trailed him to an enormous truck that sparkled in the desert sunshine. With our permission, he lifted the boys into the cab and introduced them to the life of a trucker.

After each had their turn at the wheel, he proceeded to the back of the truck as the boys followed like three ducks in a row. Lifting the door, he reached in, pulled out some bags and handed each child a package of blueberry bagels.

Bill and I thanked him for his kindness.

"No, thank *you*," he spoke with a gentle drawl. "I've been on the road a long time, away from my family. Thanks for sharing yours."

To this day, when we're vacationing, one of the boys will inevitably pipe up, "Remember that trucker? You know—the one with the bagels?"

If we could only see through the eyes of a child—rather than through the eyes of a "grown-up child of God"—how much more abundant our lives would be. Thinking back on "our encounter," I can see how simple, yet how awesome the exchange was. The trucker shared his abundance with us (his bagel, truck and need for family); we shared our abundance with him (our children); and our children shared theirs (wonder, exuberance and love). And we all basked in the simple glory of it all.

. . . if it is showing mercy, let him do it cheerfully.

> At your next family gathering, have each person share their favorite memory from your vacations.

August 5

Static That Interferes With God's Voice

JAN JOHNSON

God is not in need of anything, but all things are in need of him.

—MARCIANUS ARISTIDES

*J*t's difficult to be aware of God's presence when certain influences create static. Sometimes their clamor drowns out all
inclinations toward God; other times, we mistake these influences
for God's voice. God allows this to happen because, "generally
speaking, God will not compete for our attention." God wants us
to draw near to Him and learn to listen for His voice.

Cultural distractions. Advertisements and newsletters tell us
we've missed something important if we don't see this movie, try
that restaurant, read this book, hear that speaker, buy this
gadget, make that phone call. Striving to be busy and important
crowds out hearing the still, small voice.

The New Testament asks us to set aside the frantic craze for doing
more, acquiring more, and persuading more and simply enjoy God.
Keeping busy is a subtle way to run from the communion with God
we most desire. If we resist this temptation and instead stay close to the
heart with an inner solitude, we will find the treasure of enjoying God.

Pursuit of fulfillment. Our culture teaches that happiness flows out
of self-worth, which can be cultivated by achieving more and loving
one's self more. Biblical teaching reminds us that we will never be
enough or do enough (Romans 3:23). (Our brokenness reminds us too.)

Self-sufficiency. Striving to be loved and valued leads to what
A.W.Tozer calls the "hyphenated sins of the human spirit:" self-righteousness, self-pity, self-confidence, self-sufficiency, self-admiration,

and self-love. To these, I would add self-aggrandizement—making our-selves greater in power and stature than we really are. Tozer said of people in his day: "Promoting self under the guise of promoting Christ is currently so common as to excite little notice." We begin serving God for various reasons, one of which may be our love for God. But then the love of praise creeps upon us. Soon, we would rather be stars than servants.

Inner neediness. It is human nature to be self-obsessed. If we're honest, we all want to be loved and appreciated. We worry about how we look and what others think of us because we have a deep need to please others. Some of us numb the pain of not being appreciated and fill this neediness with eating, spending, busyness, drugs, and alcohol. These cravings fill our self-talk and crowd out the conversational flow between God and ourselves.

This inner-neediness flows out of wanting to be loved and valued, and expecting to find that fulfillment in people and work. Part of what it means to know Christ is to be in the process of learning that God loves and values us no matter what we do. The task is to make that truth so real that it permeates motives, longings, and actions.

I want to know Christ and the power of his resurrection and the fellowship of sharing in his sufferings, becoming like him in his death.
PHILIPPIANS 3:10

Every time you hear static on the radio, let it remind you of any static that is preventing you from hearing God's voice and make a fresh determination to eliminate it.

August 6

The Primroses

SUSAN KIMMEL WRIGHT

I wanted to live deep and suck out all the marrow of
life . . .
—THOREAU

I come from a place where summer days linger like butterflies riding a barely perceptible breeze, and long winter evenings burn down like embers glowing on a grate. I've long ago left that place, though it hasn't left me.

Memory comes as a dull ache of longing. Once I knew something better than this endless push and crush. Recently, just for an evening, I found it again.

My mother's friend Trudi had invited mom, my three children and me to watch the evening primroses open in the garden behind her cottage. She greeted us with a cut-glass pitcher of fresh lemonade. The children tumbled out, dashing onto the long wedge of smooth grass beside the creek.

"Last night I had eight people here to watch the flowers," She said gesturing at white, cushioned chairs arranged in a semicircle around the flowerbed. Herbs and roses spread out in spokes from narrow brick walkways. Out front, in the position of honor, stood the evening primroses, their pale-green stalks swollen with tens of ready buds.

At 8:45, the adults settled into chairs as dusk came down like a hazy transparency. The children circled the plants, searching like sentinels, hoping to be first to send up the cry.

A seam split in one long green bud, revealing a sliver of yellow. Sudden crowding, but nothing more.

Someone pointed to another bud. "Look."

One petal popped forth and the bush seemed to quiver, gentle encouragement to the opening flowers.

The green bud casing peeled back, drawn by an invisible hand to reveal a flute of sun-colored silk. Other buds began splitting and the children ran. Where to look first?

Unseen cicadas and katydids chirred in the grass, a late summer symphony accompanied by childrens' shouts. The flowers opened in a rhythmic ballet, dancing to this natural score, "Fantasia" brought to life.

Out of the gathering darkness hummed a sphinx moth to hover over a newly-opened blossom. Suspended in air, it drew up the nectar, drinking deeply for its life.

At the evening's end, we all felt refreshed and renewed. Then it hit me. We'd had evening primroses in our garden in the past, but somehow we always seemed to forget to be there at 8:45. We had a TV show or a telephone call or dishes in the sink. How easy it is to refuse God's invitation to enjoy His show of nature.

Yet He continues to be faithful in revealing His wonders. Can you and I make a new commitment to take the time to appreciate them?

Teach us to number our days aright,
that we may gain a heart of wisdom.
PSALM 90:12

> What show of God's nature have you been neglecting?
> Respond today.

August 7

Effective Paper Filing System

BARBARA HEMPHILL

Human behavior is not like a computer program. It
cannot be installed—it has to be nurtured.
— BARBARA HEMPHILL

*J*n order to have an abundantly simple office, be faithful in
organizing your filing system. If it's not working, ignore it and start
over. It is unnecessarily depressing and time consuming to spend time
organizing information you are not using. It is much easier to start over
than to try to fix it. Clean out your most accessible file space and put
those files into less accessible space if you are not comfortable throwing
them out. Begin your new system, and as you need information from
the old files, incorporate it into the new system.

File information according to how you will use it, not where you
got it. For example, file seminar handouts you received under the topic
of the seminar. To determine where to file a piece of paper, ask yourself,
"If I need this again, what word will I think of?" The answer to that
question is the file title. Arrange the files alphabetically.

The key to the continuing success of your filing system is a "file
index"—a list of your file titles. Use your file index to determine where
to file a piece of paper just as you would use a chart of accounts to
determine which account to charge an expense. Keep a copy near the
filing cabinets and see that co-workers have a copy. It is easier to locate
where a paper might be located by quickly scanning the file index than
by thumbing through drawers of files (and possibly missing the very
one you needed). The file index not only helps you locate a particular
document, but will avoid creating a file for "car" when you already have
"auto." Remember to keep it in an active document. Hand write
changes as you add or delete files and print out new copies as necessary.

Faithfully following these ideas will bring simplicity and effectiveness
into your workplace and life.

The fear of the Lord is the beginning of knowledge;
but fools despise wisdom and discipline.

PROVERBS 1:7

When traveling on business, play a game with yourself to see how much you can get in the wastebasket before you get back to the office.

August 8

Life From The Press Box

MAX LUCADO

> Unfortunately the world today does not seem to understand, in either man or woman, the need to be alone. Anything else will be accepted as a better excuse. If one sets time aside for a shopping expedition, that time is accepted as inviolable; but if one says, "I cannot come because it is my hour to be alone," one is considered rude, egotistical, or strange.
>
> —ANNE MORROW LINDBERGH

It made sense, after someone explained it to me, why our high school football coach would always disappear in the middle of the third quarter. I remember during my first game on the varsity squad, I looked up from the sidelines (where I spent most of my time) and noticed that he was gone. (It was a lot quieter.) I couldn't figure out what had happened. I was afraid the other team had kidnapped him. Or maybe he had gotten sick on his chewing tobacco. So I asked a senior "sideliner." (They know everything.)

"Where's the coach?" I asked, thinking I was the only one to notice his absence, which made me feel important.

"In the press box," he answered.

"Getting coffee?" I asked.

"No, getting perspective."

Now that makes sense, doesn't it? There's no way a coach can really keep up with the game from the sidelines. Everyone yelling advice. Parents complaining. Players screaming. Cheerleaders cheering. Sometimes you've got to get away from the game to see it.

Occasionally we need to try that on ourselves, too. How vital it is that we keep a finger on the pulse of our own lives. How critical are those times of self-examination and evaluation. Yet it's hard to evaluate ourselves while we're in the middle of the game: schedules pressing, phones ringing, children crying.

I've got a suggestion. Take some press box time. Take some time (at least half a day) and get away from everything and everyone.

Take your Bible and a notebook and get a press box view of your life. Are you as in tune with God as you need to be? How is your relationship with your mate and children? What about your goals in life? Perhaps some decisions need to be made. Spend much time in prayer. Meditate on God's Word. Be quiet. Fast for the day.

Now, I'm not talking about a get-away-from-it-all day where you shop, play tennis, and relax in the sun (although such times are needed, too). I'm suggesting an intense, soul-searching day spent in reverence before God and in candid honesty with yourself. Write down your life story. Reread God's story. Recommit your heart to your Maker.

I might mention that a day like this won't just happen. It must be made. You'll never wake up and just happen to have a free day on your hands. (Those went out with your braces.) You'll have to pull out the calendar, elbow out a time in the schedule, and take it. Be stubborn with it. You need the time. Your family needs you to take this time.

Getting some press box perspective could change the whole ball game.

Yet the news about him spread all the more, so that crowds of people came to hear him and to be healed of their sicknesses. But Jesus often withdrew to lonely places and prayed.
LUKE 5:15-16

Write into your schedule a half-day or full day to get alone with God.

August 9

Keep On Keeping On

RUTH M. RINK

Never give in. Never give in. Never. Never, in nothing great or small, large or petty, never give in.
—WINSTON CHURCHILL

Drizzle slid down the pane as I stared out the window. "Another dreary day," I pouted, tears threatening to spill over. "What in the world can I do on a day like this?"

A long-retired English teacher with limited income and energy, at that moment I silently asked God to bring new meaning into the dull routine of my days.

I turned as the phone rang. It was my dear friend, Bobbie, an author, her voice aglow over a writers' conference she had just attended with another friend. "We're going to start meeting together regularly to critique each other's work. Do you want to join us?" she asked.

My head spun at the opportunity of working with two professional writers. What followed were months, then years, of writing and re-writing. I felt a bit like Grandma Moses, beginning a new "career" in my ninth decade. Mostly, however, no matter how much I polished my pieces, I received rejection slips. Well-intentioned slips they were, each assuring me that certainly some other publisher would gladly print my submissions—but at this moment mine did not fit their "editorial needs." Somehow, those words failed to lift my spirits.

Yet an inner drive pushed me on, each effort bringing eager expectation. *Keep on knocking,* I thought to myself. Finally, on a blustery March day near my eighty-third birthday, I found an envelope in my mailbox from a Baptist devotional publisher. Trembling, I ripped it open before I even shut the front door. It was my first acceptance letter.

"Glory hallelujah." I winged my way to the kitchen phone, sharing my delight with Bobbie. Both friends continued helping me with articles, rejoicing with each small printed victory and persuading me to "keep on keeping on" as my rejection pile grew.

"Make your readers see and feel. Cut out those adjectives. Create word pictures. Show, don't tell." they prodded when my writing stagnated like the bottom of a murky pond. Slowly, my acceptance pile grew to include more devotional pieces, nostalgic articles in the local newspaper, a testimony in a counseling center newsletter. Eventually I edited a booklet of inspirational writings for my church, encouraging others to share their thoughts on paper.

Even now, I'm amazed at how graciously and faithfully God answered my simple prayer for direction. Close to eighty-eight, I've just assembled my own collection, "Memories and Musings," reaching back to my papers written as a starry-eyed English student at Columbia University in the 1920's. But that doesn't mean I'm finished.

Do you have a dream that has been set aside because you've found it too difficult to persevere in faithfulness? Get it out and blow off the dust. If I can do it, so can you.

For everyone who asks receives; he who seeks finds;
and to him who knocks, the door will be opened.

LUKE 11:10

Everyone has a story to tell. Write yours.

August 10

Transformed By Insight

OSWALD CHAMBERS

He does not believe who does not live according to his belief.

—THOMAS FULLER

*T*he outstanding characteristic of a Christian is this unveiled frankness before God so that the life becomes a mirror for other lives. By being filled with the Spirit we are transformed, and by beholding we become mirrors. You always know when a man has been beholding the glory of the Lord, you feel in your inner spirit that he is the mirror of the Lord's own character. Beware of anything that would sully that mirror in you; it is nearly always a good thing, the good that is not the best.

The golden rule for your life and mine is this concentrated keeping of the life open towards God. Let everything else—work, clothes, food, everything on earth—go by the board, saving that one thing. The rush of other things always tends to obscure this concentration on God. We have to maintain ourselves in the place of beholding, keeping the life absolutely spiritual all through. Let other things come and go as they may, let other people criticize as they will, but never allow anything to obscure the life that is hid with Christ in God. Never be hurried out of the relationship of abiding in Him. It is the one thing that is apt to fluctuate but it ought not to.

And we, who with unveiled faces all reflect the Lord's glory, are being transformed into his likeness with ever increasing glory, which comes from the Lord, who is the Spirit.

2 CORINTHIANS 3:18

August II

This Little Piggy Went To Market . . .

GEORGIA CURTIS LING

Guard well your spare moments. They are like uncut diamonds. Discard them and their value will never be known. Improve them and they will become the brightest gems in a useful life.

—RALPH WALDO EMERSON

There are some things you shouldn't put off. Grocery shopping before a snow storm hits is one of them. But honestly, I was oblivious to the snow report. Besides that, it's not supposed to snow before Thanksgiving. I just happened to have grocery shopping on my list for Monday night, and moved it to the next day. I didn't know I would wake up to nine inches of snow with all my cupboards bare.

Sometimes I think I would rather go out and hunt my own food or buy a farm and raise a garden and livestock than to go grocery shopping. I personally don't know anyone who really enjoys this thankless task. It's time consuming, hectic and definitely depressing when you see your weekly grocery bill cost more than your first car.

If you watch, you'll see different types of shoppers. There's *Mother Hubbard* who only goes to the store when there is nothing left in the house and the children are begging for fresh bread. A friend of mine said one morning she was completely out of bread and had to resort to baking homemade biscuits. The funny thing was her kids thought she was wonderful and wanted to know what they were celebrating.

Then there's *Mrs. Busy*—the one who goes shopping every day of the week, planning her evening meal in the car on the way home from work. The Grocer loves her. He sees dollar signs, because research shows she'll spend a lot more money that way.

My favorite is *Mrs. Commando*—the shopper who declares war on shopping. Her strategy is laid out, the list completed, the menu decided weeks in advance, coupons clipped and her weapon, the pocket calculator, grasped tightly in her hand. She marches in the store single minded, grabs a cart and begins dodging enemy fire (you know, those nice little ladies with the tempting sample carts of goodies). *Mrs. Shopping Commando* puts on her imaginary blinders as she quickly goes through the store, aisle by aisle, placing only approved items from her list in the cart. In order to avoid friendly fire, she never, ever takes her kids or husband with her, for they might try to sneak an unauthorized item in the cart.

I didn't always appreciate this shopper until I was recruited and now I can say, *I have declared war on shopping.* Since enlistment and boot camp, I am now *Mrs. Commando,* saving precious hours that I can spend at home with my family counting the money saved by these new tactics. Life is too short to be standing in the so-called "express" lane with eight items or less.

Being faithful with grocery shopping may not seem exciting but our families are depending on us. Plus, we'll have more time for our families, and isn't that what abundance is all about?

> *When it snows, she has no fear for her household . . .*
> PROVERBS 31:21

If you usually aren't *Mrs. Commando Shopper,* make a list this week and stick to it.

August 12

A Finely Pruned Tree

JEAN FLEMING

> If a man has no time or only a short time for seeing people, you can be fairly sure that he is neither very important nor very busy.
> —JOHN SPENCER CHURCHILL

On a finely-pruned tree, the trunk and limbs are prominent. The limbs grow out of my relationship with Christ and sprout many new branches each year. I must examine my tree and determine which branches need to be pruned back or hacked off at the base. Life is always changing. My tree must undergo changes too.

This is the process I use to prune my life. Three or four times a year, I spend half a day with the Lord to evaluate my life, examine my schedule, and set some new directions for the months ahead. I spend most of the time reading the Bible, praying, and singing to the Lord. This quiet time acts like a knife to cut through the illusions and mirages of everyday life. It enables me to focus my attention, to set my heart on things above, where Christ is seated at the right hand of God. I set my mind on things above, not on earthly things (see Colossians 3:1-2).

Then I lay out my tree before the Lord. I make lists of current obligations, activities, and opportunities. I pray, "At this point in my life, Lord, what is it you want me to do? What must I do to keep my relationship to You vital? What do You want me to say yes and no to?"

Whenever I say yes to something, it means I will be saying no to something else. For example, if I say yes to being treasurer of the PTA, it may end up crowding out my time with God, my time with the family, my preparation for Sunday school, or my Sunday afternoon nap.

Looking at life this way helps me insure that I don't become too busy or fragmented to maintain my relationship to the Lord, to have vital time with my family, or to have a part in influencing the world for Christ.

As I evaluate my life before the Lord every three or four months, I remind myself that life is seasonal. There is a time and a season for everything (see Ecclesiastes 3:1). I can't do everything at once, nor should I. The question is—At this point in my life—what *should* I be doing?

The wisdom of the prudent is to give thought to their ways, but the folly of fools is deception.
PROVERBS 14:8

Read *Finding Focus in a Whirlwind World*, by Jean Fleming (Treasure Publishing).

August 13

A Simple Gift From The Heart

GAIL GAYMER MARTIN

When true simplicity is gained, to bow and to bend
we shan't be ashamed.
—"SIMPLE GIFTS," SHAKER TUNE

In our simplicity we best reflect our Christian life. Creating a book of remembrances preserves memories and artifacts of an individual, thus providing loved ones with a special and unique gift—a simple gift from the heart. Why not create a Memory Book for your family of your life and God's faithfulness?

Sharing recollections and past experiences brings the "family tree" to life. Old photographs, letters buried in an old chest, newspaper articles, and yearbook salutations trigger vivid memories. They are a special part of you that may be lost if not preserved.

To begin, divide your memories into time periods: elementary school days, high school days, young adults years, mid-years, and present. Search through old photograph albums. Pull out special pictures that bring to mind a day or time in your life. Write a narrative about each picture, not only what was happening, but how you felt at the time. Tell secrets that will be fun to share with your family.

Old letters, greeting cards with handwritten messages, paragraphs from your teenage diaries, and saved gift tags have stories to tell. What was the occasion of the gift? Why did you keep the card or letter? Answers to these questions tell so much about who you are.

Can you draw? Make sketches of events in your life. Remember to describe what the pictures, the letters, and the drawings mean to you. Explore the feelings you had at the time of the event. Did you go to the prom, but thought you might not be asked? Tell about it.

Make lists. They could include your top ten favorite hymns, foods, books, vacation spots, and top ten pet peeves. Describe your walk with God. Describe your wedding day, graduation day, the day of your marriage proposal, the first day on your first job, and the day of each child's birth. Narrate your most embarrassing moments and your most thrilling experiences.

When you have gathered the memorabilia, purchase a scrapbook and assemble your materials creatively. The Memory Book makes a wonderful gift for your children and grandchildren who will learn who you are, where you have been, and where you are going. You and your loved ones can relive those special memories over and over again.

This Memory Book will be an abundant source for chronicling your life and God's faithfulness. It's a simple gift for others, but one which will be cherished by future generations.

Oh, that my words were recorded, that they were written on a scroll, that they were inscribed with an iron tool on lead, or engraved in rock forever. I know that my Redeemer lives, and that in the end He will stand upon the earth.

JOB 19:23-25

August 14

Rewards Of Stillness

ANITA J. ANDERSON

Nature abhors a vacuum.

—OLD ADAGE

It has been said that nature never leaves an empty space without filling it up. It seems to me that humans operate on the same principle. Even when I don't consciously plan every minute of each day, I arrive at bedtime almost before I know it. I may plan to live a simple life, but somehow it frequently eludes me.

I thought that when I quit working for pay in the marketplace that I would have a lot of time for meditation and prayer. I believed it would be easier to be faithful. But I have not found it to be so. The demands from house, garden, and family members quickly consume all the time I can give them. When I worked outside the home, I just did less housecleaning, less cooking, and no gardening at all.

So, lately, when I get up in the morning, I view the hours until bedtime as an entity of substance, instead of empty slots to be filled on a calendar. I look at the substance of the day ahead and actually carve out a place for time spent alone with God. Then, when that meditation time arrives, I have to consciously command my feet to enter my quiet place, order my mind to stop cycling about pressing concerns, and focus on the Lord. Otherwise, I will be tempted to do just one more thing and let it slip away.

Also, I don't schedule an exact number of minutes for meditation with the Lord, and I know He is not dependent on time anyway. Nor do I have to meet at the same time every day with Him, remembering that He is always available. What is important is that I take time to quiet myself and listen to Him each day, have Him search my heart for barriers to fellowship, and clear the vessel that I am for His use.

When I'm not faithful in having a quiet time with the Lord, invariably I feel shredded and worn, because I have not rested in Him and because I have not sorted out His plan for the day from mine. The rewards for sitting quiet before Him are beyond measure.

Have you been faithful in having your time with God this summer? If your children are home, that may be difficult. But think of it this way: you'll develop spiritual dependability—that's faithfulness—within them by modeling a love for time with God.

Be still, and know that I am God . . .

PSALM 46:10

> Include your children in your Quiet Time with God by having them color a Bible story coloring book and talking about the story.

August 15

One Life

HELEN LUECKE

A man can have but one life, and one death, one heaven, one hell.

—ROBERT BROWNING

*A*fter a few days my colorful bouquet of roses began to die. The petals faded and dropped to the table. My young son made a comment, "They were pretty, but they sure didn't live long."

His statement made me stop and think. Who knows how long we'll live? Am I placing too much emphasis on future plans?

A calmness filled my heart. If we accept Jesus and live in His will, God will take care of our tomorrows, whether it be on earth or in His presence. Each new day the Lord grants me, I will faithfully place Him first in my life. Then I go ahead and make plans for the future.

If you have fears about the future, trust that God has your days planned. You just have to faithfully live each one out. That's abundant life in a nutshell.

. . . What is your life? You are a mist that appears for a little while and then vanishes.

JAMES 4:14

> Spend a few minutes looking at the stars tonight and committing your future to God.

Call Me Bobo

LAUREL B. SCHUNK

Faith is: dead to doubts, dumb to discouragements, blind to impossibilities.

—ANONYMOUS

"Sorry, Laurie, the 'Big Deal' fell through," Sara, my agent, said. *Big Deal* was right. A twelve-book mystery series for a big publisher *was* a big deal. At last, I'd anticipated receiving some income for the years I had dedicated to full-time writing. Now, nothing.

"I'm so sorry," she went on. "I told you too early and set you up for disappointment."

"Oh, please don't feel bad. It gave me a dose of confidence when I needed it. And I got to celebrate the possibility, at least."

But once I got off the phone, I was deeply disappointed.

Sulking, anger, fear, and frustration overwhelmed me. All the things that I, as a Christian, feel but shouldn't indulge. I indulged it, however, for a full twenty-four hours.

This was a disappointment for my agent too, as well as for the editor with whom she had hatched the series idea. I hurt for them too. The next day, however, I was fine, and I explained why to Sara.

When these disappointments come my way, I'm a lot like a toy our oldest son used to have, a vinyl clown called Bobo that was about three feet tall. We blew it up and set it on the floor. Sand weighted its rounded bottom so that a child could punch the clown, it would fall over, then bob right back up, its dumb, painted-on smile in place.

I'm a lot like Bobo, but I didn't used to be. I used to be able to get into weeks-long snits. It was hard for me to trust God's faithful plans for me.

So now I go to my room and sulk a while. I rail at God and try to tell Him how to handle my calling as a full-time Christian writer. Then I cringe to think of the pride and arrogance I show before my Lord and my God.

He doesn't zap me with lightning, He just holds me for a while. I suffer simply and totally, and then I'm better. I wait a few days, then call a couple of special friends and share my pain with them. They pray for me. From time to time the pain comes back, but it's a little lighter each time.

Do I sometimes look as dumb as that smirking Bobo? Perhaps, but my smile isn't painted on, it's real. I've learned that after the initial disappointment, choosing to faithfully trust God releases me from those unpleasant feelings. I can't do anything about the situation anyway and feeling pained doesn't change them. So I praise God, instead, for what He sees in my future, and I continue on in faith.

And the God of all grace, who called you to His eternal glory in Christ, after you have suffered a little while, will Himself restore you and make you strong, firm, and steadfast.

I PETER 5:10

> You can maintain the balance between energy and demands by eliminating unproductive emotional drains and adding self-replenishing activities. (Carol Tannenhauser)

August 17

Not Called To The Front Lines?

RENEÉ S. SANFORD

If any one of our Christian workers ever felt our prayers for him had been dropped to the "optional" category, he would drop to his knees in despair.

—RENEÉ S. SANFORD

The future of Europe, Africa—of the world was at stake. The raging battles of World War II hemorrhaged region after region. In a gauging lab, huge shipments of bullets came in daily. One bullet from each load was tested to see that it measured up to exact specifications.

This particular lab received and tested ammunition manufactured in the USA for British use on the war fronts. The leading man in charge of drafting and revising designs for the gauges couldn't have been more qualified for the job at hand. He was a master at what he did.

But burning inside him was a yearning to serve his country on the front lines of the war effort. Finally, he received his orders, said farewell to his staff at the lab, and went out to the front lines of Africa. Within a short time, he was missing in action. His assistant, Pamela Reeve, despite her comparable lack of qualifications, was left in charge of the lab at a crucial point in the warfare.

How tragic that Pamela's boss didn't see the significance of his contribution to the war effort—behind the scenes—insisting instead to be sent to the front lines.

Pamela's story reminds me that God has not called all of us to the "front lines" of Christian ministry. But we must take seriously our faithful mission of supporting and supplying the soldiers we send out.

God has given us the privilege of sending out a large group of high caliber people on the front lines, taking the Gospel to different parts of the world. They are such outstanding people, in fact, that we can easily applaud their efforts, without realizing the crucial role we faithfully play in the spiritual warfare they fight. Like the man in charge of the gauges, we are indispensable to supplying our pastor, our missionaries, and other Christian workers with the weapons of warfare—most particularly, prayer.

How is your faithfulness in praying for God's front-line warriors? You *are* needed. Supporting others is an essential in the abundant life God wants for us.

Now it is required that those who have been given a trust must prove faithful.
I CORINTHIANS 4:2

> Pray for five minutes for a missionary today.

August 18

How Do I Discover God's Will For My Life?

DEBBIE PIPER

Has it ever struck you that the vast majority of the will of God for your life has already been revealed in the Bible? That is a crucial thing to grasp.
—PAUL LITTLE

God has revealed His will through His Written Word, the Bible, and through His Living Word, Jesus Christ. In the Bible, you will find directions for living a godly life, and in Jesus, you will find that life personified in one human life. As you faithfully take time to grow in your spiritual understanding, and as you become more familiar with Jesus, you will begin to understand the basic spiritual principles that should direct your life as a Christian. This is the foundation of the simple Christian life.

The most basic of these is love for God and love for others, but you will also discover a new way of looking at life and decision-making from God's perspective. Increasingly, you will want to be sure that you are moving in the direction that will bring you closer to God, fitting in with His desires and honoring Him day-by-day. The Holy Spirit living within you is a faithful Guide who will direct your thoughts and confirm your decisions when they honor God. He will cause you to be aware of the times when you are out-of-step with God's will.

Do you first seek direction from the Bible when you have a decision to make? Faithfully doing that will save you from many needless difficulties. He wants you to know His will. That's why He wrote you His Love Letter.

And whatever you do, whether in word or deed, do it all in the
name of the Lord Jesus, giving thanks to God the Father through Him.
COLOSSIANS 3:17

Ask, "What would Jesus do?" as you make decisions today.

August 19

The Simplicity Of Good Books

ROBERTA L. MESSNER

Lord, make me respect my mind so much that I dare
not read what has neither meaning nor moral. Help
me choose with equal care my friends and my books,
because they are both for life.
—H.H. BARSTOW

Several weeks before my 41st birthday, I was feeling quite old. One evening when my husband, Mark, and I were shopping, I visited a Bible book store, thinking a good book might lift my sagging spirits. "Tolley's," Mark commented on the name of the business. "Wasn't that the lady at church who used to loan you books?"

"No, that was *Tillie*," I corrected, smiling at the memory of Tillie Robinson. When I was a teenager with limited funds, she generously loaned me books from her extensive library of Christian classics.

Tillie always added a generous helping of wisdom. "The person you become, Roberta, will be largely determined by the people you spend time with and the books you read," she often told me. And I believed her, not only because she was a Bible scholar and a marvelous mentor, but because I knew she really cared about me.

As I browsed through racks of books, I realized I was the only middle-aged woman in the whole store. I felt conspicuously dowdy among the size-four teenyboppers gabbing about cheerleading and biology tests. One, with a flawless porcelain complexion and delicate features, dressed in a perky plaid jumper, approached me: "You must read a lot," she said shyly, taking in the growing stack of books in my arms. "I was wondering, what would you buy if you could only afford one book? I just have $5.00."

"Have you read *In His Steps* or *Not My Will?*" I asked, combing the racks for some of my all-time favorites. "They'll change your life." Other teens began to swarm around me, buzzing with questions like I was an old sage. Some spoke of their own treasured volumes, read and re-read.

Tillie's time-tested advice, spoken almost three decades before when she was about my age, formed on my lips: "Girls, the kind of ladies you'll become will be largely due to the books you read." To my amazement, they leaned closer, hanging on every word. Feeling very young, I advised. "Keep reading good books."

Good books are faithful friends and faithfully filling our minds with the truth of them will strengthen us to choose simplicity and abundance. What have you filled your mind with this summer?

Likewise, teach the older women to be reverent in the way they live . . . to teach what is good. Then they can train the younger women . . .
TITUS 2:3-4

> Enjoy browsing in the your local bookstore and come away with an unexpected topic.

August 20

Story Time

TIM REAVES

Anecdotes are stories with points. They are tools—nail sinkers to drive home arguments firmly. They are the origin of all teaching.

—EDMUND FULLER

Somewhere along the way, we have convinced our adult selves that the practice of reading Bible "stories" like we might have done as children is something we outgrow. George Bernard Shaw once said that Englishmen. . . "think that they are moral when they are only uncomfortable." Similarly, we often think that we can only say that we have spent quality time in God's Word if we feel we have just finished doing our taxes . . . and we owe.

Instead of wrestling with the Scriptures, determined to wring every little truth from its pages (as if we could achieve illumination through sheer effort), sometimes we need to sit at the feet of the Master and just listen to the stories He has given to us in the Bible.

Please understand, this is certainly not a warning against in-depth Bible study. Far from it. Just a reminder that there is a time to be the diligent student, and likewise a time to be an adoring child. Occasionally, the microscope needs to be set aside to benefit from the big picture.

The Book of Esther contains one of the more remarkable dramas ever written, in real life or fiction. A heroic woman putting her life in danger to save her people; a wise counselor brimming with integrity; an all powerful king whose weakness is his own pride; and a despicable villain seeking to destroy anyone who would get in his way; add to that an ironic and totally satisfying conclusion, and you have a story that would have made Shakespeare proud.

Esther has a story that is enjoyable, and in its entirety, paints a vivid picture of how God protects His people, and blesses character and obedience.

The writer of Hebrews encourages believers by reminding them of the stories about faithful men and women through the centuries. Hebrews 11 builds a sturdy wall of outstanding examples that could withstand the worst the world has to throw against it. These stories—of people like Abel, Sarah, Joseph, and Moses—inspire as they convict; displaying what we need to do while reminding us why we strive to do it.

Have you been faithful in enjoying the "big picture" of the Scriptures as told through its inspiring stories? For your devotional time today, delight in reading one story and let it again reveal God in a simple—yet powerful—way.

Therefore, since we are surrounded by such a great cloud of witnesses, let us throw off everything that hinders and the sin that so easily entangles, and let us run with perseverance the race marked out for us.

HEBREWS 12:1

August 21

Always Enough

LAURA SABIN RILEY

A little thing is a little thing, but faithfulness in a little thing becomes a great thing.

—PLATO

During the beginning years of our marriage, my husband and I got caught up in a business venture which we were sure was going to bring us to financial independence at an early age. We quit two good paying, stable jobs to pursue this venture full-time. In less than a year, we were in a huge amount of debt. The opportunity we thought would bring us financial freedom had catapulted us into financial disaster. During this time, we were not tithing faithfully to our church or any ministry at all. We justified this decision by saying, "We can't even pay our bills, surely God understands that we can't tithe right now." We continued to sink deeper and deeper into debt, unable to meet our monthly bills. But finally, we decided it was time to get back to two stable jobs that brought weekly paychecks. We were in so much debt, however, that we still didn't tithe.

One night shortly after we had made the transition, my husband was reading his Bible and came across Proverbs 3:9-10. He was convicted that God was speaking to him. Taking my hand, he said, "Laura, we are making a terrible mistake. We need to begin tithing, regardless of our financial position." I agreed with him and we made a commitment from that night forth to faithfully give to God from the first of our income, not from the leftovers.

An amazing thing happened. Somehow, every week after we tithed, we had enough money to pay the bills that were due that week. Often, money came from unexpected places. Week after week, month after month, we always had just enough to meet our needs. We lived without any frills for a couple of years until we paid the debt off, but we never went hungry.

Ten years later, we faithfully practice the principle of tithing, no matter how strapped for cash we are, and God continues to meet our financial needs. Many times, by obeying that single simple principle, and giving back to God what is already His, we have opened ourselves up for an abundance of blessings. He has blessed us tremendously, and not just financially, but in many other ways as well.

Have you been faithful to God in this area? If you are, God will be faithful to you. He promises it as a part of His abundant plan for you.

Honor the Lord with your wealth, with the firstfruits of all your crops; then your barns will be filled to overflowing, and your vats will brim over with new wine.
PROVERBS 3:9-10

Remember that wealth lies not in the extent of possessions, but in the fewness of wants. Live within your means, not beyond them.

August 22

Confessions Of A Sunday School Teacher

MARY LOU KLINGLER

To be glad instruments of God's love in this imperfect world is the service to which man is called.
—ALBERT SCHWEITZER

I was one of the teachers of a large first grade Sunday School class. As I told the Bible story in front of the whole room, I felt moved to give an invitation to accept Jesus as their Savior at the conclusion. We didn't do this often since six-year-olds tend to follow other children and sometimes don't really understand.

Instead of asking for raised hands or to come forward, I asked any child who sincerely wanted to ask Jesus into their hearts to stay in their seats after workbook time. I planned to talk and pray with them one-on-one.

The bell rang. Sunday School was over.

One little shy boy, Alan, sat quietly in his seat unobserved. I tidied the room and gathered up materials we'd used to store in our cupboard before Junior Church leaders came to teach the second hour. When they arrived, I was free to join my husband for our own church service.

At the years end, the first graders were promoted and there were always a few that I would remember. I remembered Alan, mostly for his attentiveness and shyness. When Alan grew to high school age, he came into our first grade class where I still taught and gave puppet shows. I felt proud of him. The children loved him even though he was still very shy. Hidden behind the curtain and puppets he expressed himself well.

Fifteen years after I'd taught Alan in first grade, I happened to see him again at our local Bible College, where he attended. He smiled shyly and came over to me. "Mrs. Klingler, for years I've been tempted to tell you that I accepted Jesus as my Savior when I was in your first grade class."

"Really, Alan? I don't remember that," I confessed.

"That Sunday you asked us to stay after class if we wanted to accept Jesus. I waited and waited. The kids came back in from recess and then we had Junior Church. I thought you might come back so I waited again. No one came. The room was empty. Finally my Dad came looking for me to go home. I told him what had happened. I still wanted to ask Jesus into my heart. My Dad understood and prayed with me. I felt so good and I think he was glad he was the one who actually led me to the Lord. I just thought you'd like to know."

He didn't mean to embarrass me, but I felt ashamed. "Thank you for telling me, Alan." He smiled shyly and walked away.

I knew I would never forget it. I wondered if I had blown it other times, too. What if Alan's father hadn't been a Christian and had made fun of his decision? What if Alan had come from a family who didn't know the Lord?

"Oh, Lord, forgive me," I prayed silently, "and keep me more aware of the needs of your little ones."

God wants us to faithfully share His wonderful gift of salvation with others. As we see the fruit He brings, we'll know assuredly the joy of the abundant life.

> *. . . how shall we escape if we ignore such a great salvation . . . ?*
> HEBREWS 2:3

Rejoice in the knowledge that you may have led someone to the Lord, or drawn them closer to Him, by your action, word, or deed.

A Dipperful Of Water

CORA LEE PLESS

Our grand business is not to see what lies dimly in the distance, but to do what lies clearly at hand.
— THOMAS CARLYLE

*A*nticipating squeals of delight, I lowered my daughter Carey into the plastic wading pool. She was about fifteen-months-old and at a perfect age, I thought, for a little pool. Carey thought differently. Instead of crying out in delight, she shrieked in protest.

Even though Carey hated being *in* the water, she enjoyed playing *with* the water and soon invented a way to do so. She would stand beside the pool and bend over to play, content as long as her feet were planted on dry ground.

One day, using one of those plastic measuring scoops from a drink mix, she bent over and scooped up a dipperful of water. Carrying the dipper, she gingerly toddled toward a yellow sand bucket several yards away. With each tottery step, water splashed out. By the time she arrived at the sand bucket, she had little water left in the dipper. But what water she had, she triumphantly poured into the bucket and hurried back to the pool for another dipperful.

She repeated this process over and over while I watched with mounting frustration. *What is she trying to do? Surely she doesn't plan to fill up the sand bucket.*

Then I understood. Carey wasn't trying to accomplish any great feat. She was simply trying to carry one dipperful of water at a time to the best of her ability.

Carey taught me an important lesson that day. Often I become discouraged as I view the difficulties in our world. The needs are like an empty bucket waiting to be filled. My help seems feeble. How can I make any difference?

Carey taught me to focus, not on the magnitude of the problem, but on doing what I can. I can't alleviate world hunger, but I can faithfully give to a hunger fund or help out in a soup kitchen. I may not preach to large numbers of people, but I can ardently share God's love with a neighbor or teach Sunday school. I cannot cure loneliness, but I can consistently visit, make a phone call, or send a card.

Discouragement still slips in at times and sometimes I hear whispers that my work for the Lord is meager and unimportant. Then I think of Carey and her dipperful of water. I focus again on faithfully performing whatever task God has given me to do—carrying my little dipperful of water to the best of my ability in God's power.

What dipperful does God want you to carry? Be faithful to do it and leave the results to God.

And if anyone gives even a cup of cold water to one of these little ones because he is my disciple, I tell you the truth, he will certainly not lose his reward.

MATTHEW 10:42

Read *Love's Little Recipes for Life* by Linda Shepherd (Multnomah, 1997).

August 24

Calendar Clutter

DEBRA SMITH

Be not careless in deeds, nor confused in words, nor rambling in thought.

—MARCUS AURELIUS ANTONINUS

Take two adults with after-hours commitments, church, and many other responsibilities. Add a daughter taking piano or dance, and maybe Girl Scouts. Then there's the son with ball practice or games almost every day. Include birthdays and dental appointments, and the family calendar begins to resemble King Tut's bulletin board. Unfortunately, few of us can read hieroglyphics.

When our children reached the "age of involvement" and we began to miss appointments because of calendar clutter, something had to be done. Our solution was color coding. Each person's activities are written in a different ink and they are responsible for checking the calendar. Birthdays that mustn't be forgotten are given special decoration. This simple step has helped our crew organize its activities and nearly eliminated those two words that wilt a parent's spirit, "You forgot."

If you have trouble faithfully keeping all your commitments figured out, try this simple step. You won't hear "You forgot." either.

For God is not a God of disorder, but of peace . . .

I CORINTHIANS 14:33

> Keep each person's favorite color of fine-point marker
> in a container near the calendar. Younger children
> enjoy stickers and rubber stamps.

August 25

Sticking Together

MURIEL LARSON

These Christians love each other even before they are
acquainted.

—St. Celsus

The new missionary heard a vast rustling sound in the distance.
Something about it made the hair on the back of his neck stand up.
His native guides paused and listened. A look of terror glazed their eyes.

Another native came running up and cried, "Army ants. They're
coming. Hurry, turn off at the fork up ahead."

A little later as they stood on a hill and looked down, they could
see a huge army of the stinging ants swarming, eating and cutting a
swath through the forest. Nothing seemed able to stand before them.
The missionary even saw a small animal disappear before his eyes, the
fast dinner of countless ants. Not far ahead was the river. "Surely the
river will stop them or turn them aside, won't it?" the missionary asked
his bearer.

The man shook his head. "No, just watch."

As the ants reached the river, they came together and formed
themselves into balls, rolled into the river, and rode with the current to
the other side. There they disengaged from one another and continued
their march.

What do you think would happen if those who love Christ would
faithfully stand together like those army ants? People would really take
notice—just as the natives do when the ants surge by.

Also, the cause of Christ would go forward in a way that it has
seldom gone since the early days of Christianity. People in those days
said of the Christians that they "turned the world upside down" (Acts
17:6). Their unity and love for one another were marveled at by all

who came into contact with them. Many came to know Jesus Christ as their Savior because of the Christians' unity, testimony, kindness, and good lives.

If we know the Lord Jesus as our personal Savior, and follow Him, it should become second nature to us to want to help others and work together for His glory. The Bible says that one sign that we know the Lord is the love we exhibit toward Him and others.

Those army ants are a great reminder of how we need to band together. Let's show the world a faithfulness in loving others that will be stronger than those ants. Can you think of something that will show that today?

Carry each other's burdens, and in this way you will fulfill the law of Christ.
GALATIANS 6:2

How's your exercising during these hot summer months? Find a friend who needs it too, and walk during the cool of sunset.

August 26

A Plan For Aerobic Spiritual Fitness

STEVE FARRAR

Habit is a cable; we weave a thread of it each day, and at last we cannot break it.

—HORACE MANN

*A*s I lay out this plan, I'm going to assume you are not spending *any* time during a given week with the Lord. You may be, but for the purpose of explaining this plan, I need to start at square one.

I believe there are four necessary components in an effective plan for "aerobic" kneeling.

1. *Plan a time.*

A good rule of thumb is to begin your day by meeting with the Lord. Not everyone's schedule allows for this. But if possible, plan to have a morning briefing with the Lord.

As you look at your schedule, what time will work for you?

2. *Plan a place.*

We are constantly planning places. The same is true with prayer. It could be your den, office, or bedroom. The only criteria is that it needs to be a place where you can have some privacy and not be disturbed.

I have a friend who has such a long commute to work that it's impossible for him to have time with the Lord first thing in the morning. So he takes four lunch hours a week and spends those with the Lord. His office is his place. What's going to be yours?

3. *Make a list.*

Write down the people and issues you want to pray about. I have a daily section, under which I include the things I need to pray for each day. Other items are listed under different days of the week. On Tuesday I pray for my extended family. I pray for my wife and kids every day, but on Tuesday I include aunts, uncles, brothers, parents, cousins, etc. I use Thursday to pray for my colleagues in ministry around the country, guys I know who carry large ministry responsibilities. When I run into one of them, I can truthfully say I pray for him once a week.

As you work your way through your list, it's a good idea to pray specifically instead of generally. Say, "Lord, give each of my children wisdom today to stand for what is right instead of giving in to peer pressure." "Lord, please give their teachers wisdom in understanding my children as they teach them today."

4. *Begin with Scripture.*

I usually begin by reading a portion of Scripture that I'm working through. That helps me to warm up to prayer. *There is no magic formula.* Keep at it, and you will find what works best for you.

Private time with the Lord in prayer and Scripture will yield tremendous benefits. Approximately fifteen minutes in the Scripture and fifteen minutes in prayer three times a week will keep you aerobically fit. That's something any of us can do.

Give yourself six weeks with a certain time in a certain place with a certain list, and you will be well on your way to establishing a systematic habit.

Blessed is the man who does not walk in the counsel of the wicked or stand in the way of sinners or sit in the seat of mockers. But His delight is in the law of the Lord, and on His law he meditates day and night.

PSALM 1:1-2

Make a list of the activities that waste your time or energy and work on replacing one of them today with a higher priority.

After Wipe-Out

CARL WESTLING

Failure is the line of least persistence.

— ANONYMOUS

J recently read in the newspaper of a man who experienced wipe-out in his business. His story is repeated in different scenarios many times over all around us. It's happened to all of us in different ways, at different degrees. At that point of seeming defeat, you may ask yourself, *What is left? What happened to the abundant life?*

You will be left with the experiences, the memories, and also the consequences of your past actions. The consequences can also have an impact on your future and may also affect the lives of others. So, what can you do? How can you handle it?

Accept the past as history that cannot be undone. Time is an essential ingredient in recovering from the shock and remorse of the past, before there can be hope about the future. God uses time to bring healing, allowing a renewal of attitude and a redevelopment of your confidence in yourself and in God.

Soon you'll start thinking, "Being wiped out doesn't mean I have to quit. Maybe, just maybe, I can benefit from that wipe-out. Maybe I've learned a lesson or two that can be applied to the future. I'll seek the Lord."

Visualize a tree on a rocky windswept hillside. The adversity of the elements actually help to strengthen the tree for ongoing survival. The wind-torn scars and fire marks visible on its trunk and limbs become part of its character, evidence of past wounds and struggles that have been overcome. Below the surface, under the skin, bark, and roots, the source of its strength remains healthy and strong. Water and nutrients are faithfully being absorbed for new strength and growth.

Think of yourself the same way. Past events are the foundation for God's future plans for you. You can believe there are seeds of the future beginning to sprout within you, and then turn the results over to God.

With God, there is always hope. Faithfully seek Him because trials are a part of the abundant life meant to bring ultimate glory to God.

And the God of all grace, who called you to his eternal glory in Christ, after you have suffered a little while, will himself restore you and make you strong, firm and steadfast.
I PETER 5:10

Read *Bounce Back*, compiled by Diana L. James (Horizon Books, 1997).

August 28

Don't Boast About Tomorrow

MARJORIE K. EVANS

Tomorrow cheats us all. Why dost thou stay,
And leave undone what should be done today?
—HUGHES

I will never forget that day years ago as I was driving to the credit union to cash my check. I had a strong impression that I should tell Mr. and Mrs. Everett, the credit union managers, about Jesus. But immediately fear arose within me and I thought, *They're so sophisticated. They'll probably laugh at me or ridicule the idea.*

Part of my fear stemmed from the fact that during my growing-up years, the pastor of our church emphasized that he should be the one to pray with and to lead people to the Lord.

After coming to California, I joined a church where our evangelical pastor taught that all of us who are Christians are to tell others about Jesus and the plan of salvation.

While standing in line to deposit my check, the urging to talk to the Everetts about the Lord persisted. But witnessing was still somewhat new to me. By the time I arrived at the counter, even though there was no one behind me, I was too intimidated to say anything. So I merely transacted my business.

Feeling uneasy, I left and slowly walked towards my car. But I had no peace, so I turned around and went back into the office. By then there were several people in line. I thought, *The Everetts don't have time to talk to me today.* So I left again.

Driving home, I consoled myself, *I'll talk to them about the Lord the first of August when I deposit my next check.*

But on the first of August, when I walked into the credit union, the only person working there was a young woman. Puzzled, I inquired, "Where are Mr. and Mrs. Everett?"

"Oh, haven't you heard the terrible news?" the woman asked. "They left on vacation Saturday. They were on their way to Washington when their small plane crashed, and they were both killed instantly."

Devastated, I exclaimed, "How tragic."

Later, as I hurried to the car, I thought of how my Bible teacher always emphasized that if the Lord impressed on us to tell someone about Jesus we should instantly obey, for we might not have another opportunity.

Tears welled up in my eyes as, in deep contrition, I cried, "Dear Lord, forgive me for my disobedience in not talking to the Everetts about Jesus. Give me the courage to tell others about You."

Since that day I've had many chances to witness to others about the saving grace of our Lord Jesus Christ. It has not always been easy, and often I've been tempted not to say anything. But when I think of the tragedy of the Everetts and the opportunity I missed, I'm now bold in speaking out. For I do not know what will happen tomorrow.

If the Lord wants you to speak of Him, be faithful. You may be surprised at a person's receptivity for He has most likely already been faithfully preparing their hearts. They want the abundant life—they just haven't heard about it yet.

Do not boast about tomorrow, for you do not know what a day may bring forth.
PROVERBS 27:1

> Share with someone today one thing God has done for you.

August 29

Time Is A Gift

MILDRED WENGER

Dost thou love life? Then do not squander time, for that is the stuff life is made of.
—BENJAMIN FRANKLIN

*U*sing time wisely is part of being a good steward of God's gifts and a part of the journey toward abundant living. Time is a gift—a most precious one. But worrying about all the things I need to get done, and sometimes forgetting something important, used to be very upsetting to me.

Then I read somewhere that making a daily list is a good way to manage this problem. The article advised the reader to make a list each evening of every single thing you need to do the coming day. Then cross off each item as you finish doing it. At the end of the day, transfer the unfinished items to tomorrow's list.

I've found this works for me. I begin each day's list with some obvious items: pray, exercise, comb hair, soak my teeth, make the bed, play piano, play organ. You probably think I should be able to accomplish this much without a written reminder. Yes, I probably should. But when I'm going to have a difficult day, like, facing an appointment for another mammogram, it helps to see the routine side on the list, too.

Besides, it's hard to discipline yourself to take time for yourself, unless you schedule it right in with other activities. Things like exercising and playing the piano might not mean much to some folks, but I need the exercise and the lovely old songs of the church lift my spirits like nothing else can. If the day is too short, these things can be skipped over, and sometimes that happens. Each person must decide for themselves how much private time they needs.

My daily list also includes all *necessary* phone calls, such as scheduling doctor visits, business calls, anything concerning church activities, and calls to my family. The list also includes seemingly insignificant jobs like sewing a button on hubby's blue shirt, or putting a patch on his gray work pants. Otherwise I might forget.

I studied Gregg shorthand in school. This gives me the advantage of being able to write very personal reminders and I don't have to worry that someone else will read them. But if you don't know shorthand, you can make up your own abbreviations for items of a private nature.

Faithfully managing time is a major undertaking and a part of simplicity. I love the passage in Ecclesiastes 3:1-8. It assures us that God expects us to fill our days with many different activities, each in its own proper time and place.

Although the summer is often a more laid-back time, activities still abound. Be sure to make your list and faithfully use it. It'll make life more enjoyable and abundant.

There is a time for everything, and a season for every activity under heaven.
ECCLESIASTES 3:1

When shopping for groceries, list the items you need in the order you'll find them at the store.

Traveling Tea Time

EMILIE BARNES

A woman is like a teabag. It's only when she's in hot
water that you realize how strong she is.

—NANCY REAGAN

*M*y friend Marilyn Heavilin told me a wonderful tea party story
about a time when she took her teacups traveling and created
a precious and durable memory.

My friend Diana had been through a very rough year. Her husband
had had a stroke at the age of 47 which had forced him into retirement.
Diana was caring for him as well as working full time at an outside
job. She loved to attend the outdoor concerts in the summertime at
the Redlands Bowl. We arranged for a night that she could have
someone else stay with her husband. We told her we would go early
and save seats so she could come as late as she needed to. When she
arrived, I opened my picnic basket and we had a tea party. Diana is
from England and loves tea and teatime. I had hot tea in a thermos,
and I served it in my most delicate china cups. I had bought yummy
desserts from a deli . . . and served them on china plates. I used my
best silverware and linen napkins. I also gave Diana a beautiful picture
book about English teatime. We had a crowd watching us and drooling
. . . . The setting was perfect, the music was inspiring, the sky was
filled with stars, and my friend Diana felt loved and pampered. She
will never forget that night, nor will I.

I have had similar experiences many times, and I have never
regretted packing up a tea party and taking it to make a memory. Once
I took a tea party in a basket to a friend who had been sick. I told her
to relax on the couch while I cleared off the coffee table and opened
my basket, which contained all the makings of the tea party except the
hot water. I put her kettle on to boil while I unpacked a tea cloth and
napkins, a candle and a candleholder, a little potted plant (which I left
as a gift), and all the other tea things. We enjoyed a delectable teatime
together. Then, after tea, I rubbed her feet.

What a wonderful experience for me as well as my friend. That
kind of giving and receiving not only makes memories; it forges
powerful bonds between people. It ministers health of body and spirit.

Let us not become weary in doing good, for at the proper time we will reap a harvest if we do not give up.

GALATIANS 6:9

Take a traveling teatime to a sick or needy friend.

August 31

R.G. Letourneau:
In Business With God

D. LEROY SANDERS

A man's treatment of money is the most decisive test of his character—how he makes it and how he spends it.
— JAMES MOFFATT

When R.G. LeTourneau spoke at our church, he almost jolted us out of our seats with a blockbuster statement. "Today I give ninety percent of everything I make back to God." Not ten percent. Ninety percent. "But you don't need to take up an offering for me. I'm not a poor man. The ten percent is more than I will ever need." Tongue in cheek, he acted almost apologetic.

At sixty-five years of age, he sold his fabulous earth-moving business for thirty-one million dollars. By the time I got around to inviting Bob LeTourneau to be our guest in Cincinnati, it was the mid 1950's. He was enduring a "temporary" retirement by traveling around at his own expense and sharing his amazing story.

He made and lost fortunes through his inventive genius and unorthodox behavior. Finally in his golden years, world leaders heaped praise on him for his unequaled accomplishments.

LeTourneau's factories had built over fifty percent of the earth-moving equipment used in World War II combat.

This high school dropout eventually founded an engineering, technology, arts, and sciences college. And left an industry with several thousand employees. His credits are stunning. Yet, nothing compared to his relationship with God.

"After I was converted, I turned my life over to God. I even offered to become a preacher or a missionary. My pastor wisely counseled me that God needed dedicated businessmen perhaps more than another preacher. On my knees, in the pastor's study, I vowed to take God as my business partner. And I also promised to tithe everything we made."

It really worked for LeTourneau. He prospered and faithfully tithed. He felt his Heavenly Partner was then asking for twenty, then thirty, forty, and eventually fifty percent. "At last, my Partner and I will share and share alike," he thought.

"Surprise," explained the inventor. "One day I seemed to hear a familiar voice. 'Are we still partners?' 'Yes, Lord.' 'Do you have all you need?' 'Yes, Lord, and more.' 'How much did you take for all those early years?' 'Ninety percent, Lord.' 'Now it's my turn. Ten percent will meet your needs. I will take the ninety percent.'"

The rest of the story? "We have had the joy of giving away more than fifty million dollars. Our remaining ten percent is now multiplied millions. More than we could ever spend."

Evidently it's good business to take God as your partner.

Are you faithful in hearing God's voice regarding giving to Him? He promises abundance when we surrender all.

On the first day of every week, each one of you should set
aside a sum of money in keeping with his income . . .
I CORINTHIANS 16:2

How are you doing in your commitment to tithe? Even if you can't give as much as you'd like, increase it by just a little this week.

September

*". . . with all humility and gentleness,
with patience, showing forbearance to
one another in love."*

Ephesians 4:2

*T*he gentle beauty of Fall is coming. This month's readings reflect God's gentleness and the gentleness that will result from our abundant walk close to Jesus. Although we may be tempted to be harsh when we are annoyed, or bitter toward those who disappoint us, God wants us to always respond in gentleness. He abundantly forgave us. He wants us to extend that same simple grace. This month's readings will inspire us to experience that rich kind of life that frees us to live positively.

Speak Gently

MARY LOU KLINGLER

Speak gently, 'tis a little thing,
Dropped in the heart's deep well,
The truth, the joy, that it will bring,
Eternity will tell.

—ANONYMOUS

*M*y Mother would often quote this poem. As we begin this month further on our journey toward the abundant life, gentle words are a necessity, as expressed in that poem. I have no idea who wrote it, and I hope I remember it correctly. When my twin sisters and I were young, we were outspoken and argued a lot. Mother tried vainly to get us to speak softly and gently, but we'd forget.

Mother finally came up with the idea of ordering us each a ring with initials on it. It would be like tying a string around your finger to remember something.

When the rings arrived, we were delighted. They were shiny black with the initials S.G. in tiny silver letters on them. Only we knew that it stood for "Speak Gently." If anyone asked, we told them it was our grandmother's initials, which was true.

The ring reminded us constantly to speak gently—and it worked. Sometimes it takes a concrete reminder of what we know to do.

Is "S.G." written on your heart? We can't fully live the abundant life without gentle words toward others. God will reward us with gentle words in return.

A gentle answer turns away wrath, but a harsh word stirs up anger.
PROVERBS 15:1

> If you struggle with keeping your words or actions gentle, make several little signs throughout your home with the letters "S.G." on them.

The Sound Of Silence

H. NORMAN WRIGHT

How can you expect God to speak in that gentle and inward voice which melts the soul, when you are making so much noise with your rapid reflections? Be silent, and God will speak again.

—FRANCOIS DE LA MOTHE FÉNELON

We live in a polluted world. There are many kinds of pollution, but let's talk about one—noise pollution. You can't even go into a nice restaurant for dinner without having to contend with loud music. Noise—noise—noise—radios, TV, horns, airplanes, people talking and yelling, electric lawn mowers and blowers, freeways. Isn't there any place where there's no sound?

Can you handle the stillness of solitude? Is it unnerving to sit and listen to . . . nothing? Are you an activity addict? Are the noises in your head so loud you can't hear God talking to you? His still, small voice won't try to out-shout the noise. It will always be a still, small voice. He's waiting for you to be quiet, to listen, to relax, so that you can be restored.

It's difficult to become a man of God without the sound of silence.

My soul finds rest in God alone . . .

PSALM 62:1

Find a quiet place to spend one hour reading, praying, and meditating. Listen specifically for God's still, small voice.

Gnarly Roots And A Red-Winged Blackbird

SHIRLEY A. REYNOLDS

Stars may be seen from the bottom of a deep well,
when they cannot be seen from the top of the mountain.
So are many things learned in adversity, which the
prosperous man dreams not of.

—Jo PETTY

J walked with a friend who was crushed by falsehoods and unjustly fired from a job of fifteen years. The beach offered a safe, gentle haven from phone calls. We breathed in the fragrance of wet moss, blackberries, hyacinths, and pine woods creating a potpourri of fragrance.

The wind swirled in gusts as we followed the trail down the cliff. A warble of a bird crept through the mist, and a red-winged blackbird disappeared into the wooded thicket. "Must be a sign from God," we laughed.

As our feet sunk into wet sand, we sensed a different atmosphere from the wooded glen. Small pools of water dotted the shoreline. Gnarly, twisted tree roots blanketed the beach. Recent storms had reeked havoc. Waves pounded the shoreline. "Please God, send my friend, Judy, a miracle," I prayed silently.

Judy looked at me with a smile. "You know what? My life may be in turmoil, but I don't have to stay there, do I? Look at this beach."

We stared at the carcasses of trees that had stood for centuries. The beach was littered with death. I looked at the torn landscape. "The beach is quite different than the top of the cliff, isn't it?"

We had felt a gentleness as we walked through the woods. But this? I never saw such desecration.

The sky darkened. The acrid smell of the sea, and wet seaweed surrounded us. Sea gulls flew above us in defiance of our presence. We looked at the storm clouds, and nodded in agreement. Time to go home.

We climbed over uprooted trees, tossed like toothpicks. Our feet made pathways through the pine needles as we trudged up the trail. I turned to look back at the beach. The violent storms of the past week had raped the coastline.

Judy turned to me with a gentle expression. "You know what I think God revealed to me? When we walked through the woods, I thought only of nature. There was contentment. As soon as we approached the beach, there was chaos. Nothing but gnarly, uprooted stumps, and twisted driftwood. The storm took its toll. God wants me to leave the gnarly wood and look for hyacinths. It's up there on top, not down here with the gnarlies. That's life, isn't it?"

We listened to the whistle of the wind in the trees as we approached the top of the trail.

I turned to face the shoreline. "The storm is gaining fury. We left just in time. Listen . . . do you hear it?"

A faint song of a bird crept through the trees. "Is it the blackbird?"

We smiled at each other.

At times of crisis, God's voice may be the gentle song expressed in nature, letting us know He's still in charge. We each have a choice: to focus on the "gnarlies" or the "blackbird." Which will you choose?

> We have escaped like a bird out of the fowler's snare;
> The snare has been broken, and we have escaped.
> Our help is in the name of the Lord,
> the maker of heaven and earth.
> PSALM 124:7-8

If you have children going back to school, send away for pencils imprinted with their names. If you don't, then have your name imprinted on them.

September 4

A Tea Time Of Friendship

EMILIE BARNES

We taste with our eyes as well as our mouths.
—CHEF AARON PATTERSON

I love to arrange a simple tea tray for someone who is a guest in my home—a tiny vase with a single rosebud, a gleaming miniature oil lamp, a pocket-sized book of poems or pictures, and of course an elegant floral teacup and plate.

I also love to host a larger gathering of friends. A shining candlelit buffet table, an elaborate assortment of tea foods, the hum of conversation as guests gather around the fire—all these bring me immense pleasure, and part of the pleasure is knowing I helped put this lovely event together.

Creating beauty in this way is hard work, of course, but that is part of the joy. When I invite my friends to tea and offer them a lovely time, I benefit too, because the work of creating something beautiful enhances the satisfaction of it.

> *. . . Whatever is lovely . . . think about such things.*
> PHILIPPIANS 4:8

Plan to bless a friend with a tea party, either simple or ornate, within the next week.

September 5

Nancy

RUTH M. RINK

There would be no great ones if there were no little ones.

—GEORGE HERBERT

I looked up from the desk of my seventh grade classroom and saw Nancy standing in the doorway. She looked like a little rag-a-muffin in a torn, plaid dress; dark stringy hair, tears streaking her cheeks. For an instant I felt like hugging her, but it was the first day of school and I was distracted by routine responsibilities. Nancy was just another new student.

"Find a seat, please," I said, and continued with student registration.

Not until years later did I discover the trauma of that first week for this twelve-year-old whose mother was hospitalized when school began. As her peers preened for junior high, Nancy filled the role of surrogate mother and homemaker for her three younger siblings and father. During a "reunion" luncheon, Nancy recalled additional struggles surrounding her initiation to the "big school."

"Before I even found your homeroom," she said, "I'd already been stranded in the corridors, lost my sixth-grade report card, been pushed on the stairs—remember my torn dress?—and mistakenly assigned to an 'all boy' ninth grade classroom."

Though now able to smile at the episode, she admitted, "That first day was so traumatizing, I almost didn't come back."

Listening to Nancy, I thought, "If I'd been less consecrated to routine and more attentive to the fears of an insecure country girl, I might have noticed God handing me an opportunity to make a difference. If I'd yielded to my initial urge to 'take her' instead of 'send her' to the Home Economics room for a few stitches to her torn dress, perhaps Nancy would not have felt so alone."

We all should learn daily to keep our eyes open for opportunities God provides to be His arms and legs, offering a shoulder or steady hand to those who are lost, alone, frightened or confused. When our hearts are attentive, He gifts us with times to gently share joy, success, growth, and sorrows with family, friends, and even strangers, like a little rag-a-muffin named Nancy. The abundant life is filled with such God-encounters.

. . . Whatever you did for one of the least of these brothers of mine, you did for me.
MATTHEW 25:40

Volunteer the first few days of school to welcome any new students.

September 6

Meaningful Touch

GARY SMALLEY AND JOHN TRENT

I never like the giving of the hand, unless the entire body accompanies it.
—RALPH WALDO EMERSON

Over one-third of our five million touch receptors are centered in our hands. Our hands are so sensitive that some blind people are being taught to read without Braille, by seeing through their fingertips. At Princeton University's Cutaneous Communication Laboratory, "vibratese" is an experimental procedure where blind people are able to read a printed page by translating the words into vibrations on their fingertips.

Interestingly enough, the act of laying on of hands has become the focus of a great deal of modern-day interest and research. Dr. Dolores Krieger, professor of nursing at New York University, has made numerous studies on the effects of laying-on-of-hands. What she found is that both the toucher and the one being touched receive a physiological benefit. How is that possible?

Inside our bodies is hemoglobin, the pigment of the red blood cells, which carries oxygen to the tissues. Repeatedly, Dr. Krieger has found that hemoglobin levels in *both* people's bloodstreams go up during the act of the laying on of hands. As hemoglobin levels are invigorated, body tissues receive more oxygen. This increase of oxygen energizes a person and can even aid in the regenerative process if he or she is ill.

How would you like to lower your husband's or wife's blood pressure? Protect your grade-school child from being involved in an immoral relationship later in life? Even add up to two years to your own life? (Almost sounds like an insurance commercial, doesn't it?) Actually, these are all findings in recent studies on the incredible power to bless found in meaningful touching.

But Israel reached out his right hand and put it on Ephraim's head, though he was the younger, and crossing his arms, he put his left hand on Manasseh's head, even though Manasseh was the firstborn. Then he blessed Joseph . . .
GENESIS 48:14-15A

Make a point of giving the blessing of a gentle touch to each member of your family today.

September 7

The Child As A Whole

MARILYN SCOGIN

Girls will be girls and boys will be boys but the question is "what kind?"

—ANONYMOUS

As I watch our children at school and at play
My heart sometimes breaks at the close of the day.

Their faces are young, but full of care
Just watch them when they don't know you're there.

They should be carefree this time of their life
But instead their days are full of much strife.

They come to school expected to learn,
But things have happened of larger concern.

Some cannot think because of pain that has
Been shown them daily
And hammers down like rain
They do not take it lightly.

Or maybe they couldn't get any sleep
Afraid to close their eyes
No one there to tuck them in
And assure them they're all right.

Some are hungry, but thankful,
For their only meal, "at school"
Some of us don't think beyond our class and
Say, "You broke the rule . . ."

Maybe if we take the time
To look at the child as a whole
We can teach them
And help their lives unfold.

Let's take a look into each face
And see what we can see
It may help us understand why this child may be
Too unruly, so hard to reach
A child that we just "cannot teach."

Let's take some time, if we may,
To look at the child as a whole
So when school's out at the close of the day.
We've helped their lives unfold.

As I watch our children
At school and at play
My heart sometimes breaks
At the close of the day.
What have we taught our children today
To help their futures grow brighter?

Train a child in the way he should go,
and when he is old he will not turn from it.

PROVERBS 22:6

SEPTEMBER

September 8

God Paved The Way

MARY LOU KLINGLER

The same love of God that melted the icy fingers of
death now warms my heart.
— DAVID CARPENTER

When three-year-old Tommy was diagnosed as having cancer in one eye that had to be surgically removed, it was a shock to his parents. Nevertheless, love for their active little son and a deep faith in God gave them the strength and courage to learn how to care for the new glass eye that routinely needed to be removed and cleaned.

There was one problem. When Tommy became boisterous, as was his nature, the glass eye often popped out. It horrified visitors in their home. Tommy's parents realized that until their son grew older they were confined at home to care for him.

Weeks passed. They missed the fellowship at church. It was almost impossible to find a baby sitter. Tommy's parents prayed. They claimed 1 Peter 5:7, and it gave them peace.

They decided to return to church and hoped if what they feared might happen, that the teacher wouldn't faint.

Sunday morning they took Tommy to the three-year-old's room. His parents explained the problem—waiting for the horrified look they saw on other baby sitter's faces. Instead the parents' eyes misted as the teacher answered, "No problem. I've had an artificial eye myself for years."

The parents left Tommy, reassured that God had indeed paved the way. How precious to know He does provide for even the small things. His gentle care communicates His great love for us.

Cast all your anxiety on him because he cares for you.
I PETER 5:7

Real Listening

H. NORMAN WRIGHT

We make a living by what we get, but we make a life by
what we give.

—WINSTON S. CHURCHILL

*I*s there a difference between listening and hearing? Yes, there is.
Hearing is gaining content or information for your own purposes.
Listening is caring for and being empathic toward the person who is
talking. Hearing means that you are concerned about what is going on
inside yourself during the conversation. Listening means you are trying
to understand the feelings of your spouse and are listening for the sake
of the other person.

Let me give you a threefold definition of listening. Listening means
that when your spouse is talking to you . . .

*You are not thinking about what you are going to say when he or she
stops talking.* You are not busy formulating your response. You are
concentrating on what is being said and are putting it into practice
(Proverbs 18:13). It also means you are looking at the person and
listening with your eyes as well as with your ears.

*You are accepting what is being said without judging what he or she is
saying or how it is being said.* You may fail to hear the message if you're
thinking that you don't like your spouse's tone of voice or words. You
may react to the tone and content and miss the meaning. Perhaps your
spouse hasn't said it in the best way, but why not listen and come back
later when both of you are calm and discuss the proper wording and
tone of voice? Acceptance does not mean you have to agree with the
content of what is said. Rather, it means that you understand that what
your spouse is saying is something he or she feels is important.

*You should be able to repeat what your spouse has said and what you
think he or she was feeling while speaking to you.* Real listening implies
an obvious interest in your spouse's feelings and opinions and an
attempt to understand them from their perspective. It means you let
your partner know, "I hear what you're saying, I understand what you're
saying, and I want to respond."

When you listen to another person, you can actually disarm him
or her, especially when you are being criticized. Arguing with a critic

rarely works but agreeing builds a closer relationship. When you listen you don't defend yourself, but neither do you have to agree with all that is said. If you can find some small element of truth to agree with, your spouse will be less on the offensive and more open to listening to you and considering your request. As a result, your desire for him or her to change may receive consideration.

. . . everyone should be quick to listen, slow to speak, and slow to become angry.
JAMES 1:19

> The next time you feel attacked by spouse or friend, resist all tendencies to defend yourself and repeat back what they're saying in your own words.

September 10

No Reruns

JENNIFER NYSTROM

When it comes to our children, there are no reruns.
—ANONYMOUS

I was a stay-at-home mom but seemed to fill every spare minute of time with some kind of project. I was volunteering at church and my older kids' school, constantly dragging my youngest child here and there, from meeting to meeting. She was always a trooper and rarely complained.

But one afternoon, after a considerably busy morning, we finally got home at lunchtime. Knowing that I had only a few minutes to prepare something before we had to leave again, I asked Amy if she wanted a peanut butter and jelly sandwich or a frozen burrito. She replied, "I'd like the frozen burrito, but could you please heat it up before I eat it?"

My first instinct was to laugh out loud and tell her, "Of course, I will. How silly."

But then I realized that my dear little four-year-old thought we were too busy to heat her burrito.

God had given me the wonderful opportunity of having children, yet I was blowing it. I was able to be home with my kids but was too busy to really give them the attention they needed. Then I reminded myself that I wouldn't have any "reruns" in raising my children and I had better get it right the first time.

We parents have an awesome responsibility when God blesses us with a child. We should never take that responsibility lightly. Our time with them is limited, therefore we need to take seriously our role as a parent. Once we put our children first, everything else will fall into place.

Take time for your kids. Treat them with gentleness, for they are precious and fragile. That way they won't think they have to eat a frozen burrito.

> *Let the little children come to me, and do not hinder them,*
> *for the Kingdom of God belongs to such as these.*
>
> LUKE 18:16B

As school begins, don't let work or volunteer activities rob you of giving "eye-to-eye" contact with your children. Spend at least fifteen minutes each day giving them undivided attention.

September 11

Establishing Family Traditions

NAOMI RHODE

Traditions and rituals give importance to a moment, a
sense of grace. They allow us to acknowledge an
important moment or change in our lives.

—JAY O'CALLAHAN

When my mother married, her Icelandic mother, my *Amma*, took some wool from the sheep on their farm, carded and spun it, and then made a quilt as a wedding gift for my parents. My mom and dad used it until dad died; then mother chose not to sleep under it without him. When I got married, she re-covered the quilt and passed it on to me. After twenty-four years, the quilt pulled apart and needed to be redone. I divided the wool inside into three parts, and when each one of our children was married I had a quilt made with the original wool in it. Each of our kids had a part of that quilt under which my mom and dad slept all of their married life and under which my husband and I slept most of our married life. When mother gave the quilt to Jim and me, she said it was more than a quilt—it was a "comforter." It was a reminder of my parents' love, warmth, and care, since they couldn't always be with us. This "gift of continuity and care" was one we wanted to pass on to our children in their new homes.

If you're humming "Tradition" and pretending to be Tevye in *Fiddler on the Roof*, you're on the right track. Tradition is that sense of continuity, wholeness, immovability, changelessness, and stability. That single thread which unites and which brings comfort in lives bombarded by unceasing, unpredictable change.

Traditions don't need to be expensive, but they are one of the greatest gifts you can give to your family. Our family traditions included family hugs, when all five of us would come together and hold hands and pray and hug one another.

The children made a tradition of climbing in bed with us every Saturday morning when they woke up. Although it eventually became rather crowded, it was a fun and warm way to start our weekend times of relaxation together. Now, our five grandsons carry on this tradition when they visit us.

Each Tuesday night was family night. And each week a different family member planned the dinner menu. After dinner we had a family meeting and discussed the family calendar, any problems or concerns, and played games, sang, and laughed together. "Rhode Games" were our favorite. Any member of the family could think of a question that the other members would then answer. Two of my favorites were: If you could spend one day with any person who has ever lived, who would it be and why? And, if you could be a drop of water in any form, anywhere in the world, what would it be and where?

It's not terrifically important what the tradition is, other than your values and beliefs, just that your family has some.

Long after Jim and I are gone, I believe the traditions we established and practiced in our family life will live on and serve as a warm memory of our love and affection.

As iron sharpens iron, so one man sharpens another.
PROVERBS 27:17

Read *The Gift of Family* by Naomi Rhode (Thomas Nelson, 1991).

Six Steps To Connecting With A Friend

STU WEBER

A friend is a present you give yourself.
—ROBERT LOUIS STEVENSON

What does it mean to "act like a friend?" Let's walk through some simple, effective "how to's" to practice when working at being and gaining a friend.

1. *Know yourself.*

Ask yourself a few tough questions, and don't let yourself squirm away from the answers. Am I positive and winsome? Or am I complaining and pessimistic? Would I like *myself* for a friend? Am I defensive? Do I let my past failures hold me down or am I ready to get on with life? And, very importantly, am I honest? Can I be counted on?

2. *Identify your vision.*

Vision is the stuff of which friendships are made. Friends stand side-by-side looking at the mountain, contemplating the task, measuring what matters. And it is that common vision that *drives* the friendship.

3. *Take the initiative.*

Can you remember a time when you were "new on the block" and no one stretched out toward you? It was uncomfortable, embarrassingly awkward, and frustrating. Don't let it happen. Beat that awkward moment to the punch. *You* be the one to reach out.

4. *Focus on the friend.*

Part of what made Jesus such a great friend was His self-free focus upon the other person. He did the little things in a big way. From noticing a little child while in the midst of teaching (Luke 18:15-17) to recruiting help for His mother while He was enduring searing torture on the cross (John 19:26-27), Jesus focused on others.

5. *Keep both your promises and confidences.*

Say what you mean. Mean what you say. And keep it between you. The use of your tongue is a key to your friendships. Friendship absolutely *soars* in an environment of acceptance, transparency, trust, and promises made and kept.

6. *Stay steady, strong, and faithful–no matter what.*

Remember, friends are like trees. There is refuge beneath their branches. There is safety. There is a haven to come to, no matter what. No matter the time (day or night), the weather (fair or foul), or the circumstances (pleasant or painful), trees and friends stay steady, strong, and faithful. Like a deep-rooted oak, friends weather the storms, hang on through the droughts, and grow stronger through the years.

So let's get on with it.

. . . but we were gentle among you, like a mother caring for her little children.
1 THESSALONIANS 2:7

Contact a person who can be a mentor for you in your area of needed learning or growth.

September 13

Angels With Skin On

SUSAN TITUS OSBORN

A Christian is one who makes it easier for others to believe in God.
—ANONYMOUS

*A*t one point in my life, I reached what might be called "my darkest moment." My mind was fragmented and clouded by stress and indecision.

Today I am asked, "How did you cope during that time? How did you survive?"

"People who treated me gently," I simply reply. "God brought unexpected angels into my life who could see through the smile pasted on my face." They realized that even though I said, "I'm fine," I was actually hurting, and they did something about it.

One couple invited me to go to the theater with them. They insisted I go out and relax for an evening. They didn't ask me about personal problems. They just provided a fun time, which helped me return home and face my situation with a better attitude.

Another friend listened and listened and listened as I poured out my heart to her. I knew she was a woman of integrity, and everything I said would be held in strictest confidence. She didn't offer solutions because she realized there were no pat answers. Yet, by talking to her,

I could gain a clearer perspective regarding my problem. She helped me realize that I was not alone—others cared about me and my feelings.

At that time in my life, God seemed far away. I was so stressed I could not concentrate on the Bible. At times, I could not pray. I wondered how I could reach Him again. I never doubted that He was there, but I was incapable of reaching out to Him.

In time, I realized that God used all these people to gently help me reach Him again. My friends made it possible for me to see Jesus. Through the concern in their hearts, through their actions of good will, and through their words of encouragement, I saw Jesus. God knew I needed angels with skin on to restore me to wholeness and to a relationship with Him—and He provided.

Are you looking for people who need gentle encouragement? For them, you can be an "angel with skin on." To live out your abundant life, help them to see Jesus in you, and, as a result, they'll move closer to Him. And you may not have to say a word.

Praise be to the God and Father of our Lord Jesus Christ, the Father of compassion and the God of all comfort, who comforts us in all our troubles, so that we can comfort those in any trouble with the comfort we ourselves have received from God.
2 CORINTHIANS 1:3-4

The next time you're with a hurting friend, don't try to solve their problem, just listen and make them laugh.

September 14

A Simple Solution

GAIL GAYMER MARTIN

It is easier to attract flies with honey than with vinegar.
—OLD ADAGE

One September, returning to my high school counseling office, I discovered that the alphabetical division of the student caseloads had changed. Instead of the usual last names beginning with T-Z, my responsibility now included students with last names beginning with "S."

Previously, I had always given thanks to God that my co-worker Bill had the "S's." It meant that he had Sandy Schwartz—and her father, an angry man. This year it was my turn to calm and appease him.

Shortly after school began, Sandy was removed from a class for misbehavior and received two detentions. I cringed, waiting for the inevitable telephone call. It was worse than I anticipated. Instead, one afternoon, I looked up from my desk and stared into the face of the 6' 3" Mr. Schwartz. He towered over me, his angry voice booming demands for immediate attention. My prayer soared to heaven. Bill walked slowly past my door, and I felt safer knowing that all 5' 8" of Bill was ready to come to my aid. I thought of David and Goliath.

As Mr. Schwartz ranted, I felt anger taking hold of me. But then the words of Jesus and the verse from Proverbs, "A gentle answer turns away wrath, but a harsh word stirs up anger" came into my mind. I bit my tongue, as the Lord asks, and responded calmly, "Please have a seat, and let's work together to solve Sandy's problems. I don't blame you for feeling frustrated."

His angry eyes softened, but he remained on the edge of the chair. I reviewed the problems and possible solutions. Suddenly, he asked, "Got a pen and paper?"

I gave him paper and a pencil, and he knelt on the floor before my desk, placing the paper on the corner. He stayed in a kneeling position as we worked out a plan of action. I knew God was definitely involved. By the time he left my office, he spoke softly and shook my hand in thanks. As he exited the counseling center, Bill hurried into my office.

"How did you do that?" he asked. "I couldn't believe my eyes."

"It was surprising, wasn't it? He finally listened."

"No, that's not what I mean," he said. "He was raving, and the next minute, he was down on his knees. How did you do that?"

I laughed, imagining the picture Bill saw—Mr. Schwartz humbly on his knees in front of my desk.

"It was easy," I said with a grin. "I didn't do anything. God did."

Whether at work or at home, the simplest and surest way to solve a problem is to remember God's Word. Is there some way that God has been wanting you to turn away wrath with a gentle word? Ask Him to strengthen you and you may find your enemy kneeling before you. That's abundant living.

A man's wisdom gives him patience; it is to his glory to overlook an offense.
PROVERBS 19:11

Memorize Psalm 15:1.

Cockatoos And Howdy-Do's

BONNIE COMPTON HANSON

The greatest sweetener of human life is Friendship.
— JOSEPH ADDISON

I was out front trimming my roses when an old friend stopped by. "Sorry not to call first," she apologized. "But I was in the neighborhood and—"

She looked around appreciatively. "My, the lawns on this street are well-kept. And everything's so quiet."

But just then—

"AAAWKKKK."

My visitor nearly jumped out of her skin. "What in the world was that?"

That was Cocky, the gorgeous white cockatoo next door—the very cross and cantankerous cockatoo next door. And the end of any quiet for that morning.

It's not that Cocky lacks would-be friends. Mike, his teen-aged master, spends time with him every day after school. The family dogs romps around him, coaxing him to play. Songbirds call from nearby trees. Even our cats often stop by to investigate their feisty, feathered neighbor.

But Cocky will have none of this. His magnificent feathers attract everyone, but when they come close, he drives them away with his constant, cross shrieks.

Just like Cocky, you and I are sometimes just as stubborn, selfish, and unfriendly, cutting ourselves off from the rest of humanity and gaining new friends.

At home, we hide behind our own TV, books, precious possessions, daring anyone to interrupt us. In a store, on a bus, at a concert, we keep our heads down, our eyes busy to prevent eye contact or communication.

Oh, what we are missing. For one of the greatest joys in this world at any age is in having a friend. And *being* one. Did you know that there are almost 150 references in the Bible to "friend," "companion," and related words? God made us to need friends, including Himself and His matchless Son. "What a Friend We Have in Jesus." That's one reason He has given us churches.

Since Jesus wants you to have friends, reach out to those around you with a welcoming smile, a warm handshake, gentle words, and an open heart. Throw away prejudices, stereotypes, any "chips on your shoulder." Be available, be vulnerable, be willing to help, listen, share, both funny incidents and deep hurts.

For your role model, think how God is to us. He doesn't just *act* interested in our lives, He *is* interested. Even the shyest of us can ask Christ's help to love others. "Reach out and touch someone"— and your life can soon be filled with abundance through loving friends also are reaching out to you. Just remember Cocky's bad example and avoid it.

> *Perfume and incense bring joy to the heart, and the pleasantness of one's friend springs from his earnest counsel.*
>
> PROVERBS 27:9

Let God's warm love flow through you today. Smile and thank a checkout clerk, a postal carrier, a peace officer. Better yet, all of them.

September 16

Gentle Caregiving

IRENE CARLONI

Care giver is who you are to me, Lord. May I give care to others in return.

—PATTI NORMILE

*H*ave you seen attendants walking or pushing wheelchairs with their patients through the malls of America? Patients are physically and/or mentally handicapped and they are in all ages, sizes, and colors. Is there someone you know who is held captive between sheets in a bed, or who has become a parent to their own parent due to an illness? Do you ever wonder about the caregiver who helps these

People become caregivers either by accident because of the need of a family member, or by choice as a trained professional or volunteer. Caregivers find many challenges in working with their patients. At times, patients do not have the most pleasant personalities. There are some circumstances that lead to hurt, anger, and frustration. A great amount of love, gentleness, and stamina is required to bond with a patient.

My own challenge as a caregiver to my son, afflicted with Multiple

Sclerosis for 21 years, was learning the art of communication. In trying to help him with everyday living, he often ignored what I said. We usually ended up yelling and arguing with each other. At wits end, I prayed to the Lord seeking comfort and confessing my anger and hurt. I continued to pray, "Lord, I don't know what to do anymore; please show me. Give me gentle words."

After a time "Make a joyful noise . . ." from the Book of Psalms sprang to my mind. I started singing simple songs as "Frere Jacques," "Row Row Row Your Boat," and even "Ring Around the Rosie." At first my son laughed at me, but then he joined in and we would finish the song together. A breakthrough. Through His grace, my attitude changed, although the situation did not. Singing became a way to break through the anger and express gentleness.

To begin their day in a joyful manner, children in kindergarten sing a song. I remember the words to an old song, "You've got to start off each day with a song, even when things go wrong." When things go wrong, I get rid of my anger by changing my attitude and praising the Lord. Then I sing, make up my own rhymes, and laugh and joke about the problem.

If you are facing the challenge of being a caregiver, you'll need to seek the wisdom of the Lord in order to gain the gentleness of an abundance-focused attitude. Always remember, when times are bad, your support system is the Lord, who cares for you. If you are a caregiver, you are special.

> Be joyful always; pray continually; give thanks in all circumstances, for this is God's will for you in Christ Jesus.
> I THESSALONIANS 5:16-18

The measure of a true person is being able to admit when you are wrong. Show your humanness some time today.

Steady Reins

DAVE GETZ

Reason lies between the spur and the bridle.
—GEORGE HERBERT, 17TH CENTURY WRITER

I hadn't ridden a horse in over a year. My instructor, Penny, chose Sarge for my first lesson. His years of jumping would make up for my lack of experience.

After a refresher course in horsemanship, I was finally ready to soar with Sarge over the first fence. My mouth became dry as we approached the barrier. The last thing I wanted was to hold back my trusty mount when he jumped. I moved my hands forward along his neck. Every muscle in my body tensed. The adrenaline flowed. I leaned forward. And then—

Sarge stopped in his tracks.

Momentum carried me onto his arched neck. I slid back down to the saddle and tried to regain some sense of dignity.

"That was your fault." Penny hollered, adding insult to my injured pride.

My fault? I thought in disbelief. *I was ready for the jump. The stupid horse is the one who messed things up–not me.*

"What do you mean?" I eventually asked.

"You gave the horse too much rein and he lost confidence."

I scratched the back of my head. "But aren't I *supposed* to give him more rein when he jumps?" Just in case my instructor didn't know better, I added, "Otherwise I'd hold him back."

"You're almost right," she admitted. "If you pull too hard, he'll be afraid to jump . . ."

I sat a little straighter in the saddle.

"But if you relax your hold too much," Penny continued, "the horse doesn't know what you expect from him. Then he won't jump."

"Oh."

"Try it again. Wait for Sarge to pull your hands forward. There's a fine line between holding him back and giving him too much freedom."

I remained unconvinced, but determined to try.

Sarge cantered into position to clear the barrier ahead. When his head lunged forward, my hands followed, keeping a gentle pull on the reins. We sailed with ease over the obstacle.

Years later, I found my horse jumping lesson could apply to raising children. My kids need guidance to clear the many obstacles in life. If I pull too hard on the "reins" of freedom, my children will fight me every step of the way. But if I give too much leeway, they'll lose confidence in their moral direction. Either way, conflict erupts and life becomes complicated.

How are the reins on your children? Are you gently giving them enough freedom along with steady reins of direction? It's a fine line and we often wish it were more simple; but our gentleness will, in time, result in an abundant relationship with them.

Fathers, do not embitter your children, or they will become discouraged.
COLOSSIANS 3:21

> Place a note in your child's lunchbox telling something about them you appreciate.

September 18

Be Strong And Courageous

PENNY SHOUP

Lord, either lighten my burden or strengthen my back.
—THOMAS FULLER

In Joshua 1:6-8, God tells Joshua to be strong and courageous. That encouragement was what my Heavenly Father gave me when He called me to home school three of my four children. I faced uncertainty that I was doing the right thing. I was fearful that my children would miss out on the social life they needed to grow and develop. I wondered whether I could be patient and gentle in my teaching. And I was frustrated with the demand that both teaching and homemaking was putting on our family. There were many struggles: physical, spiritual and mental, but the promise never failed and God's truth rang strong. God gave me strength and the courage to continue.

Now two years later, my sixteen-year-old son has an inner peace that is far from the confusion and turmoil of two years ago. He has self-esteem where he once felt worthless and a failure. He has a strong faith in God. Academically he is doing well. My thirteen-year-old daughter is happy and isn't plagued by the unrealistic expectation peers had put on her. My eleven-year-old is content and can read, which was a big hindrance in school. They are all doing well academically, but the most important growth has been spiritual. God gave my son back when he had quickly been sliding away. My daughter deeply senses the need to pray for her friends and my youngest has a love that overflows to others.

Whatever challenge you're facing, whether it's homeschooling or something else, may God's words to Joshua give you strength and courage to achieve the calling God has given you. With His help, you won't lack for gentle and caring words.

Have I not commanded you? Be strong and courageous. Do not be terrified; do not be discouraged, for the Lord your God will be with you wherever you go.
JOSHUA 1:9

Pull out—or rent—videos of old movies and enjoy them again.

September 19

Reaching Out Times

SANDY CATHCART

Beware of no man more than thyself.
—THOMAS FULLER

Why doesn't anyone come to visit? I wondered. I was stuck for three months without a phone or transportation in our wilderness home. I spoke with my young children and shared evenings with my husband. But I craved woman-to-woman talk. *I need some gentle words of encouragement. I wonder if Amber ever thinks of me?*

As days passed, my heart began to grow bitter. I imagined my friends busy with their own lives. *If they were really my friends,* I thought, *they would come visit.*

When my husband finally fixed our Jeepster, I drove to the doctor's office for a check-up. Amber sat in the waiting room, her shiny black hair forming perfect waves around her flawless complexion. She wore a wrinkle-free red suit with matching shoes. By contrast, my old dress was faded and my hair fell in its usual tangle of strings about my shoulders.

Amber barely greeted me, nodding her head and quickly looking away. "How are you?" I asked, more out of habit than curiosity.

"Not very good," she whispered. Then she burst into tears.

Surprised, I dropped to a chair and embraced her. She poured out the story of her on-going battle with deep depression for which she was seeing the doctor. At first, I was shocked. I would have never guessed such a beautiful lady could be depressed. Then I felt guilty. Hadn't I done the same thing to her that I was angry for other people doing to me? I had never visited her house or invited her to mine. She was turning to a doctor for help when her Christian brothers and sisters (including myself) should have been available. I had been so wrapped up in feeling sorry for myself I had failed to see the needs of others.

Amber told me later that our little visit in the waiting room held more healing benefits for her than the actual appointment with the doctor.

"It did a lot for me too," I said. "I learned a life-changing lesson."

"How can that be?" she laughed.

I told her how I had been feeling sorry for myself, allowing bitterness to sneak in. "But not any more," I said. "Now, I'm making an effort to turn my sorry times into reaching out times." It's such a better way to live.

If you are feeling lonely, think of others who might be feeling lonely as well. Pray for them and plan a visit or phone call or maybe a note of gentle encouragement. If no one greets you at church, look around for someone else sitting alone. Reach out and say, "Hi." In meeting the needs of others, your own will be met and you'll also experience the joy of knowing you're doing exactly what Jesus would do: living the abundant life with the fruit of gentleness.

. . . your brothers throughout the world are undergoing the same kind of sufferings.

1 PETER 5:9

Read *Love's Little Recipes for Friendship* by Linda Shepherd (Multnomah, 1997).

Hugs

PAUL LIPPARD

> I feel that God would sooner we did wrong in loving
> than never love for fear we should do wrong.
>
> —FATHER ANDREW

J once asked a child, "How do you know if Jesus is in your life?" He replied, "Because the Spirit is with me. It's like a hug from God."

According to psychologists, everyone needs daily: four hugs to survive, eight hugs for maintenance, and twelve hugs for growth. Researchers have discovered that hugging can help you live longer, protect you against illness, cure depression, alleviate stress, strengthen family relationships, and help you get to sleep at night without medication. Hugs reduce blood pressure, body temperature and heart rate, and help relieve pain and sadness.

Hugs are fat-free, sugar-free and calorie-free. They're not fattening and they don't cause cancer or cavities. They are all natural with no preservatives, artificial ingredients, or pesticide residue. They are cholesterol-free, naturally sweet, 100% wholesome. And they are a completely renewable natural resource.

They require no batteries, tune-ups, or x-rays. They are non-taxable, fully-returnable, and energy-efficient. They cost nothing, but can mean the world.

In Mark 10:13-16, we are told that Jesus hugged the little children, laid his hands on them and blessed them. But Jesus still hugs today. I know. In my life, the Lord has covered me with His arms of love. He has embraced me with his compassion and gentle words.

Jesus is a wonderful role model. Hugs are one way we can be the arms of Christ. Who would He like you to hug or give gentle words to today?

> *Dear friends, let us love one another, for love comes from God.*
> *Everyone who loves has been born of God and knows God.*
>
> I JOHN 4:7

> Give five hugs today.

An Encouraging Word

MARY LOU KLINGLER

Correction does much, but encouragement does more.
Encouragement after censure is as the sun after a
shower.

—JOHANN WOLFGANG VON GOETHE

*J*oey tried to help Mom in the kitchen, but somehow the dish dropped and went crashing to the floor breaking into many pieces. Mom scolded and went for the broom and dustpan to sweep up the broken fragments.

Joey felt badly but tried to keep from crying. It seemed like the more he tried to help the worse things got.

A few days later another incident occurred. Mom in exasperation asked, "Joey, can't you do anything right?"

Joey answered as he hung his head, "If I do, no one ever tells me."

We may smile at Joey's answer and yet, when we had youngsters at home and chaos reigned many times during the day, we rarely put ourselves in the child's place. Their tender spirits can be broken and we aren't even aware of it.

Oh, how they need a dose of gentle encouragement.

As adults, we too need an encouraging word when we're trying our best. I know a couple where the husband habitually puts down his wife and criticizes her in public. I've wondered if he does this when they are alone. I've never heard him say anything nice or compliment her about anything; yet she is a giving and loving person.

Even as a child is known by his doings—so adults are also known by theirs. A gentle word of encouragement at the right time can change a life. We all need a lift and even though we blunder now and then, with encouragement we will try again.

Is there someone at work, at home, or church, or even at the grocery store who could use a gentle encouraging word from you? Ask God to give you such an abundance of vision, that you'll see their world from their perspective.

Even a child is known by his actions, by whether his conduct is pure and right.
PROVERBS 20:11

September 22

Perfect Love

CATHY MESSECAR

Perfect love has a breath of poetry which can exalt the relations of the least-instructed human beings.
— *Silas Marner* BY GEORGE ELIOT

*R*eturning from my daughter's scoliosis check-up, we stopped at her favorite fast-food restaurant. After receiving our order, the two of us sat in a booth next to the rest rooms, the last available space. Near the end of our meal, a teenage male employee, dressed in his uniform of gray trousers and gray and white striped shirt, rolled a bucket toward the rest rooms, the industrial type with a mop wringer mounted inside. He steered the sloshy contents with the mop handle.

We were finishing our fries and ketchup when, suddenly, the young man had a seizure. He fell to the floor and knocked over the bucket of water. My brain kicked into high gear. How could we help him? I hadn't been around a person having a seizure in over 20 years. I only knew outdated emergency assistance. I felt helpless, hoping someone would assist him.

Everyone stopped eating. The boy continued having what seemed to be a grand mal. But no one moved to help. Finally, another employee became aware of the situation and yelled to the front: "Get the manager. John's having another seizure."

At the first cry of alarm, a patron stepped away from the crowded lunch counter and walked toward the back. Dressed immaculately—white shirt, gray flannel slacks, tie, and textured jacket—he looked almost out of place in the casual, jeans-clad crowd.

John's muscles were racked by spasms; his teeth gnashed; his limbs jerked. The man's up-to-date medical knowledge caused him to move the mop bucket away from John's thrashing head to avoid further injury. Then squatting, he placed one knee in the water; he bent over John and told him, "John, I'm a doctor. John, relax. This will be over soon. John, you're okay." Each of his words was saturated with gentle guidance and pleading. "Relax, John. This won't last much longer."

Again and again he reassured the writhing boy. And, finally, John's body relaxed, responding to internal signals and the gentle voice of the doctor.

Because of limited space and the on-going emergency aid, my daughter and I had remained seated until the crisis passed. Then we gathered our remaining food and tiptoed through the puddle. The last thing John needed was a gawking crowd.

The picture of John and the physician remain vivid in my memory, one a person in need of help and one willing to stop and help a neighbor. We witnessed the royal law that day when two pair of gray trousers were soaked, one by circumstances, one by choice.

If you are called upon to act in an emergency situation, remember to use the fruit of gentle words.

If you really keep the royal law found in Scripture, "Love your neighbor as yourself," you are doing right.

JAMES 2:8

> Attend a community class soon that teaches emergency procedures like CPR.

September 23

Reach Out And Touch

TAMMI EASTERDAY

Love never has to wait for an opportunity to demonstrate itself.

—HENRIETTA MEARS

On many occasions in the life of Christ, He is seen reaching out to gently touch in healing love: the leper, the blind, the deaf are just a few illustrations. His example lets us know that our touch can be healing as well.

Not long ago, my husband and I were sorting through a number of boxes. I suddenly came across the baby book I bought for our baby when we were first married over 14 years ago. Because of injuries I received in an auto accident, that book will never be used. It suddenly hit me hard and I began to cry. Seeing my distress, Bob didn't know what to say so he reached out, took me gently into his arms and held me. Though my pain was not erased, my sense of being alone in it was. His hug showed that he cared and that he was standing with me in my time of need. His touch was both comforting and healing.

We add to God's abundance in our lives and the lives of others when we use outstretched arms to show our love and concern. We may not know what to say, but at least we can reach out and hug those who might be hurting around us. This gentle hug can be a physical touch, or can be shared through other loving actions.

One easy way to extend this embrace to others is to do what you enjoy. It may be gardening, cooking, reading or even shopping. There is someone you know who could use assistance in your favorite area of interest. Touch their lives by showing up to attend to their neglected flower bed or lawn. Another way to draw them near would be to make a favorite recipe and take it to them. Hold them close by observing if their eyes aren't seeing as clearly as they used to. If not, then arrange a visit when there is time to enjoy reading their favorite book, magazine, or Bible verses to them. Another idea would be to make a tape recording of the desired material if a convenient time can't be worked out. Give them a loving squeeze by offering to take them shopping with you, pick up their groceries, or other necessities when you're going out.

These are just a few ideas to start your creativity flowing. Pray about how you might gently "hug" someone the Lord has place on your heart. For by embracing a hurting individual through the giving of yourself, your time, or abilities, you'll deepen their abundant life and your own.

Dear children, let us not love with words or
tongue but with actions and in truth.

1 JOHN 3:18

Allow preschoolers to "graze" from healthy food all day rather than requiring long sit-down meals.

When You Don't Know How They Feel

PAT PALAU

> There is no exercise better for the heart than reaching
> down and lifting people up.
>> —JOHN ANDREW HOLMER

The other day I heard a Christian woman describe how a friend had made several "mistakes" while trying to comfort her during a time of difficulty. She complained that her friend offered advice, solutions, and even dared to quote Scripture.

When a friend needs comforting, don't draw back with uncertainty, thinking you haven't the experience or the right words to say. Comforting and encouraging our brothers and sisters in the Lord is not an assignment reserved only for some "expert" or salaried staff person at church. It is the duty and privilege of the entire Body.

Although there always will be a few insensitive individuals who glibly quote Scripture at random and have an answer for every instance of life, we must not overlook the fact that in times of stress and difficulty, nothing, absolutely nothing, takes the place of Scripture.

Often people experiencing loss and difficulty are left alone because would-be comforters don't know what to say. When Luis and I heard that some friends had lost a child, our first impulse was to avoid the grieving parents. But as Christians, we knew that we had to reach out to them. So I dialed their phone number, took a deep breath and reminded the bereaved parents that we were thinking of them and praying for them.

Later that night I wrote a short note to let them know we cared. I refrained from offering advice because hurting people don't need advice; they simply need our love, support and prayers.

Then on 3 x 5 index cards I wrote some Bible verses regarding the promise of the Lord's presence in difficult times. I wrote the entire verses and not just the references. People coping with loss are mentally and physically exhausted and may not look up verses. My favorite verses to include are, *Cast all your anxiety on him because he cares for you* (1 Peter 5:7) and *Surely I will be with you always to the very end of the age* (Matthew 28:20).

No one can go far wrong in quoting the Word of God. Scripture is what God says it is—powerful and living. When you feel the gentle urging of the Spirit to reach out, do it. Reach out in a sensitive, caring way, not talking down to a person. In love, as a fellow disciple of Jesus Christ, you can share Christ and His Word with those who hurt.

Rejoice with those who rejoice; mourn with those who mourn.
ROMANS 12:15

Send a book to a hurting friend.

September 25

A Postcard Ministry

DELORES ELAINE BIUS

Biblical orthodoxy without compassion is surely the ugliest thing in the world.
—FRANCIS A. SCHAEFFER

How often do you send someone a postcard? If you are like most people, it is only when you are on a vacation.

Almost by accident, I discovered that sending postcards can become a real ministry. The postage rate is a lot cheaper than that of a regular greeting card or letter. Postcards also take less time to write than a letter.

While visiting a church out of town, I met a lovely lady who was house-bound most of the time caring for her 26-year-old son. Ken was a quadriplegic as a result of an automobile accident when he was 18. His mother mentioned that her son watched avidly for the mailman every day but that the volume of mail he received had dwindled over the years.

When I returned to my home, I began not only praying for my new friend and her son, but also sending Ken postcards often. When she wrote saying how much Ken treasured them, I made it a point to send him one every week. Not only did I send those with scenic views of my city, but I also found some with clever cartoons.

During a trip to our local zoo, I discovered a packet of twelve different cards showing animals there and bought them for Ken, so he could vicariously enjoy a trip to the zoo. Museums also provide postcards as well.

Knowing a number of elderly people who are confined to their homes, I realized they, too, would welcome postcards. I discovered that

I could take old greeting cards I had received and convert them into attractive postcards.

Some mail order catalogs feature unusual postcards for purchase. I bought several humorous ones along with some of Victorian style for an elderly friend.

At a local discount store, I discovered packets of thirty-six postcards for under two dollars. They featured floral designs, cats, dogs and even panda bears on the front, with plenty of room for an address and a message on the back.

Soon I began carrying postcards with me in my purse along with my address book and stamps. Whenever I had to wait somewhere, I would get cards ready to mail.

An elderly aunt who was hospitalized for two weeks with knee replacement surgery, and later three weeks in a rehabilitation clinic, later told me, "I counted up the cards you sent me while I was away from home and discovered you had sent me seventeen." She was most grateful for them.

Perhaps you know people who would be pleased to receive a postcard. You might not have time to write a letter or have a greeting card on hand that is appropriate. Start collecting postcards, buy some stamps and you are all set for this gentle—yet powerful—ministry.

You will bring great joy to friends and relatives at little expense or time on your part.

And do not forget to do good and to share with others,
for with such sacrifices God is pleased.
HEBREWS 13:16

> Write a postcard note to your spouse expressing your "delight" at something romantic they did in the past, then mail it.

September 26

Is This Your Church

DURLYNN ANEMA-GARTEN

The tears of strangers are only water.
—RUSSIAN PROVERB

$\mathcal{H}$ow often do we recognize the stranger in our church service? As travelers, my husband and I always try to attend church services each Sunday, no matter the location. These church experiences vary, as the examples below indicate. All are true, so ask yourself which one may have been your church.

"Ah, you must be visitors," the charming woman said as we walked into a large, beautiful edifice.

How did she know? This church obviously had a membership in the thousands, its buildings stretched for blocks and the sanctuary held at least 2,000 people. We acknowledged our guest status and were asked to sign the guest book.

Then the greeter added, "We have cake and coffee downstairs and we'd love to get acquainted."

We couldn't agree more and retained the feeling of love throughout and after the service.

    *   *   *

The white church looked like something from a postcard. We were eager to say hello and be a part of this fellowship. Not more than 150 people could crowd into the warm pews and the sanctuary was full.

We slipped into a small pew midway down the aisle. People at our side and back stared, but did not smile. At no time were "hands-of-fellowship" given during the service, nor were any greetings offered when we left. The minister did not shake hands and no one said, "Thanks for coming" or "Hope you return." All we received were a few stares at the strangers who dared to join their worship that day.

    *   *   *

This next huge edifice, which was of our denomination, was in a foreign country, beautiful and crowded with a mixture of ethnic groups. The usher politely greeted us, quite unimpressed by strangers. However, we were impressed by the people around us, who warmly shook our hands.

The warmest greeting came from the lovely woman sitting next to us, both a friendly handshake and a smile of greeting.

The service was outstanding from the music to the sermon. Then came communion. As the elders moved to our aisle, they glanced at us and recoiled. They were not going to serve communion to us, obviously strangers.

At this point, the woman beside me interfered. She insisted that communion be passed to us and finally we were served the Lord's supper. Following the service, we learned she wasn't even a member of that church.

    *   *   *

The church services were held in a dingy middle school multi-purpose room. We sat on uncomfortable folding chairs that scraped the floor every time we moved. The choir could hardly be heard because of the poor acoustics.

But the greeting was warm. "Welcome," said the usher, smiling broadly. A man rushed up and shook our hands. "Welcome," he said smiling broadly. We learned later he was the pastor.

"Hands-of-fellowship" were equally warm, as were the smiles and inquiries about us. At the end of the service a big circle was formed around the room, which no longer seemed dingy. We all held hands and looked across at our fellow worshipers. None of us were strangers.

Many churches, many edifices, many people, many greetings. Which one is your church? Which of those people were you? Do you give a gentle welcome on Sunday mornings?

Do not forget to entertain strangers, for by so doing some people have entertained angels without knowing it.
HEBREWS 13:2

> Say hello to someone new at church or invite them over for lunch after services.

September 27

No Response

CORA LEE PLESS

Sympathy is your pain in my heart.
—ANONYMOUS CHILD

Shoulders slumped, head bowed, the frail woman sat silently on the bench in the corridor of the mental health hospital. As our group of student nurses approached her on our way to another part of the hospital, our instructor paused.

"Good morning," she said to the woman.

The small, elderly woman didn't respond, and we continued on our way.

The scene repeated itself on several mornings. Each time our instructor greeted the woman with a "Good morning." Each time the woman made no attempt to respond.

One day our teacher extended the usual greeting. But this time when the woman did not react, our instructor sat down on the bench beside her and said, "It really isn't a very good morning, is it?"

Like a statue come to life, the woman looked up and spoke, "No, it's not."

Since that encounter, I've met many people in everyday life who are emotionally hurting, people who battle loneliness, depression, or fear. Many times I feel I need to offer some solution to their problem. Sometimes I'm tempted to say, "You just need to have more faith," or "You've got to snap out of it," or "Smile, and you'll feel better."

Yet, such pat answers actually proclaim a lack of gentle caring and offer little in the way of true help. Plus, it closes the door to communication. I seldom possess a quick answer to another person's problem. What I do possess is the opportunity to listen without judging, to share tears and understanding, and to say "I'm sorry."

Certainly I must be aware of the times when I can encourage another person, when I can help bolster another's faith, when I can witness for my Lord. But the woman in the corridor taught me that gentleness is often first acknowledging and accepting the pain that person is enduring.

The next time you're trying to share God's gentleness, don't feel compelled to give a solution. They most likely just want someone to listen and feel their pain.

Like one who takes away a garment on a cold day, or like vinegar poured on soda, is one who sings songs to a heavy heart.
PROVERBS 25:20

> Careful listening is an art—God gave us two ears to rely on, not one. Words alone don't paint the whole picture — use your eyes to see not only *what* is being said, but *how* the words are being said.

September 28

Gentle Confrontation

PATTY R. STUMP

Those who throw dirt lose ground.

—ANONYMOUS

$\mathcal{A}$ll of us have been impacted by the words of others. Can you recall the last time someone's words encouraged you—or wounded you? Our words can have a tremendous impact on others, with potential to be honoring or hurtful.

That certainly applies when we need to confront someone. Confrontation is awkward for most of us to give and receive, but when done wisely and gently, it can strengthen relationships and result in personal growth for those involved. Before we express comments that may be critical or potentially hurtful, it is wise to explore our thoughts and emotions, as well as consider what words to use in expressing our perspective. A few simple steps carefully applied can enable the Lord to work in the situation for His good.

• Always involve only the individual(s) directly involved in the situation, taking time to explore the motives of your heart before you confront them.

• Be sure that you have accurate information on the issue to be discussed.

• Seek to affirm the *person* while exploring the *issue*. To criticize a person can produce lasting wounds, yet criticism of an incident or issue can be more easily received when expressed with an attitude of respect for the person(s) involved.

• Seek to stay focused on the subject at hand. To overreact or lump multiple issues together is counterproductive.

• Lastly, seek to work towards a solution and resolution. God desires restoration and reconciliation.

Which of these guidelines do you find easiest to use and which are hardest? Work on strengthening the difficult ones so that you can give gentle confrontation.

Let your conversation be always full of grace, seasoned with salt,
so that you may know how to answer everyone.

COLOSSIANS 4:6

Make sure you get enough sleep each night as a means of dealing with conflict.

Shadows

MARCIA KRUGH LEASER

More than in any other human relationship, over-whelmingly more, motherhood means being instantly interruptible, responsive, responsible.

— TILLIE OLSEN

It had been a long day getting ready for guests, but at last, supper was over, the children were in bed and we were relaxing at the table with a second cup of coffee.

The men were discussing "men things" and my friend and I were solving the problems of the world, when I heard a noise in the hall to my left. Turning to see what had caused it, I found Dawn, my three-year-old, standing just beyond the light from the dining room.

"What's the matter, honey?" I asked.

"I'm scared," she responded meekly, chewing on a chubby finger.

Not wanting to be disturbed I said matter-of-factly, "Just go back to bed, sweetie, God will hold your hand."

Even though I felt a twinge of guilt for not jumping up to help, I dismissed it and watched until she reluctantly disappeared into the shadows.

I then returned to the conversation at the table. Only seconds later I heard the noise again. Sighing heavily, I turned and saw Dawn standing alone with one tiny arm stretched toward the ceiling. "God's got this hand, Mommy, won't you hold the other one?"

Reach out in gentleness to that little one who needs your comfort and reassurance. The world is a scary place without it. Let that child know they deserve abundant life too.

But if anyone causes one of these little ones who believe in me to sin,
it would be better for him to have a large millstone hung around
his neck and to be drowned in the depths of the sea.
MATTHEW 18:6

When giving items to a charity, make use of their receipt on your income tax. Small amounts add up and may lower your tax bracket.

Listening To God's Gentle Voice

FLORENCE LITTAUER

Trouble and perplexity drive us to prayer, and prayer
driveth away trouble and perplexity.

—PHILIPP MELANCTHON

*L*istening prayer is a way of freeing your mind so that God can
speak to you and reveal whatever burdens are keeping you from
a full relationship with Him or others. When Fred and I teach our
seminars, we have our students write a letter to the Lord. It might go
like this:

> *Dear Lord Jesus,*
> *When I think about the situation I'm in today, this is how I feel about it.*
> *As I look in my background to come up with the reason why I feel this way,*
> *I don't have an answer. I'm awaiting what you want me to know.*

After you've written some thoughts, sit quietly, pen in hand. Then,
write down whatever thoughts come into your mind. Fred and I have
been amazed by the way the Lord starts speaking when you open your
mind to Him and begin to record the thoughts He reveals to you. The
students can hardly contain their excitement over having the Lord
directly speak to them. Most likely, though, they've never heard Him
because they haven't taken the time to listen.

A close friend describes listening prayers as follows: "If I went over
to visit Florence one afternoon, sat down, and told her everything that
had happened to me in the last two weeks, and as soon as I got to the
end of my story I said, "Well, thanks for listening. Good-bye." how
would Florence feel? She'd think, "Wait, I didn't have a chance to
respond." That's the way it is with God. Too often we say, "Lord, here's
my problem," and then we shut the door and expect Him to break it
down and force us to listen. God doesn't do that. We need to allow
Him time to speak.

Listening prayer also helps us bring specific concerns or problems
to the Lord, so we can hone in on certain trouble spots, such as guilt.
So many times we offer generic prayers to God like, "My marriage is
terrible. Fix it." What God wants is for us to come to him with the
specifics and say, "Lord, I've spent some time on this. I know that I
have a guilt problem. Why do I have it?" Then listen. Write down what

He says. Think about it. Pray about it. Be specific. The Lord will clean up the garbage in our life, but He'll only take away the trash that we put out.

The knowledge of the secrets of the kingdom of heaven has been given to you . . .
MATTHEW 13:11

Look into taking a hot air balloon flight to start off the fall.

October

"For God has not given us a spirit of timidy, but of power and love and discipline."

2 Timothy 1:7

By now, the Fall's luster is fully evident and we begin to view the end of this year coming towards us. Yet, before we are catapulted into the holidays, we need to focus on an aspect of God's abundant touch in our lives: self-control. This characteristic must be strengthened before we can live a simplified life, free from both spiritual and material depletion. The world says "get more," but God says "find Me." In Him is true abundance.

Controlling Your Tempo Of Life

BILL AND PAM FARREL

Serenity comes not alone by removing the outward
causes and occasions of fear, but by the discovery of
inward reservoirs to draw upon.

—RUFUS M. JONES

*A*re you running from one activity to another? Do you miss the days when you sat around after an activity enjoying conversation and reveling in its success? Are you tired of being late to events because you are squeezing so much into one day?

Then your activities are too numerous. For a family to function best, a natural rhythm or pace has to form. In long-distance bicycle riding, each rider has a natural tempo that can be maintained almost indefinitely. Going faster or slower than the tempo causes the rider stress. Too fast a tempo and the rider exhausts his or her resources. The loss of energy can cause the rider to lose focus, resulting in possible injury or failure to complete the race. A tempo that is too slow is hard on the body but even more tedious to the mind. The rider feels held back and may give up hope.

Each individual has a pace. Couples and families also have a pace. You may have a personal pace that is quicker than that of the rest of your family. That's okay as long as you learn ways to go at your pace without ignoring your family's needs. On a bike trip, the person with the quickest tempo rides in front of the other cyclists. The riders are sheltered from the force of the wind and can actually speed up their tempo because there is less resistance.

For a group to ride together, different individuals take turns being the lead rider and wind breaker, because the job can get exhausting. The others then "draft" behind, almost being pulled along by the tempo of the group. Families can function this way. Different members can take responsibility for a variety of tasks; then the rest can just fall in line and draft behind their energy. Bicyclists who ride in a group and draft in this way can outdistance individual riders.

You and your spouse are in the race of life, going for the distance. Your family is a group that needs to find its own pace. You may ride out front for a while; you can even sprint out ahead, then come back, check on the rest and ride with them for a while; then do that all over again. The key is to communicate the pace.

. . . but I press on to take hold of that for which Christ Jesus took hold of me.
PHILIPPIANS 3:12

> Discuss with your spouse how your paces differ. Make any needed adjustments.

October 2

Take Time To Smell The Roses

JOAN K. WEAVER

God's fingers can touch nothing but to mold it into loveliness.

—GEORGE MACDONALD

J was in the mall recently and visited a shop which sold products for aromatherapy. The salesgirl explained how simmering herbs and scented candles could relieve stress and heal my soul. As I thought about her pitch, I knew that there was truth to what she said. The sense of smell is more powerful than we usually give it credit. But rather than candles and potpourri, I would suggest thinking back to the fragrances of childhood. These can often be recreated at little expense and with much greater benefit and satisfaction.

Perhaps today you could make some homemade soup and let it simmer on the back of the stove (or in the crock pot) all day. The wings, neck, and back of a chicken can provide the stock of a soup which will not only nourish your olfactory glands, but feed your body as well.

Or do you remember the aroma of fresh homemade bread? Begin with smelling the yeast as it bubbles and foams. Watch with satisfaction as the dough rises. Then see your family gather when the smell of the brown loaves emerge from the oven. Today, don't make them wait until dinner. Let them immediately cut off generous slices, watch the melting butter soak in, and savor the warm taste.

Perhaps the smells of a walk in the woods, or along a lake or ocean shore will conjure up memories of childhood explorations and adventures. For me, the smell of a small pillow stuffed with balsam needles brings back the simple, childhood vacation pleasures of a north woods cabin.

Perhaps you could open a small bottle of the perfume your grandmother wore, mow the grass just to smell the freshness, burn the leaves, or visit a friend's newborn baby to nuzzle in the aroma of powder and lotion. Take time today to know what Mary knew when she filled her home with fragrance in adoration of Jesus who brought abundant beauty, peace and love into her life.

Then Mary took about a pint of pure nard, and expensive perfume; she poured it on Jesus' feet and wiped his feet with her hair. And the house was filled with the fragrance of the perfume.

JOHN 12:3

What smell from your childhood is most endearing?
Try to recreate it and share it with your family.

October 3

Five Votes Of Confidence

MAX LUCADO

The greatest truth is most simple.

—BEVERLY J. PLAUGHER

Today is a new day. Hence,

1. I refuse to be shackled by yesterday's failures.

2. What I don't know will no longer be an intimidation—it will be an opportunity.

3. I will not allow people to define my mood, method, image, or mission.

4. I will pursue a mission greater than myself by making at least one person happy they saw me.

5. I will have no time for self-pity, gossip, or negativism . . . from myself or from others.

Finally, brothers, whatever is true, whatever is noble, whatever is right, whatever is pure, whatever is lovely, whatever is admirable—if anything is excellent or praiseworthy—think about such things.

PHILIPPIANS 4:8

October 4

Organizing Your Office For Less Stress

BARBARA HEMPHILL

You don't *have* to do anything. You *choose* to do it. You choose to have balance or imbalance.

—KATE LARSEN

What is an "organized office?" Do not confuse organization with neatness. Remember that old adage, "A place for everything and everything in its place?" In my experience, it's *half* right. A place for everything is very important, but everything in its place may not be. The stress comes, not from the clutter, but when you would like to clean up the clutter and don't know where to put it so that you can find it again. To put it another way, organization gives you the "ability to recover." We often find ourselves in a crisis mode. Good organization makes it possible to recover from these inevitabilities in the least stressful way.

My definition of "organized" is very simple: "Does it work?" and "Do I like it?"

1. Remember that clutter is postponed decisions. The reason that desks and filing cabinets become inundated with paper (and our computers) with files is that there are decisions we have not made. In fact, there are only three decisions you can make about any document: toss (or hopefully, recycle), file, or act. In my experience, in a typical day's mail, you can toss 40 percent and file 40 percent, which leaves only 20 percent to clutter your desk.

2. Use your wastebasket frequently and encourage others to do the same. Ask:

• Does this require action?
• Does it exist elsewhere?
• Would it be difficult to get again?
• Are there any tax or legal implications?
• Is it recent enough to be useful?

If the answers are "no," but you are still not sure, ask one last question: "What is the worst thing that could happen if I did not have this?" If you can live with the results, toss it.

3. Implement a good system for keeping track of names, addresses, and telephone numbers. Many of the pieces of paper that clutter up your life are deemed valuable because of a name, address, or phone number. Choose a system for tracking this information and use it consistently.

Abundance and simplicity require us to take control of our environment. What do you need to do today to grow closer to those objectives?

> *That everyone may eat and drink, and find satisfaction in*
> *all his toil—this is the gift of God.*
>
> ECCLESIASTES 3:13

Buy a Rolodex or business card holder and organize your telephone directory information.

October 5

Exercise Your Way To Fitness

GEORGIA CURTIS LING

Unless we form the habit of going to the Bible in
bright moments as well as in trouble, we cannot fully
respond to its consolations because we lack the
equilibrium between light and darkness.

—HELEN KELLER

Our son thought he was big stuff. At age four he was the proud owner of his first real bike. No more of those Big Wheel toys. He had moved on up to two wheels (with training wheels, of course) where he could ride faster, weave in and out of obstacle courses and ring that bell as he passed by. He described his bike as "really cool." (This all sounds very similar to when my husband got a new recreational vehicle—except for the bell.)

Needless to say, we spent quite a few hours out on the driveway after his new purchase. I decided to make some of those minutes productive so I joined the bicycling ranks and pulled out the old exercise bike so I could ride it in the garage as I watched him. I'm sure the neighbors got a kick out of that.

I found it tucked away in the shadows of the garage. I scooted it across the concrete and climbed on, but to my dismay, when I tried peddling, it wouldn't budge. I turned it upside down, began my investigative work and everything looked fine. Turning it back over, I tinkered with the tension pads. They wouldn't move either. Upon closer examination, I discovered they were rusted to the metal wheels. With some prying they began to spin freely. Yeah! (Now that will give you a hint as to how long it had been since that bike had a good workout. True confession time.)

Have you ever found yourself wanting to get spiritually fit only to find that when you turn to your first exercise of reading the Bible, the pages are stuck together? Or you start to pray and since you're out of the habit, you're short of breath and quit quickly? Or you are out of the regime of regular worship and you can't seem to remember the church service times?

Just like our physical fitness, our spiritual fitness needs exercise on a regular basis. Loosen and turn those Bible pages, strengthen your stamina and communicate longer with God in prayer. Have self-control and don't let anything keep you from worshipping God with other believers.

Before you know it, you'll be abundantly fit, ready and strong to face those every day challenges of life.

I pray also that the eyes of your heart may be enlightened in order that you may know . . . his incomparably great power for us who believe.
EPHESIANS 1:18-19A

The next time you have your devotional time, light a candle to remind you of God's presence and that the Spirit is praying for you right then.

October 6

Worship

OSWALD CHAMBERS

It is only when men begin to worship that they begin to grow.
—CALVIN COOLIDGE

Worship is giving God the best that He has given you. Be careful what you do with the best you have. Whenever you get a blessing from God, give it back to Him as a love gift. Take time to meditate before God and offer the blessing back to Him in a deliberate act of worship. If you hoard a thing for yourself, it will turn into spiritual dry rot, as the manna did when it was hoarded. God will never let you hold a spiritual thing for yourself, it has to be given back to Him that He may make it a blessing to others.

Bethel is the symbol of communion with God; Ai is the symbol of the world. Abraham pitched his tent between the two. The measure of the worth of our public activity for God is the private profound communion we have with Him. Rush is wrong every time, there is always plenty of time to worship God. Quiet days with God may be a snare. We have to pitch our tents where we shall always have quiet times with God, however noisy our times with the world may be. There are not three stages in spiritual life—worship, waiting, and work. Some of us go in jumps like spiritual frogs, we jump from worship to waiting and from waiting to work. God's idea is that the three should go together. They were always together in the life of our Lord. He was unhasting and unresting. It is a discipline, we cannot get into it all at once.

There he built an altar to the Lord and called on the name of the Lord.
GENESIS 12:8B

The next time you spend time with God, only worship. Refrain from giving requests. You could sing a praise chorus, read a Psalm, and meditate on one or more of His attributes.

October 7

Taking A "Byte" Out Of Grocery Shopping

LYNETTE S. MCBRIDE

Feeding our families is certainly a major part of our lives.
For the working woman, it can be a monumental task . . .
—EMILIE BARNES

Computers are so much a part of our daily lives that I decided to put ours to good use to help solve a problem for me. I was very unorganized when it came to grocery shopping and it was something I never really looked forward to very much. In fact, I rather dreaded the chore. I found myself going to the store every night after work to get something for dinner that evening. Then I ended up purchasing lots of junk food along with that night's dinner ingredients. I spent too much money and brought home extra calories and fat.

One weekend, I decided to try something different. There had to be a better way. So, I gathered together all my favorite recipes and sat down at the computer.

First, I made up several menus which had a variety of meals, one for each night of the week. These I labeled "Menu One," "Menu Two," etc. Then, for each weekly menu I made a list of all the ingredients needed to prepare all seven meals. This list of ingredients was divided up into categories according to the sections of the grocery store, as follows: FRESH FRUITS AND VEGETABLES; DAIRY; CANNED AND PACKAGED; BAKERY; SPICES; FROZEN; and MEATS. After entering all this information in the computer, I labeled these lists "Shopping List 1," "Shopping List 2," etc. to correspond with the appropriate menu. Initially, this required extra time, but it was well worth the effort. In the long run, I saved time and money by being organized.

Now, when it is time to do the shopping each week, I simply go to the computer, look at the menus, and pick out the one that sounds good. I print up that menu and the corresponding shopping list. The menu is placed on the refrigerator so my family can easily see it, and I don't have to continually explain what's for dinner. I then go through the shopping list in the kitchen and mark off everything that is already there so there won't be needless ingredients sitting around. At the bottom are added any other things which need to be purchased such as paper towels, cleaning supplies, and all non-food items. Then, it's off to the grocery store for a quick, well-organized time of shopping. It's a much more pleasant experience. Maybe even fun.

Being self-controlled in our food shopping will bring abundance in our purses and wallets—we'll save money.

She is like the merchant ships, bringing her food from afar. She gets up while it is still dark; she provides food for her family and portions for her servant girls.
PROVERBS 31:14-15

Put a list on the refrigerator for writing down items you use up and need to buy again. If you want to do more, put your menus on your computer.

How Busy Is Too Busy

JEAN FLEMING

Many could forego heavy meals, a full wardrobe, a fine house; it is the ego that they cannot forego.
—MOHANDAS K. GANDHI

It isn't wrong to be busy. Serious involvement in promoting God's Kingdom requires activity. Jesus was busy—too busy to eat on one occasion (see Mark 3:20). He worked to the point of exhaustion on another occasion (see Mark 4:38). Read the book of Acts; Paul was busy. But a busyness that isn't God-directed and God-motivated is not God-blessed. Busyness can ravage the soul as thoroughly as idleness can.

Somehow the phrase *I'm busy* makes us feel secure. If we're busy, we must be important, perhaps even indispensable. Mistakenly, we equate busyness with production or contribution. The busiest people must be accomplishing the most. Or are they?

Toru Nagai, a Navigator staff man in Japan, wrote, "Whenever you ask a Japanese how he is doing, he almost always replies, 'Oh, I'm quite busy.' Even if he has nothing to do, his response is the same. Rest and relaxation in this culture are almost looked on as sin, so people stay busy, even if it is with activities of little importance. This tendency is so deeply rooted in the Japanese that it remains in many after they become Christians."

Like our Japanese friends, we may complain about the endless parade of demands facing us, but unconsciously we may have designed the lifestyle of hectic, unrelenting activity as protection.

Busyness may be our shelter from the hard, cold fact that our relationship with Christ has become perfunctory. We may live in an illusory world, remembering greener days without recognizing that our zeal has waned. But if we keep busy enough, the truth can't penetrate and expose our spiritual condition. Our visible, external life may be laudable, but our inner, spiritual life has shriveled.

. . . but let him who boasts boast about this: that he understands and knows me . . .
JEREMIAH 9:24

Read *Running on Empty* by *Jill Briscoe* (Harold Shaw Publishers, 1995).

The Price Of Commitment

NAOMI RHODE

In an effort to ensure my children's tomorrows, I have
lost their todays.

—DANNY THOMAS

What is your family committed to? Are you committed to building
your dream home? Retiring at an early age? Reaching a certain
income level or social status? Committed to achieving a certain
position of power or prominence? Are you committed to each other?
To the protection and fulfillment of each family member? To supporting each other and helping each other? Are you committed to giving
your children the best possible home life? Are you committed to their
education? Are you committed to your religious beliefs and values? Are
you committed to your marriage? To parenting? Or is your primary
commitment to your career, money, power, or status?

When you commit to your family, you stick with them regardless
of unforeseen circumstances, physical or mental problems, substance
abuse, negative attitudes, reckless spending habits, personality problems, insecurities, or outside interference. It includes sustaining the
loss of a family member, your job, youth, health, or anything else you
deeply care about.

Commitment is necessary in life to see a project through to
completion. Your family is a project given to you by God. Your
commitment to your family is going to determine the happiness and
outcome of your family. Commitment is part of the support system
that holds your family together. It's always going to cost more than you
anticipated. Are you willing to pay the price?

Times get rough when you are raising a family or are just part of a
family. Things don't always turn out the way you anticipated. Strong families
learn to adapt. They change their priorities. They reassess their values. They
put the needs of their family above their own individual desires. They find
ways to communicate when communication seems impossible.

Commitment is required to build families. It involves being willing
to pay the price in terms of time, money, and lives. Hopefully, you
won't need to literally give your life for your family, but you do need
to give your family your time, your energies, your personality, your gifts,

your talents, and most of all, your love. Without commitment to your family, your dreams for them will never become a reality.

Greater love has no one than this, that he lay down his life for his friends.
JOHN 15:13

Make a commitment to drink eight glasses of water a day.

October 10

No More Games

LIZ CURTIS HIGGS

Stop dieting. This means start eating regular
meals, including appropriate sweets and snacks. Many
people who have struggled for years find that when
they give up dieting they do not gain weight.
—DAVID GARNER, PH.D.

*H*ere is an outrageous idea: fill your house with healthy foods. Pack the refrigerator with fresh fruits. Keep the crisper filled with veggies, and stock the shelves with whole grains, legumes, and pasta. Replace your soda cans with fruit juices, toss some frozen yogurt in the freezer, along with chicken breasts and fish. And, yes, go ahead and throw in some Twinkies, nacho chips, or whatever rings your bell. The things you really do crave on occasion. Then eat what you need, when you need it.

Oh, my stars. I will gain two hundred pounds.

Really? Ever tried it? Spontaneously eating healthy foods is the best thing you can do for your body. Sure, sometimes you'll reach for the stuff with a little less nutritional value. But so what? Everybody does that. Thin people, healthy people, old people, young people. Everybody eats potato chips and nobody has died from them yet.

What's an "appropriate" sweet or snack? Well, it's your body: ask it. When you're hungry, have some healthy choices available for the nutrients they provide, and give your body the fuel it needs to function. (When only a cupcake will make you happy, that's what you should eat, guilt-free.)

Whatever you do, enjoy what you eat. If you are not hungry for carrots, for heaven's sake, don't force them between your lips. One woman said dieting conjured up, "ugly, ugly thoughts of carrot sticks pounded into my heart like a stake." —Transylvania time.

Restricted eating, better known as dieting, gets us primed for the day we'll go off that diet and binge on whatever foods we deprived ourselves of. Don't be deceived. The body will not be mocked. This divinely-designed machine needs fuel at regular intervals in sufficient amounts. It will run best on the high octane stuff, but is so remarkable a contraption that it will run on almost anything—for a while. Dieting is like driving on fumes. It's hard on the engine. You could run out of gas at any moment. The smart driver keeps her tank filled and her engine tuned up, and she heads out for a spin regularly, just to keep her gears oiled. And, remember: the big Cadillac looks just as sharp on the open road as the little Honda.

> *If you are wise, your wisdom will reward you; if you are a mocker,*
> *you alone will suffer.*
>
> PROVERBS 9:12

Read "One Size Fits All" and Other Fables by Liz Curtis Higgs (Thomas Nelson Publishers, 1993).

October II

Writing Your Goals And Action Steps: Your "Reason For Succeeding"

LYNN D. MORRISSEY

> If you have built castles in the air, your work need not
> be lost; that is where they should be. Now put
> foundations under them.
>
> —HENRY DAVID THOREAU

Your goals are the foundations for your dreams; without self-control to fulfill them, they will not succeed. You can dream all you want, but as Mary Kay Ash, founder of *Mary Kay Cosmetics* says, "Without goals you can waste an entire life." She organizes her life as she would a vacation, planning every little detail. Her goals have become the road map leading to her destination.

Written goals and action steps empower your self-control and provide a blueprint for accomplishing your goals. Otherwise, they'll remain "pie in the sky," with clouds for whipped cream—all froth and no substance.

Goals should have SMARTS. They should be:

1. Specific and Measurable: Are they vague or do they specify a single, major outcome? Will you know when progress is made?

2. Achievable: Are they realistic and possible to achieve given your available time and resources?

3. Relevant: Are they related to your mission and dreams so that these ultimately will be accomplished?

4. Transformational: Do they stretch you to become a better Christian and impact others to help them grow spiritually?

5. Sacred: Are they worthy of God's approval, reflecting His will?

It is helpful to write both short-term goals (covering a six month to two year period) and long-term ones (ranging from three to five years).

Follow this simple goal-writing formula: I will (verb / end result) by (target deadline). Here is an example of one of my personal goals: I will write two articles to submit to *Today's Christian Woman* magazine by May 15th.

In order to accomplish goals, break them into small "do-able" projects called action steps and schedule deadline dates for completion on your calendar. Here are action steps and deadlines compatible with my goal: 1) read sample copies of the magazine to familiarize myself with the writing style (by April 1st). 2) write to request writers' guidelines (by April 1st). 3) list article ideas consistent with guidelines (by April 5th). 4) write two articles (by May 1st). 5) let the articles "cool" for a week, proofread, and correct (by May 8th). 6) type articles and allow them to "cool" again (by May 13th). 7) type final draft, proofread, and mail. 8) follow up by telephone with editor if I haven't heard in three months.

Writing and implementing goals simplifies life and develops self-control by keeping your actions consistent with your mission. You actually accomplish what you've dreamed you could. For what goals do you want to write down your plans?

The plans of the diligent lead to profit . . .
PROVERBS 21:5A

> Place "goal posts" in strategic places like mirrors, refrigerator door, dashboard, etc. These are one word prompters on "post-its" to remind you of your goals.

Unique Measure Of Sensitivity

FLORENCE LITTAUER

I feel the capacity to care is the thing which gives life
its deepest significance.

— PABLO CASALS

God created each of us with a unique measure of sensitivity. No
matter how emotionally tough we appear to be, each of us has areas
where we are vulnerable. Some channel this gift of great sensitivity
outward in the form of compassion and feeling for others. Because I
have lost two children, I have a heart for grieving mothers. Because
my husband was molested as a child, he is willing to spend many hours
each week ministering to those in emotional pain.

Others, though, keep their sensitivity focused inward, causing
them to harbor many hurts and wounds imposed by the perceived
callousness of those around them. While all of us are hurt from time
to time by the thoughtless words and actions of others, more often
than not it is pride and self-centeredness that turns an off-the-cuff,
innocent remark into grounds for a pity-party. By being aware of the
areas where we feel most vulnerable emotionally and then committing
these to God, we can begin to bolster ourselves emotionally.

Therefore, as we have opportunity, let us do good to all people,
especially to those who belong to the family of believers.
GALATIANS 6:10

Let your husband have his needed "trance" time when
he first comes home from work.

He Sees Beyond

HELEN LUECKE

> One reason sin flourishes is that it is treated like a
> cream puff instead of a rattlesnake.
>
> —BILLY SUNDAY

J discovered a necklace tucked back in my jewelry box. I held it up
in the bright sunlight and stared at the balled up chain filled with
knots. I should break it, retrieve the pendant and get a new chain, I
thought. "No," I said out loud, "I know how that chain looks when
it's straight."

For the next hour, using a toothpick and a straight pin, I picked,
tapped, and shook the chain. I got a crick in my neck, pricked my finger
with the pin, lost my temper, and finally put the necklace away.

The next day, along with the pin, I used a pair of tweezers and a
magnifying glass. After about an hour, I saw my original chain emerging.

Thirty minutes later, all the knots were out except a tiny one at the
latch. *Just leave it in,* I thought, *no one will see it.* I held it up. I would
know. I worked the remaining knot out.

Does your life seem like it's knotted with sin? You may feel trapped
and unworthy—ready to give up. You are valuable in Jesus' eyes, and
He sees beyond those knots. He waits to hear from you. He can loosen
the knots and set you free. As He does, you'll be farther on your journey
toward the abundant life by becoming more self-controlled.

> *Before I formed you in the womb I knew you,*
> *before you were born I set you apart . . .*
>
> JEREMIAH 1:5

Leave a little "love note" in lipstick on the bathroom
mirror for your husband.

Fearfully And Wonderfully Made

PATSY CLAIRMONT

The greatest discovery of my generation is that human beings can alter their lives by altering their attitudes of mind.

—WILLIAM JAMES

There's no doubt we are fearfully and wonderfully made. All we have to do is listen to our bodies and respond with good choices. Some of you already are disciplined and wise in caring for yourselves. But, like me, many of you don't listen until you're in trouble. We could all benefit by answering the following:

How much water do you drink in a day? (No fair counting the water in coffee or cola.)

How many hours of sleep do you require a night to feel "normal?" (My husband, Les, requires seven hours but prefers six. I need eight hours but enjoy nine. Les catapults from the bed each morning, while I have to be jump-started just to ignite a pulse.)

Do you have an exercise regimen? (Getting out of bed each morning does not qualify as weight lifting.)

When was your last eye exam? (I took my mangled glasses in last week for repair. I had sat on them . . . for the third time. The woman looked at them and said, "Lady, do you know which end these were made for?" "Evidently not," I replied sweetly, "or I wouldn't be here again.")

Write down the date of your last dental appointment. (If B.C. follows the date, it has been too long.)

Are you listening to your body when it says, "Enough is enough" (food, work, rest)?

When was your last physical? (Talking to a friend who once took a first-aid course does not count.)

Did it include a pap smear? (This is an uplifting experience.)

Have you had a mammogram? (That's where the technician thinks she's a magician and tries to turn a cup into a saucer.)

Have you ever had a change in your weight without a change in your eating? (My mother-in-law thought she was fat. Her "fat" turned out to be a tumor the size of a watermelon. My husband was losing weight while eating like a buffalo. (Maybe that's why he could lift them. It turned out he was diabetic.)

Are you having frequent headaches, stomachaches, backaches, rashes, sleeplessness, spotting, mood swings, urination, unquenchable thirst, and so on? It's time to find out why.

How many pills do you take in a week? In a month? Are you masking a growing health issue? (Our plop-plop, fizz-fizz mentality covers our pain but doesn't resolve it.)

Trust the way God has designed your body to let you know when you need to make a life adjustment or a visit to your family doctor. This body is just a temporary time suit. (Can't you hear it ticking?) It's the only one we get before heaven's new, improved version, which will be complete with eternal vision.

Speaking of vision, remember that in this life, your glasses belong on your nose. Take it from someone who knows.

> *Therefore, having these promises, beloved, let us cleanse ourselves from all defilement of flesh and spirit, perfecting holiness in the fear of God.*
> 2 CORINTHIANS 7:1

Write down five things you like about yourself.

October 15

Back To Basics

KATHRYN HARTZELL

> If you agree with God's purpose He will bring not
> only your conscious life, but all the deeper regions of
> your life which you cannot get at, into harmony.
> —OSWALD CHAMBERS

What is a Christian to focus his or her energy upon? What is God's overall plan for each of us? The answers to these questions are found in three basic principles for Godly living.

First, we are to develop a relationship with God whereby we are constantly growing in our knowledge of Him.

This is accomplished through daily Bible reading and prayer, recognizing God at work in and around us, spending time with other Christians, worship, and our obedience to God. As with any relationship, the more time spent in these activities, the more intimate the relationship becomes.

The second principle is to develop our character to be Christlike, using the gifts and talents God has given us to serve others. God has given each of us unique gifts and talents which He asks us to use to bless others. Once we identify ours, we need to determine how and where we can use them to serve others. Usually these gifts and talents are in the same area as our God-given passion in life.

The Bible instructs us to produce "fruit." There are two types of fruit—external and internal. External fruit is produced whenever we are able to assist someone in drawing closer to God. This is done by reaching out to non-Christians or helping a fellow Christian. God's family works as a team and everyone involved in a particular outreach will reap the rewards it produces.

Internal fruit deals with our character development and developing the fruit of the Spirit. Such fruit includes love, joy, peace, patience, kindness, goodness, faithfulness, gentleness, and self-control—the very fruit *God's Abundance* is focused upon. Some of these characteristics we can work on, while others come as a byproduct of other activities.

The third principle is to have the same attitudes and desires in life as Jesus Christ did. Our attitudes toward the world are to be: do not conform to it, do not love it, do not be friends with it, and do not be entangled with it. We should seek the salvation of unbelievers while reproving and praying for them.

Our attitudes toward other Christians should be to love one another, be in unity, and use our gifts to encourage and build up each other. Our attitude toward ourselves is to turn the focus away from us in order to love and serve others.

Having the self-control to obey God's principles and specific guidance brings freedom from the grip sin could have on us. The result? Abundant life.

> . . . *acknowledge the God of your father, and serve him with*
> *wholehearted devotion and with a willing mind . . .*
> I CHRONICLES 28:9

When you first go through your mail, have a wastebasket available to immediately throw away unnecessary items.

October 16

Work Has Its Place

JILL BRISCOE

Teach us, Good Lord, to serve Thee as Thou deservest:
To give and not to count the cost
To fight and not to heed the wounds
To toil and not to seek for rest
To labor and not to ask for any reward
Save the joy of knowing
That we do Thy will.

—ST. IGNATIUS OF LOYOLA

Work is a part of life as God intended it to be. But when our work becomes a snare to us, it's time to sit back and listen to what Jesus says about it.

The Lord certainly appreciates those who work hard. He considered work important enough to make it a part of Paradise. "The Lord God took the man and put him in the Garden of Eden to work it and take care of it" (Gen. 2:15). Work had its place even right in the middle of the Garden of Eden.

God worked hard himself, too. After all, he was pretty busy during those days of creation. He didn't stop for cups of tea (which he definitely would have done had he been English), or a midday snooze (which he would have indulged in had he been Italian), or even to watch the California Angels play (which he would certainly have done had he been American). He didn't, in fact, stop at all until he was through. But after God had finished his work, he did stop for a rest—and he expects us to do the same. There is a busyness that is blessed and there is a busyness that isn't.

God thought work was so important that he used up one of his Ten Commandments to deal with it. The Ten Commandments, as someone has said, are not Ten Suggestions. They are God's mandate for all people. Sin didn't change God's mind about work—it just made it necessary for him to command us to get it done, how to go about it, and when to stop.

"Six days you shall labor and do all your work," says the Scripture (Exod. 20:8). Notice it says, all your work—not some of your work, not just the work you like doing (there will always be thistles), not even the work you feel you are being properly remunerated for. It says all your work.

We live in a world where it is assumed that the only work worth doing is work for which we are monetarily rewarded. But just think how much work you do that is not rewarded by money—and how worthwhile it is. Have your children ever given you a paycheck at the end of a busy week and said, "Well done, Mom. Good job. And we put in some extra for the overtime you spent with us Tuesday?" Of course not. For this kind of work, we receive another kind of reward. What money can buy an "I love you, Mom" at the end of the day? And for our Christian service we are paid in Heavenly currency. I'm sure Adam and Eve never saw a dollar bill in the Garden of Eden. Yet God intended their labor to be rewarding and fruitful.

> *Better a poor man whose walk is blameless than a*
> *rich man whose ways are perverse.*
> PROVERBS 28:6

Anticipate waiting time and use it to your advantage. Have paper, pen, book, blank cards, tape recorder, etc. with you when you think you may be waiting. (*Finding Time*, Paula Peisner).

October 17

Without Faith It's Impossible

PAT VERBAL

My most memorable lessons have been taught by children.
—PAT VERBAL

*H*earing the distant screech of the school bus, I knew Ronnie, my youngest son, would soon bounce through the door. During lunch, we'd watch Green Acres on television and talk about his morning at Kindergarten.

It can't be twelve o'clock already, I thought. All morning I'd prayed over a problem at church. I served on our church board, where a heated issue was causing tempers to flare. Well-meaning friends called daily. I didn't know what to say and hated the gossip. Hearing the side door open, I tried to put on a smile for my adorable five-year-old.

Ronnie stopped abruptly, throwing his backpack, jacket, and library book on the kitchen floor with a thud. His bright blue eyes flashed.

"I blew it again, Mom." he wailed. "I messed up on my Bible verse and I caused the whole class to miss out on a perfect record." His lip quivered. His disappointment broke my heart. I slumped to the floor and wrapped my arms around his waist. His shaking little body went limp on my shoulder.

"Ronnie, I'm so sorry. You know that verse," I assured him.

"It's easy to say it to you, but I get nervous saying to it Mrs. Shillinger," he whimpered. "She made me start over, and then I got confused. Now our class won't get to stand up in chapel tomorrow."

"Well then, you still have one more chance in the morning before chapel," I encouraged him. "Stand up straight now and say your Bible verse for me again."

Ronnie threw back his shoulders and in a tone matching a military cadence, he loudly exclaimed, "Without faith it is impossible to please God, because anyone who comes to him must believe that he exists and that he rewards those who earnestly seek him." Beaming, he then proudly added the reference, "Hebrews 11:6."

Tears filled my eyes. Somewhere in the middle of his recitation, I'd heard the voice of God. For a split second I forgot about my son's problem. I recognized the answer to my own need . . . a powerful promise spouted by a little child speaking an eternal truth.

"Ronnie, say that verse again," I said. "Mommy needs that verse today."

He sat down beside me and together we repeated Hebrews 11:6 until I could say it all by myself. We missed Green Acres on television that day, but I was changed.

When the phone rang, I quoted my verse. When I felt confused, I quoted my verse. As I drove to the next board meeting, I quoted my verse. Because God existed and our church was seeking him, I confidently said, "His reward is on the way." It didn't come instantly, but soon the issue was resolved.

Ronnie successfully said his memory verse before chapel on Friday. Later in fifth grade, he memorized one hundred and five Bible verses to earn his way to camp. He also continued to teach his mother that memorizing Scripture was one of the best ways to hold onto our faith in troubled times.

Have you chosen to control your mind through the memorization of Scripture? It'll impact your actions and attitudes, empowering you to simply obey God.

. . . and a little child will lead them.

> Get a music tape that puts Scripture to song and
> memorize Scripture that way.

October 18

Disciplined Abundance

KACY BARNETT-GRAMCKOW

Seek the first possible opportunity to act on every
good resolution you make.

—WILLIAM JAMES

"*J* hate myself. This is not me."

It was a moment of total self-honesty. No more excuses, no
more self-justification, no more willful denial of the truth: I was forty
pounds overweight. A grown woman unable to control her own eating
habits. My joints ached. My back and my feet would scream for mercy
the instant I crawled out of bed each day. And a simple walk down our
long driveway to get the mail would leave me breathless and exhausted.

I grew up in a busy, loving family, with four brothers and thousands
of games of kickball, hide-and-seek, tag, and the ever-popular keep-the-
doll-away-from-Kacy game. I never imagined I would one day fit the
clinical definition of *obese*. But now, facing a size sixteen pair of jeans
filled me with shame. My family must be concerned about me. Not to
mention my active, average-weight husband, who gently hinted at his
care for my health. My doctor would be concerned as well; I had failed
the glucose test while pregnant with my second child, and diabetes was
a definite threat. Already, I was experiencing fatigue, shakiness, even
faintness.

These were mere physical symptoms, however. The spiritual side
was even more depressing. My ample, growing curves were obvious proof
that I was abusing God's gifts. I was being self-indulgent, self-willed, lazy,
and rebellious against what I knew was right for my body. Now, I knew
I had to change. Miserably, I searched for my "lost" copy of the diabetic
diet, and submitted to the agonies of calorie counting, all the while
praying, "Dear God, help me to resist chocolate."

Deciding to "ease" myself into dieting, I concentrated on eating

1800 calories a day; eight servings of fruits and vegetables, the leanest meat available, and measuring *everything*. Knowing I could not trust myself to resist treats, I planned for them in my diet. "One Bread Exchange and one Fat Exchange equals one plain cake donut." I exclaimed to my ever-cautious husband. "And I can make them equal one cookie too." Wisely, he kept silent as I began to read every nutrition label in the house.

Two weeks later, still "easing" myself into the diet, I realized I was actually losing almost two pounds a week. And because my job outside the home was very physical, with lots of standing, lifting and walking, exercise was not a problem. On my vacations, I took at least three brisk half-hour walks a week. True hunger was rare; if I had eaten my quota, I had a fat-free salad and tea. Despite my infrequent lapses, I lost the entire forty pounds within twenty-four weeks. One year later, I'm still at my "ideal" weight. My doctor is thrilled, and so is my husband. I know I will always be "watching my diet." But God, in His infinite mercy, has led me to that simple plan of balance.

In what area of your life do you want more discipline and self-control? Take "baby steps" to put a plan into action.

> . . . *you give them their food at the proper time.*
> *You open your hand and satisfy the desires of every living thing.*
> PSALM 145:15-16

For a week, write down everything you eat and then evaluate what changes need to be made.

October 19

Simply Unburdened

LAURIE A. FULLER

God has left his signature on many things in this world, and the hardest thing for us sometimes is to open our eyes and leave all the excuses behind and accept what God has for us.

—RICH BARCELONA

For my friends, Rich and Lori, God's signature was very plain. My husband and I met them in a Sunday School class led by Rich. Rich had a good job in construction, and Lori stayed at home with their two children, home-schooling. They had bought their second house with a pool in the yard. God had blessed them.

Soon, however, the construction industry slowed down, and Rich lost his job. Confident that things would pick up soon, Rich took his family on vacation. He had seen God at work enough to know that He would provide. But after a series of brief temporary jobs, he couldn't make the house payments. It was time for serious soul searching.

Between jobs, Rich and Lori joined a church trip to Mexico. Shaken by the appalling needs of the rural Mexicans, their hearts hurt to bring them the message of Christ. Returning, Rich and Lori committed their lives to serve God in Mexico.

Eventually, they sold their house with a sense of relief. Possessions had become a burden and a barrier to service. They sold or gave away most of their belongings and purchased a small travel trailer. It was parked on the church property, where they worked as caretakers while taking correspondence Bible School courses. During this time, two more children were born.

As I write, Rich and Lori still live in the trailer—with five children—as they finish up an intensive Spanish language program in Texas. Their church is building a house for them in Mexico. Rich and Lori are a living challenge to those around them, representing a control over themselves that few possess. Their resources are stretched, but simply depending on God instead of their own power or possessions teaches them and others the abundance of living under God's provision.

Our closeness to Rich and Lori forced me to consider how much of my energy is centered on my possessions. Can I as easily give them up? What, after all, is important? As a Christian desiring to serve God, I need to make sure my lifestyle reflects my mindset. Many of my selfish desires melt away insignificantly under scrutiny. An "at home" mother, I see myself as a local lay missionary solely supported by my husband, financially. This radically changes how I spend my time and money, and it wipes away the fog on the mirror in which I see God's image.

Is there some possession that has greater control over you than the Lord does? If so, it's choking your ability to experience the abundant life. Let it go, you'll never regret it.

Do not store up for yourselves treasures on earth, where moth and rust destroy, and where thieves break in and steal. But store up for yourselves treasures in heaven, where moth and rust do not destroy, and where thieves do not break in and steal. For where your treasure is, there your heart will be also.
MATTHEW 6:19-21

> Initiate a church garage sale to benefit missions, or quietly donate the proceeds of your own sale.

October 20

Life Without TV?

KATHRYN HARTZELL

Yielding to Jesus will break every form of slavery in any human life.

—OSWALD CHAMBERS

We know the majority of TV is a waste of time, yet it gets turned on out of habit. Breaking this habit is possible with the help of Jesus and a solid plan. To quit watching TV requires self-control and some pre-planning.

First, make a list of everything you want to do but never seem to find the time. These can include projects, spending quality time with the family, reaching out to friends, doing a Bible study, developing skills to enhance the gifts God has given you, volunteer work, or a myriad of things.

Be specific when you list each item: what it is; how it can be accomplished; others whom it may involve; the time duration; the benefits you expect to achieve; the deadline to have it accomplished; and other projects which may result as an offshoot of this activity. Do you have all the materials you'll need to get started?

Next, communicate your plan to your spouse or family. Invite them to join you in this experiment. As a parent, you may assert that the family will be doing this together. Let everyone give input on ideas and family projects.

Although parents may come up with projects for their children, be sure they are not just jobs. Children must be able to do things they enjoy or want to experiment with, otherwise it will be drudgery for them.

You will need to set an initial duration for this experiment. The minimum should be two weeks. Discuss ahead of time that the experiment will be difficult at first. However, if everyone has prepared their list of projects, it will be easier.

Set the date to begin.

The first few days are the most difficult. When there are dry spells, find another person to talk with or team up for the next project. If you're single, call a friend and let them know what you're trying to accomplish. Just sharing your vision will encourage your self-control.

I am single and my personal experience revealed that after only ten days on the experiment I didn't have enough time to get everything accomplished. I felt so good because I was getting things done. If I need to, I turn on the radio for background noise and to catch up on the news.

After the initial time period has elapsed, determine if TV watching will be allowed. I can boldly say life is more fulfilling without TV.

Would you like to stretch your self-control through such a project? Give it a try. Your life will become more simple and abundant.

I will set before my eyes no vile thing.

PSALM 101:3A

> For at least one night, instead of watching TV, go outside and meditate on God's awesome power by focusing on the stars.

October 21

One Verse A Week

BOB TURNBULL

It ain't those parts of the Bible that I can't understand that bother me, it is the parts that I do understand.
—MARK TWAIN

One morning as I completed my work out at our fitness center and was walking past a treadmill, a voice yelled out, "Good morning, Bob." I turned to see that the voice belonged to Diana, a Christian sister who serves with the Los Angeles Fire Department. My wife, Yvonne, and I hadn't seen her for quite some time.

I paused to chat with her and when she sensed I had a moment, she opened up and shared her many frustrations in the workplace. She asked, "Do you have any good Bible verses about hope you can leave with me?"

I smiled, and said, "Yes, Romans 15:13, *May the God of hope fill you with all joy and peace as you trust in Him, so that you may overflow with hope by the power of the Holy Spirit.*"

She shouted, "Wow, I needed to hear that one." We laughed and as I left I could see her mouth repeating, "Romans 15:13."

The reason I smiled is that verse is the one Yvonne and I had just memorized the day before in fulfillment of our promise to each other and the Lord: to memorize a biblical verse once a week throughout this year. We want these verses to be "hidden in our heart"—stored in our memory—and available to use in both counseling and public speaking.

We both have seen our Lord honor this discipline in all of the above areas. In Yvonne's speaking at a woman's retreat recently, new verses came to her mind at just the right moment of her message. I did a recall of a verse at our local post office talking to a Christian clerk I know. When giving a "close" at a recent marriage seminar, at just the right moment the paraphrase of Romans 12:1-2 came to mind.

Would you like to make this a simple, fun family project? It may not take as much self-control for the children as for you, but it will encourage your growth in that fruit. At dinner share and discuss your verses. It'll bring your family closer together and you'll all be strengthened in the abundant life.

> *All Scripture is God-breathed and is useful for teaching, rebuking, correcting and training in righteousness.*
>
> 2 TIMOTHY 3:16

Put the verses you're memorizing on 3 X 5 file cards to carry with you and review.

October 22

I Can?

JAN WOODARD

Never make a case against yourself.
—DR. NORMAN VINCENT PEALE

*M*y hubby, Jim, is a do-it-yourselfer. After he chopped down a tree threatening to smash his mom's roof, he hauled a wagon load of spruce branches to the bottom of our hill with his little red tractor.

That tractor is one of his favorite handyman contraptions. Naturally, it works perfectly with Jim in control. For me, it growls and stalls.

This morning I sipped coffee, watching through a glass door as Jim and his tractor wrestled with a stubborn cement mixer he left squatting outside before an unexpected snowstorm. Now entrenched in mud, the mixer won the first round. Sure as sunrise, however, Jim will figure out a way to move that ugly brute. He never gives up.

Challenges like that sometimes overwhelm me. Due to a painful muscle condition called fibromyalgia, I often can't join in. Observing my Mr. Fix-it, I was tempted to make an "I can't" list. When I mentioned that to a friend on the phone, she chided me. God used her to nudge me into creating an "I can" inventory, instead.

"But there's so much more I can't do," I argued.

God's Spirit whispered back, "Paul wrote, I can do all things through Christ, who strengthens me . . . and he was chained in jail at the time."

"All right already, I'll try."

I was surprised at the symmetry I ended up with, God's way of keeping our lives in balance:

Jim can cut down trees; I can pray as he does it.

Jim can hunt deer; I can make venison stew.

Jim can lead worship; I can teach Sunday school.

Jim can build a house; I can do the laundry.

I can write cards and notes; Jim can buy stamps to mail them.

I can wash the dog when she roles in smelly stuff; Jim can coax her into the kitchen to dry off.

I can help kids study history; Jim can help with math.

The list got pretty long. Looking it over, I discovered God didn't put us together to compare but to complement and support each other, with contributions based on the "I can" attitude of St. Paul.

Thought up your own list yet? Like a little red tractor that can do practically anything with the right person in control, our "I can'ts" become "I cans" when we're God-dependent and Christ-controlled.

By myself I can do nothing . . . I seek not to please myself but Him who sent me.
JOHN 5:30

Make a list of things you can do in the Spirit's power and see how they relate to being self-controlled.

Microwave Prayers

BETTY CHAPMAN PLUDE

There is nothing that makes us love a man so much as praying for him.

—WILLIAM LAW

"Yes, I will pray for you." How many times I have said that and by the time I reached the car I'd already forgotten, my mind focused on my busy day.

But for several years now, I've found something to solve that. In my garage where I have an exercise bike, I taped names and pictures of family and friends so that I could pray for them and keep my mind off the boring pedaling. These pictures and names turned the exercising into a rewarding experience. In winter, though, it is too cold in my garage to work out, so I go to the local college for an exercise class. I needed to devise a better year-round plan.

Little by little, I starting adding unique post-it notes, with names, to the door of my microwave. It's amazing how many times a day we use our microwaves. While food is heating, I pray for the people on my notes. I am standing before the microwave, but in my heart I am kneeling before God. Sometimes I talk to the note saying, "Hi, my friend, I hope you are feeling better today. Wish you were here to visit and have a cup of tea."

As time has gone by, I've become known as the microwave lady. Friends (and people I barely know) call and ask if I will put their name on my microwave and pray for them. On many of my post-it notes only the name appears and not the circumstances, for confidentiality is important when company is in my kitchen.

From time-to-time I call those that I don't see frequently and get an update. They are so grateful to know that I have been praying. If their situation has been resolved, I put their name and the details in my praise journal.

I use my praise journal along with my Bible study lesson each morning. What a great way to start the day.

If you're not yet in the habit of a regular time with God, get up early tomorrow when it is quiet and be sure to praise Him for all the answers to prayer He gives.

And pray in the Spirit on all occasions with all kinds of prayers and requests.
With this in mind, be alert and always keep on praying for all the saints.

EPHESIANS 6:18

> Find a place where you can put the names of the people you're praying for.

October 24

Time For Aerobic Kneeling

STEVE FARRAR

If you add a little to a little and do this often, soon the little will become great.

—HESIOD

Consider with me an idea I've been chewing on for awhile. If exercise in the physical realm requires thirty minutes, three times a week, then why not apply that same principle to the spiritual? I realize Kenneth Cooper didn't get aerobics from the New Testament, and I'm not suggesting my idea has any scriptural basis. It's only an observation from the physical that may have application to the spiritual.

If thirty minutes, three times a week, provides the necessary endurance for the physical, then would it be off-base to suggest the same schedule might give me endurance for the spiritual life? I don't think so. Especially for the person who currently isn't exercising at all.

If something is important to us, we usually can find three or four thirty-minute segments in our schedules each week to accomplish it. Let's say you decided to shoot for this goal. If you did it three times a week in a year's time, you would have spent approximately seventy-eight hours in one-on-one time with the Lord. If you had four thirty-minute appointments annually, that would give you one-hundred and four hours. Seventy-eight or more hours in a year with the Lord in concentrated, one-on-one time is nothing to feel guilty about.

. . . train yourself to be godly. For physical training is of some value,
but godliness has value for all things, holding promise for both
the present life and the life to come.

I TIMOTHY 4:7-8

Read *Homesick for Eden, A Soul's Journey to Joy* by Gary W. Moon (Servant Publications, 1997).

October 25

True Beauty

SUSAN KIMMEL WRIGHT

> Before we can adorn our houses with beautiful objects the walls must be stripped, and our lives must be stripped, and beautiful housekeeping and beautiful living be laid for a foundation . . .
>
> —THOREAU

The old expression, "Less is more," explains why my house tends to burden rather than restore me. Between my husband and me, three kids and assorted animals, we seem constantly to accumulate truckloads of trinkets and piles of paper.

While we have some lovely things, they're barely visible because of the clutter. If one knickknack is attractive, shouldn't twenty be even better? And real soon now, we'll get around to picking it all up so we can dust. Maybe we can just pull the drapes and dim the lights . . .

No amount of decorating can compensate for out-of-control clutter. In fact, the more we try, the more we have to take care of, and the more we feel as if it's all closing in on us.

Our lives are like our houses, constantly barraged by the wasteful, the trivial, and the damaging. Both need constant weeding out lest we find ourselves sinking beneath the weight of all that we've mindlessly gathered. True beauty begins with a bare canvas and a thoughtful hand.

It may take self-control to diminish clutter, but the rewards will be worth it. Do some today.

Like a gold ring in a pig's snout is a beautiful woman who shows no discretion.
PROVERBS 11:22

What clutter could you toss today and not miss it a year from now?

October 26

Abundantly What?

He who wins consistently at Monopoly should handle
the money.

—JERI CHRYSONG

J am a single mom. Single moms have abundant lives, too.
Abundantly sleep-impaired, abundantly broke, yet abundantly
fly-by-the-seat-of-your-pants spontaneous.

I am also organizationally-impaired. I shouldn't even be in this
book. I must be mad for trying. However, I believe my racing through
life doubly-hindered has taught me some valuable lessons for gaining
greater self-control.

First, I have divided my thinking into two sides: my feminine side
and my masculine side. Usually, when faced with a situation which
requires action, I, using my feminine side, react emotionally and
impulsively: "I want it now. I want to buy that. Isn't that cute, I must
have it." which brings me to another realization: I can't afford my
feminine side.

Secondly, I have learned to ask God for wisdom and guidance in
all things, whether it be child-rearing or shopping. He has answered
my prayers by helping me develop a logical, realistic, masculine side, a
tough "Hammer-of-the-Law" side, a "No, we don't have the money"
side. I don't like my masculine side. Yet, I've learned to consult and
trust it because it usually keeps me out of trouble.

For example, when totally undecided about whether to do something for the kids I really can't afford, or go away for the weekend and
be totally self-indulgent, I first consider my feminine side's feelings and
desires, then consult my logical, masculine side for advice. If my
masculine side can afford my feminine side, I go with that. On the
other hand, if my masculine side cannot afford it and dictates a
resounding "No," I have come to accept this as the Lord saying "No."
Sometimes hard-to-swallow, it does, however, save me from plunging
headlong into a financial pit of despair.

Perhaps you may be thinking, Jeri, you are abundantly-crazy with
your masculine side this and feminine side that. No wonder you're
schizophrenic half-the-time.

OCTOBER

But maybe you feel the same way sometimes, especially if you're a single person who is solely responsible for the needs of a family. Hang on. Your feminine and masculine sides may fight at times but you're learning self-control. The abundant life has got to be around the corner. And in the meantime, God will hold your two sides together.

> . . . in Him all things hold together.
>
> COLOSSIANS 1:17B

To take better care of yourself, allow family members the opportunity to take care of themselves.

October 27

The Collection

JANICE H. STROUP

Let thy mind's sweetness have its operation upon thy body, clothes, and habitation.

—HERBERT

*M*y house is big enough. At least it should be. So why is every drawer and closet and shelf filled to overflowing? Why do books, papers, and clothes collect on every available surface? Why is it I have no room to bring anything new into the house?

It's the collection of a lifetime. All five of us in this household have our treasures, our equipment, our clothing, and our junk.

My kitchen shelves are cluttered with disposable containers, old pots and pans I never use, "one-of-a-kind" drinking glasses, and too many of this and that.

I will eliminate the extras.

How about my clothing? I have things in my closet that used to fit, but no longer do. Or they never did fit and never will. I own clothes that are the wrong color for me or are out of style. And things I wish I had never bought and now feel obligated to keep.

I will give them away.

I need to take a close look at my reading material. Am I ever really going to read all those back issues of magazines when new ones come flooding in every month? How about books on subjects I was once interested in but no longer care about? And I have books I hope to be interested in some day. But, since life keeps giving me more and different interests, I will probably never read them.

I will free my mind of obligations and my shelves of extras.

My recipe collection is mind-boggling. I cook the same ten or twenty meals over-and-over, yet store thousands of recipes. Am I just dreaming when I clip yet another exotic or unusual recipe that I might need some year? I can probably find anything I might need at the public library. I will let them manage the material, while my files stay useful and efficient.

I will think differently.

It may take a while to change the habits of a lifetime, but sometime—soon, I hope—my home will be uncluttered. Each drawer will hold only what it should, and no more. My closet space will be more than adequate for my clothes and belongings. There will be room in my home and in my life for the things that matter.

I promise.

Will you promise with me? And then let's do something. We can do it with the Spirit's control.

She watches over the affairs of her household . . .
PROVERBS 31:27

> For every piece of clutter, ask yourself, "Do I toss it, file it, or act on it?"

October 28

In The Long Run . . .

LIZ CURTIS HIGGS

Getting your priorities straight and sticking to them is one of the most difficult tasks in life.
—DR. KEVIN LEMAN

What makes keeping to my priorities easier is consciously listening to God's voice, my husband's voice, and my own voice as they all resonate in my heart. This requires ignoring the voices of media and peer pressure and filtering out the you-shoulds from well-meaning but ill-informed sources.

Some questions worth asking ourselves might be:

- Will this activity matter one week from today? One month? One year?
- Is there someone who does it better than I, to whom I might delegate this activity?
- Does it satisfy a heart need for me or someone I love very much?
- What are the ramifications if I *don't* do it?
- What are the outcomes if I *do* do it?

This exercise might be a little much for considering whether you should take out the trash. The answer there is yes. But for any activity that will require even a modest drain on our time/money/energy resources, it could provide the pause we need to reconsider and say, "No, thanks."

My daughter, Lillian, who turned five while I was functioning in Passion Mode of recently writing a book, declared, "The next time they ask you to write a book, just tell them, 'No way—I have to tuck my children into bed.'" I laughed, but I listened too. At night when the words flowed most easily, Bill would often kiss them goodnight with a promise, that "Mama will see you in the morning." After Lillian's comment, I knew that Passion Mode needed to be parked for a moment while I went upstairs to hug my children and hear their prayers.

After all, look at the five questions above in light of that nightly tuck-in:

- *Yes*, in years to come, those precious times will matter to both of us.
- *No*, there is no one else who can do "Mama" better.
- *Yes*, it satisfies a heart need for me *and* for my loved ones.
- Ramifications if I don't? Disappointment for them. Guilt for me.
- Outcomes if I do? They sleep better, and I work better, knowing I took time to do something that *really* mattered.

> *Better a meal of vegetables where there*
> *is love than a fattened calf with hatred.*
> PROVERBS 15:17

Mark on your schedule times for family or friends and consider it as important as any business commitment.

How To Run And Not Be Weary

DOTTI CUMMINS

Hurry is the death of prayer.

—SAMUEL CHADWICK

"I'm going to win the race," declared our eight-year-old son Josh, as he readied himself for the 3K race near our home. "Good luck," I shouted, as both he and his seven-year-old brother Danny, shot out from the starting line once the race began.

Sometime later, I stood at the finish line peering into the distance, anxiously looking for the sight of either of my blond, curly-headed little guys. Suddenly, I saw what appeared to be Danny out near the front of the myriad of runners. But where was Josh? Unfortunately, Josh didn't show up until long after Danny had been declared the third place winner.

What happened? Both sons were equally athletic and both wanted to run the race well. Yet, one ended full of energy and stamina way out in front and one ended totally depleted and near the rear.

It became immediately apparent that Josh had been weighted down by the sweat suit he had chosen to wear on that cold, gray, October day. Danny, on the other hand, sacrificed comfort and warmth wearing a little tank top and pair of shorts. The weight they carried on their backs made all the difference.

Starting our day without prayer first, is like running a race with a sweat suit on. It's choosing to run out the door in the morning weighted down, encumbered, and heavy laden. Though the load may not feel so heavy at the start, the energy, and the strength needed to combat the pulls of home, work, church, community, and our own personal needs, will leave us drained, weary and worn by day's end. We will have carried on our back what God so lovingly and ably desired to carry for us.

We may try to "catch up" with God during the day and call on Him as we have need for His help and guidance. But the control, patience, joy and peace we need will not be ours in abundant measure. We'll get through. We'll finish. We'll cross the day's finish line as we plop into bed thankful night has come. But we won't have finished nearly as well as we could have.

Like Danny, who deprived himself of comfort at the beginning of the race and finished well, so is the person who starts the day with prayer. It may seem inconvenient, even a waste of time, but he or she knows how they start will affect how they end.

How do you start your day? With a spiritual sweat suit on or lean and mean through prayer? Your self-control may be determined by that very choice. Choose today abundance gained through early morning devotions.

O God, you are my God, earnestly I seek you.

PSALM 63:1

> If you're not a morning person, consider your evening devotions the beginning of the day. The Jewish day starts at sundown.

October 30

Losing Perspective

JILL BRISCOE

It matters not how long you live, but how well.

—PUBLILIUS SYRUS

When I lose my perspective on life because I'm running on empty, I can soon lose my perspective on God himself. I need to be still and feel his loving touch and hear him say to me, "Go to sleep, rest awhile; the journey is too great for you." I am the sort of person who always seems to need permission to go to sleep—to relax, to walk the fields, smell the flowers, or recuperate. So, unless "have fun" is entered on my weekly schedule, I'll never have it.

Does that sound familiar? Has the journey suddenly become too great for you—not because everything is all wrong with your relationship with God, but because everything has been all right and you've simply run yourself into the ground? What swept you off your feet and sent you hurrying away from your responsibilities? Actually, it matters not what caused the changes, but only *Who* waits for you with hot cakes and cool water for your hungry, thirsty soul, assuring you of his love and great concern for your well-being.

The Lord's answer to Elijah's dilemma was a physical one. My own tendency is to open my Bible at such times and begin feverishly skimming the Scriptures for a cup of spiritual cream. If the Lord gets my ear, I'm often amazed to hear him say to me, "Put away your Bible and go to sleep. We'll talk about this in the morning." We need to be careful not to look only for spiritual answers to physical problems.

> *You will keep in perfect peace him whose mind is steadfast,*
> *because he trusts in you.*
>
> ISAIAH 26:3

Read *The Pumpkin Patch Parable* by Liz Curtis Higgs to your children or grandchildren. (Thomas Nelson,1995).

October 31

A Word Fitly Spoken

RUTH E. MCDANIEL

Let thy speech be better than silence, or be silent.
—DIONYSIUS THE ELDER

If you knew that whatever you said would come to pass, wouldn't you have the self-control to think twice before speaking?

Well, it's true. And, yet people treat the power of the spoken word with little thought to any consequence. We're all guilty of speaking thoughtlessly. How often have you said, "My memory is terrible," and found your memory becoming progressively worse? Or, when someone asks, "How are you?" and you reply, "Oh, I feel awful," are you surprised that your illness worsens? You shouldn't be. You've put the power of the spoken word into action.

From the beginning, mankind has been informed and warned about the blessings and the dangers of words. The Bible gives wonderful guidelines for speaking at the right time, in making our words attractive, and for avoiding idle words. Words have the ability to change lives—for better or worse. What you say can alter someone's thoughts and actions.

Do you control your mouth and pray that your words will build and not destroy? You can faithfully plant word-seeds of hope and faith and love, then watch your garden of influence grow. And, at the abundant harvest time, you will hear the Lord say, "Well done, thou good and faithful servant" because of your self-control.

May the words of my mouth and the meditation of my heart be pleasing in your sight, O Lord, my Rock and my Redeemer.

PSALM 19:14

Think of someone who has blessed you with uplifting words, then call and thank them. Then bless someone else in a similar manner.

November

"... always giving thanks for all things in the name of our Lord Jesus Christ to God, even the Father."

Ephesians 5:20

November always brings Thanksgiving and with it, a fresh challenge to be grateful for our many blessings. Although not a stated "member" of the Galatians' lineup of fruit of the Spirit, we must agree that having a thankful heart is at the core of living an abundant, simple life. Without it, we'd never notice how rich our lives are.

Gratitude In Having Less

BILL AND PAM FARREL

If you own something that you cannot give away, then
you don't own it, it owns you.
—ALBERT SCHWEITZER

*I*s your car a disaster area? Can you never keep up on housework? Is
the grass a foot high? When things break, do you have no time to
fix them and no money to hire the job out? Can you only halfway shut
your closet doors and no longer actually park your car in the garage?

If all your answers are yes, you don't own your things; your things own
you. Everything you possess can possess you. Material possessions are
necessary, but they are also demanding. How much stuff do you really need?

For example, how big a house do you need (not want)? How much
do you need to spend at Christmas (not: how much do you feel obligated
to spend)? How many clothes are there in a necessary wardrobe (not a
desired wardrobe)?

Try these exercises:

1. You are a pioneer in the Old West. You can take only what will fit
in two covered wagons. What will be left behind?

2. You are moving to the mission field. Each barrel you ship costs an
amazing amount to send. The dishes and kitchen equipment fill one
barrel. Pack everything else for the house in one barrel, and then allow
one barrel per family member. (The barrels are the size of a large trash
barrel, not a dumpster or truck.) What would stay and what would go?

3. Consider the phrase *Everything you own costs*. Think about cutting
your possessions in half. Would that be workable? Could you still keep
your family running with half the possessions?

*I know what it is to be in need, and I know what it is to have plenty. I have
learned the secret of being content in any and every situation . . .*
PHILIPPIANS 4:12

If there's a possession that makes you feel tense at the
thought of losing it, then "it owns you." Surrender it to
the Lord by envisioning giving it to Him.

Manna Burgers Again?

NANCY E. PETERSON

No unhappiness is equal to that of anticipation
unhappiness.
—EL MAYOR MONSTRUO LOS ZELOS BY CALDERON

"Nothing ever goes right. Everything's falling apart," I complained again. We didn't have enough money for our bills, my schedule was jammed full with clashing events, and my son lost another text book. "God, why don't you make it better? I've prayed and prayed."

That night He woke me at one o'clock and didn't let me go back to sleep for three hours. He had a point to get through my thick skull—that I was like the Israelites. As they wandered in the wilderness, they complained of hunger. In His loving way, he sent them manna. They didn't have to till the ground and grow it, just pick it up and put it in their baskets. Like salvation itself, it was a free gift. What did they do? Instead of being thankful, they continued to complain.

During those three hours listening to God, I would think of one blessing and thank Him. Then another would pop into my mind. In twenty years of marriage God has rescued our family from many messes, sent us enough money through various sources so that ours is one of the few houses in the neighborhood that is paid for, and healed us of many types of illnesses (physical, emotional, and spiritua) I know this is only part of the list).

Even so, like the Israelites in the wilderness who said, "What, manna again? Can't we have steak?" I continued to complain.

I confessed my sins, the primary one of ungratefulness, then slept peacefully for the next half hour until the alarm went off.

The next day, reminders of His many blessings surfaced over and over again. Even when we thought He was being cruel or had His back turned, He eventually turned it into a blessing. I recalled when our truck was stolen, the settlement from the insurance company helped us out of a financial jam. God knew we didn't really need that truck.

I made a fresh commitment to prevent "Israelite complaining" from stifling a mature walk with God.

If you find that kind of thinking stealing your gratitude, reflect on the many blessings God has given you. And be thankful. It's so much better than being miserable complaining.

Enter His gates with thanksgiving and His courts with praise;
giving thanks to Him and praise His name.

PSALM 100:4

When you find complaining overtaking your thoughts, make a list of all your blessings. You'll thank God He's working in your life.

November 3

Today I Will Make A Difference

MAX LUCADO

Not failure, but low aim, is a crime.

—ERNEST HOLMES

Today I will make a difference. I will begin by controlling my thoughts. A person is the product of his thoughts. I want to be happy and hopeful. Therefore, I will have thoughts that are happy and hopeful. I refuse to be victimized by my circumstances. I will not let petty inconveniences such as stoplights, long lines, and traffic jams be my master. I will avoid negativism and gossip. Optimism will be my companion, and victory will be my hallmark. Today I will make a difference.

I will be grateful for the twenty-four hours that are before me. Time is a precious commodity. I refuse to allow what little time I have to be contaminated by self-pity, anxiety, or boredom. I will face this day with the joy of a child and the courage of a giant. I will drink each minute as though it is my last. When tomorrow comes, today will be gone forever. While it is here, I will use it for loving and giving. Today I will make a difference.

I will not let past failures haunt me. Even though my life is scarred with mistakes, I refuse to rummage through my trash heap of failures. I will admit them. I will correct them. I will press on, victoriously. No failure is fatal. It's OK to stumble . . . I will get up. It's OK to fail . . . I will rise again. Today I will make a difference.

I will spend time with those I love. My spouse, my children, my family. A man can own the world but be poor for the lack of love. A man can own nothing and yet be wealthy in relationships. Today I will spend at least five minutes with the significant people in my world. Five *quality* minutes of talking or hugging or thanking or listening. Five undiluted minutes with my mate, children, and friends.

Today I will make a difference.

> . . . *Forgetting what is behind and straining toward what is ahead,*
> *I press on toward the goal to win the prize for which*
> *God has called me heavenward in Christ Jesus.*
>
> PHILIPIANS 3:13-14

Spend five minutes listening and giving total eye contact to each member of your immediate family or those living in your home.

November 4

Getting The GRR Out

GLENNA CLARK

Gratitude is attitude with the 'grr' taken out.
—ANONYMOUS

*D*riving home alone from a friend's party, I wavered between feeling envious and then feeling guilty. Edith's home, like many of our friends' homes, seemed more like a palace to me. Our home seemed to lack much in my lopsided comparison.

God had graciously provided our home and I usually appreciated it. But sometimes I gazed with envy at the grass on the other side of the fence.

"Lord," I complained, "She doesn't appreciate her fabulous kitchen. And everything matches. Everything. And that built-in planter is the ultimate."

By the time I arrived home I felt drained. If my husband had been awake, I might have vented on him. Instead, as I padded around our quiet little home, I began to sense the Lord's tender hand of conviction. I confessed my bitterness and jealousy.

"Lord, You know this isn't the first time I've felt dissatisfied after being with our more affluent friends. Please forgive me and show me how to overcome this sin. Please teach me how to remain strong and victorious."

Before falling to sleep, I meditated on all the verses I could recall that dealt with "things" and jealousy. Then Matthew 6:21 gently crept into my mind, "Where your treasure is, there will your heart be also." The Lord tenderly impressed me with the long-forgotten principle that I should be grateful for what He chooses to withhold as well as for what He chooses to grant. Peaceful sleep enveloped me as I sensed His forgiveness and love.

The next morning I woke with a song of praise in my heart for God Himself, not just for what He gives. Before the day was half gone, I realized that when I'm choosing to be thankful, I'm not complaining. Gratitude is a matter of attitude and it's the way of escape from the bondage of discontent.

Finding a notebook, I jotted down my heart's prayer. "Lord, I want to write a 'Thank You' note to You every day, expressing my gratitude for something money can't buy. May the prevailing attitude of my life be one of gratefully, joyfully majoring on Your grace."

Now, some years later, I can still enjoy others' luxuries and return home contented. And God has enabled me to write a daily "Thank You" to Him . . . thus making every day "Thanksgiving Day" in my heart.

How about you? Would you like to increase your abundance by focusing on gratitude for something money can't buy? If you do, it'll change your life.

. . . give thanks in all circumstances; for this is God's will for you in Christ Jesus.
I THESSALONIANS 5:18

> If you struggle with a lack of gratitude, write a "thank you note" to Jesus every day through the end of November.

November 5

Meaningful Touch In Our Relationships

GARY SMALLEY

It is better to be alone than in bad company.
—GEORGE WASHINGTON

Every day, researchers are discovering more and more information about the importance of touch. If we are serious about being a source of blessing to others, we must consider and put into practice these important points.

Some nursing homes and animal shelters can be havens of despair, not places of hope. Residents in both can be isolated and alone.

Residents in either can spend hours dreaming and longing for a family or friends; and in many cases, the loneliness in an older person's heart can be just as confining as the bars that forsaken animals live behind.

Thankfully, some nursing homes and animal shelters seek to meet their residents' needs. Almost by accident, residents of a nursing home and a local animal shelter were brought together. At first, it was just thought of as a recreational activity for the nursing home patients. Soon, however, more significant results began to surface. Those residents who had a pet to touch and hold not only lived longer than those without, but they also had a significantly more positive attitude about life.

What had changed? The pets still had to go back to the animal shelter, waiting for adoption, and family visits were still nonexistent for many of the elderly. But the few hours when they had someone—even a pet—to touch, to talk to, to love, added new life and energy to those dear, aging folk. We don't usually think of a mutt as being a source of blessing, but for these elderly people they were angels in disguise.

What brought about these physical changes? Studies show that touching can actually lower a person's blood pressure. Low blood pressure is an important part of staying healthy. But that's not all. In a recent study at UCLA, it was found that just to maintain emotional and physical health, men and women need eight to ten meaningful touches each day.

At a marriage seminar I was conducting, I told the couples that an important part of the blessing was given through meaningful touch. When I cited this UCLA study, I noticed a man in the second row reach over and begin patting his wife on the shoulder and counting, "One, two, three . . ." That is not meaningful touching. These researchers defined meaningful touching as a gentle touch, stroke, kiss, or hug given by significant people in our lives (a husband or wife, parent, close friend, and so on).

This study estimated that if some "type A driven" men would hug their wives several times each day, it would increase their life span by almost two years. (Not to mention the way it would improve their marriages.) Obviously, we can physically bless those around us (and even ourselves) with meaningful touch.

Love must be sincere . . .

ROMANS 12:9

> For one full day keep track of how much you touch each person in your home. If it's not eight to ten times, make a new commitment to bless them through additional loving touches.

Un-Thanksgiving

DAVID SANFORD

Giving thanks is one course from which we never
graduate.

—VALERIE ANDERS

May I make a radical proposal this Thanksgiving season? This month, instead of counting your blessings, I recommend that you:

1. Make a list of everything you're *not* thankful for. Include anything you're tired of, frustrated about, or worried over.

2. Review every area of your life and family, school, work, church, neighborhood, friends, finances, schedule, hobbies, activities, and interests. Make sure you don't forget anything you're *not* thankful for.

3. Include as many specifics as possible. Don't simply list "current job." Specify exactly what's bothering you about every area of your life.

4. Review your list with your spouse or a close friend. Again, try to think of *everything* you're not thankful for.

5. Once your list is complete, congratulations. That was quite a bit of work, wasn't it? But don't stop yet.

6. In the tradition of the Psalms and other great prayers of the Bible, take your list to God. Pour out your complaints to Him. Don't forget, however, that prayer isn't meant to be a monologue.

7. In response, listen to what God says to you: "Yes, I *know* what you're going through (Hebrews 4:15). But, listen, rejoice. In your trials? Yes. (Romans 5:3, James 1:2). When it's your turn to help in the church nursery again? Yes. (Matthew 10:40-42, Luke 9:48). Even if (worst case scenario) everyone turns against you? Yes. (Matthew 5:10-12, 1 Peter 4:12-14)."

8. Listen to what else God says to you: "My son, My daughter, My child, I know how you feel. But, listen, rejoice always, pray without ceasing, and give thanks in everything, for *this* is My will for you (1 Thessalonians 5:16-18)."

9. "Yes, rejoice always. Again, I say, rejoice. Let your mind dwell on whatever is true, honorable, right, pure, lovely, good, excellent, and praiseworthy (Philippians 4:4,8)—not on what you're *not* thankful for."

10. "Yes, make a list of what you're not thankful for. But don't let that list become your focus. Instead, look to Me. Dwell in My Word.

Spend time in My presence. Remember, My joy is your strength (Nehemiah 8:10)—today and always."

Devote yourselves to prayer, being watchful and thankful.
COLOSSIANS 4:2

It's hard to be grateful when you're exhausted. Promise yourself a full night's sleep tonight and keep to it.

November 7

God's Presence In Temptation

JAN JOHNSON

If you would master temptation, you must first let
Christ master you.

—ANONYMOUS

*P*erhaps the moments when God's presence is most unwanted or scary is during temptation. Who wants to talk to God, much less enjoy His presence, when they're about to eat two submarine sandwiches or trash someone's reputation? But practicing God's presence during temptation is part of what it means to "stand firm" (Ephesians 6:14).

To rest in God's companionship in the midst of temptation provides a lifeline of strength. As an acquaintance and I were complaining about a company we had both worked for, he stopped in mid-sentence and said, "God's yanking my chain. I don't need to talk this way. They did their best and I appreciate it." His mid-sentence repentance modeled for me the importance of listening to God's nudges and responding to them as soon as I'm able.

Sometimes, temptation is so invasive that it seems to crowd out God's presence. While wrestling with a tough temptation once, I felt the need to physically escape into a place I reserve for enjoying God's presence. Armed with my walking shoes and worship tape, I spent hours walking a nearby canyon road, crying out to God. I picked up wads of sagebrush and tossed them over the steep bank of the creek to show my resolve. "I'm sick of being so weak. I want out," I yelled. "This is crowding You out of my life, God. I want You back."

A week later, on the canyon road again, I stamped my foot and said, "When will You take away this problem, God? When will I give it up? Tell me what to do." As you can guess, nothing happened. So I kept walking. As I stared at the canyon walls, I thought of my son who skillfully rappels down the sides of cliffs. *That's not me*, I thought. *I'm scared, I'm weak. I'd never rappel. I'd be clinging to the sides of the cliffs.*

Cling? Didn't the psalmist *cling*? The line of the worship song resonated within me: "You have been my help in time of need. Lord, unto You will I cling." I saw that my error had been in trying to perform stunts for God, trying to be a temptation-proof Christian. I could stand firm against temptation only by clinging to God as I would to the side of a cliff.

Because you are my help, I sing in the shadow of your wings.
My soul clings to you; your right hand upholds me.

PSALM 63:7-8

What temptation are you facing right now? If it surprises you that you're experiencing temptation, make a list of feelings you have about it, and then write across it, "This is normal."

November 8

How To Cultivate Simplicity

JILL L. FERGUSON

Cultivate simplicity . . .

—CHARLES LAMB

One cold and windy winter afternoon in rural Pennsylvania, a man trudged through the glass double doors of the church where I worked. He was thin; his beard and hair were scraggly and unkempt. His face, hands, and ears were a wind-chapped red. His denim jacket had ripped-out elbows and he wore it over a long, beige raincoat that had seen better days. His canvas deck shoes were a dark gray, far from the white they had once been. His clothing was frozen.

"I was directed here from the restaurant," he said, pointing to the little café across the street. "They said you could help me."

The man, who said his name was Fred, explained that he had been hitchhiking from Georgia, trying to make his way to Canada. He had lost his job, had no family, and thought he might be able to find work easier up North. But he hadn't eaten in two days and had tried to sleep on a park bench the night before, but was buried in the foot of snow that had fallen.

His soft-spoken voice said all this without a complaint, just matter-of-factly.

The pastor and I decided that we had to help this man. Reverend Clark called the local hotel and booked a room for Fred for the night while I ran across the street to the café and ordered bowls of soup, coffee, and sandwiches.

Our church ran a clothing bank so we could provide Fred with much-needed warmer clothing. He was outfitted in a winter coat, boots, gloves, knit cap, turtleneck, wool sweater, heavy knit socks, and jeans.

At the time, I felt good about being able to help someone in need. Then Fred surprised me and did something that will stay imbedded in my memory forever.

He folded the dirty clothes he had just taken off and handed them back to the lady who ran the clothing bank.

"I no longer need these," he said. "Someone else may need them more."

Here was a man who owned nothing but the clothes on his back, who had been traveling for two weeks, gone without food and shelter that someone else may be more needy than he. (He was a man truly content in his simplicity.)

I was in tears. I knew I hadn't always been content and frequently wanted more than I had already acquired. I did not need fifteen pairs of jeans and twenty sweaters. I had not cultivated simplicity, as Fred had. By encountering Fred, I learned that the accumulation of possessions is only valuable if you can give them away.

What makes you feel tense if you were called upon to give it away? Your car, house, clothing, or job? It may be your tension shows it possesses you, instead of you possessing it. Reconsider how you'd like to cultivate simplicity by offering everything up to the Lord.

But godliness with contentment is great gain.
I TIMOTHY 6:6

To take a further step toward contentment and a simple life, give away a valued piece of clothing or another possession. You'll experience the freedom of being content.

Feeling Out Of Sorts

JILL BRISCOE

*An optimist may see a light where there is none, but
why must the pessimist always run to blow it out?*
— MICHEL DE SAINT-PIERRE

*I*f I am out of sorts with everyone, I don't need to be around anyone who is in sorts with everyone. This only serves to make me feel even more uncomfortable about my own attitude. And yet, this is the time I really need someone around to help me. If we could only learn not to isolate ourselves in times of deep trouble, we would receive ministry to our wounded spirits that would bless not only us but also those who minister to us. But type A personalities have a hard time receiving; they are used to giving. Those who are in positions of authority and responsibility are used to having others look to them for strength; they have a hard time looking to others for help.

What was it Jesus told us to do? Wasn't it to get into our "closet" alone and meet with the Father?

*But when you pray, go into your room,
close the door and pray to your Father, who is unseen.*
MATTHEW 6:6

Read *A Graceful Waiting* by Jan Frank (Vine Books, 1996).

Materialism

KATHY COLLARD MILLER

*If the grass looks greener on the other side of the
fence . . . it's most likely Astro Turf.*
— ANONYMOUS

*A*bout 100 years ago, a survey asked average Americans to list their wants. They listed seventy. In a similar survey taken recently, Americans listed 500. How naturally I fall victim to the abundance cheater called materialism. And its sidekick is ungratefulness. "Oh, I must have that dress. I need it." The Lord gently taps my mental shoulder and inquires, "Kathy, you need that dress? Will you die without it?" I want to say, "Yes." but I know it's not true. How easily I use the word "need" when it's really a "want." When I can't have my materialistic wants met, I neglect being grateful for everything else I have.

Television commercials bombard us with "New!" and "Improved!" Its subtle message: we can't be living an abundant life without the newest fashions or the most expensive car. Battered by the messages of the media, we conclude that needs and wants are the same, and simple-living sadly hangs its head and backs out the door.

Let's welcome it back by facing the abundance cheater of materialism and shouting, "God promises to meet all my true needs. He is so generous, He often gives me my wants."

God knows best, and His wisdom can determine my true needs and my fickle wants. Even when God gives me my wants, I've noticed how quickly they lose their value. Only focusing my eyes on the Lord and heaven's future glories keeps me filled with thanksgiving with this temporal, unsatisfying world. Storing up treasures in heaven and building my character are far more worthy goals than maintaining the world's definition of "needs."

How does materialism subtly draw you away from the abundant life? The solution is to rejoice in how God has provided your true needs and seek to know Him better. It may seem like you'll be needy as a result, but actually your need of God will just be a blessing.

And my God will meet all your needs according to his
glorious riches in Christ Jesus.
PHILIPPIANS 4:19

Refuse to purchase anything from a mail-order catalog until you've waited at least one month. You'll usually find you can do without it, or it's no longer available.

Writing Your Spiritual Autobiography

LYNN D. MORRISSEY

The unexamined life is not worth living.

—PLATO

One of the most exciting history books ever written could be the story of your spiritual walk with the Lord. Writing such a document has many advantages. Your faith grows by leaps and bounds as you become aware of God's continuous activity throughout your life, even before salvation. You see His sovereign hand orchestrating circumstances that drew you to Him initially and His care, protection, and guidance ever since.

As you examine your life, you will understand your great significance to God and the purpose for which you were born. Your life will be simplified as you piece together the mosaic of patterns leading to your mission, thereby avoiding rabbit tracks that stray from God's will. You'll gain perspective, realizing how the past effects the present and is leading to the future.

Most importantly, you will leave an irreplaceable legacy to share with your progeny. Your spiritual autobiography has the tremendous potential of reaching your descendants, yet to be born, giving them cause to praise God for the Good News of salvation through Jesus Christ. You may reach others for Christ even following your death.

In order to write your spiritual autobiography, search for God's activity in your life and how you have changed as a result. You can cover the following topics: your family background and spiritual or church upbringing; your search and/or struggle to find God; your conversion experience; your confirmation experience; your ongoing encounters with God; your response to Him in obedience or disobedience; seeing God in nature, seeing the "sacred in the secular"—e.g., God speaking to you through poetry, books, music, art, conversations, etc.; God's specific answers to prayer; God's "still small voice" specifically guiding you; and your crises of faith and how you responded to God.

You may write from several different vantage points based on age-oriented periods (childhood, adolescence, and adulthood), relationships (who shaped your spiritual growth throughout life), or milestone events (education and graduation, military service, marriage and family, career changes, church, organization, or sorority involvement, lifetime achievements, tragedies, illnesses, and deaths).

Ask the Holy Spirit to guide your thoughts as you glean memories from friends, family, teachers, colleagues, journals, photographs, letters, greeting cards, scrapbooks, invitations, printed programs, and yearbooks.

Your autobiography will be a source of thanksgiving for yourself and for your relatives in the future.

> *Let this be written for a future generation,*
> *that a people not yet created may praise the Lord.*
> PSALM 102:18

If you feel intimated about writing your story from scratch, buy a "fill in the blanks" autobiography at your stationery store.

November 12

Successful Communication

KATHRYN HARTZELL

Change that which can be altered, explain that which
can be understood, teach that which can be learned, revise that which can be improved, resolve that which
can be settled, and negotiate that which is open to
compromise.

—JAMES DOBSON

We want gratitude to permeate our relationships, yet often, we can't talk to our loved ones about things that concern us. It may be because of fear of rejection or because past attempts always led to an argument. Since God has equipped us with the ability to communicate, let's review some effective communication skills.

Try writing things down. Whether using verbal or written skills, there are three elements of communication for problem solving: identifying the problem, offering solutions or alternatives, and affirming the positives.

Discussing problems should be done at a time when all parties are calm. It may need to be delayed until the next day. Everyone should come prepared with the issues they want discussed and with solutions. The discussion should not be one-sided. In any relationship, both parties have items to be brought to the table.

Allow the person to state his or her position without interruption. Listen with your full attention and avoid trying to pre-plan your response.

While discussing the problem, talk in terms of "When this is done, I feel this way." This approach is more effective than, "I hate it when you do this." The suggested alternatives also need to be presented in a personal manner: "I would rather have you embrace me than give me advice."

Far too many families have no communication skills. In the past, the dinner table was the time and place to catch up on everyone's life and work through problems. Today, hectic schedules prevent the family from gathering for a leisurely time to eat and talk.

When you can meet together, interact with your family by asking open-ended questions. These are questions that cannot be answered with a simple yes or no. They require a more involved answer. This is especially helpful with teenagers who don't know what to share with their parents.

Intertwine your discussions with positive attributes you see in the other person. Aim at providing more affirmations than negative comments.

Having unresolved conflicts can steal our abundance and make life complicated. What will you do this week to put these principles into action? Be sure to express gratitude for the characteristics you appreciate. Being thankful will lay a simple—yet powerful—foundation for good communication.

The tongue that brings healing is a tree of life . . .
PROVERBS 15:4

Send a love note along in your mate's briefcase or lunchbox, or leave it for him or her at home.

A Simple Faith

GLENDA SMITHERS

Lord, send me anywhere, only go with me. Lay any
burden on me, only sustain me. Sever any tie but the
tie that binds me to Thyself.

—DAVID LIVINGSTON

I tucked David Livingston's prayer into my daughter's "care package"
the day she left for college. She recently took her first bus ride home
from college and I'm ashamed that the wisdom of Livingston's simple
faith didn't stay with either of us.

Kamber Jean was anxious about spending all day on a bus, but we
reassured her that nothing could go wrong. However, this turned out
to be a false promise.

My husband, Steven, and I drove from our home in Kingsville,
Missouri, to the town where we were to pick her up. Unfamiliar with
the town, we arrived at the bus station only to discover that it was one
of four different bus stops where she could possibly be let off. It was
dark and we hurriedly drove from one end of town to the other trying
to cover each of the four bus stops.

I was worried sick that we'd miss her and she'd end up alone,
thinking we forgot to pick her up. Suddenly I remembered a verse I
had memorized for Bible study weeks ago: "Some trust in chariots and
some in horses, but we trust in the name of the Lord our God" (Psalm
20:7). I repeated it over and over until the fear left me.

I quit trusting in vehicles. We chose one of the four bus stops in
town and stayed put. In seconds, God delivered our smiling daughter
safe into our arms. I was grateful again for the power of God's Word
to guide and for the trust He instills in us in time of need.

As our year of journeying toward abundance continues, are you
learning more and more gratitude and dependence upon the Word of
God? That's one of the firm foundational stones in our building of
abundance. Keep up the good work.

*And without faith it is impossible to please God; because anyone who comes to Him
must believe that He exists and that He rewards those who earnestly seek Him.*
HEBREWS 11:6

November 14

Giving God Money

PENNY SHOUP

Money buys everything except love, personality, freedom, immortality.

—ANONYMOUS

The Bible gives a clear command on giving a tithe of what we earn. My husband, Bruce, and I have always felt very strongly about giving a tenth of what we earn back to God. We feel that it is not our money to begin with. Everything we have belongs to God and it is our privilege to give a portion back to him.

It hasn't always been easy. There were times when we needed, and used the money to pay bills. What we found was that it seemed to have a snowball effect. The next week something else needed to be paid, and then the next, and the next. It always came to the point where we had to say, "Stop. We will pay God first and then our bills."

Since then, He has always taken care of us. My Grandfather's favorite song was, "His Eye is on the Sparrow and He Watches Over Me." We have found that to be true.

Besides the simple fact of giving, we need to give cheerfully. Shortly after Scott, my second child, was born, I had just finished nursing school. Bruce was still in college. A new baby tends to change the shape of your body and I didn't have a dress to wear for Sunday mornings. I remember looking at the money we had set aside for tithe and thinking it would do nicely for buying myself a dress. I remember God saying, "No," and my feeling guilty that I had even thought of it.

We went for a visit to my parents shortly after that time. While we were there, my dad told me to get ready because he was taking me to town. My dad, who hates to shop, and had never before bought me a dress, took me shopping for a dress. The fact that *Dad* gave it to me meant more than the dress ever could. I was very grateful. That day both of my Fathers had given me a dress and it was an act of love that I would have missed out on if I had bought the dress myself.

Having a grateful spirit for God's simple generosity will enable you to tithe your money. Are you a steward or owner of what God has given you—that which really still belongs to Him? Show Him your gratitude by giving first to Him. He'll abundantly provide.

A tithe of everything from the land, whether grain from the soil or fruit from the trees, belongs to the Lord; it is holy to the Lord.

LEVITICUS 27:30

Don't waste time or money by listening to pleas for money on the phone.

November 15

The Joy Of Service

MILDRED BROWN

All service ranks the same with God.
—ROBERT BROWNING

To me the abundant life was a collection of material things such as houses, big cars, money, and jewelry. I believed that if I lived the Christian life, one day I would have such possessions.

One Sunday, our pastor asked for volunteers to work one day each week in the Feeding Ministry of the church. I volunteered for Thursdays. The Coordinator asked me to work in the dining room. As I served the residents of our community, I realized this was the only complete meal for them that day. They were also in need of clothing and money.

I felt guilty about all the times I had complained about not having what I wanted to eat or wear. I said a silent prayer of thanks with each meal I served. These prayers made me feel humble with a desire to do more for others. Serving meals in the dining room changed my life. I learned that the abundant life is not a collection of material things. It is a Spirit-filled life which comes from serving God by serving others.

How could you give back through a service of your time or talents to those less fortunate? You may find it builds your thankfulness and your desire for the simple Christian life.

I tell you the truth, whatever you did for one of the least of these brothers of mine, you did for me.

MATTHEW 25:40

November 16

To Touch A Leaf

EUNICE ANN BADGLEY

If you don't get everything you want, think of the things you don't get that you *don't* want.

—ANONYMOUS

When I enjoy the little things of nature, I often remember a remark made by a teenage boy. He was in the detention center for youth where I worked as a fill-in houseparent. John had been in and out of the center for several years, partly because he had no real home or anyone who cared enough to take responsibility for him.

I'm sure he has long since forgotten his comment to another teenager who was leaving for home: "You can reach up and touch a leaf anytime you want." It seems such a little thing, but it would have meant so much to John.

I hope that John now has a better life and is able to touch a leaf. When I think of him, I take time to reach out for a leaf or walk barefoot on the grass or listen to a bird's song, just because I can.

You and I can easily take our freedom, blessings, and talents for granted. It only takes exposure to one who isn't as fortunate to remind us of our blessings. Thank God today that you can touch a leaf and go anywhere you want, that you have people who love and want you to be there with them. These are the true blessings of life.

So if the Son sets you free, you will be free indeed.
JOHN 8:36

What common simplicity are you taking for granted? Stop and smell the roses.

Life In A Load Of Laundry

RENEÉ S. SANFORD

If a man has limburger cheese on his upper lip, he
thinks the whole world smells.

—ANONYMOUS

Surely two certain things reign supreme in housekeeping: dishes
and laundry. Dishes defeat me, but laundry, I can see life there.

As I face my Monday morning cleaning, or anytime the house is
in total disarray, I always start with the laundry. "Pick a corner," a
friend recommends for handling stress. Laundry is my favorite corner
in which to begin.

Something about taking overflowing baskets of jumbled, limp
clothing and grouping them into logical piles does my heart good. It
represents a transformation from disorder to order.

Piles of laundry, each piece in its place, give me a taste of what I'd
relish for the rest of my life—order and accomplishment. Of course,
those small human beings who generate the content of those piles also
help generate the hecticness that keeps my life spinning happily. So I
enjoy my islands of order when I can and let them spur me on to
accomplish other tasks.

On warm summer days I like to take the time to hang my clothes
on the line. Some people do it for the fresh scent in their clothes, but
I simply savor the chore of hanging them out, one by one.

As those shirts and skirts, pants and panties dance in the breeze,
they make a colorful company. I enjoy the collection of colors as much
as any bouquet of flowers. A rack of embroidery floss or tubes of paint
are enough to make my senses spin with delight. How much more these
colors on my line. These are the colors of my life: purples and pinks
from two little girls; turquoise that graces a green eyed beauty, and
jade to accent the dark eyes of my strawberry blonde.

How many times have I handled this garment, first for Elizabeth,
then for Shawna? I can mark the passing years by the clothes in my
basket. Little sleepers and Humpty Dumpty socks in rickety piles have
given their place to solid stacks of pants and shirts with sock balls in
coordinating colors tossed in for spice. Fingering these pieces of cloth

that hug my children's bodies, I try to grab the tails of days and years and memories. Slow down for just a moment more.

But the hourglass fills up as quickly as the hamper. Someday my girls will graduate from just folding towels and sorting socks to doing all the clothes for quarters. I will be glad to have help, but I will keep my hands in the basket. I see my life in a load of laundry, and I don't want to miss it rushing by.

Yes, simple things, even the laundry, can help us focus on the abundance of life. It's all a matter of perspective—the mental glasses we look through. Do yours have smudges on them? Clean them off and look through a lens of gratitude.

. . . making the most of every opportunity . . .
EPHESIANS 5:16

> When was the last time you hung clothes on a line? Try it again soon.

November 18

Would God Label People?

ARLENE KAISER, ED.D.

Our lives will be complete only when we express the full intent of the Master.

—CHARLES R. HEMBREE

I was eagerly shopping for a unique dress ensemble for a speaking engagement. As I wear only brightly-colored, unusual clothes, I knew the task might be difficult. As my eyes scanned the boutique filled with dramatically-designed clothes, I noticed a label dangling from the sleeve of most of the garments. The label read, "This garment is designed of the finest fabric. All nubs, irregular designs are part of the unique fabric and are not a defect of workmanship or material. For best results wash in cold water or dry clean."

I surveyed the dress shop crowded with customers and sales-people. There were different sizes, shapes, coloring, and ages. I was reminded of the biblical principle that God creates each one of us unique, a designer creation.

I giggled to myself. Imagine God writing a label for every person to wear. It might read, "Dear Reader: This individual was created with selected characteristics of the finest quality. All marks, slight irregularities, wrinkles, variation of size or color, unexpected behavior or response, in no way should be taken as defects, rather as the *unique* qualities of this individual. For best results, please learn the care and self-esteem building for this *unique* individual."

As people continue to parade through my life, I imagine each person wearing that label. Just remembering this gives me the insight to be more respectful, kind, and thoughtful of my fellow human-beings. And I am impressed to be grateful for the variety that it brings into my life. What abundance.

As people come into your life, dare to label them with the characteristics as reflected in Psalm 139. And, remember, you are wearing a label too. Be grateful.

I praise you because I am fearfully and wonderfully made;
your works are wonderful, I know that full well.
PSALM 139:14

Read *Mothers Have Angel Wings*, edited and compiled by Carol Kent (NavPress, 1997).

November 19

Stop Wanting More

LINDA CARLBLOM

It is beautiful, my house. It is bare, of course, but the wind,
the sun, the smell of the pines blow through its bareness.
I am content . . . To ask how little, not how much, can I get
along with. To say—is it necessary?—when I am tempted to
add one more accumulation to my life . . . ?
—ANNE MORROW LINDBERGH

I felt it again. That sharp stabbing in my heart that made me look at a friend's beautiful, new home with envy. It was breathtaking. Floral curtains hung with an interior decorator's flair, a huge island accented the spacious kitchen, no fingerprints smudged light switches. My feet padded silently on the new carpet as I took the "nickel tour."

"It's beautiful," I told my friend. "I'm so happy for you. You deserve all this and more." I truly meant what I said. These were good people who genuinely loved and served God with their whole hearts. But I too love God, and serve Him with my whole being. Why couldn't I be "blessed" with a home like this? I felt guilty for my jealous thoughts.

That incident caused me to examine my heart and the root of my jealousy. It's not that I didn't love my home or that I lived in poverty. Far from it. I had a lovely three-bedroom home which adequately housed my husband, two children and me in sunny Arizona. We lived on a quiet cul-de-sac where our children could safely play. We had a large back yard with grapefruit, orange, and pecan trees. We were happy there. What more could I possibly want?

I wrestled with this bothersome question one morning during my quiet time with God. *Why God, do I have this disquiet within me?* On this particular morning He chose to answer me, His whiny, ungrateful child. "My grace is sufficient for thee," He reminded. "Stop wanting more and look at me." I raised my guilty eyes upward realizing that I had taken my focus off my Lord, the ultimate Provider, and turned them toward others' possessions. God wanted more for me. He wanted to give me *Himself.* Indeed, what more could I possibly want?

"Forgive me, Father, for overlooking You and all Your blessings," I prayed. "Help me to be content, even joyful, for all that I have. Even more importantly, for all that You are. Help me to simply bask in the glory of Your presence in my life."

I looked around me and saw how God had blessed me. Even my house looked radiant as the sunlight poured in through generous family room windows. I had learned to simplify my life by being grateful with what I have. And to ask as Anne Morrow Lindbergh, " . . . how little, not how much, can I get along with?" God's blessings are abundant. He is sufficient for me.

If you struggle with ungratefulness, you aren't alone. And it seems that no matter how much each of us has, it's not enough. Realizing that fact can help us choose to be grateful. For even those who have the most must do the same thing. Will you?

Keep your lives free from the love of money and be content with what you have,
because God has said, "Never will I leave you; never will I forsake you."
HEBREWS 13:5

As Thanksgiving approaches, plan a simple event that will allow you to relax and enjoy your time.

Robbed Again!

MARY LOU KLINGLER

Events are less important than our responses to them.
—JOHN HERSEY

A neighbor called to inform us that our storage shed had been broken into. I groaned, "Not again." A few years before it had also been ransacked and a few irreplaceable items had been stolen.

My husband and I hurried to the area where all the sheds for our complex were located. In horror we saw that not just ours but seven were burglarized. Items were thrown all over the open lot.

Our aluminum shed, with the lock still in place, had been pried open and bent back to gain entrance and boxes shoved outside. Boxes of personal letters from many, many years ago were opened. Lying on the ground, some trampled and wet from a recent shower, lay hundreds of my letters. "How could anyone do this?" I asked my husband. I struggled to keep from crying.

I took an empty box and picked up the strewn letters and our four daughter's elementary grade cards. Some were ink-smeared from the rain and I spread them out to dry. The next two days I read letters, most of them thirty to forty years old. They brought back memories of when my daughters were born; letters from them when they were away at college and their struggles when they fell in and out of love; letters after their marriages telling of their baby's first steps, first words and teeth.

Many of the letters were from dear friends and relatives who are now with the Lord and doubly precious to me, especially from our daughter, Sally, who died of cancer at age thirty. There were letters from a pen pal in Australia with whom I've written to since we were both ten-years-old.

Many of the letters I threw away because I knew no one else in my family would ever care to read them, but I enjoyed reading them one more time. Afterwards, I again thought of the person who'd invaded our shed to do havoc and find whatever they could that might be salable. I unexpectedly found myself praying for that person. I hadn't planned on praying for him as I still was full of hate, but I felt the hate in my heart melting. That person needed Jesus *so* much.

The two days I read old letters and reminisced, I realized how much the Lord has blessed me over the last forty years. I could almost thank them for forcing me to go back in time and see what the Lord has done. Isn't it amazing how God can use something evil for good?

What could you give thanks for that previously has been a source of pain or hurt? Your simple choice will bring abundance into your life.

Do not store up for yourselves treasures on earth,
where moth and rust destroy, and where thieves break in and steal.
MATTHEW 6:19

Forgive someone in your past that you never thought you could and communicate it verbally or by letter.

November 21

The Seeing Blind

JOAN CLAYTON

To see from the heart is the greatest sight of all.
—JOAN CLAYTON

The tree was gorgeous. Brilliant hues of deep scarlet with tiny hints of burnished gold graced the ornamental pear tree in our front yard. It was in the final stages of its dazzling beauty before the touch of frost. Our tree is lovely in all seasons, but frost has a way of tiptoeing through its treetop, painting blushing strokes of ruby red and flaming yellows.

I had never really stopped to notice the simple beauty of the tree until my beloved Aunt Mary came to visit one fall. Aunt Mary, 89, and legally blind, was always upbeat, cheerful and lovable. After church, we took her out to eat and to visit relatives.

On returning home, Aunt Mary got out of the car, took a deep breath of fresh air and exclaimed exuberantly, "It's been such a wonderful day. I loved the church service. The food was delicious. I enjoyed the visit with loved ones, and now look at that tree. Isn't it gorgeous?"

I gasped and said, "Aunt Mary, can you really see that tree?"

"No," she answered, "but somehow I know it's there. Maybe it's because I can hear the leaves rustling. Maybe I can smell it. I don't know. Maybe I can feel its beauty inside of me. But it's just such a beautiful day. The sunshine feels so good. It's just a beautiful world, so I know there's a beautiful tree over there!"

Aunt Mary, with her blind eyes, was seeing more from her heart than I had ever seen with my eyes.

I learned a lot that day from her. Now I take simple pleasures in studying the incredible design of a rose. I look for a rainbow after an afternoon shower. I sit in the swing with my cat and listen to him purr.

Aunt Mary has made me acutely aware that nothing should ever be taken for granted. She has taught me that simple things are one of life's greatest blessings. I have eyes to see, but I also want to see with my heart too.

How is your heart vision these days? Is it abundantly-colored with gratitude?

He is like a tree planted by streams of water,
which yields its fruit in season and whose leaf does not wither.
Whatever he does prospers.

PSALM 1:3

Take a nature walk and view God's beauty with new eyes.

November 22

House: Reflection Of Me?

LUCI SHAW

Be careful for nothing, prayerful for everything, thankful for anything.

—DWIGHT L. MOODY

Our homes often fulfill deep emotional and psychological needs for us. A few years ago, my son-in-law built a home for me in Bellingham, Washington. It's a place of safety, seclusion, and possibility for me, with its wood stove and skylights, surrounded by the green forest and the hush of the stream that flows below the outside deck—an anchor in times of stress. As I worked with him on designing this house, I realized that a home, especially for a woman, is an extension of herself. And as a result, on an emotional level, I wanted my home to represent my best qualities and my truest values. In a sense, creating a home is like creating a work of art.

With my home in Bellingham I tried to make it as functional as possible, but I also wanted it to be beautiful—something that would represent me so when friends came to my home they would see evidence of my taste, creativity, or organizational ability. My desire for my home to look "just right" wasn't based on my wanting it to look better than someone else's home; instead, subconsciously I realized that my home was *a reflection of* me.

A word of caution about our homes, though. While it is perfectly normal and legitimate to want to create a home that reflects our individual taste and personality, we need to take care that our self-image doesn't become too wrapped up in a physical structure and our home doesn't become our idol.

Down the street from where John and I live is an immense, three-story, seven-bedroom home. A couple lives in this huge house and, while they have no children nor do they seem to entertain, they continue to pour money into the house. Granted, I don't know what their lives consist of, but from outward appearances it seems that they don't know what else to do with their lives or their money other than improve their home. Expensive and luxurious as it is, their house seems empty and cold—a fortress that excludes rather than a home that welcomes.

A second caution about our homes is that we don't want to let them take priority over the relationships in our lives. I've known of women who spend so much time trying to create the picture-perfect home that their families end up feeling neglected. My own mother, an immaculate housekeeper, was so worried about fingerprints on the woodwork and dirt tracked into the house, that she never could relax and enjoy her grandchildren when we came to visit her, and they never felt at home with her.

But whatever was to my profit I now consider loss for the sake of Christ.
PHILIPPIANS 3:7

> At your Thanksgiving celebration, decide to not get upset about how the house looks. Your calm reactions are more important.

Baywatch

KATHY KEIDEL

> A certain simplicity of living is usually necessary to
> happiness.
>
> —HENRY D. CHAPIN

Our home for seven years had provided good shelter and certainly a spacious backyard for two active children, along with a menagerie of pets. It wasn't the dream home, but it was functional and was always "home sweet home." As the economy of our community boomed, I realized how very fortunate we were to have this home as the market around us was becoming unaffordable for many newcomers.

I began focusing on what changes I could make that would be simple, yet help to make our home more comfortable. I found myself surveying homes in other communities, perusing home-improvement magazines, note-taking and pencil-sketching ideas. I realized what I wanted more than anything was "to bring the outside in." Our home was dark and dreary with window shades in an attempt to block out the drafts created by the frequent howling wind.

Meanwhile, something else was happening. As I focused on our home, I became more focused on a spiritual essence in art work. Around my little corner of the bedroom I found myself putting up clippings of cozy rooms, next to clippings of artwork or figurines of angels or pictures that created a peaceful, celestial feeling. Ideas for my home were being interwoven with a spiritual reality.

Within a year, we had added an entryway and porch, thirteen new windows, and a beautiful bay window covered with lacy drapes. Everything was painted a country white. A white oval oak table with six, white, heart-shaped chairs invite family and friends to share stories, laughter, and friendship as we come together. The bay window lets in beautiful glowing light for each meal. Indeed, the outside comes in; we can see the trees through the curtains, we can hear the birds sing, we can feel the sunlight, see the moonlight glow and even the stars. Inside, simple artwork with a spiritual mood compliments the decor.

As we join hands at mealtime for prayer, my son reminds us to form an arch with our joined hands to create a heart. Our bay window and other simple changes have made our home a place I want to be.

With family or alone, it's a place for quiet reflection . . . to reflect on the simple joys in life—like bay windows and heartfelt prayer.

If you're dissatisfied with your home, but can't afford another, why not look for inexpensive ways to bring it closer to what you want? Choosing gratitude and the abundant life can include taking action to make it easier to make that decision.

> And we know that in all things God works for the good of those who love him, who have been called according to his purpose.
>
> ROMANS 8:28

Make one change in your home each month that is inexpensive and yet brings it closer to the way you want it to look.

November 24

Beauty

MATHEW J. BOWYER

Beauty is truth; truth beauty—that is all
Ye know on earth, and all ye need to know.
                                    —JOHN KEATS

Everybody knows what beauty is. They may not know how to define it—express just what it is, in words—but they know it when they see it. It could be said that beauty is the most valuable thing in the world. Many people have spent all the money they had on things they hoped would make them beautiful. They all finally found out that real beauty is not something that can be purchased with money.

Beauty was aptly defined by John Keats, a British poet who lived hundreds of years ago. His career as a poet lasted only seven years, but during that time the words he wrote about beauty will stand out for eternity. He was a very young man when he wrote those immortal words. Sometimes an older person wonders how a person so young could come up with such profound truths, the words of which make the whole world stand up and listen. Then we realize this person must've had a gift from God.

It was intended by his family that John Keats would be a surgeon. When very young he was apprenticed to a surgeon. He diligently studied the profession for seven years, but his heart was in poetry. He made his mark on the world with his observations.

Keats loved beauty. So much so that at age twenty-five, he gave up surgery and became a poor poet. He died when he was barely twenty-six. He saw his death coming, and for his epitaph he wrote, "Here lies one whose name was writ in water." It was his way of saying that he felt his name would not be remembered, that his life was like water that flows, then is gone. Not so. History would show he had captured infinity with just the first short sentence of one of his poems, by writing: "A thing of beauty is a joy forever."

The simple, abundant life of gratefulness is aware of God's beauty in the world. Have you stopped recently to appreciate the beauty of a flower, a face, a picture, or more ethereal things like truth, honesty, or kindness. Slow down and take notice. You'll be abundantly grateful you did.

One thing I ask of the Lord, this is what I seek: that I may dwell in the house of the Lord all the days of my life, to gaze upon the beauty of the Lord and to seek him in his temple.

PSALM 27:4

Take breaks from your work so that you can focus on the simple things of life.

November 25

I Want More

COLLEEN FRAIOLI

Content makes poor men rich; discontent makes rich men poor.

—BENJAMIN FRANKLIN

I convinced my husband that I'd be a new person if he would consent to a day of shopping with a friend. Dashing out of the house at the crack of dawn, I nearly leveled the dog and a few pieces of furniture on my way.

The day started out at my friend's new home. It was her dream house filled with picture-perfect furnishings and decor. It was the home I'd always wanted. Now it belonged to my friend. Feeling a twinge of envy, I thought of my microscopic family room fully engulfed by a fifteen-year-old brown couch. But no time to dwell on that. We were on a mission of shopping bliss and nothing was going to spoil my day.

Outside we were met by her fully-loaded new car, strategically parked next to my ancient gutless wonder. "I'll drive." she yelled.

A feeling of relief swept over me when we reached the mall. Neutral ground. Setting aside thoughts of my aged possessions, I decided to focus on the twenty dollars burning a hole in my pocket.

While my friend consulted with her personal shopper, I rummaged around the clearance racks. Hanging onto my last thread of hope, I tried to visualize the items in my closet that might match orange sweaters and lime green stretch pants. By the time we broke for lunch—she ordered the filet, I had a cup of soup—I was ready to go home and sink into deep depression.

My adoring family greeted me, bubbling with anticipation. They expected to see a fully-revived wife and mother ready to throw herself into their every need. What they received, however, bore more resemblance to a shell-shocked war veteran, armed and ready to blast anyone who dared to even breathe a word about needing anything.

Recognizing my need to be alone, my family scrambled for cover.

After storming up the stairs, I proceeded to disassemble my closet. "Everything I own is out of style." I ranted as I flung blouses and dresses around the bedroom. "I hate my clothes."

After thirty minutes of trashing my wardrobe, it occurred to me that I had a slight attitude problem. Eyeing various articles of clothing dangling off of lamps and doorknobs, I felt completely ridiculous. *God, what is my problem? How could I be so materialistic? Forgive me.*

In the minutes that followed, God reminded me that comparing myself or my circumstances with others is harmful and my brown couch, albeit ugly, is actually very comfortable.

The following week another friend asked me to go out shopping for the day. I invited her over for lunch instead.

If you're invited to attend something that will bring discontentment and a lack of gratitude, think of lunch at home instead. Why tempt yourself? Choose abundance.

For we brought nothing into this world, and we can take nothing out of it.
But if we have food and clothing, we will be content with that.
1 TIMOTHY 6:7-8

My godchild is just about my size. She loves raiding my closet for a "new" outfit. Do you know someone you could share with?

Praise The Lord

MARGARET PRIMROSE

Rejoice the Lord is King; Your Lord and God adore.
—CHARLES WESLEY

It sounds simple enough to praise God, but probably most of us spend less time thanking and adoring Him than petitioning Him. Maybe we have tried unsuccessfully to reverse that. Yet there are many easy ways to help us improve.

Start slowly and patiently. We would not begin an exercise program with a twenty-mile marathon. We would start with short periods of moderate exercise and aim for gradual improvement. Shouldn't we do the same with our prayer life?

Except in emergencies, begin prayer with praise. In the Lord's Prayer, *hallowed be thy name* comes before *give us this day our daily bread.* Probably we are not as likely to forget our wants as we are to neglect gratitude. There will, of course, still be crises when "Lord, help me." is all we have time to say.

Use unscheduled delays as times to praise God. Waits can be frustrating. Thanking God can turn a negative into a positive. Once while I waited for auto repairs, I thanked Him for the things I saw that I had not known existed and had not needed. Disposable coveralls and a lock for a polyester car cover were among them.

Schedule some prayer time exclusively for praise once in a while. This can be a wonderful accompaniment for a walk.

When wants are not needs, focus on the parallel blessings you have enjoyed. As a Nebraska farm girl I never had a turkey dinner until I was eighteen, but the beef roasts we had for Thanksgiving were choice. I have never seen the Alps, but I have lived in the Black Hills and the Andes.

Slowly read chapters like Psalm 103 and hymns like "This is My Father's World" to focus attention on worship. Pause at phrases like *who healeth all thy diseases* and thank God for your recoveries. Take time to visualize the "rocks and trees, skies and seas" for which to praise God.

Ask the Lord to help you find other innovative ways to focus on praise. It is all right to make a list of things for which you have never thanked God even if you end up praising Him for jar lids and the pores of your skin.

I will extol the Lord at all times; his praise will always be on my lips.

PSALM 34:1

Read Psalm 103 out loud.

November 27

A Glad Heart Cleans A Bathtub

DORIS CRANDALL

Education lays hold of what is best in a person but character lays hold of what is worst. It takes hold of a failing and by very skillful manipulation and training turns it into a perfection.

—FULTON J. SHEEN

*A*rmed with dust rag and vacuum cleaner, I tackled my cleaning with enthusiasm. Now and then I glanced out of the living room window. What a lovely day it was.

But when I saw our neighbors drive past in a new car, my mood changed to misery and the day became bleak.

"It's not fair," I muttered to myself. "They get a new car every year, and we have to keep driving our eight-year-old clunker." Like a jealous child, I collapsed into a chair and cried.

When the tears of self-pity and covetousness let up, I recalled an incident from my childhood involving Mrs. Kennedy, an elderly neighbor my mother loved dearly.

The day after our family moved to a different farm where we had a bathtub, Mrs. Kennedy walked the two miles to our new place. Mama opened the door and Mrs. Kennedy smilingly told her, "I've come to clean your bathtub."

Mama looked surprised but welcomed our old neighbor in—and let her clean the tub.

I could hardly wait till Mrs. Kennedy had gone. "Why did she walk all that way to clean our tub?" I asked Mama.

"It's just her way," Mama answered. "She wanted me to know that even though she doesn't have a bathtub, she's glad I have one. Such a woman. She doesn't have a jealous bone in her body. She reminds me of the verse in the Bible that says we should rejoice with those who rejoice."

That memory made me search my Bible for the verse Mama had

spoken of so long ago—Romans 12:15. I copied it on a piece of paper, along with my own words, *A glad heart cleans a bathtub.*

I memorized the words. That memory was just what I needed. I wiped my face with my apron and asked God to forgive me of the burden of coveting.

Would you clean your neighbor's bathtub? That would be the ultimate heart of abundance. Let's all seek such a grateful spirit.

> *Do not be overcome by evil, but overcome evil with good.*
> ROMANS 12:21

Read *You Don't Have To Quit* (Thomas Nelson Publishers) by Anne and Ray Ortlund.

November 28

At The End Of A Perfect Day

LOIS ERISEY POOLE

For memory has painted this perfect day
With colors that never fade,
And we find at the end of a perfect day
The soul of a friend we've made.

—CARRIE JACOB BOND

This evening I walked through my garden and watched the sun continue its journey to the other side of the world. As its light faded, I packed up all the problems I had faced today and sent them along.

The flat tire was forgotten.

My painful back was ignored.

The notice about an insurance mix-up became vague.

Even frustration over the dusty house grew unimportant.

My quiet walk startled a few of the birds, settled for the night. A drowsing finch broke the reverie with a dreamy half-song sounding like a child mumbling in its sleep.

The marigold blossoms glowed a shocking neon-orange in the twilight.

It was still, quiet. Not a breeze ruffled the fragile leaves on the mimosa tree.

A frightened coyote startled me when it suddenly darted across the field and watched me suspiciously over its shoulder.

The volume to nature's "serenade at dusk" gradually increased as the crickets began to chirp, the doves cooed goodnight, and the click beetles kept time with their staccatoed love song.

I was wrapped in a warm cape of peaceful serenity as I stood there listening and watching the evening symphony unfold. The air smelled sweetly, a potpourri of cut grass, ripe peaches, and fallen leaves.

Far away a car door slammed and a dog barked joyfully. Someone he loved had come home. Lights blinked on in houses along the road. A cool breeze roused from its afternoon nap and sent a breathy hello across the valley.

At that moment my appreciation for the gift of life was eternal. I was seeing nature the way it was meant to be seen. Quickly, the last arc of the golden sun spread its gilded wings and, with a silent sigh, vanished. A lone star trembled in the eastern sky. And I reflected upon all the good things that happened to me today:

Rising early enough to see the fiery dawn.

Miss Molly Bumbles, my Labrador, learning to "sit" and "stay."

That warm hug from a friend.

A chocolate cake waiting on the counter top, a pot of tea steeping nearby, and a few orange embers still glowing in the fireplace.

And now, this quiet moment of gratitude at sundown.

It was a perfect finale at the end of a perfect day.

From the rising of the sun to the place where it sets, the name of the Lord is to be praised.

PSALM 113:3

By shifting your focus from external to internal, you can learn what's going on inside of you.

Only Temporary

MICHELE T. HUEY

The really happy man is the one who can enjoy the
scenery when he has to take a detour.
— WINNING ATTITUDES

Years ago, we moved into an unfinished basement thirteen miles
from the nearest town, hoping to save rent money as we built our
house ourselves. I'd given up my teaching position to be a stay-at-home
mom, so money was scarce with just my husband's income from his
work at the local scrap yard.

The children were still toddlers, and boxes, clothes, and toys
cluttered every square foot as I struggled to make that concrete cubicle
a home. The furnace, on loan from my husband's boss until we could
afford a larger one, needed repair. It was already mid-November, and
winter was closing in fast. A constant fire in the wood stove did little
to warm up the concrete surrounding us. Insulating the place was still
on our "to do" list. I wore long underwear, a toboggan hat, and layers
of clothing indoors.

The plumbing was unfinished, so we hooked up a garden hose to
the water tank and fed it through the hole in the wall above the tub
for the fixtures. Lugging pots of hot water from the kitchen, I'd flooded
the bathroom floor twice getting the kids' bath ready.

My back ached from sleeping on an old, lumpy sofa bed. Our
comfortable queen-sized bed was still in the shed, where we'd temporarily stored items while we unpacked and organized.

Three days of disorganization, interruptions, and things gone
wrong left perfectionist me struggling with my emotions. *Why can't I
have nice things the easy way like everybody else?* I wondered. *Why am I
always a "have not" and never a "have?"*

Although I tried not to complain (too much), my husband sensed my
lack of gratitude and tried to cheer me up. "It's only temporary," he'd say
when my impatience oozed through the cracks of my composure.

"Hurrumph." I'd answer, turning away so he wouldn't see the
smoldering anger showing on my face.

Then an early snowstorm dumped six inches on the countryside
overnight. Every two hours I bundled up even more and shoveled

swirling drifts away from the only door. Flinging wet, heavy snow over my shoulder, I finally gave in to self-pity.

"Temporary, temporary." I fumed. "Is *everything* temporary?"

The answer came immediately. *Even if you had everything exactly the way you wanted, it would still be temporary.*

I couldn't argue with that.

When grumbling and a lack of gratitude wipes away your sense of God's abundant provision in your life, remember that whether things are good or bad, it's all temporary. Live for the moment. Enjoy right now. It's the only moment you have available.

> *Do not say, "Why were the old days better than these?"*
> *For it is not wise to ask such questions.*
> ECCLESIASTES 7:10

After turkey has been sliced, lightly pour turkey broth mixed with apple cider (or juice) over the slices to keep them moist.

November 30

The Blessing Jar

DEENA L. MURRAY

A thankful heart is not only the greatest virtue, but the parent of all other virtues.

—CICERO

Thanksgiving time is when we give thanks for the year's blessings. We started a tradition in our family we call the Blessing Jar. It began because every year at Thanksgiving we asked each person to share what they are thankful for. So many times we knew there was so much to be thankful for, but we couldn't remember all the wonderful answered prayers and blessings we had received.

Now, whenever a prayer is answered or we receive a blessing, we write it on a 3 x 5 card with the date, and drop it in the Blessing Jar (we use an old cookie jar). Sometimes during the year when I'm feeling down, I'll reach my hand in the jar and pull out a few of the cards. As I read them I am reminded of how much we have been blessed and it helps pick me up.

One example of a blessing in our jar is our trip to South Dakota. My husband and I wanted to see wild buffalo and had been told they roamed freely on some of the roads in the Black Hills region. We were driving through one of the national parks on the last day of our trip and still hadn't seen any buffalo (unless you count the two in the zoo). We decided now was the time to pray.

We were both silent for about sixty seconds as we prayed. We rounded a curve in the road and standing right in front of us was one, big, brawny, wild buffalo. He was grazing and slowly meandered off.

As we drove on, I asked my husband, "Did you just pray?"

He said, "Yes, but I expected a herd of buffalo, not just one."

I asked him, "Did you ask for a herd, or did you ask for just one?"

We had both prayed for *a* buffalo. God heard our prayer and responded with exactly what we had asked for. Although I must confess, I wish He hadn't taken us so literally. But it was still a blessing and one that went in the Blessing Jar.

Over the years, we've had to empty our full Blessing Jar many times.

Why not bless your family with your own Blessing Jar? There are so many things to be thankful for. Even the Blessing Jar will be a blessing as it reminds you of blessings you've forgotten. We shouldn't take for granted the things God does for us.

Give thanks to the Lord, for he is good; his love ensures forever.
PSALM 107:1

Create your Blessing jar today.

December

*"And the angel said to them, Do not
be afraid; for behold; I bring you
good news of a great joy which shall
be for all the people."*

Luke 2:10

*A*t the culmination of our year, we experience
the blessed season of Christmas, when Jesus
cooperated with His Father's plan for divinity to
wrap itself in a human body. Truly, we are blessed.
This month's readings will inspire you to appreciate
these blessings and not get sidetracked by the season's busyness. When we aren't overwhelmed, we'll
delight in December's great blessings.

Lighten Up On The Holidays.

MURIAL LARSON

> I have always thought of Christmas time as a good
> time; a kind, forgiving, charitable time.
>
> —CHARLES DICKENS

It's the first day of December, and yet it seems the holiday season is already in full swing. You may be facing stress factors you wish you could hide under the kids' beds, like:

• The kids will be home instead of at school.

• Prepared delicacies will once again mysteriously disappear from the refrigerator (you suspect bottomless stomachs).

• You have to buy food and gifts, and you *know* you're not going to zero in on what your latter twentieth-century teens will like. (And, of course, you're not going to serve cheeseburgers and pizza for holiday dinners.)

• If anything can go wrong, it will.

This is especially true when you have teenagers. Have you noticed how tall 13-year-old Jimbo has gotten? With those elongated arms and legs goes the word "awkward." Go ahead—hand Jimbo the full gravyboat to carry to the dining room. Odds are, he slips on the throw rug and the gravyboat lands upside down on the sleeping cat—who sets up a yowl that makes you drop the turkey.

So . . . how do you get through the season without having a nervous breakdown that causes the kids to leave home? Lighten up. Expect accidents to happen. Then take them with a sense of humor.

At the dinner table you all can share "disasters" that happened previous years, and see who can make theirs the funniest. Each person should tell his own story to avoid embarrassment over what someone else might say. It doesn't hurt to laugh at ourselves, so we parents can begin by setting the example.

We can lighten up over holiday accidents and mistakes if we seek to see the good that may come because of them, and encourage our children to do the same. Some of the "good" could include:

1. We learn to have patience and tolerance with ourselves and others by taking such things more lightly;

2. We learn to have more true faith in our Lord;

3. We improve our family relationships.

What will you do to lighten up over these following days of potential stress. Look for the positives, and you'll experience more of Christmas blessings.

So whether you eat or drink or whatever you do, do it all for the glory of God.
I CORINTHIANS 10:31

> Either buy or create an Advent calendar to focus on the true reason for Christmas.

December 2

Goody Bags

DELORES ELAINE BIUS

Blissful are the simple, for they shall have much peace.
—THOMAS A. KEMPIS

I attended a women's retreat where each participant received a Goody Bag. The small plastic bag contained a notepad and pen, a few pieces of candy, and a card that encouraged us to make prayer an important part of our lives. That gave me the idea for a goody bag ministry.

It started out with a bag in which I assembled gifts for a missionary friend who was home on furlough. I also adapted the idea for housebound friends and for newcomers to my Bible study or neighborhood.

Lest you protest, "But I don't have the finances for such a huge effort," let me explain. Most of the items I include are bought at discount stores and garage sales, or else I make them by hand. Also, the dollar stores that are springing up all over are a marvelous place to find treasures.

I used small tote bags to put things in as my original goody bags. (These can be found in dollar stores or are often free from book clubs.) I have also used baskets. Keep your eyes peeled and you will find all sorts of containers.

Perhaps you will want to use a plastic mixing bowl covered with colorful plastic wrap. Recently I got a set of four mixing bowls in graduated sizes for only two dollars and used them as goody bowls. Still another option would be a goody box that is covered with contact paper or cloth.

Remember, your goal is to lovingly fill something with trinkets to bless others, not to impress them.

Try some of these ideas for the contents of your goody bag: mug and tea bags, cocoa mix or instant coffee; refrigerator magnets; guest soaps; dried fruit or candies; dish towels or pot holders; scented tea candles, stationery and stamps; book or magazines—new or used; notepad and pen; potpourri; small stuffed animals (people never outgrow their need to cuddle); box of assorted greeting cards; homemade cookies; small plants (possibly a cutting from your own); pocket calendar; hand cream; address book; and/or devotional booklet (many churches give them out free).

A friend of mine said, "I discovered several little candy dishes in my cupboard that I never used. I filled them with homemade fudge and used all of them to put in my goody baskets."

People want to know you're thinking of them. Bless someone today with a goody bag. You'll be representing the Lord.

A gift opens the way for the giver and ushers him into the presence of the great.
PROVERBS 18:16

Learn to build and not destroy. Learn to ask, not demand. Learn to forgive, not complain. Learn to accept and Learn to smile.

December 3

Merry Christmas

BONNIE COMPTON HANSON

Christmas is coming, the geese are getting fat.
—ENGLISH FOLK SONG

Years ago, as Christmas approached, a homesick young couple were out on the road, headed for a strange city. But when they arrived, all the places to stay had "no vacancy" signs out. So they had to spend Christmas Eve in a rundown, smelly old barn.

No turkey. No fruitcake. No Christmas tree, decorations, cards, parties, family get-together. *Nothing.*

Except love. For that night Mary and Joseph had the most joyous Christmas ever known, as they welcomed into this world God's Son, the Savior of mankind.

Yes, every year about this time we all panic. Christmas is coming—and there's so much to do. How will we ever get it all done?

Here are some time, energy, and sanity-savers to help you prepare for and enjoy a Christ-honoring, truly Merry Christmas this year, based on the acrostic, MERRY CHRISTMAS:

Make your plans early, and write them down.

Estimate your expenses. Don't start with a wish list. Begin with a total dollar amount that won't put you in debt. Estimate non-gift expenses such as tree, cards, wrappings and subtract from your budget. List all those you need to buy gifts for and divide the number into what you have left in your budget.

Refrain from grandiose schemes. If a large gift is needed for someone, maybe several in your family can pitch in to buy it together.

Review what you already have on hand to use. Pull out last year's unused cards and decorations. Check bulbs. Consider loving home-made gifts: jelly, needlework, baby-sitting vouchers, gifts of your time.

You must be organized. Your daily responsibilities won't stop for Christmas.

Calendars are indispensable. Keep one on the refrigerator or by the phone to note all parties, get-togethers, practices, programs. Say no when too heavily scheduled.

Help your family help you. Even little ones can help decorate and wrap gifts.

Remember the Reason for the Season. Helping in a shelter, convalescent hospital, school, or youth center can help show Christmas as a time of giving as well as receiving.

Invite friends for informal times of fun instead of big parties. Pop-corn, decorating Christmas goodies, candy apples, ice skating, hay rides, singing Christmas carols, having Bible study times, or watching videos are simple, yet meaningful times. Why not potluck?

Shop smartly. Stick to your lists and check off when something's bought. Comparison shop. Wear comfortable shoes. Once home, wrap, label, put away or under the tree as soon as possible.

Traditions are half the fun—and it's never too late to start one.

Mail everything early in sturdy, well-wrapped containers and correct postage.

Ask for assistance from your family, relatives, friends. And take shortcuts. Children would just as soon have hot dogs or spaghetti as turkey, anyway.

Savor this joyous time; it'll so soon be past.

. . . you are worried and upset about many things, but only one thing is needed . . .
LUKE 10:41-42

December 4

Peace On Earth

PAULINE JARAMILLO

> A moment of quiet repose cannot be bought or sold.
> —M.E. BRIGGS

Hustle, bustle, hurry and wait.
Am I early? Am I late?
As I run from store to store
the lyric of a Christmas carol echoes in my head—
"Peace on earth, goodwill toward men."

I push it aside and continue my quest
with the fierce devotion of a Christian crusader.
My eyes catch sight of a perfect gift
lying just beyond my reach.
I venture forth and take it up,
assisted by another pair of hands.

I pull it forward, she pulls it back.
We both insist we had it first.
I tug, she pulls, it rips.
Only then do I relinquish my hold.
"Peace on earth, good will toward men."

Home at last I stagger in the door,
balancing packages, boxes, and Christmas things.
I'm greeted by a joyful bark and eager paws.
I topple backward.

Lying on the floor, arms free, vision clear,
I experience peace and good will
as Rex demonstrates his joy
in seeing me—
not my gifts.

Peace I leave with you; my peace I give you.
I do not give to you as the world gives . . .

JOHN 14:27

Look back through old photo albums of Christmases from your childhood. What is your most memorable Christmas?

December 5

Bring The World To Me, Lord . . .

JAN WOODARD

Evangelism is a sharing of gladness.

—ANONYMOUS

Rag in hand, I dusted a small replica of a Russian Orthodox cathedral, a brightly-painted *matrioshka* doll, and a vase of inlaid wood storing foreign coins. Fingering the coins, I smiled at the simplicity of my prayer a few years ago.

With a part-time job, a limited budget and kids in college, it wasn't often I escaped the boundaries of this small college town, hidden in the hills of Western Pennsylvania. Sometimes I used to feel buried here, as if just beyond the horizon the rest of the pulsating world whizzed by, and I was missing it all.

One January day when a gray gloom entombed our house in fog, I prayed from my depths, "Lord, you said to go into all the world, sharing your love. Since I can't go out into the world just now, please bring the world to me."

Day by day, he did just that, beginning with an invitation two weeks later to a local Finnish banquet, complete with pickled salmon. Then, as a writer, I met folks visiting our campus and church from India, Gambia, Surinam, and Indonesia. Opportunities abounded to share my faith, each new friend enlarging my heart and my vision of the world. We invited college students for dinner from Japan and Hong Kong, and my friendship deepened with an Iranian woman after I surprised her with a party celebrating her baptism.

At the year's end, our community participated in a "sister-city" project with Moscow, bridging cultural differences through mutual visits. (Using "city" to describe this rural community stretched the definition of the word a bit thin, I thought.) I couldn't travel with the delegation visiting Russia, but I offered to host Moscow's deputy mayor, Boris Bykov, and his translator for a meal.

What a great chance for us all. I thought, preparing that all-American dish, macaroni and cheese. A Christmas season luncheon followed with a fire blazing in our stone kitchen fireplace. An antique oak table stretched with extra planks to seat a crowd of relatives, and laughter and congeniality spanned language barriers.

Our guests, who lived in cramped Moscow apartments, marveled at the view of the surrounding hills and valleys, and the roomy home my husband built. My face flushed as I suddenly knew my greater abundance—my faith, family, and freedoms.

The knickknacks I now dusted were gifts from our Russian callers, memory-makers of the year the Lord turned strangers into friends and showed me how blessed I am to live in this tiny dot on the map called Indiana, Pennsylvania. Come visit, sometime.

How might the Lord bless others through your outreach to the world? You don't even have to leave home. Invite others in.

You are the light of the world. A city on a hill cannot be hidden.
MATTHEW 5:14

Ask God to show you who would be blessed by your gift of friendship this week.

December 6

Seeing The Christ In Christmas

DORIS STERNER YOUNG

The hinge of history is on the door of a Bethlehem stable.
—RALPH W. SOCKMAN

I stepped into the crisp evening air to hang the oversized star on our picture window. Festooned with bright lights and a pine garland, it represented a fourteen-year-old Christmas tradition that began when we moved into the first home of our own with our toddlers.

As I reached to secure the star on the special hooks in the window frame, memories of other happier Christmases overwhelmed me. Tears flooded my eyes causing the lights on the star to take on a blurry quality. This star, which meant so much to our Christmas, was handmade by my husband from scraps of lumber left over from building our house. The bulbs in the sockets were put there by his own hands. I clung to the star. It was my connection to Christmases past, and to him.

Six weeks earlier, my husband died unexpectedly, leaving me to carry out our family's unique Christmas rituals. I wanted to make the holidays special for my children, but I admit I felt alone and uncertain about the future. All of my relatives were 2500 miles away. I had no job and the idea of providing for three teenagers by myself frightened me. As I stepped back to admire the star's glow on the shrubbery, I tried to be optimistic, hoping the holidays would be a turning point in our grief.

Back inside we finished dinner together. As we were clearing the table, Kim said, "Mother, the lights on the star have gone out."

"I'll check the fuses," I replied.

The fuses were intact. However, half the bulbs in the star had been stolen, along with my new heavy duty extension cord. I knew there wasn't enough money in the budget to replace them. No cord, no lights. I felt like a failure. I couldn't even afford to give my children the gift of the star this year.

Soon anger overtook me. *Why did this have to happen to us when we are trying so hard to enjoy the season despite our hardships? Is there a lesson God wants us to learn from this? If so, what is it?*

We went to bed, hoping the thief would have time to repent and return what was rightfully ours. But it was not to be. The next morning those light sockets were still as empty as my pocketbook.

It was then I noticed our Merry Christmas banner had fallen from above the door. That is, the "Merry" and the "mas" were down. Somehow those sections separated from the rest, leaving "Christ" firmly in place.

At that moment I understood clearly the answer staring me in the face. The things of the earth can be taken from us at any time, just as my husband was taken suddenly in the prime of life, but the gifts of the spirit are eternal.

Christ is the answer. He would see us through whatever trials lay ahead. No thief could rob us of the comfort and the joy that comes from having Christ in our lives. It would be a very special Christmas.

If trials try to rob the awareness of God's blessings this season, take your eyes off your circumstances and see the eternal aspects of this time. Your pain is valid, but God will use it for good.

Trust in the Lord with all your heart and lean not on your own understanding; in all your ways acknowledge him, and he will make your paths straight.
PROVERBS 3:5-6

> Take pictures from past Christmases and glue them to Styrofoam pieces to make ornaments. Decorate with glitter and paint.

December 7

Giving On A Shoestring Budget

MARGARET PRIMROSE

Is not giving a need?

—FRIEDRICH NIETZSCHE

I was about ten-years-old the Christmas I discovered that it is more blessed to give than to receive. It was the time of the Great Depression, and for the first time I had hoarded enough to buy a ten cent gift for each of the family. The Great Depression is history, but for many of us tight budgets are not. Fortunately, there are lots of ways to take the strain out of giving:

Pray about it. To give an expensive gift may be a want, not a need. Drawing names is still a popular way to save.

Watch for bargains. When you see a baby blanket, toiletries, or note cards for sale, buy them. It may save time as-well-as money when special occasions come. If you end up with ten suitable but assorted gifts for ten people, put the gifts in a grab bag.

Be innovative. Dress up an old doll if you can't afford a new one. Buy a file box for a bride and put your favorite non-copyrighted recipes in it. Plan a treasure hunt of small items for a child's birthday.

Give promissory notes. "I'll baby-sit an afternoon while you shop" may be a very welcome gift. Promise to alter a skirt, trim a hedge, or change the oil in a car.

Make use of your hobbies. Woodworking, cross-stitching, or ceramics are good choices for people who like crafts. Or give fresh produce and bouquets if you are a gardener.

Cut the cost of cards, gift wrap, and postage. Choose boxes of cards, bags of ribbon and packages of picture postcards. Look for rolls of ribbon, greeting cards, and gift wrap in thrift shops or at garage sales. Enlist friends to join you in purchasing the minimum required by card-selling plans. Make your own cards or call a friend in the same city instead of sending a card. Choose small enclosures like bookmarks, books of stamps, gift certificates, and checks to cut postage. Save bows and paper from gifts if they are reusable.

Give heirlooms. Earmarked for occasions like birthdays, these are especially welcome from senior citizens who must move into small quarters.

Find some thrifty, but thoughtful ways to say, "I love you" and "You're important to me." Be a blessing to others. That's the *abundant* life.

A generous man will prosper; he who refreshes others will himself be refreshed.

PROVERBS 11:25

> It can be a lot of fun to have the family bring pictures of what they would give each other if money were limitless.

December 8

Recycled For Tradition

LYNNE LOGAN, PH. D.

The manner of giving is worth more than the gift.
— PIERRE CORNEILLE

Another birthday present to purchase. It's not that I mind giving, I love the entire process with the shopping and wrapping. I even give unexpected gifts to our grandchildren between birthdays, putting special little presents into colorful sacks. I call them "blessing bags." When we arrive for a visit, they're excited to see Mimi and Grandpa strolling up the walkway with these brilliant bags. So what's the problem?

I've grown "thrifty" in my later years. I love giving presents, but what I resist is spending four dollars on the gift bag. My husband figured it out one day. I spent approximately $200.00 a year on beautiful bags. My only consolation was passing them on to another person.

Aren't there more simple ways to adorn gifts? "But, I love gift bags." my inner child screams. The adult within me protests, "They're too expensive." I could go back to the old paper wrapping and scotch tape routine, but wadding up the paper and throwing it away seems even more wasteful.

I found a simple answer. I'll ask for the return of the gift bag after the person opens the gift. Suddenly, I realized I've turned into my own grandmother. My frugal spirit had finally arrived. But I could envision my family giving me funny looks while rolling their eyes.

How could I turn this return-the-gift-bag plan into a pleasant experience? A plan that didn't scream *miser?* Slowly, my strategy unfolded.

I purchased one large gift bag for every individual in my family. Each bag visually dramatized a personal reflection of the person. For instance, my oldest daughter loves the Victorian era and my grandson loves Winnie-the-Pooh. I purchased large bags to hold gifts of all sizes, using the same bag through the years for each family member. I decoratively wrote the person's name on their bag. Each time I gave a gift, I documented on the bottom of the bag the occasion, date, and the gift. This takes care of tradition.

Projecting ahead a few years, I envision our twenty-year-old granddaughter smile as she remembers her seventh birthday when we gave her a Barbie wristwatch. I imagine our grandson at age fifteen laughing as he recalls the giggling excitement that Winnie-the-Pooh once brought him. This provides sentimental memories.

My husband is especially happy. He calculated that over a period of fifteen years (the life of one strong gift bag used fifteen times) based on the average cost of four dollars per bag, purchasing fifty per year, we saved over $3,000. This took care of our Hawaii vacation. Simple cost-saving ideas are all around us. Turn them into traditions, and you've touched hearts forever.

Although I originally used this simple plan for birthdays, I'm sure you can see how it could be used for Christmas. See whether it can be a blessing for your family and a part of your abundant simplicity.

Every good and perfect gift is from above . . .
JAMES 1:17

Invite friends and family over to watch Christmas movies such as "It's a Wonderful Life."

December 9

An Impossible Task?

GEORGIA BURKETT

The early Christians not only moved the world, they turned it upside down.
—GEORGE JACKSON

*L*ittle did the devout young Mary realize what she was getting into. The angel Gabriel had just brought her the news that God had chosen her to be the mother of His Son, Jesus. How could it be? she wondered. She was a virgin and engaged to Joseph. How could she ever make him and her family understand? Would they stone her to death according to the prescribed punishment for such a situation?

However, when Gabriel explained how God would overshadow her and be the father of her baby, Mary agreed to God's plan. In faith, she realized that with God, nothing was impossible. If her baby was to be God's own Son, surely God would protect him, and her as well.

As I read that blessed story, I remember how often God has given me what I considered an impossible task. I've even argued that I'm not qualified to do it, I don't have the time, or I am too frightened. More than once I've turned my back on God, afraid to trust my life to Him.

I remember so well the times I refused to sing hymns like, "I'll Go Where You Want Me To Go." I thought God would want me to go to some dark dangerous jungle, a prospect that positively terrified me.

How silly I was. If God had wanted me to go to the jungles, He would have created within me such a deep desire to go that nothing could have stopped me.

Even so, there are still times when I feel God expects more of me than I am willing to give. "Why me?" I ask Him. "There are others far more qualified to do what You want me to do. Besides, they have more time and resources than I have."

But God knows me better than I know myself. He knows that I am weak. But it is then that He gives me just the right amount of courage, wisdom, and stamina I need. He has also promised that He will never leave or forsake me.

With promises like that, I can't help singing like Mary, *My soul glorifies the Lord, and my spirit rejoices in God my Savior . . . For the Mighty One has done great things for me—holy is his name.* (Luke 1:46a, 49).

If you've hesitated to surrender your will to God, consider the risk Mary took and be encouraged by her faith. God brought great blessings into her life, and He will in yours also.

It is God who arms me with strength and makes my way perfect.
PSALM 18:32

Take your family or friends to a nativity scene at a church or community center and sing Christmas carols.

The Cookie Christmas Tree

INA GESELL

Choose such pleasures as recreate much and cost little.
—FULLER

A Christmas tradition we enjoyed when my kids were young was trimming the Christmas tree with freshly-baked, homemade and individually-decorated cookies.

I baked the sugar cookies, cutting out Christmas shapes with special cookie cutters, while the kids were at school. They included Christmas balls, Santa Claus, reindeer, stars, and even the complete nativity scene. Then, on the following Saturday the children each invited a friend to help decorate the cookies.

I covered the kitchen table with newspapers, then set out several cups full of powdered sugar icing. Bright Christmas reds, blues, greens, and gold, and a large bowl of uncolored frosting for the much needed white. A dozen or so cheap paint brushes were on the table to paint the icing. The icing was simply powdered sugar, food coloring, and water, so it was easy to make another batch as the colors were depleted.

I let the children design the cookies without interference, then we hung them on the tree. I baked them with clean hair pins inserted to make them easy to hang. Of course the neighbor children took their cookies home with them for their own Christmas trees.

The tree was embellished solely with gaily-colored cookies and twinkling lights. On Christmas Day they invited their friends over to "undecorate" the tree. The cookies were eaten and shared among the neighborhood children.

As the children grew, they too, began to help in the baking and cutting of the cookies. And the project gradually grew to where I had to provide each child's classroom and Sunday School class with a cookie nativity scene. I made the stable out of gingerbread, (or frosted cardboard, in a pinch).

If you'd like to consider doing this, it may seem like a lot of work, but it will create fabulous memories for you and your loved ones. And it'll make the process of taking down the Christmas tree simple. Plus, storage is definitely no problem.

He has filled them with skill to do all kinds of work . . .
EXODUS 35:35

> Make Christmas cookie ornaments to help decorate your tree. Be sure to invite some neighborhood children over to enjoy the treat.

December II

A Christmas Bonus From God

FRANCES L. PARTAIN-MARTIN

You can never out give God.

—ANONYMOUS

Losing my job back in October was a great blow to me. My meager savings were dwindling and job prospects were not good. On top of everything else, Christmas was fast approaching.

I looked over my gift list. After eliminating several names, I sat down and wrote notes to friends saying that I would not be sending gifts. However, there were still five people that I felt I had to buy presents for, including my three-year-old granddaughter.

My dearest friend hosts a wonderful Christmas party every year for our church family. She invited me to go with her to get some items for the party and do "a little Christmas shopping." Before we left, I asked God's help in keeping my finances in check.

My friend had a long list of things to buy, and I satisfied my shopping urges by finding things that she needed and pushing the shopping cart. I could feel God's presence and a deep sense of peace. Then, as I was walking past the book section in a huge outlet store, I felt a nudge, as if God were saying, "Look over there." I found several books that would make wonderful gifts, including a beautifully illustrated book of Bible stories for my granddaughter. Most of the books were just a fraction of the original price, and I was very pleased. I was able to complete my Christmas shopping that day without guilt feelings. I'd only spent $62.30.

After dropping off my friend, I started to worry about the money I'd spent. I wondered if I should return everything except the book for my granddaughter. I was exhausted and decided I would go straight home without stopping by the post office for my mail. Again, I felt a nudge, so I went to the post office where I found just one piece of mail with a return address from my insurance company. I thought, "What a waste of time," and started to stuff the envelope into my purse. Another nudge.

I opened the envelope and inside was an unexpected dividend check for $65.15. God had provided for my Christmas shopping with a $2.85 bonus for me.

What blessings have already been given to you, yet somehow they haven't seemed "big" enough to notice. Be aware of the simple things and give God credit. He wants to bless you.

> *And my God will meet all your needs according*
> *to his glorious riches in Christ Jesus.*
> PHILIPPIANS 4:19

> If you feel pressured to give when there's a lack of money, give a gift of your help or service.

December 12

A Wreath Of Blessings

ERMA LANDIS

> Christmas is a time for giving, not swapping: giving up
> sin, giving in to Christ, and giving out to our fellow
> man that we might meet him in his need.
> — ANONYMOUS

*L*ike crocuses in late winter, Christmas cards are a harbinger of the season, a forerunner of the joyous time, the heralding of that great event when God's love was climaxed in sending the world a Savior. I want to say, "Hello. Aren't you glad? Here's a special message to help you celebrate the season" to as many people as possible. Christmas cards give that opportunity.

Christmas cards are greetings. Like all greetings they say, "I am thinking about you. I care about you."

Blessings come both in the sending and the receiving. Whether buying, mailing, receiving, or disposing of them, by hemming the activity in prayer the blessings add up and spread over a time span of months.

The blessings begin when buying them. Browsing through the shelves, I ponder their messages and artwork while breathing a prayer for help in choosing ones that will prove a blessing to the receivers.

Preparing them for mailing is another opportunity to pray for friends as I proceed down my list, choosing the most appropriate card, reminiscing and tucking a prayer of blessing into each envelope.

When the greetings arrive from friends the blessings not only add up, they multiply. The warmth of friends' greetings permeates our home. The newsy letters and notes stimulate more reminiscing and prayers of praise and gratitude.

When the season draws to a close, the cards must find another home. Before they do, however, rereading them brings one more round of blessing. Because of them, a renewed sense of reverence and awe has entered my spirit because God's unspeakable gift, His Son, was willing to humble Himself that we might live abundant lives.

Reluctantly I tuck them away in boxes, send them to craft groups or save them for my own scrapbook pages or projects. Sometimes there is no alternative but to throw them out. One friend told me, "Our Christmas cards warm us three times. Once when we receive them. Secondly, when we reread them after Christmas and a third time when we roll them up with our newspaper logs and burn them in our fireplace."

Enfolding my Christmas cards with prayer, receiving them with gratitude and praise, disposing of them with reverent care has formed this Christmas tradition into a wreath of blessings. When the calendar once more indicates Christmas is coming, Christmas cards will again, for me, like those cheery crocuses, be a harbinger, a heralding of another season of celebrating the birth of my Savior.

If you've begun to take Christmas cards for granted or they've even become a bother, appreciate them again for the blessing they can be. It's a simple tool for sharing God's love.

Today in the town of David a Savior has been
born to you; he is Christ the Lord.

LUKE 2:11

Write a Christmas newsletter to let your friends and family know how God has blessed you this past year.

December 13

Ornaments

NANETTE THORSEN-SNIPES

Christmas is bathed in the humility of Christ if we
but remember.

—ANONYMOUS

Several years ago, we brought home another scrawny Christmas tree.
How I longed for one with pink bows peeking from the branches
and slender ribbons cascading like waterfalls.

My children were thrilled to see the tree and brought in the boxes
of ornaments. I dreaded taking out faded paper chains and clothespin
reindeer with missing eyes. I felt like tossing them all out. I watched
Jamie and Jon hang bright red and blue balls while my mind wandered
to a tree dressed in pink.

Jamie rummaged through the box. "This ornament says Baby's First
Christmas," she said, her eyes sparkling. "And it has my name on it."

I recalled her birth years before—my only girl among three boys. I
cradled her against my body and kissed her sweet-smelling fingers. In the
quiet of the moment, another birth came to mind. I'm sure His mother
counted His fingers and kissed each one. I can almost hear her as she
kissed His forehead and whispered His precious name—Jesus.

My son's voice jolted me back to reality. "Mom, this is my star." I
took the tin star remembering when his father had helped him hammer
his name across it. I stood to hang the star, visualizing the star of
Bethlehem. I could scarcely imagine its brilliance announcing the
greatest birth the world has ever known.

I picked up an angel with lace wings a friend once gave me. My
thoughts raced to the year when she and I exchanged gifts following
a disagreement. When we parted, she hugged me as though no cross
words had ever been spoken. An inner joy spread through me. I smiled
realizing what we really exchanged that day was the gift of forgiveness.
What greater gift could friends give?

Placing the angel on the tree, I recalled the angel who brought the
news of the birth of the baby Jesus. Ironically, He would one day die
a cruel death on a tree and say, "Father forgive them, for they do not
know what they are doing." I bowed my head thanking God for
allowing forgiveness to take place between my friend and me.

I found it hard to believe but for every ornament there was an equally important event in my life. It's strange how I'd never noticed how much of a blessing my timeworn ornaments had become. Only when I was about to throw away my past did I realize how much the love of God was embodied in a simple ornament given to a baby, a tin star made by a child and his father, and an angel with lace wings given in friendship.

What blessings do your ornaments represent? Take time to remember.

For where your treasure is, there your heart will be also.

MATTHEW 6:21

> As you hang your ornaments, recount to your children the history behind each one.

December 14

Passing Down A Legacy

LORI WALL

I love scrapbooks. They are one of the finest ways of dejunking life and abode.

—DON ASLETT

When a co-worker approached me about attending a Creative Memories scrapbook class, I put her off. I felt my photos were in some sort of organized order sitting in a giant plastic bin and in a couple of shoeboxes.

However, during the night, the Lord woke me up and instructed me to attend the class along with my daughter, Jennifer. Getting my photos in albums were part of His plan to get my home in order and shut the door on 20 years of my life.

Little did I realize what effect the process had on the whole family. As I continue to work on individual albums for each of my three children, I see them proudly show finished pages with pictures of themselves to their friends and relatives. They enjoy reading the captions I write in an attempt to capture what happened when the photos were taken. Simple memories jotted down in the scrapbook bring forth smiles at what they were like when they were younger. The scrapbooks not only are about who they are, but simply passes down family stories and memories they can enjoy for years.

Now all of us are conscious about taking photos to remember

special family events and moments. When we went rollerskating with members of our church for the first time, my youngest quickly asked me when we arrived at the rink, "Did you bring the camera?"

Your family may groan when the camera is brought out this Christmas season but years from now they'll be blessed as they point proudly and with great interest to the photos. Be sure to take pictures during this holiday season.

. . . Surely I have a delightful inheritance.
PSALM 16:6

> When taking photos, don't discount what's in the background. The car, house, yard, etc. will capture history of the times you lived in.

December 15

Giving Away Happiness

MARGARET PRIMROSE

The best way to have happiness is to give it away.
—AUNT RACHEL G. KINNIER

Theoretically, I agree with Aunt Rachel. Opening presents on Christmas Eve always seems a little anticlimactic to me. What I enjoy more is shopping and wrapping gifts, making and sharing candy and cookies and taking friends to holiday events. Yet I have not arrived at Aunt Rachel's level of maturity.

Aunt Rachel lived alone in a big white farmhouse that once rang with the laughter of six children and a loving husband. One by one Uncle Jim and five of the children passed away. Only her son Jim remained, and she did not see him often.

Hard-of-hearing, Aunt Rachel could not enjoy the telephone much. She had no car and rarely got to go anywhere except the three miles to the village church. An invitation to spend Christmas with Jim must have been the highlight of the year, and she appreciated the fact that it would mean two 50-mile round trips for him.

However, rain had frozen the lane's ruts before that Christmas morning. If a car went off the road, it was likely to roll into a ravine.

"Don't come to get me," she told Jim when he called that morning. She was thinking of his safety, knowing she would spend the day by herself.

Aunt Rachel loved her Bible, and my guess is that she spent quite a bit of time reading the Christmas story that day. Then she began opening her Christmas cards and letters. She mentioned there was quite a stack of them. She did not mention any presents nor anything special she had to eat. It was when she summed up the holiday that she said, "The best way to have happiness is to give it away."

I still can't relate her story without feeling the intense disappointment I think I would have had. I accept it as a challenge to be thankful for what I can give up, not just for what I can give. Let that challenge be yours also during this special season. It'll bless you and others.

It is more blessed to give than to receive.

ACTS 20:35

> "Only you can make your life more interesting, more rewarding, more satisfying." (*How Do You Want Your Room . . . Plain or Padded?* —Jo Ann Larsen & Artemus Cole).

December 16

It's A Beautiful Day In The Neighborhood

PATTY R. STUMP

God's immense love must be translated to the world through us.

—TIM HANSEL

*H*aving grown up on a small farm in North Carolina, my relocation to the Arizona desert has brought with it a variety of changes and *opportunities* for personal adjustment. Carefully-manicured rock gardens with little greenery have often stirred in me a longing for the rolling countryside of the south. As well, adjusting to life in a community where homes are in close proximity has periodically left me pleading with the Lord for a change of address. The Lord knows that I tend to resist change. He also knows that I need to experience change in order to grow in my faith and dependence on Him. I am learning on a daily basis that in order to be content in *all* of my circumstances, I must have *His* perspective regarding my circumstances.

I have discovered that with a little bit of effort, a neighborhood can become a wonderful place to be an extension of Christ. If you're looking to have the same viewpoint, the first step in being used by

Him is to adjust our perspectives in order to see circumstances and surroundings through God's eyes. He invites us to move outside our comfort zones and into the lives of others.

Our initial efforts in doing that took the shape of a simple Christmas drop-in. Early one December our family went house-to-house, delivering to each of the twenty-eight homes on our street an invitation to a "Casual Christmas Drop-in." Two weeks later on a Sunday afternoon, we hosted the drop-in at our home, sharing with neighbors a simple menu of hot apple cider and holiday goodies. This Christmas tradition has become an anticipated event on our street. It has enabled families to become better acquainted with one another while simultaneously making our neighborhood an enjoyable place to live and exciting place to see God at work.

In addition to the Christmas drop-in, our front lawn has become the site for a periodic lemonade stands, watermelon meetings, and popsicle parties. Informal games of volleyball or croquet always draw small crowds of curious onlookers, and our tiny wading pool has become the final stop for neighborhood children to gather for an evening dip. We anticipate hosting a "Sunday Sundae Social" to celebrate the end of the school year and are expectant about what the Lord is doing in the lives of those right in our midst.

Not all of us will serve the Lord as missionaries on foreign soil or as pastors from podiums. But we can be used of Him to minister to others right in our own neighborhoods. We simply have to be willing to be available where and how He desires to use us. With God's perspective, any neighborhood can be an opportunity for a beautiful blessing to serve on His behalf.

> *. . . Love your neighbor as yourself.*
>
> MATTHEW 19:19

Consider having a "Casual Christmas Drop-In" for your neighbors and see how God desires to use it.

December 17

A Want To Is The Key

PAT VERBAL

All the beautiful sentiments in the world weigh less than a single lovely action.

—JAMES RUSSELL LOWELL

"*Mama*, hide the silver." Rich teased over the phone. His familiar words signaled me that he'd be bringing home another street person. He knew, of course, we didn't have any silver. But we always had another place at the table.

I wish I could say I always welcomed my son's calls. Sometimes I just didn't want to reschedule my busy day. He seemed to forget that I had a full-time job too. Yet, during Rich's years as chaplain at the Los Angeles Mission, we ministered to many needy young people. Each one told a sad story with an uncertain future. Our prayer list stayed full.

We dressed the wounds of runaways caught in domestic violence, washed soiled sheets left by recovering addicts, and housed family members during counseling sessions. We served tons of lasagna and brownies with hugs and tears.

One December they turned the tables on us. Following the death of my mother-in-law, I couldn't find my Christmas spirit. Rich suggested canceling a holiday dinner planned at our house, but I insisted I needed a task to concentrate on. I cleaned, cooked, decorated, and enjoyed watching the guys give symbolic gifts. While getting a Coke for a handsome nineteen-year-old, I was jolted by his appreciation when he said, "I thank God for being in your home tonight. I've spent the last three Christmas seasons in jail." My eyes filled with tears. His humble prayer brought Christ back into my Christmas that year.

When our friends mentioned the risk in bringing these vagabonds into our home, I told them about God's call on Rich's life. He'd carted home needy kids since kindergarten. I'm afraid my desire to serve came more from my wanting to support his ministry that it did from a heart for the homeless.

The Holy Spirit was powerfully present in our home as we cared for these hurting kids. I'm grateful I did not miss the opportunities—whether I wanted to or not.

Are there hurting people around you that need your touch of blessing? Ask the Lord to open your eyes to opportunities you've never seen before.

The poor you will always have with you,
and you can help them any time you want.

MARK 14:7

> Look for ways to reach out to the needy. Involve your children as much as possible.

A Shortcut To Service

CHARLOTTE ADELSPERGER

If you are unhappy with your lot in life, build a service station on it.

—CORRIE TEN BOOM

*M*any years ago, as a young mother, I began a December day with a sense of being pulled in multiple directions. This was a common feeling for me. I was pregnant and tired, and yet my mind bounded with things I wanted and needed to do.

Most of my energy was going into the care of our toddler, Karen, as well as into household tasks. But today, with snow coming down, a whirlwind of errands blew through my mind. One was to visit Mrs. Snead, a homebound woman from our church.

It was still early and Karen was asleep. I began my cherished "quiet time." (I prayed silently and read the Bible.) Taking a notebook, I listed what I thought were my "needed" things to do. But sensing God's presence, I felt a loving desire to put Mr. and Mrs. Snead at the top of my list.

I'll never forget trudging up to the Sneads' house that freezing afternoon. As I gripped Karen's small hand, I stepped over slick spots. Pausing at the door, I prayed for God's blessing upon the visit. Yet I wondered, *Am I foolish going out in treacherous weather or am I following God's leading?*

Mr. Snead beamed when he saw Karen and me. Yet he seemed worn and tense. A few minutes later he pushed his wife in her wheelchair into the front room. Mrs. Snead had suffered as an invalid for many years.

The couple delighted in our conversation, and they obviously loved watching Karen play with toys. They seemed to savor this Friday afternoon visit. Before I left, I prayed with them. I recall thanking God for Jesus. Then I thanked Him for each of them and asked His blessing on their Christmas.

Sunday morning brought a shock. In church our pastor announced that on Saturday Mr. Snead had died suddenly of a heart attack. I was stunned. But I now knew the Lord had guided me to go to them—only one day before Mr. Snead went to his Heavenly home.

I look back now and see that winter day as a turning point. Since then I've learned to take my "appointment with God" and include a follow-up planning period. I list each time-consuming task or goal on a slip of paper the size of an index card. Then I prayerfully stack them in prioritized order.

No more long, overpowering lists. Focused on the Lord, I am able to carry out one activity at a time. What a blessing. Some things get saved for another day. In the long run, I have had more opportunities to "build a service station" in my home or in any situation where the Lord might send me. It's a rich adventure in Christ.

If the season is making you feel pressured, relax. Remember what's really important. The opportunity for Christmas joy will soon be gone. Don't let its blessings slip through your fingers.

. . . If anyone serves, he should do it with the strength God provides, so that in all things God may be praised through Jesus Christ . . .

I PETER 4:IIB

Burnout is the result of unrelieved stress. When the stress of the holiday season begins to pile up, concentrate on completing just one task at a time and trust God for the rest.

December 19

Hassle-Free Holiday Giving

ROBERTA L. MESSNER

Sometimes my expectations lead to discouragement or exhaustion, but God's expectations bring rest and balance.

—MAYO MATHERS

We Americans spend approximately seventy percent of our discretionary income between Thanksgiving and Christmas. While it's no secret that holiday gift-giving is big business, it's also the source of frustration and frayed nerves for both givers and receivers. Would you like to choose gifts that please with minimal ease, that won't break your budget? It's as simple as 1-2-3.

1. Cultivate an attitude of sincere giving. While cultural expectations try to persuade us that bigger is better, giving in the truest sense is not synonymous with VISA or MasterCard. Real giving is an attitude

of the heart and knows no season. It's smiling at the frazzled cashier at Wendy's drive-through window, shoveling a neighbor's sidewalk, or sharing some of your tomato harvest with a co-worker. Best of all, this type of giving brings abundance and energizes the spirit. It eliminates the competition of, "Did I spend as much on her as she's spending on me?"

2. Develop a plan. Organization is the key to less-stressful gift-giving. Carry a list of sizes and preferences with you to eliminate the guessing game when you run onto a sale. Keep a supply of gift-wrapping supplies on hand so that giving gifts blends seamlessly with other aspects of your life. If you have the space, a closet is great for organizing scissors, tape, gift-wrap, and boxes, as well as gifts. This makes it as convenient as grabbing a can of soup from the pantry.

Once you designate a spot, you'll be heading there often to stash previously-overlooked treasures. You'll no longer have to organize a search party to track down those snippets of ribbon, lace, and trinkets you spied for package toppers. And you'll likely find you're stretching your gift buying over twelve months, squirreling away smarter purchases and placing less strain on your nerves and pocketbook.

3. Make it personal. Gift-giving is a joy—not a drudgery—when you get creative and come up with presents that speak to the recipient's heart. To add to your personalized touch, tie on a small gift as a package topper that hints at the contents inside (such as a bundle of recipe cards and a wooden spoon for a package that holds a cook book).

Train yourself to listen for clues (a favorite brand of tea or lotion, perhaps) and jot them down. Then you won't be overwhelmed when you go shopping and you'll make a heart-to-heart connection with your recipient. This matters so much more than how much money you spend.

For an ultra-personalized touch, compile a little book of favorite quotes on motherhood for that new mother on your gift list. (You won't have to fight the crowds on this one. Wait for a perfect June afternoon while you sip lemonade on your porch.) Stock a basket with permitted treats for a diabetic family member. Or why not pass along one of your mementos to a loved one who has long admired it? Rather than a cookie-cutter gift, your selection will tell your special someone you really noticed them. And you will have given a gift that only you could give, that brings great blessings.

Do not neglect your gift . . .

I TIMOTHY 4:14

Stop trying to be perfect—you'll only be disappointed. Focus on growing, one step at a time.

A Strange Christmas Gift

SARAH HEALTON

Make for yourself a family tradition.

—AUNT MAGGIE

A huge black nail has now become part of our family traditions. Unusual? Yes, but it was a Christmas gift from my grown-up son a few years ago. When I opened his beautifully-wrapped package, I saw a black spike nail mounted on a card. As I looked up to thank him, he remarked, "Read the card with it, Mom. Read it aloud, so all of us can hear."

I did. The instructions said: "Hang this nail on a sturdy branch next to the bark on your Christmas tree. Few will notice it, but you will know it's there. It is hung with the thought that the Christmas tree foreshadows the Christ-tree which only He could decorate for us."

Then I thought of other Christmases we have celebrated as a family. Each year since our son was three-years-old, we have had coffee cake for breakfast on Christmas morning. In the center of the cake is a birthday candle which we light and then sing, "Happy Birthday" to Jesus before eating or opening our gifts. Through the years we have continued this tradition with our children and now our grandchildren.

During my children's rebellious years, I was tempted to drop the custom because, I wasn't sure how my family felt about the birthday cake, candle, and singing, "Happy Birthday" to Jesus. The gift of the nail was our son's way of saying that he treasured family traditions rooted in our Christian faith.

To families young or old I suggest you find a way to establish family traditions that puts Christ at the center. You need not be afraid to establish family Christmas traditions or be afraid to show your love for God. They may not bless you for it now, but they will later.

*Train a child in the way he should go, and when he
is old he will not depart from it.*

PROVERBS 22:6

Tape a birthday candle on a Christmas ornament or some presents to remind everyone that Christmas is Jesus' birthday.

December 21

A Grateful Heart

SANDY CATHCART

My soul can find no staircase to Heaven unless it be
through Earth's loveliness.

—MICHELANGELO

In this world of fast food, video games, and virtual reality, it can
be difficult to muster up a grateful heart during the Christmas
season. I have found that staying away from shopping malls helps.
Then I'm not tempted to spend money on things I can't afford. Instead,
I give homemade gifts like patchwork quilts, tiny jars of blackberry jam,
and wildflower cards. The Christmas season becomes a time for telling
stories around the fireplace and huckleberry pie smothered with fresh
cream; a time of sharing a delicious home-cooked meal of venison and
roasted potatoes; a time of joining together on Sunday afternoon at
the country church for a potluck dinner and singing of carols.

Our grandchildren are learning to be thankful as well. They are
no longer disappointed in our lack of a TV and video games. They've
discovered the joy of tumbling through the snow and the special gift
of enjoying the outdoors with their parents. They're not disappointed
with handmade gifts. In fact, they look forward with great anticipation
to our traditional ornament exchange party. Each participant takes a
full year to make or choose a special ornament and wrap it in an
unmarked box. We place the boxes on a table, then form a circle. The
first person opens a box. The next can either open another box or take
the first person's ornament. If they take the gift of the first person,
then that person gets to choose another but can't take the first gift back
until later. The ornament changes hands a set number of times (usually
four) before becoming the property of the participant. This game offers
a rowdy good time and each participant returns home with a gift.

God has given us many good gifts, all free for the taking and
worthy of thanks. Even as I write this, the singing of a million crickets
surrounds me. I can look into a span of twinkling stars so thick that
the sky seems to nearly touch the ground. You probably know the
feeling. Have you ever been stuck in a long line of cars at a stoplight
and been surprised by a spectacular rainbow? What about the ocean?
Can you face it and not be awed at the power and wonder of a God

who holds back the force of its waves? Can you look at the perfect fingers of a newborn baby and not be moved in your heart at the wonder of God's creation? Staying away from the man-made glitter and focusing more on what we do have than what we don't have, is a good way of maintaining a simple heart of abundance all year.

Thanks be to God for his indescribable gift.
2 CORINTHIANS 9:15

Although it may seem impossible in the busy Christmas season, try to steal away for an hour of being quiet before God at a local park. You'll handle the holiday stress much more effectively.

December 22

Candy Cane Witness

LAURA SABIN RILEY

God has given us two hands, one to receive with and the other to give with.

—BILLY GRAHAM

The Christmas season is a wonderful time to be a witness for Christ. Evangelism is not one of my gifts, and yet I love the Lord with all of my heart and desire to see others come to know Him and love Him like I do. I have found a great way to witness for Him during the entire Christmas season. Everyone loves candy canes, and yet, most people do not know that there is a significant spiritual meaning to the candy cane. I recently discovered the meaning when a friend of mine shared this story with me:

A Candymaker's Witness

A candymaker in Indiana wanted to make a candy that would be a witness, so he made the Christmas candy cane. He incorporated several symbols for the birth, ministry, and death of Jesus Christ. He began with a stick of pure white, hard candy. White to symbolize the virgin birth and the sinless nature of Jesus; and hard to symbolize the solid rock, the foundation of the Church, and firmness of the promises of God. The candymaker made the candy in the form of a "J" to represent the precious name of Jesus, who came to earth as our Savior. It could also represent the staff of the "Good Shepherd" with which

He reaches down into the ditches of the world to lift out the fallen lambs, who, like all sheep, have gone astray. Thinking that the candy was somewhat plain, the candymaker stained it with red stripes. He used three small stripes to show the stripes of the scourging Jesus received, by which we are healed. The large red stripe was for the blood shed by Christ on the cross so that we could have the promise of eternal life. Unfortunately, the candy became known as a candy cane—a meaningless decoration seen at Christmas time. But the meaning is still there for those who "have eyes to see and ears to hear." May this symbol again be used to witness to the wonder of Jesus and His great love that came down at Christmas and remains the ultimate and dominate force in the universe today.

This powerful illustration of Christ's love spoke to me the first time I heard the story, and believing it would touch others as well, I decided to spread the word. I needed to think of a creative way to do it, so I went to work.

First, I typed the story on my computer and ran off lots of copies on red paper. I purchased several boxes of candy canes and green ribbon. I then cut the story and folded it in half, to look like a gift tag. Punching a hole in one corner of the paper, I threaded ribbon through the hole and tied the tag around the candy cane with the ribbon. Then, anytime someone came to my door during the month of December, I gave them a candy cane, and wished them a Merry Christmas. Mail carriers, delivery drivers, salesmen, and plenty of neighbors and friends received candy canes. Some of them I knew personally, some I didn't know at all. All of them were appreciative of the candy cane, and some, after reading the story, asked me questions about its meaning. One year my husband set some of the candy canes in a basket in the reception area of his office. The response was tremendous. He had opportunities to witness as well.

Every December we continue to give candy canes with "A Candymaker's Witness" tag attached by a bright ribbon. It is a simple, yet beautiful way to share the message of Christ's love. I have found that people are generally more open to spiritual things during the Christmas season. I have never had anyone refuse a candy cane. As each person leaves my doorstep, I pray that God will use the story to bring each one into a personal relationship with Him.

I encourage you to do the same. Evangelist or not, you can help to tell others the great news of the Savior. They may thank you for the blessing.

> *Call to me and I will answer you and tell you*
> *great and unsearchable things you do not know.*
>
> JEREMIAH 33:3

> Each of our children receive three gifts from us to correspond to the three gifts the baby Jesus received.

December 23

Treasures

MARJORIE K. EVANS

Happy memories are treasures we store in our hearts.
—MARJORIE K. EVANS

When our grandchildren were very young, I began putting surprises in their special dresser drawers in the guest bedroom. Each time they came to see us, they eagerly ran to find their treasures.

Bursting into the house one Christmas Day, Charity (four) and Cody (six) gave big bear hugs and kisses to their grandpa and me, then raced to the bedroom. Almost immediately, they came running out and chorused, "Grandma. There's nothing in my drawer."

"What day is today?" I asked.

Together they chimed, "It's Christmas, Grandma."

"Yes, this is Jesus' birthday and a very special day, isn't it? So today your surprises are in a special place. Would you like to look for them? When you're close, we'll say, 'You're hot,' and when you're far away we'll say, 'You're cold.'"

The hunt began, and soon there were squeals of pleasure or groans of disappointment depending on whether the children were hot or cold.

Finally Cody and Charity were close to the large wooden shoes from Holland, which stood near the front door. "You're warm, warm, warmer; now you're hot," we cried.

Suddenly Cody looked down at the shoes. "Charity." he exclaimed, "Here they are. Here's my surprise and here's yours." Grinning happily, they sat down to examine their treasures.

Our Heavenly Father loves us and delights in giving us special surprises and blessings. But many times they are not in the places we expect them to be. Perhaps they're in the simple, warm handclasp of an older person who says, "You don't know how your phone calls cheer me." Or they may be in the sweet smile of a child, or in an unexpected card or letter. And often they are found in God's Word, if we are diligent in searching them out.

Can your prayer be that the Lord will help you be more childlike in your eagerness to find the treasures He has for you today and every day. His blessing for today might be in the simplest way. Pay attention or you might miss it.

I rejoice in your promise like one who finds great spoil.
PSALM 119:162

> Take time to enjoy your grandchildren and/or children now. They'll be grown before you know it.

December 24

God's Delivery Room

MARY LOU KLINGLER

It is Christmas in the heart that puts Christmas in the air.
—W.T. ELLIS

As a nurse in obstetrics, I've seen hundreds of babies born and felt the presence of God in the delivery room. I've had the thrill of showing the babies, after their first bath, to their mothers. We didn't wrap the babies in swaddling clothes but soft shirts, diapers, and a receiving blanket.

I thought back to what it must have been like 2000 years ago. Bethlehem. How far from Nazareth it must have seemed to young Mary as she rode on a donkey. The ninth month is so uncomfortable for any mother and her baby was due to be born any time.

As they passed Jerusalem, Mary knew her time drew near. Joseph, unable to secure a room in the inn in Bethlehem, gratefully accepted a corner in the stable with the cattle.

A stable for a delivery room. Today our delivery rooms are shiny and sterile with gowned doctors and nurses. Mary's attendant was Joseph, who probably knew little of the details of a delivery. He took armloads of clean straw and made a bed for Mary to rest upon and she whispered, "It won't be long."

Next, Joseph cleaned out the manger and filled it with fragrant hay to cradle the baby after its birth. Joseph sat beside Mary—waiting as her contractions grew stronger. Suddenly a baby's cry broke the stillness of the night. Even the cattle must have paused while chewing their cud.

Mary held her Son close and kissed His precious head. She wrapped

Him in swaddling clothes and Joseph tenderly laid Him in the manger. Joseph stood in awe of this perfect little life now in his care.

God Himself was present at that unusual delivery of His only begotten Son. Almost two-thousand years have passed—yet that special birth is celebrated by believers the world over.

I also believe God is present at all babies' births. They are indeed a wondrous miracle. Being a nurse in obstetrics has been a great privilege in my life, and I thank Him for giving me a glimpse of what God can do.

Have a Blessed Christmas tomorrow. God loves you so much He gave the best blessing He could.

> *. . . and she gave birth to her firstborn, a son. She wrapped him in cloths and placed him in a manger, because there was no room for them in the inn.*
>
> LUKE 2:7

Write the Christmas story as a play to be used tonight for Christmas Eve or on Christmas Day, giving members of your family or friends parts to read.

December 25

Ultimate Giving

ESTHER M. BAILEY

> By one act of consecration of our total selves to God we can make every subsequent act express that consecration.
> —A.W. TOZER

*A*fter the Christmas gifts were opened, my nephew, Benny, disappeared. Soon he returned and approached his father. From behind his back he extended his arm with a big red bow attached to his wrist. With a flourish, Benny displayed the gift tag on which he had written, "To Dad from Mom."

Benny's creativity in relating to his father warmed my heart. It also reminded me that giving of myself to God strengthens my relationship with Him.

I gave my heart to Jesus when I was a twelve-year-old child and have given more of myself through the years. No matter how much I have already given, though, there is always more to give.

As I think of giving a Christmas gift to God, I am at a loss for ideas. What can I give to the Creator of the universe—the One who gave all for me? I focus my mind on the majesty of God and my heart stirs with praise. The emotion creates an awareness of something I can give to God. I can give more of my time to Him in praise. According to Psalm 148, God actually delights in the praises of His people.

I can give more of myself to God by increasing my Bible study time. As I put the words I read into practice, I will love more deeply, forgive an offense against me, or hand Jesus the emotional burden I carry. Changes that begin in my heart will then translate into action, causing me to mend a relationship, sacrifice something I want in order to expand my level of giving, or find a place to serve in the kingdom of God.

At best, my gift to God is small. But God has a way of transforming minimum resources into maximum value. I remember what Jesus did with the bread and fish from a lad's lunch. Sometimes I am amazed at how much good comes from a simple deed or a note sent at the right time.

While abundant-living calls for continuous surrender of myself to God, this Christmas Day is a good time to rejuvenate my commitment. In recognition of God's great gift to me, I want to give more of myself to Him.

Benny's performance suggests the value of visual evidence of what happens in the heart. Is your heart wrapped in a bow of surrender to God? If you've never made that decision, do it and you'll receive great blessings and abundant life.

Merry Christmas. But to say it even better, have a Blessed Christmas.

. . . I urge you . . . to offer your bodies as living sacrifices, holy and pleasing to God . . .

ROMANS 12:1

Many churches present free Christmas musicals. Use this opportunity to invite an unchurched friend to attend with your family.

Jesus Uses Leftovers

NAOMI WIEDERKEHR

Jesus used food (bread and wine) which are earthly, human necessities, as symbols of Himself.

—NAOMI WIEDERKEHR

Yesterday's Christmas dinner has most likely yielded you some leftovers, a sure sign that there was an abundance of food. When Jesus provided the miracle of the feeding of the five-thousand, there was an abundance of food, when everyone thought there could never be enough.

After the multitude had eaten, Jesus told His disciples to gather the fragments of food that were left and they filled twelve baskets. Did He throw these bits and pieces on the grass for the birds to eat? Did Jesus and His disciples take them to eat as they journeyed from place to place? We are not told, but we are sure they were used.

We have leftovers of our lives—indeed, we are like leftovers because of sin—which we can offer to Jesus for His use. Regardless of our past, if we offer Him our left over years and our left over talents, He can make something beautiful. He welcomes our leftovers.

Leftovers are often not appealing to the eye. They are discolored and less tasty. We consider leftovers boring, unappetizing and "old food." Yet, some good cooks are very talented at making wonderful dishes out of them.

Jesus is like those good cooks. He can take the leftovers of our lives, and when given to Him, can blend the flavors together and make something more tasty than the "original meal." Try Him.

Soon, you'll be starting a brand new year. This past year has been filled with challenges and blessings—with some leftovers. Turn them over to the Lord. He knows the recipe He wants to use. He has great plans for blending them into a wonderful, abundant life.

When they had all had enough to eat, he said to his disciples,
"Gather the pieces that are left over. Let nothing be wasted."
JOHN 6:12

To get ready for the new year, read *The Family Manager* by Kathy Peel (Word, 1996).

How Do We Return?

CORA LEE PLESS

To know whom you worship, let me see you in your
shop, let me hear you in your trade, let me know how
you rent your houses, how you get your money, how
you kept it and how you spent it.

—THEODORE PARKER

The shepherds were privileged to be a part of that first Christmas.
They heard the angelic message proclaiming the birth of Christ
and were evidently among the first to worship in Jesus' presence. What
joy must have filled their hearts. How excited they must have been to
have come into the presence of the long-awaited Messiah.

Eventually, however, they had to return to the fields. The coming
of the Messiah did not negate the need for shepherds to care for the
flocks. But the important thing is how the shepherds returned. They
did not go back in sadness and dejection because the great event was
over and now they had to return to the routine of their daily work.
Instead, they "returned, glorifying and praising God . . ." (Luke 2:20).

Once again this year, Christmas is past for us, and we too must
return—to our job, school, housework. How do we return? Is it with
a sense of sadness and dread because we have to encounter the same
routine, the same people, the same problems? Or are we able to return
with an abundantly-renewed joy and vigor in our lives for having been
reminded once again of God's great love and gift? He wants us to bless
others with that realization.

And whatever you do, whether in word or deed, do it all in the name
of the Lord Jesus, giving thanks to God the Father through him.
COLOSSIANS 3:17

What blessed Christmas attitude will you take back with you
into the workplace or in your relationships with others?

December 28

Stuff In Storage

SHIRLEY SMITH

> It is possible to give without loving, but it is impossible
> to love without giving.
>
> —RICHARD BRAUNSTEIN

"Why didn't we figure that out before everyone else did?" my husband asks as we pass a storage facility. Building units for people to lock their possessions in and pay the owner for the privilege strikes my husband as an incredibly simple way to "get rich."

I answer with another question; "What can possibly be in so many units?" My guess is those units hold "collectibles," a term which must surely apply to anything from antiques to angels . . . things people pursue and refuse to throw away. Like the man who was still solving a storage problem the night his soul was required of him (Luke 12:17-20), we can be overly-burdened with what to do with all our stuff.

A new store is announced in our area which will be selling bins and boxes for storing stuff. It promises better organization for our possessions. That seems to take consumerism to a new level . . . a store whose only purpose is not to sell things but to help us with the things we've already bought and now have no room for and likely no purpose for.

I won't be shopping at the organization store. For a Christian the question becomes: "How much luggage is enough for this trip through life? How much straining under the weight of accumulated stuff?"

Jesus cautioned that life consists not in the abundance of possessions. He counsels us to send the luggage ahead and enjoy treasures for eternity.

Our money can walk the inner-city streets with a police-officer-turned-evangelist and find young people starving for the message of salvation. We can join with a ministry that tastefully presents the message of the sanctity of life and influence some to choose adoption instead of abortion. We can encourage and enable those who crusade for morality on campuses across the country. Our dollars will send a message about corruption in government and effectively join with those who are imploring God to heal our land.

Money invested in kingdom ministries change us in at least three ways:

• We are *freed* from the burden of protecting, displaying and organizing stuff.

• We are *focused* on the issues of the day and their solutions.

• We are *fulfilled* knowing our money has been invested in the only security guaranteed to pay returns for all eternity.

Which of those "investments" are most attractive to you? Are you investing in any? If not, what could you do this season of giving or in your plans for next year? You'll really never miss the "stuff" or the needed organization storage units for them.

Then Peter said, "Silver or gold I do not have, but what I have I give you . . ."
ACTS 3:6

"Give to the charity of your choice," is better used as a motto for the living than a memorial for the dead.

December 29

Simple Pleasures

CATHERINE DUERR

I adore simple pleasures. They are the last refuge of the complex.

—OSCAR WILDE

We sipped tea at a tea party in the Mad Hatter's Garden, complete with Queen of Heart's Tarts, Bread and Butterflies, and Unbirthday Cake. We enjoyed a croquet tournament on the lawn, colored the roses red and broke a white rabbit piñata. Everyone exchanged unbirthday presents and went home with a bag full of goodies from the piñata. The Unbirthday Party was a success.

I breathed a sigh of relief as I slapped together peanut butter and jelly sandwiches for Mark and Nicholas, my two unbirthday boys. I was tired. The party started at ten, but before that all the preparations had to be done. Fortunately the boys went over to their friend Joe's for a couple hours before the party so I could pull it together. I worked all morning, but it was fun.

As I set the sandwiches in front of the boys, I asked Nicholas, "So, did you have fun this morning?"

"Uh-huh."

"What did you like best?"

Nicholas thought for a bit, then answered, "Eating donuts at Joe's house."

"Eating donuts at Joe's house," I repeated through a frozen smile. *I could have gotten away with donuts.*

I realized that the extravagance had really been unnecessary. I had wanted to do something special for my children and I did. But we could have enjoyed a trip to the donut shop without having to send out invitations, spend hours making decorations or arrange for baby-sitting. It doesn't take extravagance to delight a child—just a little time. And maybe a donut.

In the midst of Christmas celebrations, evaluate whether all your activity is really what is truly meaningful and a blessing to your family. You may be surprised at what they value.

Blessed are the pure in heart, for they will see God.
MATTHEW 5:8

Take someone special (maybe a child) out for donuts. Enjoy the special time you share together.

December 30

Love . . . The Girl No One Wanted

ERNESTINE COWARD

The biggest disease today is not leprosy or tuberculosis, but, rather the feeling of being unwanted.
—MOTHER THERESA

*H*er mother had a stroke and died. Her father was an alcoholic. She went around the neighborhood dirty and sometimes hungry. No one wanted her in their home because she was marked as a bad child and a bad influence on the other children.

When she would go to anyone's home, they would run her away. My heart went out to this eight-year-old girl. I talked to my husband about her. I told him it was a shame the way everyone treated her. She was only a child and she just needed someone to love her and not scorn her. I asked him if we could take her in. He told me if I wanted such a great responsibility to go ahead.

We took her in our home, cleaned her up, and bought her new

clothes. We treated her like she was our own. She started calling us "mom" and "dad."

We found out she wasn't doing well in school. We had her eyes examined and found out she couldn't see clearly. We bought her glasses. She was so proud that she went around reading everything in sight.

She was really a happy little girl. All she had needed was someone to care and love her. She grew up to be a fine young lady. One we are very proud of.

I often wonder what her life would have been like if we hadn't cared. If we hadn't reached out to her with God's love. We gave her love but she has given us blessings.

You may not be able to take someone into your home to live but for a small amount each month, you can support a child overseas through a Christian relief organization. Why not be a blessing in that way? You'll never know until Heaven how God has used your generosity.

> And now these three remain: faith, hope, and love.
> But the greatest of these is love.
>
> I CORINTHIANS 13:13

When putting away Christmas decorations, use this as a time to declutter and condense by throwing away or giving away anything you won't use next year.

December 31

The Assignment

IRENE HINKLE FAUBION

Blissful are the simple, for they shall have much peace.
—THOMAS A. KEMPIS

"Take a piece of typing paper and line it off for half-hour periods. Write down what you do from the time you arise until you go to bed. This paper is due next week; you will receive a grade." Strangest assignment I ever heard of, but I did it.

I knew I was stressed out, but didn't seem to know how to eliminate any of the many things I had to do. Sound familiar? Is it defrauding you of your abundant life?

I got up early to prepare breakfast and help get my husband off to work. Then I went to my job teaching kindergarten. Back at home I had housework, shopping, and dinner to prepare. I faithfully logged these activities for every half-hour and turned it in. The professor returned it at the end of the week. He had written only one comment, "Wow."

I asked what that meant.

"Too much." came the answer.

Arriving home I sat down at the table with my pencil and questioned each item. Is this something I really have to do? Could it be done only every two weeks? Could I get help? I know, I'll ask Mrs. Ronquillo who cleans my classroom if she has time to help me two hours a week. She did and was delighted to have the extra work. Now my life was beginning to look more manageable. The dreaded assignment was proving valuable. Since then, when I begin to feel overstressed, I know I have three options: evaluate, eliminate, or delegate.

All stress is not bad. If the bow were not tightened we would never hear the beautiful music of the violin.

As a young preacher's wife, I thought doing everything that the church might ask me to do was the same as God's expectations. There can be a difference. I had a rude awakening. Finally I heard the Lord gently say, "I made the laws that govern your body just as I made the laws that govern the universe. Would you expect to jump off the roof and not break your leg? You break the rules of health at your own risk."

As you've concentrated on simplifying your life and as you look forward to starting a new year, what would writing down your activities every half-hour reveal? What changes do you still need to make? You have made progress. Continue on. The blessings will continue.

Before I was afflicted I went astray, but now I obey your word.
PSALM 119:67

At the stroke of midnight, thank God for life, thank a significant person for their love; think of one thing you've learned this past year, and plan one thing you want to improve next year.

Credits

Know His Purpose from *I'm Listening, Lord*, Marilyn Willett Heavilin, Thomas Nelson, TN, 1993. Used by permission.

Abundant Spiritual Gifts and *The Simple New Life* from *Returning to Your First Love*, Tony Evans, Moody Press, IL, 1995. Used by permission.

Meaningful Touch adapted from *Meaningful Touch in Relationships* from *The Blessing*, Gary Smalley and John Trent, Thomas Nelson, TN, 1986. Used by permission.

Practical Steps, Communicate, Communicate, Communicate and *Slow Down and Have Fun* from *Tender Love*, Bill Hybels, Moody Press, IL, 1993. Used by permission.

Turn Irritation into Insight, Joy Through Greater Intimacy, Controlling Your Tempo of Life, Prevent Ambition From Stealing Your Peace, Gratitude in Having Less, Good Giving and *An Important STEP* from *Marriage in the Whirlwind*, Bill & Pam Farrel, IVP, IL, 1996. Used by permission.

Worship, Will You Go Out Without Knowing, Leave Room for God, Look Again and Consecrate, Transformed by Insight and *Have You Ever Been Alone With God?* From *My Utmost for His Highest*, Oswald Chambers. Copyright 1935 by Dodd Mead & Co., renewed Copyright 1963 by the Oswald Chambers Publication Assn. Ltd., and is used by permission of Discovery House Publishers, MI. All rights reserved.

Speaking Your Spouse's Language and *Real Listening* from *How to Bring Out the Best in Your Spouse*, H. Norman Wright and Gary J. Oliver, Ph.D., Vine Books, MI, 1994. Used by permission.

Increasing Your Effectiveness and *The Sound of Silence* from *Promises and Priorities*, H. Norman Wright, Servant Publications, MI, 1997. Used by permission.

Life From The Press Box, Votes of Confidence and *Today I Will Make a Difference* from *On the Anvil*, Max Lucado, Tyndale House Publishers, IL, 1985. Used by permission.

A Solitary Tea, Traveling Tea Time, The Tradition of Tea and *A Tea Time of Friendship* from *If Teacups Could Talk*, Emilie Barnes, Harvest House Publishers, OR, 1994. Used by permission.

Static That Interferes With God's Voice (adapted from), *Rhythms Throughout the Day, Morning and Evening Rhythms, Breath Prayers, God's Presence in Temptation* and *Reminding Us Who We Are* from *Enjoying the Presence of God*, Jan Johnson, NavPress, CO, 1996. Used by permission.

The Problem of Being Driven, Satisfying Life (adapted from), *Man Is A Hard Audience to Please, A Finely Pruned Tree, Being Peace With God's Assignments, How Busy Is Too Busy?* and *Thoughtful Living* from *Finding Focus in a Whirlwind World*, Jean Fleming, Treasure Publishing, 1991. Used by permission.

Fearfully and Wonderfully Made and *Memorable Laughter* from *Normal Is Just A Setting On Your Dryer*, Patsy Clairmont, Focus on the Family Publishing, CO, 1993. Used by permission.

Feeling Out of Sorts, Reminders of God's Care (adapted from), *Losing Perspective, Work Has Its Place, Let God Do the Worrying* and *Giving God the Best Dish* from *Running on Empty*, Jill Briscoe, Harold Shaw Publishers, IL, 1988. Used by permission.

Time for Aerobic Kneeling and *A Plan for Aerobic Spiritual Fitness* from *Point Man*, Steve Farrar, Multnomah, OR, 1990. Used by permission.

Pressure Is Normal from *On Becoming A Real Man*, Edwin Louis Cole, Thomas Nelson, TN, 1992. Used by permission.

Positive Mental Attitude, Unique Measure of Sensitivity, House: Reflection of Me?, Loneliness Isn't Always the Loneliest Number, Focus on Others and *Listening to God's Gentle Voice* from *Can I Control My Changing Emotions?*, Annie Chapman, Luci Shaw, and Florence Littauer, Bethany House Publishers, MN, 1994. Used by permission.

In the Long Run . . . and *The "I Can Do It All" Route to Self-Worth* from *Only Angels Can Wing It*, Liz Curtis Higgs, Thomas Nelson, TN, 1995. Used by permission.

Establishing Family Traditions and *The Price of Commitment* from *The Gift of Family*, Naomi Rhode, Thomas Nelson, TN, 1991. Used by permission.

No More Games from *"One Size Fits All" and Other Fables*, Liz Curtis Higgs, Thomas Nelson, TN, 1993. Used by permission.

Six Steps to Connecting with A Friend condensed from *Locking Arms*, Stu Weber, Multnomah, OR, 1995. Used by permission.

Contributors

Charlotte Adelsperger is a part-time teacher and the author of two books. As a free-lance writer and speaker she has written numerous poems, stories, and articles for over 60 different publications. Contact: 11629 Riley, Overland Park, KS 66210. (913) 345-1678.

Patricia A. J. Allen is a writer of daily devotionals, personal experience articles, Bible studies and fiction. She wants to encourage you to meet her Jesus and live in harmony with him. Contact: 1848 East NC 10, Newton, NC 28658.

Anita J. Anderson is currently a housewife and fledging writer. She has had experience as a registered nurse, music instructor, and foreign missionary. Anita has post-graduate study in psychology, has been married for 35 years and is grandmother of four children. Contact: 9936 W. Moccasin Trail, Wexford, PA 15090-9309.

Durlynn Anema-Garten, Ph. D., Ed. D., is a Christian counselor and author of ten books and numerous inspirational articles. She presents at women's work-shops/retreats and for Christian schools and is Vice President of Education, Women's Ministries Institute. Contact: 401 Oak Ridge Court, Valley Springs, CA 95252. (209) 772-2521.

Eunice Ann Badgley is a mother, grandmother, and widow living in Liberty, MO. Her inspiration comes from nature and family memories. Crafts and reading are her favorite things to do.

Esther M. Bailey, a freelance writer, has more than 600 published credits and has co-authored a book, *Designed for Excellence*. She enjoys sharing the blessings of life with her husband Ray. Contact: 4631 E. Solano Dr., Phoenix, AZ 85018. (602) 840-3143.

Kacy Barnett-Gramckow also uses the pen name Elizabeth Larson. Some of her writings have appeared in *A Moment A Day* and *The Women's Devotional Bible*. She is married to Jerry and has two sons. Contact: 7803 NE 332nd St., La Center, WA 98629. Email: GRR321@juno.com.

Crane Delbert Bennett retired in 1972 from 36 years of postal service. He has sold over 1000 short stories, poems, and articles. Husband to Janie, and father of six, he is active in the Arnold, Missouri, Corps of The Salvation Army. Contact: 2410 Alcarol Dr., Fenton, MO 63026-2225. (314) 861-1201.

Andrea Biczo is a native Californian and received Christ at age 10. Her call is to boldly tell others of Christ. She teaches first grade and is married with three children. Contact: 6529 Carissa Ave. Riverside, CA 92504.

Delores Elaine Bius has sold over 1,700 articles and stories in 25 years of writing. She is an instructor for American Christian Writers and speaks at conferences and retreats. She is a widow and mother of five sons. Contact: 6400 S. Narragansett Ave., Chicago, IL 60638. (773) 586-4384.

Mathew J. Bowyer is a solo, ghost and "with" author of four non-fiction books on history, mysticism, collecting, and investing. His articles cover the spectrum of human interests. He has historical fiction and religion works pending. Contact: 5397 Summit Dr., Fairfax, VA 22030.

Joanie Brown holds a Bachelor's Degree from California State University. She has served as Poetry Editor for the *Pacific Review* literary journal. She is proud of her two children, Jennifer, 17, and Lindsay, 11, both published authors. Contact: Email: poetjb@mscomm.com.

Mildred Brown is a freelance Christian writer who has had meditations published in *Star of Zion*, *The Secret Place*, *Daily Devotions for the Deaf*, and *Pathway to God*. She is a Church Sunday School Teacher Chairperson for a scholarship committee and Youth Missionary Society.

Kitty Bucholtz, daughter of a writer, has been writing since she was a child. She writes Christian fiction and is currently working on a novel. Contact: P.O. Box 68114, Phoenix, AZ 85082-8114. Email: jkbuch@primenet.com.

Georgia Burkett is a great-grandmother and freelance writer with more than 200 devotionals published; also many historical and inspirational articles. She teaches a Juniors' Sunday School class and sings with a group of "over 55" seniors who refuse to grow old. Contact: 220 Dock St., Middletown, PA 17057.

Linda Carlblom is a freelance writer, wife, and mother of three children, ages 13, 10, and 1. She is active in her local church's women's and children's ministries. She is currently writing a book of children's messages. Contact: 1403 E. Westchester Dr., Tempe, AZ 85283. (602) 730-7960.

Irene Carloni writes newsletter, devotionals, and is an editor and producer. She has received awards for work with cable TV. Irene enjoys photography, crafts, and Bible Study. The Carlonis have three children and live in Manhattan Beach, CA.

Julie Marie Carobini is a freelance writer with more than 50 articles published. She lives with her husband, Dan, and their children in Ventura, CA, not far from Elaine F. Navarro, who is her mother. Contact: carob@juno.com.

Libby C. Carpenter is a former teacher, wife of Hugh, mother of two, and grandmother of three. She attends Covenant Writers, which motivated her lifelong dream of writing, and Bethel Evangelical Lutheran Church. Contact: 426 Aderholdt Rd., Lincolnton, NC 28092. (704) 435-2932.

Sandra Palmer Carr is a wife, mother and grandmother, and a member of the Christian Writer's Fellowship of Orange County. She brings the hope of Jesus through poetry, stories, drama, and devotionals. Contact: 9421 Hyannis Port Drive, Huntington Beach, CA 92646-3515. (714) 962-0906.

Sandy Cathcart, freelance writer, speaker, musician/singer, and Bible courier shares a message of encouragement for believers to put feet to their faith. Contact: 341 Flounce Rock Rd., Prospect, OR 97536. (541) 560-2367.

Jeri Chrysong, a legal secretary, lives in Huntington Beach, CA, with her two sons, Luc and Sam. A humorist and poet, Jeri writes for newspapers and magazines. Her work has also been featured in the *God's Vitamin "C" for the Spirit* series.

Glenna Clark and her husband are assigned to Wycliffe Bible Translators' California offices and have served in Jamaica, the Philippines, and Central America. She has three grown children, seven grandchildren and two great-grandchildren. Contact: 5318 W. Keelson Ave., Santa Ana, CA 92704-1042. (714) 775-6020.

Joan Clayton has written over 300 articles in various publications. She also has 5 books to her credit. She and her husband, Emmitt, reside in Portales, New Mexico. They are retired educators. Her passion is writing; his is ranching.

Ernestine Coward is a mother and grandmother. She and her husband, Jack, have been married for 46 years. They are both retired and have two sons and five grandchildren. Contact: 25741 Calle Aqua, Moreno Valley, CA 92551-2006. (909) 488-0859.

Doris C. Crandall has been published in many religious magazines, take-home Sunday school papers, and several anthologies such as *Guideposts*, *Friendship at its Best*, and *Guideposts Christmas Treasury*. She lives in Amarillo, TX. Contact: (806) 355-0533.

Heidi Cressley is a stay-at-home mom and writer. She and her husband, Kevin, live with their two children, Aubren and Corban. Contact: Rt. 1 Box 103B, Rochester Mills, PA 15771.

Dotti Cummins is a pastor's wife and mother of 3 sons. She has her master's degree from the Juilliard school of music and teaches piano at The University of the Pacific. Her passion is prayer which she has taught since 1984. Contact: (209) 333-0836.

Christine Davis resides in Platte City, Missouri with her husband and 3 sons. She has been published in *Flower and Garden* and *Birds & Blooms* magazines. She writes a monthly column for a small publication in southeast Missouri. Contact: 18540 Deerbrook Lane, Platte City, MO 64079.

Lille Diane is a sought after speaker and vocalist for groups seminars and retreats nationwide. Her inspiring story "From Ashes to Beauty" transforms lives, young and old. For current schedule or bookings information contact: (805) 649-1805 P.O. Box 924, Oakview, CA 93022.

Catherine Duerr is a wife and mother of three. When she isn't throwing backyard parties, she writes and is the author of *Hold Me Tightly* (Concordia Publishing House), a devotional for mothers. Contact: (805) 397-4016.

Gloria Dvorak has been a freelance writer for 8 years. She is a wife, mother, and grandmother of four. Gloria loves to draw, read, needlepoint, and belongs to three women's groups.

Tammi Easterday is a freelance writer and speaker/singer. She and her loving husband, Bob, lead out in small group, youth and church building ministries. She is a former Physical Therapist who also holds a degree in Floriculture. Contact: 17760 Churchill St., Techachapi, CA 93561.

Marjorie K. Evans, a former school teacher, has many published articles. She enjoys grandparenting, reading, church work, traveling, their Welsh corgi, and tending plants. She and husband, Edgar, have two grown sons and five grandchildren. Contact: 4162 Fireside Cir., Irvine, CA 92604-2216. (714) 551-5296.

Irene Hinkle Faubion is a published author of poems and short articles. She and her husband

Jill L. Ferguson is a freelance writer, editor, and business marketing consultant who lives with her husband. Contact: 1615 152nd Ave. S.E., Bellevue, WA 98007. (425) 637-7011.

Olga Flores is a recent graduate of the Institute of Children's Literature. She is a volunteer tutor and mentor at a Hispanic children's learning center in New Orleans. Her interest is in Christian writing. Contact: 1318 Filmore Ave., New Orleans, LA 70122. (504) 288-9287.

Mary Bahr Fritts has authored juvenile titles, *The Memory Box*, *Jordi's Run*, and *The Boy Who Loved Snowflakes*. The winner of nine writing awards, she has published 125+ stories, columns, reviews, and articles. Contact: 807 Hercules Place, Colorado Springs, CO 80906. (719) 630-8244.

Laurie A. Fuller is a graduate of Bethel College in St. Paul, MN. She has been a Graphic Designer and homemaker in MN, IL, and CA. Now a freelance writer, she resides with her husband and son. Contact: 970 Sunny Field Court, Lawrenceville, GA 95376.

Joy P. Gage is a speaker, travel writer, and author of 13 books. Her magazine credits include *Saturday Evening Post*, *Moody Magazine*, and others. Joy travels throughout continental U.S. and Hawaii as a women's conference speaker. Contact: 2370 S. Rio Verde Drive, Cottonwood, AZ 86326.

Ina Gesell has written many newspaper columns and produced her own TV show. Her first work was published in *Christianity Today* and most recently was published in *God's Vitamin "C" for the Christmas Spirit*. Contact: 1201 W. Valencia #212, Fullerton, CA 92833.

Dave Getz lives with his wife and three children. Many outdoor activities provide ideas for stories, including the ones in this book. Contact: 323 E. Auburn Dr., Tempe, AZ 85283. (602) 838-7169.

Lynell Gray, an elementary teacher and freelance writer, is the author of professional materials for teachers, as well as poems and devotionals for inspirational books. Contact: 2867 Balfore St., Riverside, CA 92506. (909) 788-2638.

Ruth Giagnocavo lives in Akron, Pennsylvania, and is mother of seven and grandmother of ten. Ruth helped to run a bookstore for twenty years. She writes poetry and has been published in several Christian magazines.

Sandra Hinnan Griesmeyer has traveled the world with the Navy. Sandra resides in Southern California with her husband. Christian writing gives her a new way to use a gift she has always loved. Contact: 74137 Pinon Drive, Twentynine Palms, CA 92277.

Bonnie Compton Hanson is formerly with Scripture Press and has written curriculum. Co-author of three books, she enjoys both freelancing (over 415 manuscripts sold in the last 1 1/2 years), and her own lively family. Contact: 3330 S. Lowell, Santa Ana, CA 92707. (714) 751-7824.

Jeremi Harnack likes hiking, reading, and enjoying God. She has her BA in English Education and her MS in Meteorology. She homeschools her daughter, writes published poetry and coordinates the prayer ministry of her church. Contact: 1258 Aaron Road North Brunswick, NJ 08902. (908) 821-9625.

Kathryn Hartzell does freelance writing while working as a legal secretary. After ten years of volunteering on crisis hotlines, she is writing a book on handling problems biblically. Contact: P.O. Box 8155, Huntington Beach, CA 92615. (714) 964-9401.

Judith Hayes has been a professional freelance writer since 1993. She and Michael have been married 27 years, and Sasha (25) and Annabelle (21) are their children. She has a strong faith that is a recurring theme in her writing and life. Contact: (818) 701-9775.

Sarah Healton, Ed.D. is retired and co-author, with daughter Kay, of the *Anytime Craft Series*. She is published in *God's Vitamin "C" for the Spirit of Women*. She loves reading, writing, sewing, and traveling. Contact: 6669 Belinda Dr. Riverside, CA 92504. (909) 787-4811.

Barbara Hemphill, a pioneer in professional organizing, is the author of *Taming the Paper Tiger* and *Taming the Office Tiger* (Kiplinger Books). Barbara is past-president of the National Association of Professional Organizers, and appears on national television and writes for national publications.

June Hetzel has been a classroom teacher, curriculum specialist, administrator, author, and editor. She teaches at Biola University and the Orange County Department of Education. Contact: DJuneH@aol.com or 241 W. Patwood, La Habra, CA 90631.

Jan Hoffbauer and her husband, Mike, of 31 years love to visit their children and grandchildren. She has over 400 articles in *The Advertiser-Tribune* and has presented over 50 motivational talks. Contact: 8395 South SR 231, Tiffin, OH 44883-9245. (419) 927-2729.

Cher Holton, Ph.D., works as an Impact Consultant with corporations focusing on customer service and cross-functional team relationships. Contact: 4704 Little Falls Dr., Raleigh, NC 27609. (800) 336-3940/(919)783-7088.

Ed Horton is a Senior Business Analyst of a major corporation. His favorite pastime is freelance writing. Ed is published in *Keys for Kids, Alive!, The Upper Room,* and *God's Vitamin "C" for the Spirit of Men.* Contact: 5652 W. Pontiac Drive, Glendale, AZ 85308. (602) 561-6789.

Michele Howe is a freelance writer living in LaSalle, Michigan with her husband Jim (a public high school instructor) and their four homeschooled children. Contact: 6154 South Otter Creek Rd., LaSalle, MI 48145. (313) 242-5250. Email: jhowe@monroe.lib.mi.us.

Michele T. Huey is a wife and mother of three. She writes feature articles and devotionals, plus edits for her local newspaper's weekly devotional column. She enjoys teaching, camping, and music. Contact: R.D. 1, Box 112 Glen Campbell, PA 15742.

Pauline Jaramillo is a journalist and an award winning freelance writer in a variety of genres. She is bicultural and bilingual (Spanish/English) and has recently received her Master of Arts Degree in Rehabilitation Counseling. Contact: P.O. Box 225, Rim Forest, CA 92378.

Nelda Jones is a freelance writer with poetry and articles published in several publications. A grandmother, she received her journalism degree in 1994. Nelda is Director of Media Ministries at Edgewood Church of God, and editor of the church newsletter.

Veda Boyd Jones, an award-winning author, writes inspirational romance novels for adults and historical fiction for children. She and her husband Jimmie have three sons.

Arlene Kaiser, Ed.D., professional speaker, teacher, and author celebrates life with her inspiring and humorous message for Christian, educational, and business organizations. She is the author of 3 books to be published in Fall, 1997. Contact: 3424 Spring Creek Ln, Milpitas, CA 95035-7211. (408) 946-4444.

Kathy Keidel is an elementary school teacher in Buena Vista, Colorado, where she resides with her husband and children, 9 and 12. She is active in her church and community and enjoys sharing special times with her family.

Pamala Kennedy is Ms. California—Mom '97/'98, founding director of Women In Touch, pastor's wife, mother of three, and grandmother of Chelsea. She is a speaker and author of *Where Have All The Lovers Gone?*

Helen Kesinger, a freelance writer of published stories, articles and poems, is committed to "setting the captives free" by sharing how God works extraordinarily through ordinary people. She is currently weaving her first inspirational romance novel. Contact: 221 Brookside Drive, Paola, KS 66071. (913) 294-2937.

Tina Krause is an award-winning newspaper columnist, public speaker, and freelance writer of over 650 columns, feature stories, and articles. She is the wife of Jim, a mother and new grandmother. Contact: 223 Abington St., Valparaiso, IN 46385. (219) 531-2729.

Erma Landis is a wife of 46 years, grandmother of 17 and a mother of 6. Her work has appeared in *Christian Living, Christian Digest,* among many others. She also enjoys photography, bird watching, and traveling. Contact: 690 East Oregon Road, Lititz, PA 17543. (717) 581-8361.

Dr. Muriel Larson has published 17 books and thousands of articles, columns, curricula, and songs. She teaches at Christian Writers Conferences, and is also a counselor, child evangelist, musician, and columnist. Contact: 10 Vanderbilt Circle, Greenville, SC 29609.

Marcia Krugh Leaser is a freelance Christian writer who has been writing fro twenty years. Her poems and articles have appeared in magazines like *Ideals, Decision,* and *Standard.* Marcia's song ministry includes her original poems. Contact: 2613 C. R. 118, Fremont, OH 43420. (419) 992-4307.

Georgia Curtis Ling is an entertaining speaker, writer and newspaper columnist who shares about faith, love, and life. She is published in numerous magazines, and newspapers. This is her third appearance in *God's Vitamin "C" for the Spirit* book. Contact: 4716 W. Glenhaven Drive, Everett, WA 98203. (206) 257-0377.

Diane Lehman is a Physical Therapist, Dietitian, and has a Masters Degree in Health Education. She has helped hundreds regain hope, health, and a better quality of life. Contact: P.O. Box 374, Oak View, CA 93022. (805) 649-4459.

Paul Lippard has worked in Religious Education and Youth Ministry for 20 years. He is presently the Director of Family Life and Christian Formation at St. Gertrude Parish. Contact: 28801 Jefferson, St. Clair Shores, MI 48081. (810) 775-5820.

Dr. Lynne Logan is the director of Woman-To-Woman Ministries. She has written for *Moody Magazine*, *Home Life*, *Power for Living*, and has appeared on several national talk-shows. She is a mother and grandmother, and married to her best friend, Neil. Contact: website: http://wwwjs-net.com/drlogan. (909) 336-3626.

Helen Luecke is a freelance writer. She has been published in numerous Christian magazines including *Home Life*, *Mature Living*, *Secret Place*, and *Standard*. Contact: 2921 S. Dallas, Amarillo, TX 79103. (806) 376-9671.

Brendalyn Crudup Martin is Poet Laureate of the Arizona Supreme Court. She was born in Hot Springs, Arkansas and currently resides in Phoenix, AZ. Brendalyn is married to Ronald and is mother to James.

Gail Gaymer Martin is retired as a professional licensed counselor and presently teaches English at Detroit College of Business. She is a freelance writer with five books and over forty published articles and short stories. Contact: 27335 Eldorado Place, Lathrup Village, MI 48076.

Carole Mayhall works with The Navigators in the field of marriage, giving seminars nationally and overseas. Carole has written seven books and co-written two with Jack. She also frequently speaks at women's retreats. Contact: 5720 Velvet Court, Colorado Springs, CO 80918. (719) 534-9999; FAX: (719) 534-9490.

Jack Mayhall works with The Navigators with his wife, Carole. He is a speaker and the author of *Discipleship: the Price and the Prize* and two other books. They have been with The Navigators since 1956. Contact: 5720 Velvet Court, Colorado Springs, CO 80918. (719) 534-9999; FAX: (719) 534-9490.

Jane E. Maxwell, RN, is a freelance writer of inspirational and health articles, essays and devotionals. She is also involved in a ministry for single parents, a childrens' ministry, and volunteer work for various community agencies. Contact: 1704 Pearl Street, Vestal, NY 13850.

Renee McClellan lives in Southern California with her husband of 17 years and their two daughters. Her hobbies include reading science-fiction novels and riding their Morgan horse. Contact: 425 E. Arrow Hwy., #341, Glendora, CA 91740. (909) 599-0621.

Lucinda Secrest McDowell is a speaker and author of *Amazed by Grace* and *Women's Spiritual Passages*. A seminary graduate, she directs Caring Ministries for a 365-year-old New England church. Cindy is married and mother of four. Contact: Box 290707, Wethersfield, CT 06129. (860) 529-7175.

Cathy Messecar writes light humor, inspiration, devotionals, essays, and short stories for newspapers, magazines, and church bulletins. She is a featured speaker at local women's retreats. Contact: P.O. Box 214, Montgomery, TX 77356. (409) 597-4141 or 449-4396.

Roberta L. Messner, RN, Ph.D., is a free-lance writer with over 500 contributions to healthcare, home decorating, and inspirational publications. Her latest book is entitled, *Increasing Patient Satisfaction: A Guide for Nurses* (Springer Publishing Company). Contact: 1878 Crossroads, Kenova, WV 25530. (304) 453-3836.

Kathy Collard Miller is the author of 29 books including the best-selling series, *God's Vitamin "C" for the Spirit*. She speaks nationally and internationally both in Christian and business settings. Contact: P.O. Box 1058, Placentia, CA 92871. (714) 993-2654. Email: Kathyspeak@aol.com.

Rosalie J.G. Mills is a free lance writer and the mother of one grown son. She sings, speaks, writes plays, poetry, lyrics, and music, and is active in her church. She is a secretary in a property management firm.

Lynn Morrissey, *Words of Life Ministries* founder, writer and speaker, specializes in workshops on prayer journaling, spiritual autobiographies, discovering gifts/missions, writing, and volunteer management. Contact: 155 Linden Ave., St. Louis, MO 63105. (314) 727-8137.

Jeanne Mott, after having lived in various states, has returned to the state of her birth, North Carolina. She is kept busy with teaching school, church activities, writing, and playing with her nineteen-month-old grandson. Contact: P.O. Box 50, Dallas, NC 28034. (704) 922-5221.

Deena Murray is Editor of *Sharing Hope & Joy* published by Caring Hearts Ministry. She is a speaker and invites subscribers to her newsletter. Contact: 2251 Coachman Cir., Corona, CA 91719. (909) 279-9224; Email: murray@pe.net.

Lynette McBride lives with her husband and their two teenage children. Lynette's Christian speaking and writing ministry, *Vision Restored*, helps women and youth. Contact: 684 Fairway Lane, Gunnison, CO 81230. (970) 641-4238.

Ruth E. McDaniel is a freelance writer, author, poet, caregiver, and frequent writing instructor who seeks to use her talent for the glory of God. Contact: 15233 Country Ridge Dr., Chesterfield, MO 63017. (314) 532-7584.

Louisa Godissart McQuillen has written since childhood, at times falling asleep at the table (with pen in hand and nose on paper). She lives with an orange Somali cat called "Milo" and with "Shar," a slightly crabby Siamese. Contact: 525 Decatur St., Philipsburg, PA 16866-2609.

Elaine F. Navarro is a vivacious grandmother, passionately in love with life. She began writing in earnest six years ago, and won 2nd Place in the 1996 Biennial Competition sponsored by The National League of American Pen Women, Inc. Contact: Email: eldorado@jetlink.net.

Deborah Nell lives with her husband Craig and three year-old daughter Sophie. She is a stay-at-home mom, writer, and visual artist. She and her husband enjoy ministering to their neighborhood. Contact: 12571 Sunswept Ave. #7, Garden Grove, CA 92843. (714) 265-1364.

D. J. Note is a freelance writer and homemaker. Contact: 9821 Hwy. 62, Eagle Point, OR 97524.

Jennifer Nystrom is a mother of three, ages 15, 12, and 8. She is the preschool and nursery director of Northshore Christian Church and a freelance writer of Children's literature and curriculum. Contact: 7021-76th Dr. N.E., Marysville, WA 98270. (360) 659-2542.

Luis Palau is an internationally renowned evangelist. He's spoken to hundreds of millions through television and radio in 95 nations, and face to face to more than 12 million people in 64 nations. He is the author of 42 books. Contact: P.O. Box 1173, Portland, OR 97207. (503) 614-1500.

Pat Palau and her husband, Luis Palau, have extensive speaking and writing ministries, including contributing to *Keeping Your Kids Christian* (Servant Publications) and co-authoring *How to Lead Your Child to Christ* (Multnomah Press). Contact: P.O. Box 1173, Portland, OR 97207. (503) 614-1500.

Frances Partain-Martin, a native Californian who has traveled extensively throughout the world, now lives in the desert near Twentynine Palms. Several of her Christian poems have been published nationally. She is now concentrating on Christian short stories and articles.

Nancy E. Peterson has been a Christian writer and cartoonist for ten years. Her work has appeared in publications including *Housewife-Writer's Forum*, *The Press Enterprise*, and other publications. Contact: 28626 Tulita Lane, Menifee Valley, CA 92584. (909) 679-5137.

Patricia Phipps has been a pastor's wife for 28 years and they are currently pastoring at Family Life Assembly of God in Frontenac, KS. She began freelance writing in 1993 and enjoys music, reading, writing, and painting. Contact: P.O. Box 377, Pittsburg, KS.

Debbie Piper (BA, Biblical Education) is a Christian writer and speaker, and the author of *I'm a Christian, Now What?*, a question and answer guide on Christian living and faith. Contact: P.O. Box 2223, Windermere, FL 34786-2223. (407) 578-7069.

Cora Lee Pless has articles published in *Guideposts*, *Decision*, *The Christian Reader*, and others. She enjoys teaching Sunday School and is an inspirational speaker. Contact: 127 Overhead Bridge Road, Mooresville, NC 28115. (704) 664-5655.

Betty Chapman Plude is a freelance writer and speaker. She is the author of *A Romance With North San Diego County Restaurants*, numerous articles, and two newsletters. Contact: 834 Cessna St., Independence, OR 97351.

Lois Erisey Poole is a well known national writer and author of the book, *Ring Around The Moon*, a celebration of life's simple pleasures. She and her husband have 3 children and one grandchild. Contact: P.O. Box 3402 Quartz Hill, CA 93586. 1-800-476-5758.

Dr. Kathryn Presley is Associate Professor of English at Lamar University—Port Arthur (Texas). She was born to a sharecropper family in Oklahoma's Dust Bowl. Along with teaching, she enjoys "Grandmothering," writing, and speaking to women's groups.

Margaret Primrose is a retired employee of Nazarene Publishing House who was office editor of *Come Ye Apart* magazine. She has authored two children's books and numerous devotionals and other pieces.

Dortha Edith Osborn is a freelance writer and has been published in *St. Louis Lutheran*, *Celebrate Life*, and Word Aflame Publications. Contact: 4300A Arrow Tree Dr., St. Louis, MO 63128. (314) 892-7269. Email: DodiO@aol.com.

Susan Titus Osborn is Editor of *The Christian Communicator*. She is also an adjunct professor at Pacific Christian College in Fullerton, CA. Susan has authored 12 books and numerous articles, devotionals, and curriculum materials and teaches at writers' conferences across the U.S. and internationally.

Tim Reaves is crazy about his wife, Marianna, and adores his daughters, Alison and Faith. He is an award winning writer and humorist and is the creator of "Word In Edgewise," a ministry using storytelling to share the Scripture.

Shirley Reynolds has recently become a housewife due to cancer treatment. But it has freed up her time to write, sing in a church choir, and volunteer with youth at risk programs and a local food bank. Contact: 5228 170th Pl. S.W., Lynnwood, WA 98037.

Laura Sabin Riley is a homemaker, speaker, and freelance writer of articles and short stories in various Christian publications. She is currently writing a devotional book for stay-at-home moms. Contact: 10592 Del Vista Dr., Yuma, AZ 85367. (520) 342-7324.

Ruth M. Rink graduated from Indiana State Teachers College in 1930 and later received her M.A. She has taught elementary school and student teachers. She retired at 62 and traveles widely. Contact: 580 North Ninth Street #9, Indiana, PA 15701. (412) 465-8677.

Peter N. Robbins, Ph.D., is a speaker, writer, psychologist, marriage counselor, and radio talk-show host. Contact: website: www-turningpoint.org. or 620-B N. Diamond Bar Blvd., Diamond Bar, CA 91765. (800) 99-TODAY.

D. Leroy Sanders, long-time chaplain at the Motion Picture and Television retirement facility in Los Angeles, has written about encounters with Bob Hope, Ronald Reagan, Pat Boone, and many more. Contact: 216 Strongbox Court, Roseville, CA 95747. (916) 771-8254.

David Sanford is a husband, father, adjunct professor of journalism at Western Baptist College, director of print media for the Luis Palau Evangelistic Association, and coauthor of *God Is Relevant* (Doubleday, 1997). Contact: 6406 N.E. Pacific St., Portland, OR 97213. (503) 239-5229.

Rene'e S. Sanford is a wife, mother, free-lance writer, conference speaker, and lay leader for missions and women's ministries at Spring Mountain Bible Church in Portland, Oregon. Contact: 6406 N.E. Pacific St., Portland, OR 97213. (503) 239-5229.

Doug Schmidt is a curriculum editor with Cook Communications Ministries in Colorado Springs, CO. Contact: E-mail: Bugsley@aol.com.

Laurel Schunk is a full-time Christian writer. Her first book was a romantic suspense novel, *The Voice He Loved*. Three easy-reader books will be published in 1998. She loves teaching writers how to improve their writing. Contact: 4200 E. 24th, Wichita, KS 67220. (316) 683-6090.

Jim Schweitzer is grandfather to three small boys and works as chaplain at the Dallas Retirement Village in Dallas, OR. He and his wife, Carol, enjoy theater and gardening. Their 30 acre farm provides leisure and therapy.

Marilyn Scogin teaches special education, writes, and is an avid guitar player. She is a wife, mother, and grandmother. She and her husband teach Bible classes in their home. Contact: 16109 Jersey Dr., Houston, TX 77040. (713) 466-6598.

Penny Shoup was born on a farm in Ohio, and currently lives in Columbia, TN, with her husband, Bruce. She has worked as a Registered Nurse and now homeschools her four children. She loves children, horses, dogs, and writing, and has just finished a novel, *In His Time*.

Debra Smith is a wife and mother of two teenage children. Her work includes books in the *Hattie Marshall Frontier Adventure* series and articles for the Baptist Sunday School Board. Contact: 9158 Arnold Road, Denham Springs, LA 70726. (504) 664-4982.

Shirley Smith has pursued her love for writing after retiring from a thirty year teaching career. She and her husband had two sons and a daughter when they began foster/adoptive parenting for a neglected three-year-old girl.

Winona Smith is a wife, mother, homemaker, and church secretary, who loves to write in her spare time. She desires to have God use her words to bless others. Contact: 9060 Roundtree Drive, Baton Rouge, LA 70818.

Glenda Smithers lives in Kingsville, MO. She is a preschool director, Sunday school teacher, public speaker, and author of three children's missions books.

Janice Stroup works part-time in the family business, a jewelry store, teaches piano part-time, and writes in her "spare" time. She lives with her husband, Joe, and three teen-aged sons, Joshua, Caleb, and Joel. Contact: 403 S. Cedar St., Lincolnton, NC 28092. (704) 735-8851.

Patty R. Stump is the wife of a Youth Ministries Consultant, mother of two, Christian Marriage and Family Counselor, and writer. She speaks for women's retreats and special events. Contact: P.O. Box 5003, Glendale, AZ 85312. (602) 938-1460.

Trisha Throop is 19 and an English/Communications major at Western Baptist College. She hopes to freelance write or work for her hometown newspaper in Colville, WA when out of school. She enjoys singing, butterflies, bubblebaths, and daydreaming.

Nanette Thorsen-Snipes, 1994 "Writer of the Year" of the Georgia Christian Writers Conference, has authored a small inspirational book and over 250 articles, short stories, and devotionals. Contact: 355 Pinecrest Terrace, Buford, GA 30518. (770) 945-3093.

Doris Hays Toppen is an author, teacher, and speaker who lives at the foot of Mt. Si and finds inspiration in camping with her four children and families, friends, jogging by the river, biking, gardening, and "spring that never ends."

Bob Turnbull is an author, speaker, former football coach, and television and radio personality. His most recent book is *Marriage Mentors: Guiding and Encouraging Couples Toward a Healthy Marriage*, co-authored with his wife, Yvonne. Contact: P.O. Box 4170, Mission Viejo, CA 92690. (714) 457-1410.

Marcia Van't Land is the author of *Living Well with Chronic Illness* and is available for speaking in the Southern California area. Contact: 12648 Ramona, Chino, CA 91710. (909) 627-2024.

June L. Varnum is the author of articles and devotions, amateur photographer, and speaker. She has taught Sunday school and led Bible studies, prayer groups, and retreat workshops. Contact: P.O. Box 236, Loyalton, CA 96118. (916) 993-0223.

Pat Verbal speaks and writes on behalf of today's kids. She is the founder of "Ministry To Today's Child" and co-authors the *My Family's Prayer Calendar* with Shirley Dobson. Contact: 503 E. Leadora Avenue, Glendora, CA 91741. (818) 963-4326.

Pam Waian is the co-founder of Caring Hearts Ministry, dedicated to sharing the hope and joy we can have in Jesus Christ. She is a talented writer and speaker and is available to speak to your group. Contact: (909) 698-2474.

Lori Wall is a single parent of three children. Her talents range from poetry to playwriting. She has written for Plastow Publications, and presently is the in-house playwright for Pasadena's Exodus Theatre Troupe. Contact: 5418 Dahlia Drive., Los Angeles, CA 90041. (213) 257-0274.

Joan Weaver lives on a farm where she spins, weaves, writes, and portrays historical ladies involved in the textile arts, including Delilah, Lydia and Mary. She published the booklet *Spinning and Weaving in Biblical Times*. Contact: R.R. 2 Box 52, Lewis, KS 67552. (316) 659-3253.

Mildred Wenger has had children's stories published in the papers of many church denominations. She also teaches piano and organ. She and her husband, Daniel, live in Stevens, PA, and have five grown children.

Naomi Wiederkehr has written over one hundred articles, devotionals, and book reviews. She's still seeking publishers for her two children's books. She has worked in libraries for thirty years. Contact: 705 Stucky, Apt. A., Berne, IN 46711. (219) 589-2445.

Lois A. Witmer is a retired school teacher. She taught for 29 years in elementary, high school, and junior high. She is an active member of Willow Street Mennonite Church, presently serving as Sunday School Superintendent, secretary of church council, and an adult ladies' class teacher.

Cheryl Williams was born in 1941 and founded Project Share and Granny's Ink as a special "Thank You" to God who scooped her up from the ashes and made her whole, late in life. Contact: 26411 NE 98th, Exelsior Springs, MO 64024.

Carolyn C. Wilson, a speech-language pathologist, has authored 10 professional books, including *Room 14* (LinguiSystems). She and her husband, Russell, share a nursing home ministry. Contact: 4317 Willow Way Road, Fort Worth, TX 76133. (817) 370-8255.

Jan Woodard, a wife and mom, writes for *Guideposts* and other publications. She believes everyone has stories to tell and shares some of her own with presentations on "Opening Your Memory Box" and "Angels Among Us." Contact: 270 Sunset Dr., Indiana, PA 15701. (412) 465-5886.

Keith Wright is a graduate of Westmont College and Fuller Theological Seminary, and Pastor of Evangelism at Colonial Presbyterian Church. Contact: 9500 Wornall Road, Kansas City, MO 64114. (816) 942-3272.

Susan Kimmel Wright lives in an old farmhouse with her husband, three children, and assorted animals. She has written many articles and a children's mystery book series (Herald Press). Contact: 221 Fawcett Church Road, Bridgeville, PA 15017-1512. (412) 746-2517.

Robert Yocum no longer has the "incurable disease." He currently works with two lupus support groups to encourage patients and their families. He wrote *My Adventure With Lupus*. Contact: P.O. Box 6133, Tehachapi, CA. (805) 822-5395. Email: Yocum@lightspeed.net.

Martha B. Yoder left the nursing profession because of post-polio problems and began to write. The multiple handicaps within her family gave much material through which she can encourage others. Contact: 1501 Virginia Ave., Harrisonburg, VA 22301.

Doris Sterner Young has a BS in Communication and retired from nursing in 1995. Doris has been published in *The Christian Communicator, Across the Universe*, and in Campus Comedy of *Reader's Digest*. Contact: 2060 East Cairo Dr., Tempe, AZ 85282. (602) 838-9063.

Jeanne Zornes is a widely-published speaker and writer whose book credits include *When I Prayed for Patience . . . God Let Me Have It* (Harold Shaw Publishers). Contact: 1025 Meeks St., Wenatchee, WA 98801-1640.

Books by Starburst Publishers
(Partial listing—full list available on request)

God's Abundance
—Edited by Kathy Collard Miller

This day-by-day inspirational is a collection of thoughts by leading Christian writers such as, Patsy Clairmont, Jill Briscoe, Liz Curtis Higgs, and Naomi Rhode. *God's Abundance* is based on God's Word for a simpler, yet more abundant life. Most people think more about the future while the present passes through their hands. Learn to make all aspects of your life—personal, business, financial, relationships, even housework can be a "spiritual abundance of simplicity."

(hardcover) ISBN 0914984977 **$19.95**

Revelation—God's Word for the Biblically-Inept
—Daymond Duck

Revelation—God's Word for the Biblically-Inept is the first in a new series designed to make understanding and learning the Bible as easy and fun as learning your ABC's. Reading the Bible is one thing, understanding it is another! This book breaks down the barrier of difficulty and helps take the Bible off the pedestal and into your hands.

(trade paper) ISBN 0914984985 **$16.95**

The Frazzled Working Woman's Practical Guide to Motherhood
—Mary Lyon

It's Erma Bombeck meets Martha Stewart meets cartoonist Cathy Guisewite. The author's extensive original cartoon illustrations further enliven a sparklingly humorous narrative, making her a new James Thurber! *Frazzled* is an essential companion for any working woman who thinks she wants a baby, or is currently expecting one. Especially if she could use a good laugh to lighten her load and her worries. This book also offers an innovative update on effective working-mom strategies to women who are already off and running on the "Mommy Track."

(trade paper) ISBN 0914984756 **$14.95**

The Miracle of the Sacred Scroll
—Johan Christian

In this poignant book, Johan Christian masterfully weaves historical and Biblical reality together with a touching fictional story to bring to life this marvelous work—a story that takes its main character, Simon of Cyrene, on a journey which transforms his life, and that of the reader, from one of despair and defeat to success and triumph!

(hardcover) ISBN 091498473X **$14.95**

The Remnant
—Gilbert Morris

How far will the New Age philosophy with it's "politically correct" doctrine take us? *The Remnant*, the second futuristic novel in The Far Fields series, continues the story which began in *Beyond the River*—that of a world where a total authoritarian government has replaced family and rewritten history.

(trade paper) ISBN 0914984918 **$8.95**

Beyond The River
—Gilbert Morris & Bobby Funderburk

Book 1 in The Far Fields series is a a futuristic novel that carries the New Age and "politically correct" doctrines of America to their logical and alarming conclusions. In the mode of *Brave New World* and *1984*, *Beyond The River* presents a world where government has replaced the family and morality has become an unknown concept.

(trade paper) ISBN 0914984519 **$8.95**

Health, Happiness & Hormones
—Arlene Swaney

Subtitled: *One Woman's Journey Toward Health After a Hysterectomy.* A frightening and candid look into one woman's struggle to find a cure for her medical condition. In 1990, when her story was first published in *Prevention* magazine, author Arlene Swaney received an overwhelming response from women who also were plagued by mysterious, but familiar, symptoms leading to continuous misdiagnoses. Starting with a hysterectomy Swaney details the years of lost health that followed as she searched for an accurate diagnosis. Her story is told with warmth and compassion.

(trade paper) ISBN 0914984721 **$9.95**

Books by Starburst Publishers—cont'd.